Your Complete Guide to Financial Security

Your
Complete Guide to
Financial
Security

How to Invest and Prepare for Your Future Peace of Mind

TWO BESTSELLING WORKS COMPLETE IN ONE VOLUME

Investing
for the Future

Preparing
for Retirement

Larry Burkett

Inspirational Press . *New York*

First Inspirational Press edition published in 1998.

Inspirational Press
A division of BBS Publishing Corporation
386 Park Avenue South
New York, NY 10016

Inspirational Press is a registered trademark of BBS Publishing Corporation.

Published by arrangement with Chariot Victor Publishing and Moody Press.

Library of Congress Catalog Card Number: 97-73420

ISBN: 0-88486-170-8

Printed in the United States of America.

Contents

I

INVESTING
FOR THE FUTURE

Contents

Introduction

WHEN I WAS first approached by the editors at Victor Books about writing a book on investing, I declined. My feelings then were the same as now. I am not an investment advisor, nor do I desire to be. A genuine concern I have is that someone might misinterpret what I say and lose some hard-earned money. If that person makes money by investing money it would be bad enough. But many of the people I know make their money by investing their labor. Advising them on how to risk that money is a grave responsibility that I have no desire to assume.

But, as you can tell by now, I decided to write a book on investing. My reason for doing so is that, as a teacher and counselor, I have seen most of the mistakes that can be made with money—including investing. As a result, I believe I can help you to avoid some bad decisions and make some good ones. I hope you will find this book unlike any you have ever read. In reality it is not one book but several related topics put under one cover.

First, it is an overview of the economy and how it affects investment strategy.

Next, it is a basic overview of what God's Word has to say about investing, and the biblical principles of multiplication.

Then it shifts to what I call "the hall of horrors": the investment errors that usually result in the maximum loss for those who choose to risk their resources foolishly. I believe that I have seen virtually every way someone can lose money. The investments may change from time to time, but the same strategies persist.

The next section is dedicated to understanding which invest-ments to use at the different stages of life. This is an age-related study on how to develop sound investment strategies. The goals at each stage (20–40, 40–60, 60+) all differ, but the end result is to become debt-free and develop enough surplus to live comfortably while pleasing the Lord in the process.

The last section evaluates the various investment groups (se-cure, long-term income, growth, speculation, and high-risk) and places them in a five-tiered strategy to help determine which is best at any stage of life.

I have tried not to duplicate work done by others who have written on this subject where I believe their efforts are valid. In-stead I refer to their works in the Appendix as resources for those seeking more in-depth analysis on specific investments.

Investing is anything but an exact science, as anyone who has ever lost money on a "sure thing" can testify. But there are basic rules that apply to investing, just as there are basic rules for phys-ics. For example, the law of gravity says that an object will be drawn toward another object of greater mass. Thus when you jump into the air you ultimately come back down to earth. If you fill a balloon with helium it will seemingly defeat the law of grav-ity, but only until the helium leaks out; then it will return to earth again.

Investing's law of risk and return works the same way. The higher the promised rate of return, the higher the risk of losing your money. Economic upturns and inflationary markets can tem-porarily make that law seem defeatable, but eventually the market deflates and the high-return investments plummet to earth again, along with your hard-earned savings.

If you gain but one perspective from this book, I trust it will be this: *The rules from God's Word about investing still work.* Apply them and you will prosper over the long run. Violate them and you will lose all that you have worked so hard to accumulate.

I am grateful to many friends who have contributed their col-lective knowledge to *Investing for the Future.* Not one of them boasts of never having made an investment mistake. Most will readily admit that they are wrong sometimes and they are right sometimes. The saving feature of their counsel is that they are right more often than they are wrong, and they try to minimize the downside risk while maximizing the gain, so over the long run their clients prosper.

I am especially grateful to one of my best friends, a skilled professional in the field of medicine. It was from him and his colleagues that I learned a valuable insight: It is possible to attain a nearly perfect track record in the area of investments while relying almost exclusively on intuition and the advice of others. How do I know this, you ask? Because he and his colleagues have been nearly 100 percent wrong in every investment they have made. Therefore, if one would simply study the techniques they employ and do the exact opposite, he would come out ahead. It's not always perfect, but it comes pretty close.

I will confess from the outset that I am personally a very conservative investor. I stay with things that have proven their worth over several decades, and try not to vary during good times or bad. The so-called "dollar averaging" approach usually pays off in the long run. If you're not familiar with this technique, you will be by the time you have finished this book.

I also don't want to get up in the morning and have to rush out to buy a copy of *The Wall Street Journal* to see how my investments are doing. I am more than willing to pay someone else a fee to do that for me. In my case, I elect to use good quality mutual funds with professional management. You may prefer to do your own investing, which is totally your choice. What I will try to do is evaluate what the professionals have done so you can decide if you have done better or worse. The bottom line with any financial management fee, regardless of whether it is a financial planner's fee or a fund management fee, is: Can they cover their fees and still do better than you can on your own? If so, it would be silly not to use them. If not, then their service is a waste of money.

The one area of investment counsel that irritates me the most is to have someone present an investment in glowing terms, only to find out later that he didn't reveal the whole truth. Therefore, in this book I will try to be brutally honest. I know this will alienate some Christians who sell investments, but I believe it is preferable to alienate a few salespeople rather than allow more of their clients to lose money because of ignorance.

Good reading, God bless you, and I trust you will decide this book is one of the best investments you have ever made.

1

The Economy

THERE IS VIRTUALLY no way to write a book on investing without first discussing the economy. After all, what is an investment except an idea to make money? If that idea is not matched to the economy it is almost certainly doomed to failure. For instance, an investment of $1,000 in the Ford Motor Company in 1912 would have grown to nearly $12 million by 1950. Inflation consumed about half of its buying power during the intervening years, so an investor in Ford was left with a mere $6 million on which to retire. Not a bad deal.

The equivalent investment of $2,000 in 1950 in the same stock would have been worth about $50,000 in 1990. Still not a bad return, except that inflation would have eroded its buying power to about $10,000. Clearly the economy had a major effect on the value of investments made in the early and latter part of the twentieth century.

What might you have done with your $2,000 in 1950 to improve your retirement income? You might have guessed that the world would have a computer revolution in the next 40 years and invested your money in IBM. If you had purchased $2,000 worth of IBM common shares in 1950, your investment would have grown to nearly $700,000 by 1990.

Or you might have chosen a new investment idea called a mutual fund. This is a plan in which many investors pool their assets and invest in a wide spectrum of stocks or bonds. Several of the top funds would have yielded a return of nearly $2 million on your original $2,000.

Or you could have invested in Symmetrics Engineering (as I did in 1959) and watched your stock value go from $2 a share to $30 a share in just four years, only to plummet to zero five years later when the Japanese entered the electronics business.

Now that we have established that the economy has a direct bearing on which investments do well or poorly, I would like to give a short refresher course on how our economy operates.

Prior to the twentieth century our economy operated by what was called monetarist, or free market, economic theory. Simply put, monetarist theory means that the government plays little or no role in determining the direction of the economy. Prior to this century if the economy slumped into a recession (or depression), the government did not feel compelled to step in and bail it out. Nor did the average American expect direct government intervention. After all, if private businesses caused the problems, they should solve the problems, right?

Prior to this century, no Americans drew welfare from the government. No farmers were paid not to grow food. No homes were subsidized by government loans, and the "homeless" who wouldn't work were called "bums." One side benefit of free-market economics was that Americans were allowed to keep 100 percent of what they earned. Taxes were collected through the sale of goods, through tariffs, not income confiscation. Governments ran lean and efficient; because if they didn't, they shut down.

A New Theory of Economics

World War I made an indelible impact on this nation. From an isolationist country we emerged with much more of a global mentality. Certainly that was true where economics was concerned. The devastation of Europe presented unparalleled opportunities for Americans to expand their businesses. With the industrial revolution in full swing, American businesses exported automobiles, telephones, food, and technology worldwide.

Unfortunately, what American business schools imported was an idea that had just begun to take root in Europe: socialism. Professor John Maynard Keynes, a British economist, and an avowed socialist, had succeeded in establishing his doctrine of government intervention in private business throughout European academics.

Simply put, Dr. Keynes believed that it was the role of governments to manipulate the economies of their countries so as to lessen the effects of economic cycles. He taught that during good economic times a government should confiscate funds from the economy and use them to promote socially mandated programs such as health care, shelter, jobs, and such: the Robin Hood syndrome, if you will.

Then during economic downturns the government would supply capital as needed to stimulate growth and economic recovery. (The difficulty arises when the social programs expand during bad times and the governments are enticed to borrow to continue their operations.)

In the poorer nations, where the economies were already controlled by the governments, this concept was adopted wholeheartedly, but they lacked the resources to give the theory a platform from which to experiment. So what better place to experiment than in America, where free market economics, based on a biblical heritage, had built the strongest economy in the world with tremendous surpluses available to pilfer.

Keynesian economics swept the world. From it was born the International Monetary Fund and the World Bank. In America came the Federal Reserve system, the federal income tax system, the Social Security system, the Job Corps program, the Farm Bank, the Federal Depositors Insurance Corporation, and on and on it went. The real impetus to adopt Keynesian economics came during the Great Depression of the 1930s. In reality the Great Depression was exacerbated by President Hoover's ill-advised decisions to raise taxes on consumer goods to feed the government's growing need for funds, and the incredibly nearsighted move to establish import quotas on foreign goods, which triggered a worldwide protectionist movement.

Herbert Hoover was booted out of office and Franklin Roosevelt was voted in with a mandate to implement Keynesian economics at every level of government. Adding momentum to these social changes was America's entry into World War II. During this period the checks and balances of the Constitution were suspended in favor of almost dictatorial powers for the president. Coming out of the war the expanded role of the central government grew until it touched the lives of virtually every American.

What we see and accept as normal today would have sparked a revolution in *any* generation prior to this century. When the federal income tax system was first suggested in 1912 it was promoted as a "voluntary" system because the supporters were fearful that the electorate would revolt if the government tried to force compliance. When Congress voted to accept the voluntary tax system, it was argued that a 1.5 percent cap should be placed on what the federal government could raise in income taxes. The resolution was soundly defeated on the basis that Americans would never allow their government to take such large sums from their wages. It was argued that if the Congress approved such a limit some future politician might be tempted to seek that outrageous amount.

From those humble beginnings we have evolved into a full-blown Keynesian-run economy. Nothing happens that does not in some way involve the federal government in everyday business affairs. The average American now believes it is the duty of our government to control the economy.

The difficulty with government manipulation of the economy is that each action creates a greater reaction and requires more manipulation. Lowering interest rates and producing credit out of thin air definitely stimulates the economy. But the laws of supply and demand swing into play, and with more people competing for the available products, prices go up and we have inflation.

When I went to college in the sixties, it was accepted that we could live with an inflation rate of 1 percent a year, and long-term interest rates as high as 4 percent. After all, with an inflation rate of 1 percent it would take 50 years or so for prices to double. And with interest rates at 4 percent your savings would double in just 18 years. No problem—right?

Except that the inflation rate didn't stay at 1 percent. Inflation is a ratio of how much new or unsecured money is put into the economy versus how much real money and assets exist. So as the government created new money out of thin air the ratio changed rapidly. Allow me to use an example.

In 1960, gold (the standard for real value for about 3,000 years) traded for about $35 an ounce on the world market. (Franklin Roosevelt had outlawed the ownership of gold in America in order to create fiat money.) The price for an ounce of gold didn't change significantly until it became legal to own gold in the U.S. again. In the meantime people began to figure out that the United States had printed a lot of new dollars with virtually nothing of any real value to back them up. Gold prices climbed rapidly once it was legal to own it again, and even ignoring the rapid speculative runup in gold prices during the late seventies, gold leveled out at around $350 to $400 an ounce—an increase of about 1,000 percent! Very few fixed-dollar investments kept track with that increase. But gold didn't actually inflate by over 1,000 percent. Gold was merely acting like an inflation barometer, reflecting the inflation that had taken place in our economy. In real buying power, investors holding paper money had lost much of their savings.

One might argue that prices didn't increase by 1,043 percent during the last 30 years, and interest rates increased to help make up some of the inflation.

I would agree (to some extent). Interest rates leveled out in the eighties at around 10 percent a year. At 10 percent, paper money investments doubled about every seven years or so. In fact, interest rates paid to investors really only reached the 10 percent level in the late eighties. But even if the rate had been 10 percent for the 30-year period from 1960 to 1990, an investor's assets would have increased about 1,600 percent. That is impressive sounding, but not compared to an inflation increase of 2,000 percent.

What about real assets? An average three-bedroom home in 1960 sold for about $10,000. In 1990 that same home (not a new one—the *same* home) sold for approximately $108,000, yielding an inflation rate of nearly 1,080 percent!

A family-sized Chevrolet sold for about $2,600 in 1960. In 1990 the same (but smaller) model sold for approximately $16,800, an inflation increase of about 650 percent. And on it goes. . . .

The point I am trying to make here is that the economy has a *direct* effect on anyone's investment philosophy, whether we want it to or not. So understanding something about the economy is essential to long-term saving. The shorter the time period, the more difficult it is to project the direction of an economy. What any knowledgeable investor must do is look at trends. Trends often develop over years, not months, and certainly not weeks.

Since this is not a book on economics I won't discuss the background of our economy any further. (For more detail on that subject, I would refer you to my book, *The Coming Economic Earthquake*, Moody Press, 1991.) But it is important to discuss where we seem to be headed. If you believe we are going to have significant long-term inflation, then your long-term investment strategy should be aggressive and diversified. But if you believe the economy will slump into a decade-long depression (as some project), then your strategy should be maximum protection of your capital.

The difficulty is that good arguments can be made for either scenario (and several others). Eventually, you must pick a side and commit yourself. I personally believe that a balanced strategy, where assets are invested in a variety of categories, is the wisest approach.

The Future Economy

With some degree of certainty I can say that the economy of the nineties, and well into the twenty-first century, will not be like that of the past 40 years. In the fifties we were the world's industrial leader with a huge surplus of trade and very little government debt. It was a wise investor who would borrow at 4 percent and invest in growing businesses that would yield 6 to 12 percent.

The sixties and early seventies was the era of massive debt funding, and by the late seventies inflation was raging and interest rates had soared. Those who borrowed money to make investments found themselves saddled with 20-percent loans in 10-percent investments. Only the incentives of ill-conceived tax shelters enticed the foolish to follow this path.

In the early eighties "Reaganomics" lowered interest rates and income taxes to stimulate a depressed economy. The eighties will surely be known as the era of junk bonds, tax shelters, and huge debts. The legacy of "Reaganomics" is the demise of the savings and loan industry, as well as several hundred banks that engaged in the debt expansion.

The debt bubble has burst and the fallout is still being determined at this time. The nineties will present unparalleled challenges to retirees trying to salvage their life savings from the ravages of a fluctuating economy and plodding inflation. A debt-ridden government gone spending-crazy will turn over every economic rock possible to generate the capital it needs to feed the "system" just a little while longer. Social Security will need huge infusions of capital as the baby boomers approach retirement. The cash reserves that should be held in trust have been spent by the government, and the wage earners of the twenty-first century will be tapped as no generation before them. You can be sure that the eligible voters of the next century will demand reform of the system that would rob them of a reasonable standard of living. Therefore, a prudent investor would do well to look to his own reserves for the retirement years. But we'll discuss that more fully later.

Recessions, Depressions, and Recoveries

Almost everyone has a theory about where the economy is headed. There is the depression theory, the inflation theory, the deflationary-inflation theory, the inflationary-depression theory, and so on. I also have an opinion, but I prefer to keep it to myself until later because if you don't hold to my opinion you may get distracted and stop reading.

The one certainty is: The economy won't stop; none ever has. The economy periodically slumps into what is commonly called a recession. A recession is neither mystical nor inexplicable. Generally speaking, a recession is caused by consumers reducing their level of spending from what it was previously. Usually the cycle of comparison is three months. In other words, if consumer spending drops for three consecutive months, the economy is considered to be "in a recession."

Obviously there are several other factors that are measured, such as consumer confidence (whatever that is), durable goods output, the wholesale index, the inventory index, the Federal Reserve index, etc. I'm convinced that most of these are created to employ economists who otherwise would have very little to talk about on the evening news.

The reasons for any economy to suffer through a recession are varied. In our generation the primary cause of recessions is consumers who take on too much debt and then have to cut back on spending to pay it off. The reduction in new debt is reflected in lower sales—hence a recession. Certainly the recession of the early nineties can be traced directly back to the credit binge of the eighties. The same can be said of the larger recession of the mid-seventies.

Recessions occur about every seven to eight years and last from a few months to as long as three years. They rarely affect the entire economy, and seldom encompass the entire country. These economic downturns are called recessions, rather than depressions, primarily because of the depth and breadth of the down-turn. In reality, a recession is simply a less severe and more local-ized depression.

Generally, depressions occur in 50- to 70-year cycles. Again, this is not some mystical timing. It is the normal operation of market cycles. As debt becomes more pronounced in an economy, the prices of goods (land, stocks, buildings, etc.) are bid higher and higher. The shorter recessions relieve the upward pressures somewhat, but often the very thing that helps the economy to recover from a recession—more debt—is what leads to the longer, more severe depression.

Ultimately the economy cannot handle any additional debt as loans have been extended for 30-, 40-, or even 50-year periods. Prices begin speculative runups based on the availability of easy credit, and even the most conservative of investors wants to get in on the action. Suddenly bankers get very nervous when they see loans being maintained through more borrowing and defaults be-coming more common, and they pull the plug. Marginal loans get called, borrowers default, and the downward spiral begins.

Usually a depression is not a steep drop into an economic abyss. Instead, it is a series of recessions followed by an increasing abundance of government-sponsored debt to shore up the flagging system. One event can often trigger the collapse. It can be as simple as a sudden drop in stock market values, as in 1929. Or it may be as insidious as the government printing money to pay its bills, as Germany did in 1919, before their great depression.

Eventually the economy will recover; it always does. It may be altered somewhat and no longer be tied to the gold standard, as happened to the U.S. in the Great Depression. After the next de-pression (and I do believe there will be another one), we may find that we use no currency at all. Predicting when and how the next depression will occur is almost impossible without a great deal of speculation. One logical projection is the last half of this decade when government debt reaches the $10 *trillion* mark, and the annual deficits reach $1 trillion a year! Depression in a debt-run economy is as certain as death. The question is not "if," but "when."

Again, the point I would like to make here is that the economy *will* recover and, if you can wait it out, so will you. The key to surviving in the short run is to carry as little debt as possible into the downturn, avoid selling when prices are down, and have enough cash on hand to buy good assets when the prices are down. Those who are in debt and in need of quick money to pay the bankers will be the losers because they will be forced to sell regardless of the loss. The economic principle is simple: It's better to be a buyer during a down cycle; then sell when the economy recovers. What is the key principle? *No debt!*

As I close this chapter, I would like to acquaint you with two key facts that should motivate you to watch the economy and make some changes in the way you perceive the future.

1. *The "on-budget" debt of the federal government is rapidly approaching $4 trillion.* "On-budget" refers to the posted amount uncontested by the Washington bureaucrats. The real debt is closer to $8.5 trillion. This includes the funds pilfered from the Social Security trust, deposit guarantees to cover the deficiencies at the savings and loans and banks, projected income deficiencies for federal retirees and service personnel, defunct retirement accounts, and insurance company defaults. There is perhaps another $500 to $600 billion in debt to secure home loans, farm loans, school loans, etc.

2. *By 1996, at the current rate of deficit, it will take all of the taxes paid by all taxpayers to pay the interest on the national debt.* The federal government will be spending money at the rate of approximately $7 billion per minute! If a husband sent his spouse out to spend a million dollars at the rate of $1,000 per day, she would return in about three years. If he sent her out to spend a billion dollars at the same rate, she would return in about 3,000 years.

Why the U.S. Economy Must Ultimately Fail

I personally believe we will see a severe decline of the U.S. economy because God's Word promises it. In Deuteronomy 28:43-45 God gave His people a warning:

> The alien who is among you shall rise above you higher and higher, but you shall go down lower and lower.
>
> He shall lend to you, but you shall not lend to him; he shall be the head, and you shall be the tail.
>
> So all these curses shall come on you and pursue you and overtake you until you are destroyed, because you would not obey the Lord your God by keeping His commandments and His statutes which He commanded you.

Observe what is happening in America. This curse is being fulfilled. Perhaps the people of this nation can turn their direction back toward the Lord. But in the long history of civilization there has never been a society that has done so.

This does not mean that there won't be people who will prosper during the decline of America; there will be. I pray it will be God's people because they willingly choose to follow His path. Our prosperity can be a great witness to many unsaved who will lose all they hold so dear—but only if we take a stand for God's way first. God's provision for our needs in a time of great turmoil will certainly be a witness, but only if we commit to using our surpluses to help others who are in need. In the final analysis, that is the only true motive for investing beyond our own needs: to meet the needs of others, in the name of the Lord.

2

Three Important Principles

THERE ARE APPROXIMATELY 12 basic principles of investing found in God's Word. During the course of this book I will discuss and amplify most of them at one time or the other. But this is not designed to be a Bible study on investing, or a theological debate on the principles of borrowing and lending. If you are interested in those topics, I would refer you to the bibliography listed in the Appendix. This particular work is designed as a "how-to" help as opposed to a "why-to."

Without question, the majority of people I have ever counseled who lost more than they made through investing violated one or more of the three basic principles taught in God's Word. Let me make it clear. Even if you follow the principles in the Bible there is no guarantee that all your investments will prosper. Since investing is more of an art than a science, losses are possible as the likes and dislikes of people change.

For instance, you may have invested in the Cord Motor Car Company, which did quite well in the twenties. However, as more modern production methods developed, Cord refused to change and the company failed. If you had Cord stock you lost your investment, even if you had followed biblical principles. Although God's Word guarantees no sure profits, the one thing that *is* guaranteed is peace and contentment. That's worth a whole lot more than money.

Principle #1—Surety

The term *surety* means "to take on a contingent liability." The most common example found in the Bible is cosigning for the debts of another person. For example, Proverbs 20:16 says, "Take his garment when he becomes surety for a stranger; and for foreigners, hold him in pledge."

The logic behind not signing surety is simple: When you sign for a debt without knowing how or when it might come due, you jeopardize your future. When it's the debt of another person, you absolutely don't know when it might come due. It's like the joke about the definition of a distant relative: a close relative who owes you money.

Let's assume that as an investor you know better than to cosign for the debts of another. Does that mean you have successfully avoided all surety? Not necessarily. When you sign *any* note payable and do not have an exculpatory clause you have signed surety.

The term *exculpate* means "to hold harmless." When you exculpate a loan it means that the lender agrees to clear you of all blame (literally to hold you harmless) if for any reason you fail to pay the loan off according to the terms of the contract.

But why would a lender be willing to exculpate a loan agreement? The fact is that most lenders won't anymore, but if they will it is only because there is more than enough collateral pledged against the loan to ensure that the lender is protected. Until the early eighties, most banks would exculpate a home mortgage contract if the buyer financed 75 percent of the appraised value or less. The assumption was that the property would always be worth more than the outstanding mortgage. Since the decline of the housing market in many areas, no commercial lenders that I know of are still willing to exculpate.

There are still some loans that require no personal guarantee (surety), but these are generally where a savings account or certificate of deposit is pledged as collateral. When cash accounts are pledged, the lender knows with certainty that the loan will be repaid—in full.

How important is the principle of surety? Surety is the primary reason many otherwise wealthy people go broke. If an investor with significant assets borrows to invest and pledges all the previous assets against each new loan, it is not a question of *if* he will go broke—only *when*.

One Christian investor, whom I'll call Martin, reflects the typical consequences of signing surety on investment loans. Martin came from a well-to-do family and inherited about $400,000. He used good business sense to parlay his inheritance into several million dollars. He was a committed Christian and well-known in evangelical circles for his giving and his personal testimony. Martin made his initial fortune in the oil business in Texas and Oklahoma and then took advantage of the blossoming real estate market in those areas to diversify and expand. By the mid-seventies his personal worth was estimated to be nearly $50 million and included oil wells, office buildings, and vast undeveloped real estate holdings in and around Dallas.

His personal net worth and unerring ability to spot good deals made him the darling of the commercial lenders. He regularly had bankers and S&L officers calling him with offers to lend huge sums of money for his development projects. At any given time he could call any of several bankers and arrange a million-dollar loan on the telephone.

The Arab oil embargo of the late seventies did nothing but enhance his financial position as his properties and oil-related assets skyrocketed in value. Using his asset base he borrowed several million dollars more to invest in oil and gas development, as well as entire city blocks of commercial real estate in the "oil patch."

Then, in 1981, the oil market collapsed as the OPEC nations began to cheat on their partners and export more oil than agreed upon. Prices plummeted in the oil industry; and commercial real estate in the oil patch, woefully overbuilt, stood empty.

Martin struggled under the debt load but was confident that eventually the oil market would recover and the recession in Texas and Oklahoma would end. After all, his family had ridden out the Depression years and survived; he would too.

But Martin had signed surety on every loan he acquired since the early eighties. When he borrowed, he pledged everything he had accumulated up to that point, whether he realized it or not.

Even so, he wasn't really worried. His properties were good, sound investments. The negative cash flow was well within his ability to manage until the economy turned around. At least it was as long as the bankers were willing to extend more credit on the basis of his total net worth.

Then the oil market collapse became front-page news as giant lending institutions failed because of non-performing loans. In their typical overreactive fashion known as "close the barn door after the horses have left," the government moved in and shut down many of the struggling savings and loans. They immediately declared all the outstanding loans due and payable. Within one month Martin found himself in default with no one willing to lend him another dime.

Property after property was foreclosed by the government regulators and suits were filed against Martin and his companies for recovery. By 1989 Martin owed the government (the Resolution Trust) nearly $60 million. His total asset base was down to less than $12 million by then; statistically he was bankrupt.

Then the next blow came from the IRS. With each foreclosed property came what is called "phantom income" through forgiveness of indebtedness. He owed the IRS nearly $4 million in taxes.

In 1990 Martin saw his home and cars being auctioned off by a court-appointed administrator. They allowed him and his family to retain their clothes and a few personal items of jewelry that were family heirlooms. Had Martin even excluded his home from surety it could have been sold for enough for his family to live comfortably for the rest of their lives. But he didn't. Every asset he owned was pledged against every loan he negotiated.

In a generation where surety is accepted as normal, a prudent investor would do well never to borrow if it means risking everything made up to that point. As Proverbs 17:18 says, "A man lacking in sense pledges, and becomes surety in the presence of his neighbor."

Principle #2—Risk

If you are going to invest, even in a certificate of deposit, you will assume some risk. The general rule is: the greater the potential return, the greater the potential risk. That's why a corporate bond usually promises a higher percentage than a government bond. In order to attract investors they must offer a higher rate than the government does. Otherwise, why take the risk?

Risk, in and of itself, is not necessarily bad. After all, that's what the free market system is all about. The people who take the risks have the potential of great return, and therefore create more goods and jobs. But when the risk goes beyond common sense it is poor stewardship, and losses become the norm. Some people take risks that are so ridiculous they make no sense at all. It's like tossing a coin and having it land heads three times in a row and then betting double or nothing that it will do so forever. It won't, and you will eventually lose.

With a few exceptions, those who take excessive risks do so because they lack the knowledge and ability to evaluate the actual risk. As Proverbs 21:5 says, "The plans of the diligent lead surely to advantage, but everyone who is hasty comes surely to poverty."

Not long ago I was counseling with a couple in their late sixties who had lost their entire life savings in one of the riskiest investments possible—commodities speculation.

When this elderly gentleman shared how they had lost their savings I was honestly astounded. Over the years I have counseled with many high-income people who lost money (a lot of it) in commodities, but never a retired couple who had made their money the old-fashioned way, by hard work.

"Why," I asked, "would you take such a risk? Did a friend or relative talk you into it?"

"No," he replied in an apologetic voice, his head down. "I attended a one-day seminar on investing where the man said we could double our money in commodities. Since we didn't have quite enough to live on comfortably, I thought it would be a good way to make the money we needed."

"Didn't you object?" I asked his wife.

"I didn't know enough to object. I thought he was investing in some pigs since he said he was in pork bellies. And I thought soybeans would be a good investment too."

Unfortunately this couple learned the hard way that you cannot only lose what you have, but even more than you have sometimes. The husband had opened a margin account to buy commodities and lost not only their savings but owed nearly $5,000 to the exchange as well. Fortunately the broker was willing to absorb the loss and let them keep their home. Nevertheless, this husband was forced back into the sign-painting business at age 68.

Remember that risk is not the issue. Every investment carries some degree of risk. Just be very certain you know what the actual risk is, and decide if you're willing and able to absorb it. Remember the counsel of Proverbs 27:12, "A prudent man sees evil and hides himself, the naive proceed and pay the penalty."

Principle #3—Diversification

In an ever-changing economy no one can say with certainty what will be a good investment over the next 10 years and what will be a loser. Over the long run there are basic areas of investing that do well. These include food, housing, transportation, health care, etc. But even a casual observer of economics will tell you that each of these areas has gone through some major cycles during the twentieth century. An investor who had his or her total funds in any one area would have found it difficult to survive during a major down cycle without a large cash reserve and very little debt.

Who would have believed 50 years ago that farmers today would not be able to sell their products for what it costs to grow them? And yet in the second half of the twentieth century we live in a starving world, with a surplus of food, but no one to buy it. Why? Because our American standard of living is so much higher than theirs that they cannot afford our produce.

Or who would have imagined that in a nation of 100 million drivers, who own 70 million automobiles, an investment in one of the big three car companies would go sour? But then along came the Japanese who took a large part of the market away, and the Big Three had to fight for their very survival.

In 1974 investors were begging oil and gas developers to take their money. The OPEC embargo was on; oil was in short supply, selling at $36 a barrel; and the major media networks told us the world was going to run out, remember? In the mid-eighties investors were calling the developers to see why they hadn't heard from them, except to ask for more money. Oil was selling for less than $20 a barrel again, and natural gas could not be sold at any price most of the time.

When the EPA began its terrorist attack on small oil and gas developers, threatening massive fines for even the slightest infractions of their unintelligible pollution standards, investors, facing potential fines of millions of dollars, panicked and shut down producing wells, plugging them with concrete just to satisfy the EPA.

The point is, there are no sure things; so diversification is essential to long-term stability. The world's wealthiest man, King Solomon, once wrote, "Divide your portion to seven, or even to eight, for you do not know what misfortune may occur on the earth" (Ecclesiastes 11:2). That advice is still as sound today as it was 3,000 years ago. As my grandfather's generation used to say, "Never put all your eggs in one basket."

As you will see later, diversification means more than just splitting your money between stocks and bonds. It means investing in some assets that are "paper," such as stocks or bonds, and some that are real, such as real estate. It also means investing in assets that are not totally dependent on one country's economy:

European stocks and bonds, Japanese companies, mortgage loans in the Eastern bloc nations, etc. This may all seem too complicated to someone with $1,000 to invest for future college needs, and it is. But for others, with $10,000 to invest toward retirement in 30 years, it is a necessity, and really is not very complicated if you know where to look.

3

Why Invest?

THERE ARE SCRIPTURALLY sound reasons for investing, and there are unscriptural reasons for investing. If you are investing for the wrong reasons it's like having your ladder leaning against the wrong building. It won't matter how high you climb, you still end up on the wrong building.

Right Reasons for Investing

From a biblical perspective, only three legitimate reasons to invest money exist:

Right Motive #1: Multiply to Give More
Take a fresh look at the Parable of the Talents Jesus told in Luke 19:12-26:

> A certain nobleman went to a distant country to receive a kingdom for himself, and then return. And he called ten of his slaves, and gave them ten minas, and said to them, "Do business with this until I come back."
>
> But his citizens hated him, and sent a delegation after him, saying, "We do not want this man to reign over us."
>
> And it came about that when he returned, after receiving the kingdom, he ordered that these slaves, to whom he had given the money, be called to him in order that he might know what business they had done.
>
> And the first appeared, saying, "Master, your mina has made ten minas more." And he said to him, "Well done, good slave,

because you have been faithful in a very little thing, be in authority over ten cities.''

And the second came, saying, ''Your mina, master, has made five minas.'' And he said to him also, ''And you are to be over five cities.''

And another came, saying, ''Master, behold your mina, which I kept put away in a handkerchief; for I was afraid of you, because you are an exacting man; you take up what you did not lay down, and reap what you did not sow.''

He said to him, ''By your own words I will judge you, you worthless slave. Did you know that I am an exacting man, taking up what I did not lay down, and reaping what I did not sow? Then why did you not put the money in the bank, and having come, I would have collected it with interest?''

And he said to the bystanders, ''Take the mina away from him, and give it to the one who has the ten minas.''

And they said to him, ''Master, he has ten minas already.''

''I tell you, that to everyone who has shall more be given, but from the one who does not have, even what he does have shall be taken away.''

This parable from the Lord tells us that God entrusts wealth to some of His stewards (managers) so that it will be available to Him at a later date. The management of wealth requires that it be invested or multiplied, as the parable reflects.

Right Motive #2: Meet Future Family Needs

The indication throughout God's Word is that the head of a family should provide for his own. To do this in our generation requires the sacrifice of some short-range spending to meet future needs such as education, housing, or a start in business.

Even though retirement is completely out of balance in our society (everyone seems to want to quit work), it would be very shortsighted for most people to assume they can earn as much at age 70 as they do at 50, or that they will be able to live off of Social Security. Good planning requires laying aside some of the surplus for future needs. Proverbs 6:6–8 says, ''Go to the ant, O sluggard, observe her ways and be wise, which, having no chief, officer or ruler, prepares her food in the summer, and gathers her provision in the harvest."

The same can be said of education for our children. Not every young man or woman should attend college. But everyone needs some advanced training in our generation to reach his or her full potential. Wise parents lay a small amount aside each month to help their children reach their full potential.

No one can argue that basic housing is beyond the reach of most young couples today, and apparently will be so for the foreseeable future. Once you have reached your own financial goals you should be able to help your children purchase adequate housing for their families. As long as parents don't go overboard, there is little danger of spoiling children by helping them get into a home, especially if it's a two-bedroom, one-bath starter home.

Right Motive #3: Further the Gospel and Fund Special Needs

Most of us as Christians give to several organizations regularly. As the Apostle Paul said, "Now concerning the collection for the saints, as I directed the churches of Galatia, so do you also. On the first day of every week let each one of you put aside and save, as he may prosper, that no collections be made when I come" (1 Corinthians 16:1–2). Such giving is necessary to maintain and promote the Gospel. But often additional needs come up that require special funding. These include building programs, special emergency relief funds, opportunities to send Bibles into countries that had been closed (such as those in Europe's Eastern bloc), and so on. Investing wisely allows you to do this kind of giving, provided that you always keep some of the funds in cash reserves.

If the "church" is ever to break out of the borrowing habit then Christians who invest must maintain some surpluses and be willing to give to legitimate needs. Just think of the advantage of being able to fund *reasonable* building programs without debt. The interest saved could feed millions of hungry people and fund most of the training for worldwide evangelism.

One principle taught in Proverbs always comes to mind when I consider the biblical rationale behind investing for future needs:

"There is precious treasure and oil in the dwelling of the wise, but a foolish man swallows it up" (Proverbs 21:20).

Wrong Reasons for Investing

I rather suspect, based on my observations of people I have counseled, that the majority of Christians who engage in speculative investing do so for the wrong reasons. If someone is trying to invest to be able to give more, his pattern of giving will reflect it long before he "strikes it rich." Giving is *not* easier as you make more; it is actually more difficult. A stingy person doesn't get more benevolent as he prospers, he gets increasingly more stingy. Charles Dickens understood this principle well when he wrote about Ebenezer Scrooge in his famous *Christmas Carol.* Only when someone's heart is attuned to God's are more resources an asset. As the Lord said in the Parable of the Rich Fool recorded in Luke 12:16–21: "This very night your soul is required of you; and now who will own what you have prepared?" (verse 20)

Wrong Motive #1: Greed

Greed simply means that a person always wants more than he needs. In our generation that is an easy motive to rationalize. After all, things might happen that would wipe out what we already have. So just a little more is always necessary.

As you will see as we progress through this book, ultimately God is our resource. If you lose sight of that truth no amount will ever be enough. Perhaps the most crucial question any Christian (or non-Christian) must ask is, "How much is enough?" For Howard Hughes, $2 billion wasn't enough. For Donald Trump, $1 billion was too little. Michael Milken's $100 million a year apparently wasn't enough.

At some point a Christian has to stop and decide why he (or she) is trying to make and store more. I would hate to die and find out that the epitaph on my tombstone read, "The Richest Fool in the Cemetery."

Not long ago I read about a professing Christian businessman who was reported to be worth $3 billion. I don't know anything about his living or giving habits, nor do I need to. What I do know is that he could probably get along quite well on $1 billion, or maybe even $100 million or so. I wrote him a letter (that he never answered) challenging him to give away the surplus above what he actually needed. Think of the testimony of a Christian committed enough to voluntarily give away $2 billion to spread the Gospel.

The unsaved of our world are not impressed by how much a Christian can make and keep. After all, few Christians can make as much money as a rock star. The one thing that normally does impress them is someone who gives away everything for what he or she believes in.

It has been my observation that those people who lose the most money typically do so because of greed. The get-rich-quick con men rely heavily on greed to blind the people to whom they sell. Greed is what motivates high-income professionals to risk money in abusive tax shelters. Most could pay their taxes and still have plenty to live on comfortably. But the desire to hang on to a little more tempts them to take excessive risks.

One doctor came in for counseling complaining that a Christian investment advisor had talked him into risking money in an opal mine in Brazil (that he subsequently lost). The opals were appraised at a highly exaggerated value (my assessment) and then donated to museums as tax write-offs.

On paper the deal looked great. The doctor invested $10,000, signed an unsecured note for another $90,000, and received a tax deduction of $100,000 the first year. He committed to lesser investments, but with the same ratios, over the next five years. Since he was in a 50-percent tax bracket at the time, he stood to gain well in excess of $100,000 over the next five or six years. The $90,000 note was to be repaid in Brazilian currency which was being devalued at the rate of nearly 20 percent a month. So in one year he could pay the note off with about 2,000 American dollars—all saved from taxes he would have paid anyway.

Unfortunately, the 1986 tax act killed all such abusive tax shelters and tagged the users with 50-percent penalties as well. One could argue that the law wasn't fair; what tax law is? But it is the law, and this doctor got stuck for all the original taxes, plus the penalty, plus interest—and to add insult to injury he lost the original $10,000 he invested. All told he repaid $140,000 for the two years he was in the deal. Had he paid the original taxes that were due he would have owed only $75,000.

My question to him was, "What is your complaint?"

He was taken back a little and replied, "Should I sue the advisor who steered me into such a bad deal?"

I believe that, according to 1 Corinthians 6:1, Christians shouldn't sue Christians. But I didn't even raise that issue, because there was a more fundamental issue at the heart of this problem. So I asked, "What was your motive in investing?"

"What do you mean?" he replied irritatedly. "I wanted to reduce my taxes."

"Why didn't you just give the money away, then?" I countered. "That would have reduced your gross income, and consequently your taxes."

He didn't answer so I offered an alternate explanation. "You invested out of an attitude of greed, because that's what a get-rich-quick attitude is. You expected to get something for nothing, and ended up with nothing for something."

He got up angrily and stormed out of my office, saying that he had come to me because I had introduced him to the investment advisor and I had a responsibility to help him get his money back. I knew that he expected me to confront the errant advisor, and although he didn't know it, I had already done so even before he came to see me. Unfortunately, rather than face the consequences of his actions, the advisor fled the country to avoid prosecution by the IRS.

It was almost three years later when the doctor called and asked if we could have lunch. At that meeting he apologized for his attitude and the fact that he had been angry at me for three years, particularly because I didn't seem all that sympathetic to his plight at the time. "I wanted you at least to accept some of the blame," he said.

"But," he added, "you were absolutely right. I acted out of greed, and was arrogant enough to think that I could outsmart the IRS. I have forgiven the advisor (who is still missing) and have committed myself to a more reasonable lifestyle" (an offshoot of repaying the IRS).

Then he added, "I have even forgiven you!"

I told him how much I appreciated that, and I had heard of a great investment in an atomic plasma car engine and wondered if he would be interested. "Just kidding," I added.

Wrong Motive #2: Slothfulness

It might seem strange to say that slothfulness is a motive for investing, but it is. Often people don't plan well during the earlier years of their lives and consequently, when faced with college expenses for their children or retirement, they panic and try to generate in five years what they should have saved over the previous 20. That's a little like counting on the lottery for the majority of your retirement funds.

A regular habit of spending less than you make (no matter what you make) and saving the difference is the proper investment plan. Hasty speculation, on the other hand, is characterized by Proverbs 20:4 which says, "The sluggard does not plow after the autumn, so he begs during the harvest and has nothing."

My favorite example of good planning is a pastor I met several years ago who worked with Village Missions. I was teaching a conference for some Village Missions pastors in California, and had been discussing the need to be good stewards of what God gives us, whether it is a little or a lot.

I knew approximately what each of the men attending the meeting made, because I had discussed their average compensation with the ministry's director. At that time a young pastor with a family made about $8,000 a year; an older pastor made as much as $10,000. At those income levels I knew I would not be talking about investment principles to most of them, so I concentrated on budgeting instead.

During one of the breaks a pastor, who appeared to be in his late sixties, came up and asked if we could meet to discuss his financial problems. I set up a time for later that day, knowing that I was probably dealing with a pastor facing retirement with virtually no savings and no Social Security available.

Instead, what he shared was an incredible story of how he had saved a sizable fortune out of his meager earnings over the previous 40 years.

He had invested his savings in small parcels of land in each community where he had ministered. By selling off pieces of the land they had accumulated, he and his wife had been able to send their four children through college, and one even through medical school. All with no debt!

He had recently sold off most of the remaining properties and his problem was what to do with the income his nearly $300,000 was generating in the bank!

I know of many people who earned 1,000 times what this man ever made as a pastor and retained nothing at his age. He was a diligent steward who handled a little well so the Lord entrusted more to him. As Matthew 25:29 says, "For to everyone who has shall more be given, and he shall have an abundance; but from the one who does not have, even what he does have shall be taken away."

Wrong Motive #3: Ego

Many people, Christians included, invest to bolster their pride and ego. Why else would someone who already has millions of dollars spend countless hours and risk everything he owns to make more?

I am reminded of the wealthy Texas oil family in which the brothers inherited a fortune so vast that it could not be calculated. The best estimate was somewhere between $4 and $7 billion— certainly a sufficient amount for several lifetimes. In the early seventies they risked a large amount in the commodities market and lost it. Then in the late seventies they risked their entire fortune in the silver market and lost everything. Why? To "corner" a world commodity. In other words, ego (my opinion). Certainly it was not a *need* for more money.

On a lesser scale I have observed individuals who were risking all that they had (and then some) because they were jealous of the success of others they knew. In a scriptural context that is ego. As Proverbs 29:23 says, "A man's pride will bring him low, but a humble spirit will obtain honor."

Wrong Motive #4: The Game of It
To some people, making money is simply a game. They have no particular attachment to the money; it's winning that's important to them. In many ways this is perhaps the most destructive of all wrong motives because it becomes an addiction just like alcohol or drugs. Everybody and everything becomes a pawn in the game: family, friends, even God.

I have known several people who professed to be Christians but were totally absorbed by the game of making money. There are some outside indicators that serve as warnings: They can never accept a loss; they will do whatever is necessary to win; they will cheat when necessary.

The worst thing about it is that usually these people refuse to see themselves as they really are and refuse to accept any responsibility for their actions. As Proverbs 28:6 says, "Better is the poor who walks in his integrity, than he who is crooked though he be rich." I also like what Proverbs 16:2 says, "All the ways of a man are clean in his own sight, but the Lord weighs the motives."

An individual I'll call Mike was one of the first people I counseled to whom making money was truly just a game. He came to my office one Monday after attending a Christian Financial Concepts seminar the previous weekend. His reason for coming was to share with me how good he was at the "game" of investing.

After reviewing some of the financial statements he had brought with him, I was impressed that indeed he had been extremely successful with his investments. He had parlayed a few thousand dollars into nearly $3 million in less than five years using a fairly simple, straightforward strategy. He bought distressed properties, particularly residential rentals, fixed them up, and sold them back to the tenants using "wrap-around" mortgages. Usually he could secure mortgages for more than his total purchase and remodeling costs. Essentially he had no money in the properties and nonrecourse loans. He cleared from $10,000 to $50,000 per sale.

What impressed me most about his strategy was that there was very little actual risk involved. I thought it was generous that he would be willing to share his knowledge with others so I asked him to join me at an upcoming conference. (I have since learned not to do this, but back then I was somewhat naive.)

At the conference he spent nearly an hour telling everyone how great and successful he was. Finally as his time was running out he shared just enough about what he was doing to attract a large group to him after leaving the platform. Right then I knew I had made a fundamental error in judgment. Mike wasn't interested in helping others. He was interested in letting others know who he was, and how successful he had been. His ego was showing through the thin Christian veneer.

Over the next several years Mike made an assortment of investments with some of the people who attended the first and only conference at which he taught. With virtually no exception they all later reported that, although the investments appeared to do well, they received no return for their share. Each time Mike would pressure them into paying him "management" fees that absorbed their profits.

Mike did not need the money. He lived well on his own investment income. The truth was that everything he did was for the game of it, and he was heard to say more than once to a disgruntled partner, "That's the golden rule: He who has the gold makes the rules."

Some signs that anyone should look for in dealing with the Mikes of this world are:

- A lot of braggadocio and self-promotion.
- Total control of everything and everyone where money is involved.
- A lack of accountability, including financial statements.
- A track record of using others, and never taking a loss themselves.

I will end this discussion on motives with one last comment: *Set your goals and pray about them before attempting to do any investing.* If you or your spouse sense that your motives are anything but biblical, it would be better to give the money away now rather than risk losing something far more important than money—your relationship with the Lord. There is a nonfinancial passage recorded in Matthew 5:29–30 that I believe fits this situation well:

> And if your right eye makes you stumble, tear it out, and throw it from you; for it is better for you that one of the parts of your body perish, than for your whole body to be thrown into hell.
> And if your right hand makes you stumble, cut it off, and throw it from you; for it is better for you that one of the parts of your body perish, than for your whole body to go into hell.

4

Risk and Return

WILL ROGERS AND his friend, Wiley Post, had invested in several "opportunities" that Wiley had suggested, most of which lost money. Wiley Post was perhaps the best-known aviator of his day and was prone to risk-taking. Will Rogers was certainly the best-known political humorist of his day and had lived from hand to mouth so long in the early days of his career that he felt a strong compulsion to put something aside for his later years. He knew that a fickle public might shift its attention to another performer at any time.

The string of failures Will and Wiley experienced was nothing shy of miraculous. Rogers once told a reporter, "You couldn't pick that many losers by chance." One morning as Rogers and a reporter sat eating breakfast at a hotel in Washington, Wiley Post popped in to the restaurant, spotted Will, and came over to his table. Rogers could see that his friend had something on his mind, and asked, "What's up, Wiley?"

Post looked first at the reporter and then in a low whisper replied, "I just got a call from one of the biggest oil men in Oklahoma. He's got the best deal I ever heard of and wants us to have a part of it. He says the return on this deal will be bigger than anything he has ever done."

Will Rogers sipped his coffee for a couple of minutes and then responded, "You know, Wiley, I guess I'm more concerned with the return *of* my money, than I am the return *on* my money."

The reporter used that quip in his article, and it became one of the most commonly quoted bits of humor during the oil bust of the early thirties. The principle is still just as sound as ever: The return of your money is the highest priority. Anything beyond that is a blessing.

Rating Systems

There are a myriad of ways that investment advisors and counselors grade the risk of an investment. Almost without exception the degree of risk is rated based on the guaranteed return of the principle, not how much earnings the investment might yield. For example, most government securities—Treasury bills, savings bonds, and the like—are graded as the lowest risk of any investments. This is primarily because it is assumed that the government will always repay its debts. This may or may not be a valid assumption, given the current state of our government. But, nonetheless, ratings services have accepted the primary debts of the U.S. government as the baseline upon which all other investments are graded. This means that when the government offers its debt to the public, the interest rate it must pay to attract the funds it needs is usually the lowest of all securities.

Thus we can also equate rate with risk. The lower the risk, the lower the rate of return. The higher the risk, the higher the rate of return. Although this is not an absolute by any means, it is a good general rule to observe. So when you see an investment that promises a high rate of return you can logically assume it is because the risk is proportionately higher also.

Obviously other factors must be analyzed to determine true risk. One might argue that since a government bond carries a fixed interest rate its value can be eroded through inflation, which is true. So if the future worth of the money is brought into the equation, the concept of risk becomes more clouded.

On this basis, a good argument exists that gold is the most risk-free investment since it traditionally holds its value even in an inflationary economy. But nothing in the sales structure of gold guarantees the return of the original investment. Therefore it fails the initial test we prescribed: the return of our principal. So having come full circle on evaluating risk, and even though inflation may erode the buying power of an investment in government securities, such an investment still carries the lowest risk rating. Later, when we evaluate various investments, we will evaluate the risk of all other investments in relation to government securities.

Any rating system must also factor in the potential loss of principal and buying power through what is called "the future worth of money." In order to evaluate the future worth of an investment it is necessary to balance risk, return, and time.

For example, suppose that I arbitrarily assign a U.S. Treasury bill (T-bill) a risk factor of 1 (the least risk on a scale of 1 to 10). On the same level would be U.S. savings bonds, Treasury bonds, etc., because they are all primary obligations of the government. But do they all actually carry the same degree of risk? Not when inflation and future value are considered. A T-bill which matures in seven years may return between 8 and 9 percent in a given market, while the savings bonds would yield only 6 to 7 percent for the same period. Therefore it would not be logical to give both the same rating, even though they are both primary obligations of the federal government.

So let's add to our rating system another factor: *yield*. Assuming that our rate of return is a low of 4 percent and a high of 9 percent in government securities, we would then have the following rating:

T-bill: Risk = 1, Return = 7
Savings bond: Risk = 1, Return = 4

So you would be better off, all other factors being equal, to invest in the T-bill than in the savings bond. Why? Because you assume no higher risk and yet get a higher return.

When the time factor is added, the equation gets progressively more complicated. For instance, with no annual inflation (current or anticipated), a one-year T-bill paying 6 percent and a three-year T-note paying 7 percent would carry the same risk. But if the annual inflation rate was 5 percent, the three-year T-note must be considered a higher risk for "future value" because it cannot be adjusted during that time. The one-year T-bill could be adjusted annually for inflation through higher yields.

Rating any investment is not always simple, but I will return to this approach throughout the book when discussing specific investments. What any logical investor wants is a way to reduce risk while increasing yield. Just as obvious is the fact that it makes no sense to take on a higher risk without the potential for higher yield. Successful investing means determining what risk you must take to accomplish your long-term goals.

For example, a 35-year-old businessman making $100,000 a year who is able to save $25,000 annually toward his retirement in 30 years need not take excessive risks with his money. His total objective can be accomplished by investing in low-risk securities that offset inflation.

However, a 50-year-old man earning $40,000 a year who is able to save $10,000 annually toward retirement could not accomplish his objectives in 15 years without seeking a much higher rate of return, along with the higher risk. He would need to match the inflation rate, plus double his principal over the next 15 years. To do so would require a return on investment of approximately 20 to 25 percent a year. He won't do that in T-bills.

A widow, whom I'll call Betty, came in for counseling about her investment strategy. Betty's husband, Jim, had died the previous year and left her an estate consisting of $200,000 in insurance and about $150,000 in income properties. She also had their home, which was worth approximately $125,000, with a mortgage of $50,000.

Betty was 56 years old, did not desire to work, and would not be eligible for Social Security for another six years. At age 62 she would be eligible to draw approximately $600 a month in retirement benefits.

She needed approximately $1,400 a month to live comfortably. So her investment strategy had to be designed to provide her with that amount for six years (plus inflation), and then $800 a month for the rest of her life (estimated, statistically, to be 30 years).

A financial planner had recommended that she invest the life insurance in an annuity paying a guaranteed 7 percent a year for life. That would provide her with a monthly income of $1,166 for as long as she lived. In addition, with $600 a month rent from the income properties she would have a total long-term income of nearly $1,800, certainly enough to meet her needs.

On the surface, the plan she was considering was more than adequate. But I felt it had two essential flaws: First, the income properties were nearly 30 years old and required considerable maintenance. While her husband was alive he did the maintenance and leasing himself. But since she could not do the same, she was faced with an annual outlay of approximately $3,000 over the next 10 years to maintain and rent the properties. Thus her net income would be about $4,200 a year or $350 a month—a pretty poor return on an investment of $150,000 (about 2.8 percent).

The second flaw was that her annuity income was based on a single life plan. Thus, when she died, the annuity would stop. She would not be able to pass the principal or income to her children and grandchildren, a strong desire of hers. Also, since the annuity represented nearly 60 percent of her available assets, I felt that investing it in one company was too risky.

The plan we finally settled on was simple and less risky, while still accomplishing her objectives.

Step 1. She moved into one of the rental homes for three years, making it her principal residence. She then sold it for $70,000, took her one-time tax exclusion for the sale of a residence, and moved back into her original home. She used $50,000 of the proceeds to pay off her home mortgage. That was the equivalent of a 10 percent return on investment—guaranteed.

Step 2. She sold the other rental unit for about $75,000, and after taxes and tithes had approximately $60,000 left over. With the $20,000 from the first sale, she had $80,000 to invest, which she put in T-bills at 7.5 percent interest for 10 years.

Step 3. The $200,000 from the insurance was split four ways and invested in a combination of an 8-percent annuity, government bonds at 8.5 percent, tax certificates at 14 percent, and a government-backed money market fund at 9 percent.

The total income from her investments was approximately $18,500 per year. Since she paid off her mortgage she also saved $7,000 a year in payments.

The net result was to improve her income, lower her risk, and remove the headache of rental houses. As you can see, it is possible to increase yield while lowering the risks by simple planning. In addition, since the majority of Betty's money is invested in timed deposits it can be adjusted for inflation periodically. Eventually all but the $50,000 in the annuity can be passed along to her heirs.

It is amazing how much risk the average investor is willing to assume. One would think that, having earned the money to invest by trading labor and time, most people would be extremely cautious about risking it. Unfortunately, that is not always so. All too often those who labored to earn their stake are looking to strike it rich, so to speak, so that they can stop their labor. As noted earlier, another reason that many people are willing to take inordinate risks is that they feel they have waited too long to get started on a plan. The need may be to educate their children, start a business, or retire. But the closer they get to an assumed goal, the greater the temptation to take risks.

I wish I could indelibly imprint on everyone's consciousness the three basic reasons that most people take excessive risks. If you will take the time to read the next few pages and to adopt the supporting Scriptures as your lifetime guides, you can save yourself (and your loved ones) a lot of money and grief.

In spite of all the admonitions in God's Word against excessive risk-taking, I still receive letters from Christians who heard the truth but still violated these basic principles and lost huge amounts of money. I suppose *huge* is a relative term. If you lose all you have, it's a huge amount.

Principle #1: Get Rich Quick

Proverbs 23:4–5 says, "Do not weary yourself to gain wealth, cease from your consideration of it. When you set your eyes on it, it is gone. For wealth certainly makes itself wings, like an eagle that flies toward the heavens."

I have discussed the issue of "get rich quick" in other books, but I would feel remiss if I didn't cover it again, especially in a book dealing with investments. So for those who have read some of this before, forgive the repetition. For those who have not, please read carefully. This simple discussion can save you much grief and embarrassment.

It continually amazes me how gullible Christians are when it comes to get-rich-quick schemes. With rare exception, virtually all the nationwide get-rich-quick schemes begin inside Christian circles. The only logical conclusion I have been able to draw is that Christians tend to trust one another more than average non-Christians do and therefore are more easily influenced.

Perhaps one additional factor is the fact that we believe in the supernatural and will risk money in investments that require supernatural intervention. It's almost as if the more impossible the investment, the more Christians want to believe in it. This is particularly true where the promoters recite Bible verses to justify their claims.

In 1980, at the height of the Arab oil embargo, I was approached by a well-known Christian leader who told me he had been given a "revelation" from God about how to solve America's oil problems. Intrigued by his apparent sincerity, I agreed to hear his revelation. He and two other members of his leadership flew to Atlanta to present the most fantastic revelation of our generation, if it were true.

It seems that he had been approached by an angel one evening while he was praying and the angel revealed to him where the hidden oil deposits in America were located. This angel had pointed to a spot on a map where the largest oil reserves in the world lay untapped. Since it was in an area where no oil had ever been discovered previously and where the geology did not conform to any patterns established by the petroleum industry, I commented, "That would certainly explain why the oil companies have not located this vast, untapped treasure." They were looking in the "oil patch," and this was definitely not in that area.

When I asked why he felt there was oil in such an unlikely location, his response was, "Because God told me that is where it is." As far as he was concerned, that settled the issue once and for all.

"But how do you know your input is from God?" I asked.

He looked at me as if I were a heretic who had challenged the deity of Christ. "I was praying when God told me this," he said in a commanding tone.

The other two men with him nodded in agreement, certain that all my objections had been satisfied since he had received this revelation while praying. They suffered from a common delusion that prayer in itself has some supernatural meaning or power. Don't misunderstand me. I believe God can and does reveal Himself supernaturally through prayer. But the process of praying is not supernatural—God is.

"What do you need from me?" I asked, realizing further argument was useless since their minds were made up that this was a vision from God.

"We need $3 million to drill a well in this spot," the pastor replied. "It will be the biggest oil find in the world and will make us independent of imported oil. If you will endorse this project we will be able to raise the development funds."

They had already raised nearly $50,000 from people in their church to do a prospectus and brochures. But raising the rest of the money had proved very difficult.

Since I had made an absolute commitment several years before never to endorse any investment products, this helped to extricate me from an uncomfortable situation. I told them the truth, "I never endorse any financial venture. God has not gifted me to give investment advice."

I also suggested that they retain the counsel of a good securities attorney since they were offering stock in several states and it appeared to me as if they had not completed the necessary registrations.

The pastor replied that their securities registration had been blocked by Satan's forces within the state governments, and they had decided to accept money from people in those states anyway. At that point I backed away from even listening to further discussion on the subject. Circumstances sometimes warrant opposing government rules, but only when those rules conflict with the ordinances of God. Such would be the case if witnessing were prohibited by law, if worship of God were restricted, or if babies were being aborted. But certainly securities registration would not fall into that category.

The three men went through with the securities sale and a limited drilling operation, raising nearly $600,000 from Christians who heard about the project. In one instance a pastor from another state told his people they would be failing God if they didn't invest in this oil venture. Several families borrowed against their homes to do so. One 80-year-old couple risked their entire savings in the project.

The hole was dry and all the funds were lost, along with several pastors' credibility. Lawsuits flew like snowflakes as disgruntled Christians sued one another in violation of Paul's teachings in 1 Corinthians 6. The media picked up on the lawsuits because many elderly people had been duped into investing. As a result the cause of Christ was set back in the communities most affected. Ultimately the promoters of the venture—including the pastor—were prosecuted, convicted, and given prison sentences.

These weren't stupid people—neither the promoters nor the investors. Neither were they particularly greedy; although without a doubt, the promised returns influenced their decisions. They simply violated the basic rules that God's Word teaches on "get-rich-quick":

1. *Don't get involved with things you don't understand.* Proverbs 24:3–4 says, "By wisdom a house is built, and by under- standing it is established; and by knowledge the rooms are filled with all precious and pleasant riches."

It would be difficult to talk a geologist into an investment like the one I just described. Why? Is it because he's smarter than the average doctor who risks his hard-earned money? No, it is because he has acquired wisdom and judgment in the area of his expertise.

2. *Don't risk money you cannot afford to lose.* Ecclesiastes 5:14 says, "When those riches were lost through a bad investment and he had fathered a son, then there was nothing to support him." Not too long ago I risked a modest amount of money in the stock of a company that had been manufacturing computer disk drives. The company had run into some bad times due to poor management and the stock had fallen from about $20 a share to $1. I had done business with the firm several years earlier when they were the leader in the industry and I felt that perhaps under new management they could recover. So I risked $500 in their stock. I didn't want to lose the money, but I knew I could afford to. I did.

Within one month, the company filed for bankruptcy and my stock was worthless. It was a high-risk venture, but it was not a get-rich-quick scheme. I knew the risk, could absorb the loss, and was willing to take a long-term gain.

The most common source of investment capital for get-rich- quick schemes is borrowed money. When investors risk borrowed money in anything, they are being foolish. When they borrow against their homes and needed savings (education, retirement, children), they are being stupid (in my opinion).

One pastor who invested in the oil exploration scheme I de- scribed earlier actually borrowed against his elderly mother's home to do so. That goes beyond ignorance into the realm of stupidity.

3. *Don't make a quick decision.* Psalm 37:7 says, "Rest in the Lord and wait patiently for Him; do not fret because of him who prospers in his way, because of the man who carries out wicked

schemes." One of the prime elements of a get-rich-quick scheme is that the promoters want a quick decision. The way this is done is to make a potential investor believe that so many people want in on the deal that they're doing you a favor by giving you the opportunity first.

Usually the initial pitch is that you will get a discount or some other special consideration for getting in early. "But if you delay," the promoter warns, "the opportunity will be lost and you'll be left out."

In truth, there is an advantage in getting into most get-rich-quick schemes early on, because most of them don't survive long. So if you get in early maybe you can "sucker" enough friends in to make some money. But if you have a genuine concern for other people, you should discourage, not encourage, them to invest too.

The vast majority of get-rich-quick schemes are built on a pyramid base. This means that they require an ever-expanding supply of new investors (suckers) in order to sustain them. Usually those who join are given a monetary incentive to sell others on the scheme. If, for instance, you invest $5,000 for the right to sell synthetic oil, you can recoup your "investment" (and then some) by enticing others to do the same. These incentives are offered under the most innocuous of terms, such as "finder's fees," "royalties," and "bonuses." The bottom line is simple: If you are dumb enough to risk your hard-earned money, you must know several people who are dumber than you are.

Even as I write, new schemes are roaring through the Christian community. Some are so implausible that at first glance it's hard to believe any thinking person would respond; but they do. I have long since realized that in the realm of get-rich-quick there are no schemes too ridiculous to believe.

Most get-rich-quick schemes get started with a novel idea and enough biblical jargon to make it sound plausible within the Christian community.

Some time back, a novel get-rich-quick program surfaced in churches around the country. The premise behind this particular scheme was based on making loans without interest: a thoroughly

biblical concept taught in the Old Testament. In order to participate in the program, investors had to "contribute" 10 percent of
the loan they needed. If, for instance, you needed a $50,000 loan
(at no interest) you shelled out $5,000 up front—with no guaran-
tee that you would ever get the loan.

Obviously, with no further elaboration than what I have presented, few people would be gullible enough to "invest" $5,000
with no guarantee of an eventual loan. What made this scheme
work was the fact that others were receiving such loans and then
telling their friends and families.

The concept is not a new one. In the early twenties a promoter named Ponzi came up with a similar idea. He took small
amounts of money from a large number of investors, promising
them huge returns on their investment. He offered interest rates of
10 percent a month in an era when 3 percent a year was a good
return.

His "investment" worked well as long as he could attract
ever-increasing numbers of investors. The concept was simple. He
used a portion of the new money coming in to pay the existing
investors their interest. With investors sharing testimonies of the
great returns he had no lack of new investors (suckers).

The scheme continued to grow until Ponzi was recognized as
one of the leading businessmen of his generation. He pitched elaborate parties, often entertaining the "nobs" of San Francisco's Nob
Hill. Businessmen, politicians, entertainers, and grocers all fought
for the right to give him their money. No one questioned how he
was able to make such a fabulous return. After all, to question a
golden goose was to risk losing it.

Eventually the scheme got so large that the interest payments
required more new investors than existed, and cracks began to
appear in the investment. Ponzi could no longer meet the ever-
increasing payouts. For a while he solved the dilemma by promising even higher returns to those who would reinvest their earnings rather than drawing them out each month. But eventually
those who wanted their money monthly grew beyond his ability to
control, and he defaulted.

Panic struck as investors heard Ponzi could not deliver on the promises he had made. Mobs of investors stormed his business office demanding their money. Ponzi simply folded his tent and quietly walked away. The laws of that day relied on the principle of "let the buyer beware." Later, securities laws would be fashioned around the Ponzi principle.

Unfortunately, gullible people still abound today, just as they did in Ponzi's day. To believe that anyone can make interest-free loans to all who want them based on a 10-percent deposit is unbelievable—almost. Everyone wants to believe in something for nothing. In this case the promoters confused the issue with a lot of biblical jargon about prosperity. As a consequence, thousands of Christians lost what may ultimately amount to millions of dollars.

Most Christians, if they were honest, could relate similar instances of where they have lost money because of trusting a Bible-spouting huckster. The "investments" range from jojoba beans in the desert to gas plasma engines that will run on water. Perhaps the most common revolutionary idea is still the 100-mile-per-gallon carburetor. Every decade or so someone will drag that one out and bilk a lot of people out of their hard-earned money. I have often wondered why the car companies would spend millions to eke out another 3 miles per gallon on new cars when they have this great carburetor sitting in the back room!

Principle #2: Waiting Too Long

As I said earlier, risk is often related to time. I personally don't like books filled with graphs and charts, so I don't use them often. But one graph that is very revealing is the compound interest curve. Before explaining the chart, let's define our goal.

Let's assume an investor needs to save $200,000 to be able to retire at age 65 and have a $20,000 per year income. (We will also assume the average yield per year is 10 percent on his money at retirement.)

To read the chart is simple: Look at the time line on the bottom. This shows the number of years from when he starts investing until he retires. We will assume he has $5,000 a year to invest (or spend). The vertical line shows the rate of return he must have, depending on when he starts investing, in order to have $200,000 at retirement. So if he starts investing his $5,000 a year at age 30, he needs to earn 0.77 percent a year on his money. If he waits until 45 to start, he will need 6.7 percent per year. If he waits until 55 to start, he will need 28.7 percent per year.

The principle here is very simple: People who wait too long get panicky and then take excessive risks. One of the primary motivations behind state lotteries is this very mentality. Many people see the lottery as a way to make up for a lack of discipline in their earlier years. So the people living on Social Security or welfare try to hit the lottery and win a million dollars (or more). The few who do are presented week in and week out as typical success stories by those promoting the system, giving false hope to those who would rather indulge now and gamble later. Obviously, what lottery promoters don't show are the millions who risk their meager earnings and lose.

Principle #3: Excessive Risk Through Ignorance

Proverbs 13:15 says, "Good understanding produces favor, but the way of the treacherous is hard." As mentioned earlier, a case can be made that everyone who takes excessive risks with their money suffers from ignorance. That's probably true to some extent, but we need to differentiate between doing ignorant things (like playing lotteries or trusting in a Ponzi scheme), and being financially ignorant.

There is no dishonor in ignorance, provided you don't choose to display it. I have absolutely no knowledge of brain surgery, nor do I desire any. So I diligently avoid all suggestions that I take a Saturday off from what I do best and perform a brain operation. That obviously sounds ridiculous, but in reality that is precisely

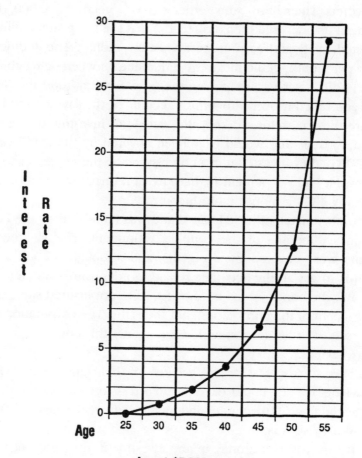

Invest $5,000 per year.

what many brain surgeons do when they risk months, or even years, of earnings in a shopping center development with no more knowledge of that specialty than I have of brain surgery.

Recently, I received a letter from an elderly couple. It seems they had retired from teaching and both elected to take their retirement savings in a lump sum, rather than take a lifetime annuity. This decision was based on the counsel of a financial planner in their church.

The annuities would have paid them a monthly income of about $600 each, which they calculated to be just barely enough to live on. Their lump sum settlement was nearly $200,000. The financial planner told them (correctly) that the lump sum could be invested safely and earn at least $1,500 a month. The additional $300 per month would mean the difference between being able to travel a little versus just paying the bills. So they took the lump sum and rolled it over into an IRA account at the savings and loan where the counselor worked. But instead of investing it in an insured account that would have been covered by the FSLIC (later the FDIC), they invested it in a bond issued by the savings and loan because it had a 2 percent higher rate of return, which amounted to nearly $300 a month more income.

Unfortunately, the S&L failed and was liquidated by the FDIC within six months of the couple's retirement. The insured accounts were covered by the FDIC, and although it took some months to get all the accounts repaid, no depositors' money was lost. But the bonds issued by the S&L were not insured since they were a debt of the corporation, not the FDIC. The corporation had no assets after liquidation and consequently this couple lost their entire savings.

They took excessive risk because of their ignorance (lack of knowledge). They could have avoided this loss simply by asking any accountant, attorney, or independent financial planner what the actual risk was.

Before you risk money in any investment, first find out what the rules are. Later in this book I'll try to provide the resources you need to evaluate any given investment area.

5

The Investment Hall of Horrors

IT'S IMPORTANT TO note that this chapter deals more with observations than it does with scientific studies. By that I mean I am offering a counselor's view of investments I have seen others make that have consistently lost money. Obviously, there are investment advisors who will disagree with my observations. That's okay too, because I would probably disagree with theirs. The criterion I use here is very simple: Of the people I have known and counseled over the years, which investments made them money and which lost?

Perhaps the simplest, most straightforward method for evaluating any investment is the percentage of people who buy into it and get their money back. The next rule of thumb is how many made a return above their investment. It's very much like evaluating your financial advisor. The rule of thumb is: If he makes you more money than he costs you, he's pretty good.

I have purposely oriented this book toward nonprofessional investors like myself. Even though I am a financial counselor and teacher, I am *not* a professional investment advisor. The difference between being a counselor and a professional investment advisor is that I don't risk other people's money.

I have always tried to limit my advice to basic financial areas such as budgets, financial goals, and biblical principles. I would personally find it rather hard to sleep at night knowing that I had the responsibility of overseeing the management of other people's money.

Most successful investors are what I call hedged risk-takers. By that I mean that they will take risks periodically if they can afford to, but they never take more risks than are considered necessary to accomplish their goals. There are investments that potentially can return great financial rewards, but most are what should be called "sucker bets." (Forgive my use of gambling terms, but that's what most of these are.)

Amateur investors who attempt to beat the odds on the high-risk investments do nothing but feed more money into the pockets of the professionals. The brokers on the commodities and stock exchanges make money whether the investors do or not. They make it when their clients buy, and then again when they sell. It matters naught whether the investors make or lose money on the transactions (as far as commissions are concerned). It would be great if a brokerage house would agree to forgo all commissions if the products they sell don't return a profit, but it doesn't work that way.

Over the years I have seen some very good investments and some very bad ones. It is impossible to categorize any single investment absolutely. Someone with specialized abilities can take a risky investment and make it less risky because of his or her knowledge and ability. As it will be throughout this book, my analysis of risk is based on the average, nonprofessional investor. If you are a thoroughly professional investor and average 25 percent a year return on your capital, you probably wasted some of it on this book. If you think you are a professional investor and average less than 25 percent a year return, you're probably fooling yourself, so read on.

The Worst Investment: Commodities Speculation

Commodities trading is the buying and selling of materials for future delivery. Perhaps the best book ever written on this subject for the average investor is *God in the Pits* by Mark Ritchie, a professional commodities trader in Chicago. Mark is a Christian and a good friend, and clearly one of the most successful commodities traders in America.

In chapter 1 of his book Mark describes the details of how the Hunt fortune was lost through speculative trading in the silver futures market. That one story should be frightening enough to convince any novice with less than $5 billion that commodities trading is not for the sane investor.

I have known Mark for many years, so I think I understand the mentality of what it takes to be a Christian in the commodities business. Unless you have the absolute conviction that everything you own belongs to God (literally) and can go to bed at night with the understanding that everything you have worked for most of your life can be lost while you sleep, don't trade commodities.

In the past several years, as the commodities business has become less attractive to the average investor, many speculators have shifted to trading in option contracts. An option contract gives an investor the right to purchase a futures contract at a future date. If that doesn't confuse you, nothing will.

Basically, it means that, as an investor, you pay a fee for the right to buy a contract at a future date. If the material goes up while you hold the option, you may elect to exercise the option and purchase the contract. More commonly, the option itself is resold at a profit.

The other side of options is that if prices decline you can elect to drop the option, forfeiting the option money. The advantage of options, as opposed to an actual futures contract, is that the downside risk is the amount you have paid for the option. In a futures contract the risk is potentially much greater.

Allow me to illustrate. Let's assume you purchase a futures contract to deliver soybeans in 90 days at $5 per bushel, and they are presently selling for $4 a bushel. A smart investor would buy a contract for 1,000 bushels to be delivered in 90 days at $5, and immediately purchase 1,000 bushels at market price for $4. You just made $1,000 and all you have to do is store the beans for 90 days; it's a good deal. But what if in three months soybeans are down to $3 a bushel? In that case you will have just lost $1,000.

The losses can be greatly magnified through credit. Suppose you bought the contract on margin (credit) and put down 50 percent. If soybeans go to $5 a bushel, you stand to make more than 300 percent in 90 days. If they go to $3, you can lose the same percentage! The risk is high, but so are the potential profits. If they weren't, who would be foolish enough to risk his money?

Commodities trading does have an honorable purpose, though it has been lost in the mad dash for instant riches. The commodities exchange was created to provide a method for farmers to presell their crops, thus assuring them a variable, but guaranteed, price each season. However, a quick check of the volume traded on the commodities exchange reveals that many more future delivery contracts are sold than crops are grown. What that obviously means is that many commodities contracts are never meant for delivery. They are paper transactions, designed and used only for speculation.

Trying to guess the future prices of agricultural commodities can be a stressful way to earn a living. I recall when the fighting between England and Argentina erupted over the Falkland Islands several years ago, the common logic was that soybean prices would skyrocket since Argentina was a major producer of that commodity. But, contrary to logic, after the English launched their attack the price of soybeans went down limit (the maximum allowed by the exchange in a single day's trading). Those speculators who guessed wrong, including my friend Mark, found themselves unable to sell their contracts. That's known as "catching a financial alligator." They're a lot easier to catch than to let go. Mark suffered his losses and survived, but I'm sure there were many others who lost a lifetime of earnings.

When the Gulf War broke out in January 1991 the same anomaly happened with oil. The common consensus was that oil prices would skyrocket to around $40 per barrel. Those who purchased future delivery contracts at the prevailing $26-per-barrel rate at the outbreak of the war saw prices plummet to nearly $20. That's called "wipe out."

There are ways to reduce the overall risk in commodities, such as buying options. But even so, this merely limits the downside risk. It does not reduce the risk of losing your investment money. My advice to anyone who does not own a seat on the Chicago Board of Trade is: Stay out of the commodities business. And to those who do own seats on the board—sell them and get an honest job.

Worst Investment #2: Partnerships

Contrary to some teachers in Christian circles, I do not believe the Bible prohibits Christians from being in partnerships. The admonition against partnerships with nonbelievers in 2 Corinthians 6:14–15 is clear, but does not extend beyond that.

Having made the point that partnerships between believers are allowable, in no way do I mean to imply that they are advisable, especially financial partnerships.

The Apostle Paul wrote to the Corinthians that "all things are lawful for me, but not all things are profitable" (1 Corinthians 6:12). That is a very good principle to bear in mind. The Lord told Peter that he should "kill and eat" (Acts 10:13). The instructions were clear that all foods and animals were allowable to eat. I would assume that would include buzzards and skunks, but they wouldn't be too palatable.

In the investment arena the most common financial partnerships are "limited partnerships," meaning that the contractual arrangement specifies a "general" or managing partner, and one or more non-managing or "limited" partners.

The intent of a limited partnership is to limit the liability of the non-managing partners to their financial investments only. Thus they would be sheltered from lawsuits, contract defaults, and future losses.

Based on observation I have often wondered if the "limited" in limited partnerships means that a participant is limited in his or her ability to get back the money invested.

Some limited partnerships require future financial participation in the event of operating losses or specified capital infusions, so they aren't all that limited. But even the limited partnerships that specify no future financial obligations have one hidden flaw—recapture.

Recapture is a nasty rule practiced by the IRS that says when a property is sold or foreclosed some or all of the previous tax deferments become due and payable, and the forfeiture of any outstanding debt becomes "phantom" income. The income may be "phantom," but the taxes aren't. They are due and payable when the loan is transferred back to the lender.

Understanding tax deferment is crucial when investing in any partnership that provides a tax write-off. There are virtually no tax eliminations where the IRS is concerned. True tax eliminations are things like tax credits, personal exemptions, operating losses, and such. All other tax reductions are called deferments, meaning that they are delayed until the investments are sold, or otherwise transferred. It's the "otherwise" that has gotten many unknowledgeable investors into trouble.

Allow me to share a typical horror story involving a limited partnership. A Christian I'll call Henry developed some limited partnerships to invest in apartment complexes. He was particularly good at taking complexes that were losing money and turning them around. The limited partners were required to invest enough money to renovate the complexes and provide enough operating capital to carry the complexes until they could be rented. There was nothing wrong with Henry's investment philosophy and, based on an estimated five-year holding period before the complexes were resold, the average return to the investors was over 50 percent a year! With that kind of return there was no lack of willing investors.

Some of the complexes were particularly desirable income properties. These were kept for income rather than sold. As the properties appreciated in value, the general partner, Henry, borrowed the original investment capital (and then some) out of the complexes and returned it to the partners. Effectively the investors had an appreciating asset that generated good income in which they had virtually no money. That's a good deal by any investment standard.

When a complex was sold the partners knew they would have capital gains taxes to pay as well as some recapture of depreciation write-offs, depending on how long the complex had been held. Since they made a sizable profit from the sale it was no difficulty to pay the taxes. But an event occurred that was ultimately to shatter the bubble of high returns with low risk.

In 1986 President Ronald Reagan proposed the most sweeping changes in the tax laws since the late sixties. One of the changes was to disallow tax write-offs from passive income investments (such as apartment complexes) against earned income. This meant that many high-income investors who bought properties and used the depreciation to shelter their regular income lost that capability. The result was an almost instant collapse of limited partnerships in general, and income property partnerships in particular. Basically there were virtually no buyers for apartment complexes that were developed to shelter taxes.

Even worse, new complexes under construction were dumped on the market at drastic discounts. Investors backed out of many new complexes and desperate mortgage lenders hired managers to rent them out at far below the going market rates. Complexes that had previously been profitable suddenly became money losers.

Many of Henry's complexes fell into arrears and were foreclosed by the lenders. Each complex that was foreclosed carried with it a tax liability for the accumulated depreciation and forgiveness of debt. The outstanding debt was considered as income to the partners when the mortgage companies reassumed the liability. The partners found themselves faced with hundreds of thousands of dollars in tax liabilities, and no money to pay them.

Many limited partners, whom I know personally, will be repaying their taxes for several years at substantial interest rates. Their homes are attached as collateral and several have had their personal assets sold at public auction. Their liability was not as limited as they had been led to believe.

Worst Investment #3: Tax Shelters

Although this category includes some of the other all-time worst investments, such as the limited partnerships just described, I decided to list it separately because it is a great way to lose everything you have and then some.

Tax shelter investments are in a category by themselves simply because they are used primarily to defer income taxes rather than for any economic value they might have. It does not mean that they have no economic value. Any investment that has no economic value is prohibited, according to tax law. But if the intent is primarily the deferment of current tax liability, then I would classify that investment as a tax shelter.

Since the 1986 Tax Reform Act, tax shelters for the average investor have been much curtailed. As noted earlier, passive investment tax benefits cannot be used to shelter earned income (in most cases). Therefore, it is usually the investor with significant passive income who is attracted to existing tax shelters.

But since all things that go around come around, tax shelters for the average investor will return; of that I have no doubt. In the meantime, there are still sufficient numbers of shelters being peddled to attract the gullible.

As you might guess, I am somewhat negative about tax shelters as investments. The reason is simple enough: I have known many fine people who have lost virtually everything they owned as a result of them. About the only people who have regularly made money from tax shelters are the salesmen, attorneys, and accountants.

Tax shelter investments prey on the uninformed and the greedy (my opinion). The simple truth is that unless you are willing to spend years in court and lots of money on accountants and attorneys, you will not beat the IRS at their own game for two basic reasons. One, they can use your own money to fight you. Two, they have the ability to change the rules in the middle of the game.

I can think of a hundred personal examples of people I have known who thought they could "beat the system." But in the interest of time and space I will share only one.

A Christian professional athlete whom I'll call Bob was being counseled by a "Christian" investment advisor on how best to maximize his income during his professional career. Bob was a fairly typical pro football player—though intelligent and skilled at his sport, he had practically no business experience. His salary of nearly $200,000 a year seemed enormous when compared to the pittance he and his wife had been living on in college. But after paying his taxes, tithes, normal living expenses, and additional in-season living expenses, he had less than $10,000 a year left over to invest.

Unfortunately for Bob, his investment advisor followed a strategy of using multiple tax shelters to save as much tax as possible and then using the tax money to invest for the future.

He put Bob into a Brazilian opal mine that would shelter $10 in taxes for every $1 invested (using leveraged notes payable). Next he suggested Treasury bill straddles (if you don't know what these are you're better off). These provided an artificial loss at the end of each tax year. Finally, he put Bob into a highly leveraged equipment leasing deal that would shelter nearly $20 in taxes for every $1 invested (again using future debt and investment tax credits).

The result was that Bob saved all of his tax liability (federal and state). This provided him with an additional $70,000 a year to invest (less the $30,000 it took to invest in the tax shelters). Bob was convinced that his advisor was a wizard.

The advisor then helped Bob invest in several real estate and business deals for which the advisor received a commission. He also had received either commissions or finder's fees for placing Bob in the tax shelters. I always thought it interesting that during this time the advisor did not invest in any of these tax shelters himself, although he did risk some money in the more traditional investments.

Bob retired from professional football in 1984, expecting to be able to live off of his investments and whatever income he could earn as a teacher and coach. Instead he got the biggest shock of his life: a letter from the IRS stating that he was being audited.

The audit quickly progressed from bad to nasty, with the agent recommending that the IRS disallow all of the tax shelters. He further recommended that 50-percent penalties be assessed, along with interest.

Bob quickly hired a tax attorney to represent him before the IRS. After investigating the shelters the attorney recommended that Bob plead for mercy. It seems that in the case of the T-bill straddles the investment company hadn't even bothered to make the trades each year. They just sent a falsified report to Bob's accountant. Even if they had made the trades the IRS would have disallowed the deduction as a sham transaction, but in this case there was no defense—not even ignorance.

When the dust settled Bob owed more than $200,000 in taxes, interest, and penalties, with the interest clock continuing to tick.

Unfortunately, Bob's money was gone by then. He couldn't get his investment money back, and the tax shelter companies had folded and fled into the night. Bob lost his home, cars, investments, and even had his retirement account with the NFL attached for taxes. He now works a full-time job, with the IRS receiving nearly one fourth of his total take-home pay.

Worst Investment #4: Precious Metals

I know I'm going to irritate some friends who believe in precious metals as investments. But I have to say what I believe, and thus far most of the people I know who have made money on precious metals are those who sell them.

There are two basic reasons why people invest in precious metals such as gold and silver. The first, as with any other commodity, is to speculate on their rise and fall. The second is as a hedge against a future collapse of the economy and/or the currency system.

One negative aspect of speculating in precious metals is the cost of buying and selling them. Unlike stocks and bonds, which have a well-organized and highly competitive market, precious metals have no such market. Investors can buy contracts for future delivery of precious metals in the commodities exchange, just as for virtually any commodity, but buying the actual metal is limited to a relatively few traders around the country.

These traders or dealers mark up the metals, usually from 5 to as much as 12 percent, when they sell them. Then when they repurchase the metals they make an additional premium by way of a discount from the quoted retail price. Essentially investors buy at retail and resell at wholesale. It takes a significant rise in price to make up the fees.

I know there are individual exceptions to this rule, but discount brokers and buyers are not available to the average precious metal investor.

In the case where an investor is buying precious metals as a hedge against a potential economic disaster, there is some justification for not listing them among the "worst" investments. After all, we haven't had a real depression since the thirties, so we don't know how metals will fare. So in fairness to those who sell gold and silver as a hedge against a collapse, I will downgrade my evaluation to merely a "questionable" investment.

Those who bought gold at $30 an ounce and saw it climb to over $500 an ounce in the seventies would probably disagree. But again, for the average investor who bought in after that one spectacular event, the trend has been level—to down.

Even the most enthusiastic precious metals advocates rarely defend the purchase of silver anymore. So many novice investors got wiped out in the great fall of silver in the early eighties that most dealers speak of silver in whispers only. In reality the depressed price of silver probably makes it one of the better speculative risks for the next decade.

The difficulty with buying precious metals (primarily gold) as a hedge against collapse is one of determining the future of gold as a currency. Traditional hard money advocates say that when a nation's (or world's) currency gets too inflated it will collapse and people will return to the gold standard. Unfortunately, that theory was developed before the communications age that we are in today. It is my strongly held conviction that the next currency will be neither gold nor paper. It will be electronic transfers, regulated and controlled by a central world bank.

If that proves to be true, and only time will tell, gold will be little more than a speculative commodity again. Those who don't believe this could happen need to read the arguments from the thirties that the United States could not remove its currency from the gold standard. We did it because of the desire to put out massive amounts of paper money without the requirement to collateralize it with gold. The same mentality (political necessity) may well divorce all world currencies from the confinements of a limited supply of gold. I am not advocating this reasoning. I am simply looking at the facts and stating my opinion.

Worst Investment #5: Gemstones

A woman may well treasure the diamond she wears on her finger or around her neck, but it is *not* an investment. For the average investor the same can be said of most precious and semiprecious gemstones. Most novice gem speculators usually buy high and sell low.

There are several factors that encourage me to list gems in my worst investment category, not the least of which is the difficulty for the average investor to tell the quality and value of gems.

There are grading organizations that will swear to a gem's quality, clarity, and estimated value. But unless you can resell to the same dealer that sold the stone to you, the next trader may not accept the evaluation. Even if the original dealer does agree to repurchase the gem(s), there is no guarantee that he will give you the current market value. The market value of gems is nebulous at best, and is not quoted daily as are company stocks.

In the mid-seventies several large traders, pooling their resources, made an attempt to create a ready market for precious gems—particularly diamonds. Unfortunately, all that came of it was a dramatic increase in the price of diamonds as the companies marketed them aggressively. Many individuals bought "investment grade" diamonds after being assured they were secure investments. "After all," the salesmen said, "diamonds have held their value better than any other investment over the last 100 years." This was true to a large extent because the DeBeers trading company of South Africa controlled the supply of diamonds very carefully, allowing only a few investment-quality stones on the market each year.

The net result of this debacle can best be demonstrated by a gift a supporter made to our ministry a few years back. He bought a one-carat "investment" quality diamond in 1982 for approximately $16,000. It was sealed in a plastic container along with a certificate issued by a certified appraiser.

In 1986 he donated the diamond to our ministry. We attempted to sell it at what was estimated to be its fair market value of nearly $20,000 (based on the opinion of the original dealer). Two prospective buyers sent the stone to be reappraised. The first appraisal downgraded the stone's quality one full point, lowering the value to about $9,000. The second came back two points down, with a value of $5,000. There were no buyers at either price, I might add.

I told the shocked donor, who immediately went to the dealer who sold him the stone. He had a written option to resell the diamond to the dealer at the original sales price at any time. The dealer told him a sad tale about his misfortune with other investors and notified him that he had filed for bankruptcy.

Over the last 20 years or so I have counseled many people who have purchased gems as investments. Some were happy because the gems were safely locked away in their safety deposit vaults appreciating greatly, according to the reports they received annually from their dealer/broker. And I am quite sure that many investors who resell their gems to friends and family do make a profit. But to date I have not met a single novice (nonprofessional) investor who has made money on gems, except by reselling to another friend who didn't know better either.

Worst Investment #6: Coins

Collectible coins, stamps, and other unique items can be good investments for knowledgeable buyers who take the time and effort to become proficient at their trade. It is not to this group that I speak. Nor is it to those who collect coins and stamps for a hobby. Basically they don't care if the items appreciate or not. Obviously anyone would rather their assets appreciate, but if they are not going to sell them, who cares?

I restore old cars as a hobby, and I really don't intend to sell them. I periodically check to see what equivalent cars are selling for, but only by way of interest. Most of the cars have so much of my labor in them that at double the market price I would net about a dollar an hour for my time. For me, it's a hobby, not an investment.

There are several companies that offer numismatic (collectible) coins as investments. In the eighties collectible coins became very popular investments not only because they could appreciate in value as collectibles, but also because the coins usually contained precious metals.

There is no doubt that many numismatic coins have appreciated over the last two decades, so why list them among the worst investments? Because, in general, it is the professional collector who has done well, not the novice investor. In recent years many trade shows have developed to buy and sell coins. These establish a market for coins and have helped to standardize the pricing through a very detailed grading system between traders.

But if the market for collectible coins were limited to dealers only, the prices would quickly settle down with little or no appreciation. Why? Because the traders would all know the true value of the coins and would not sell too low or buy too high (except for extreme cases of hardship).

For the price spiral to continue, it is necessary to market the coins to the general public. Thus a trader buys coins at their true market value at a show, then resells them to investors (usually through a recruited mailing list) at higher prices. If enough investors can be found, the dealer makes his own market.

If a novice investor attempts to resell a coin at the listed market price, he quickly discovers that what he paid was retail and the price he is offered is wholesale. The dealer buys low and sells high, so the investor is forced to resell to the dealer at a substantial discount.

If the dealer would give his investors access to his mailing list, they might be able to command his prices, but he obviously won't. Some dealers *will* offer to resell your coins, or even repurchase them at the wholesale price. But unless the coins have appreciated greatly, you end up either losing some of your investment or, at best, making a small gain.

Again, drawing on the testimonies of many people I have counseled who purchased coins for investment purposes, the vast majority said they lost money; some of them, a lot of money!

If you're not interested in studying numismatic coins, you'll probably find they are not a good investment for you. One side note is necessary here. If you ask a friend who bought coins, he will probably tell you he did well. That's because compared to some of the other investments he made, the coins lost the least. That is not exactly what you're looking for from your investments.

Worst Investment #7: Stocks

Since I have already alienated a large part of my friends who sell investments, I figure that I might as well go the whole way and

irritate the rest—so I have included stocks among my worst investments list.

Again, I would emphasize that a knowledgeable, professional
investor can and does make money regularly on common stocks.
Also, anyone can learn how to evaluate stocks and reduce the risks
involved. But for the average investor, today's market is not like
that of our fathers' day. Determining which stocks will do well and
which will not is a highly technical field that very few investors are
equipped to handle.

I would also like to make it clear that I am *not* trying to
discourage those who invest in a single stock, such as that offered
by the company they work for. I am referring to novice investors
who buy stocks based on their "gut" feelings. More often than
not, what they are feeling are simple gas pains.

If you took a portion of your savings and bought a representative sample of "blue chip" stocks and then just held on to them for
20 years you would do fairly well. From 1970 to 1990 your investment would have kept pace with inflation and earned about 3
percent a year in real growth. Unfortunately, the average investor
doesn't do that. He hears of a strong bull market and jumps in,
trying to make a big hit. Usually by the time he hears about the
bull market it has peaked, so he gets in at the top. Then the market
turns down and he sells in a panic to avoid taking the big loss. It
has been my observation that the net transaction is a loss, with
rare exception.

If you are one of those people who can dollar average your
stock purchases, meaning that you continue to invest in the blue
chips during good times and bad, you will do okay. But it also
means that you have probably just moved out of the average or
novice category, in which case you would be better off switching
your investment over to mutual funds where a knowledgeable professional with a proven track record will manage your stocks for
you.

You may or may not agree with my worst investment list, but I
developed it by observing how others have consistently lost their
hard-earned money over the years. Some people have beat the

system and walked away with their earnings. But on the average the people I counsel are not professional investors, and they range in incomes all the way from half a million dollars a year to less than $10,000. Some are college graduates, some have not completed high school. Some are senior citizens, others are just starting out. The point is they represent the average American investor pretty well, both Christian and non-Christian. Most would heartily agree that had they avoided these "worst investments" they would have been much better off financially today. But that decision is up to you. As Proverbs 18:15 says: "The mind of the prudent acquires knowledge, and the ear of the wise seeks knowledge."

6

The Best Investments

SINCE I DON'T want to seem anti-investment oriented, I decided to include a chapter on those investments that have worked out best for those I have counseled. This in no way implies that everyone who selected one of these investments made money with it, any more than those who selected the previous group always lost money. But on the average, more people made money using these investments than lost money.

The Best Investment: A Home

Without question the best overall investment for the majority of Americans has been their home. Residential housing has kept track with inflation and appreciated approximately 4 percent a year besides. That doesn't make it the best growth investment, but it does make it the best performer for the average individual.

It is also important to remember that our homes serve a purpose beyond the investment sphere. A home is something that you can use while it appreciates.

Many investment analysts have recently commented that the boom in residential housing is over. That is probably true to some extent. I believe that the expansion of single-family residences via cheap credit is winding down and housing will be more expensive for young couples. But Americans are hooked on having their own homes. If that trend changes it will only be because the country is in the midst of another Great Depression, in which case all other investments are equally at risk.

It is unfortunate that most Americans have been duped into accepting long-term debt on their homes as normal. With the prices of homes being what they are today, most young couples need extended loans to lower their monthly payments initially. But any couple can pay their home off in 10 to 15 years simply by controlling their lifestyles and prepaying their principal a little bit each month.

A simple investment strategy to follow is to make the ownership of your home your *first* investment priority. Then use the monthly mortgage payments you were making to start your savings for education or retirement. If you can retire your home mortgage before your kids go to college, they can graduate debt-free (and you too).

The most common argument against paying off a home mortgage early is the loss of the tax deduction for the interest. Allow me to expose this myth once and for all.

Let's assume that you are in a 30-percent federal tax bracket and a 6-percent state tax bracket. We'll also forget that the tax rates are graduated (based on a lower percentage at lower incomes). For each $1,000 in interest you pay on a home mortgage you will receive 30 percent of it from the IRS and 6 percent from the state, right? ($1,000 × 30% = $300; $1,000 × 6% = $60) So you will net $360 for your $1,000 interest payment. What happened to the other $640 you paid in interest?

As best I can tell, the mortgage company kept your money and you only received a portion of it back through tax deductions. What would happen if instead of paying interest on a mortgage you simply paid the taxes?

You would owe $360 in federal and state income taxes, but would keep $640. I'm not an investment counselor, but that seems like a better deal to me.

Retiring your home mortgage early pays huge investment dividends. Suppose, for instance, that you have a 30-year mortgage at 10 percent on a loan of $100,000.

The first of the following two illustrations shows how much a 35-year-old man retiring at age 65 could save in a retirement account at 6 percent if the home mortgage was retired early by paying an additional $100 per month and then the mortgage payments he had been making were saved in the retirement account.

—$100,000 mortgage at 10% for 30 years = $315,720
—$100 per month additional payment saves $90,033 in interest. Home is paid off in 19 years.
—Mortgage payment of $877/month + $100/month prepayment invested in retirement account at 6% for 11 years = $182,947 (approx.)

NET RESULT: Home paid off (at age 54, at total cost of $225,687) and $182,947 in savings by age 65.

The next illustration shows the comparison if, instead of prepaying the mortgage, the same person continued to pay the mortgage for 30 years while putting the $100 extra in a retirement account.

—$100,000 mortgage at 10% for 30 years = $315,720
—$100 per month invested in retirement account at 6% for 30 years = $100,953 (approx.)

NET RESULT: Home paid off (at age 65, at total cost of $315,720) and $100,953 in savings by age 65.

CONCLUSION: Paying off the mortgage *before* saving for retirement nets an additional $81,994 toward retirement (*plus* the savings on the mortgage).

The bottom line is, you're a lot better off financially earning interest than you are paying it. As Proverbs 9:9 says, "Give instruction to a wise man, and he will be still wiser, teach a righteous man, and he will increase his learning."

Best Investment #2: Rental Properties

It has often been said that the thing you know best, you do best. The majority of Americans know how to evaluate rental properties, particularly residential housing. Most of us have been renters ourselves at one time or another, or have bought and sold homes. Most homeowners have the ability to evaluate good rental real estate; at least when compared to buying soybeans, stocks, or coins. Therefore, rental properties are a logical source of investments—but not for everyone.

There are assets and liabilities to owning rental properties. Unless you have a strong personality and are willing to eject some nonpaying tenants from time to time, you need to avoid becoming a landlord.

A friend who has done exceedingly well in residential rentals over the years has a philosophy that I endorse. First, he sets his rent levels at less than the going market rates in his area. This is so he will attract a good volume of potential renters and can then qualify them according to the criteria he has established over the years, which include credit checks, previous rentals, and personal references. His low-rent policy also helps to attract long-term tenants who know they could never duplicate the deal he has provided them.

He establishes his rental rates on the basis of covering his mortgage payments and other out-of-pocket costs, including that of maintaining the properties. His goal has always been to use the rental income to pay off the mortgages, and then use the mortgage payment money for his retirement income. During the first 10 to 15 years he receives very little, if any, personal income from the rentals. Yet he now owns several dozen rental houses debt-free and has a sizable, and very stable, income.

Often he has shared stories of renters who have maintained the properties at their own expense, including one who totally reroofed a home because he did not want his rent to go up. This is one of the rare win-win situations with rental properties.

One of the most attractive aspects of rental property is that the initial investment is not excessively large in many areas. An additional benefit is that once the property is rented the tenants pay off the mortgage for you.

Many investors have moved up from single-family rentals to duplexes or triplexes because the risk is reduced. The chances of a unit being vacant are cut proportionately to the number of tenants it will accommodate. The flipside of the coin is that the initial costs also go up, and often to buy such a unit requires a partnership arrangement with someone else.

One additional idea is to joint venture a rental home with a couple who will live in it. Usually this means the investor provides the down payment and assumes a 50-percent (negotiable) interest in the property. The tenant couple then pays the mortgage payments and all other associated costs, including maintenance. When the house is resold, usually after no more than 10 years, the investor receives the down payment back and the two parties split the profits equally. There is a risk that the property will not appreciate, but that is the risk you run with any investment.

Best Investment #3: Mutual Funds

The whole concept of mutual funds is designed to attract the average investor. The pooling of a large number of small investors' moneys to buy a broad diversity of stocks (and other securities) is a simple way of spreading the risks.

Most of the average-income families I know who have accumulated supplemental income for education or retirement have done so successfully through the use of mutual funds. I particularly like mutual funds because (1) most allow small incremental investments, (2) they provide professional investment management, and (3) they allow great flexibility through the shifting of funds between a variety of investment assets.

As with any other area of investing, you must exercise caution and acquire some fundamental knowledge of what you're doing. There are funds that perform well in good economies and then lose it all in economic downturns. There are funds that guessed right once and basically never duplicated the feat again. There are funds that charge excessive administrative fees and dilute the return to their investors. And there are funds that have performed well for two and three decades and continue to lead the industry.

Even with these, you must exercise some caution, because their success may be built around the expertise of a single individual. When that person retires or dies, the fund may lose its edge. It is well worth an investment of $50 to $100 a year to subscribe to a good mutual fund newsletter if you have $10,000 or more to invest. It will help you to keep close tabs on the fund(s) you select. A list of some suggested newsletters is included in the Appendix.

Mutual funds offer such a diversity of investment products that it is probably safe to say that if you want to invest in anything legitimate there is a fund that will allow you to do so. Since we're going to evaluate some of the various fund types that are available in a later section, I will not elaborate here.

It is important to note, however, that in placing mutual funds in the best investments category I need to offer a qualifier. A good-quality, well-managed fund fits in that description. A poor-quality, poorly managed one does not. Later we will discuss how to find the funds that have proven to be the most reliable to the average investor.

Just remember that just as stocks are more speculative than corporate bonds, and bonds are more speculative than CDs, and CDs are more speculative than Treasury bills, mutual funds fit the same profile. So the type of fund you invest in will greatly affect the risk of your money, even in the well-managed ones. The higher the promised return, the greater the risk that must be assumed.

A growth (speculative stock) mutual fund managed by the best advisor in the world is still more risky than a mutual fund that invests only in U.S. Treasury securities. When we get into the strategy planning section of this book it is important to keep this in mind.

The question of whether to invest in a loaded or no-load fund always comes up in any discussion of mutual funds. A "loaded" mutual fund means that the sales commissions and administrative fees are taken out of the purchase price of the fund up front. For instance, a $5,000 investment in a fund with a 6-percent load would actually leave $4,700 to be invested in the fund. Additionally, you may also be charged an annual fee that can vary from a few dollars to several hundred or more, depending on the amount invested.

A "no-load" fund means that no commissions or fees are deducted up front. Logically an investor should therefore conclude a no-load fund is better since 100 percent of your money goes into the investment. That may or may not be true in the long run. If the no-load fund has higher annual fees and commissions, the money you save up front can quickly be consumed in the first few years, and then some.

I have personally found that a well-managed no-load fund will beat a well-managed loaded fund; therefore, that is what I look for. But a well-managed loaded fund is a better buy than a poorly managed no-load. So choose your fund carefully. The primary reason a loaded fund is loaded is because of salesmen's commissions. If you need individualized help in selecting or understanding mutual funds, the fees may be worth it to you. The no-load funds sell their products through advertising, not agents. They will provide any information you need by phone or mail, but use no local sales agents. It is my opinion that a subscription to a good mutual fund newsletter is better than paying a commission, but you may disagree if you know an honest, knowledgeable agent.

As with most investments today, one of the primary difficulties with mutual funds is trying to decide which type of fund best suits your individual need, and then which company's products are the best. With the hundreds of choices and every salesman (by phone or in person) totally convinced that his or her products are the best, it can be very confusing. Using the resources listed in the Appendix can help you sort it out.

Best Investment #4: Insurance Products

I have found in teaching a daily radio program on finances that there is no better way to stir up a heated debate than to discuss insurance. It really doesn't matter what position I take: If I am for insurance or against it (or totally neutral), I'm always stepping on somebody's toes because so many people earn their livings in the insurance industry.

If you would care to read a thorough discussion on insurance from a biblical perspective, as well as the assets and liabilities of term versus whole life, see my book, *The Complete Financial Guide for Young Couples* (Victor Books, 1989). But for the purposes of this particular book I'll limit my evaluation to the investment side of insurance.

Over the past 20 years or so, insurance companies have developed many investment products to tap into the private retirement savings movement. Products like cash-value insurance and annuities have been around for nearly a hundred years, but they were not really competitive as investment vehicles until more recently, in my opinion.

Generally speaking, the accumulated savings in life insurance was, and still is, too accessible to the investor. Therefore, the majority of investors look upon their cash values as a ready source of funds in a time of need. That's fine if the intent is to build a reserve account for a new car, a down payment for a home, or even a college tuition fund. But there are many places to save money at higher rates of interest than a whole life insurance policy. Besides, stripping life insurance of its cash values reduces the amount of insurance available in the event of the insured's death.

During the decade of the eighties, as retirement plans such as IRAs, Keoghs, 401(k)s, and the like became available to the general public, the insurance companies realized they had to pay higher rates of return if they were to be competitive as investment companies. The insurance companies also realized that the higher yielding mutual funds would eventually pull capital out of existing insurance policies. A knowledgeable investor would not leave money in a cash-value insurance policy at 4 to 6 percent return when mutual funds were earning twice that per year. Consequently, the major insurance companies began to offer policies with much higher yields. With the dual benefit of insurance coverage, plus higher yields, they became viable products for long-term investors.

The two basic types of insurance plans used most often (by those whom I have counseled) are annuities and whole-life insurance (usually in specialized policies such as universal life). There are endless varieties of these plans available. The difficulties are to determine which best suits your investment needs, and then to decide which company offers the highest return with the lowest risk. I have included a section on evaluating investments, which covers insurance products, so I will not elaborate on them here. Generally speaking, insurance products have been among the safest, if not the highest earning, investments. But what has been safe in the past does not automatically imply future safety. The insurance industry as a whole is very sound, but several of the larger companies have made many bad investments. The future of some insurance companies is in jeopardy. It is critical to select the company you use carefully and continue to monitor it at least annually, just as you would any other investment.

It would be far better to withdraw your cash reserves from a policy, or transfer your savings in an annuity, even if there is a penalty to do so, than to risk losing it all. The Appendix provides all the sources necessary to evaluate your insurance company, should you choose to use these types of products.

Best Investment #5: Company Retirement Plans

It almost seems unnecessary to list company-sponsored retirement plans among the best investments, but it continually amazes me how many people don't take advantage of the opportunities to use them. The jargon used to identify these plans may be confusing, with titles like 401(k), 403(b), TSA, HR-10, and the like. But, in reality, the titles simply reference the tax codes that authorize the plans.

The investments available through a company retirement plan are the same as those you might choose personally. Depending on the plan and how it is administered, your options can include annuities, mutual funds, company stock, CDs, or any combination of these.

The disadvantage of a company retirement plan is that although you may be able to select any of several investment options, the plan administrator(s) select the plan's options. They may or may not be the best options available to meet your personal goals.

One large advantage of company-sponsored retirement plans is that usually the funds invested are tax deferred (delayed until withdrawal). Additionally, many companies offer matching funds based on a percentage of what you elect to invest yourself. Some companies even go so far as to provide 100 percent of the retirement funds. I trust there is no one foolish enough to turn down an offer like that.

There are some potential problems with company retirement accounts. You need to be aware of these and take the proper precautions.

1. *The plan administrator may invest poorly, thus placing your funds in risk.*

2. *The company may reserve the right to borrow from the employees' retirement account for operating capital.* The problem here is that if the company fails, the retirement plan may fail too, especially if the company has substituted its own stock as collateral for the loans.

3. *The company may reserve the right to borrow from the retirement account and substitute an insurance annuity for the cash.* If the insurance company itself fails, then the retirement plan fails too.

Even with these potential problems, company sponsored retirement plans represent one of the best investments for any average investor. Most companies are run honestly and ethically and have the best interests of their employees at heart. Just be aware of the potential problems and do the checking necessary to verify the solvency of your plan.

Remember, the sooner you start in a retirement plan, the less risk you will have to assume in order to reach your financial goals. Sometimes it is advantageous to invest in a company retirement plan even before paying off a home mortgage, especially if the company matches the funds at a rate of 25 percent or more. It's hard to beat an investment where someone guarantees you a 25-percent return the first year—tax-free!

Best Investment #6: Government-Backed Securities

In pondering what to include in the best investments section I have tried not to get too detailed, lest we both get bogged down in whether a municipal bond from Chicago is better than one from New York. That kind of analysis is difficult at best since risk factors can change so quickly. So I purposely limited the discussion to general areas of investment. As I said earlier, government-backed investments are considered to be absolute security. Among those I have counseled who were older than 50 years of age, government-backed securities dominated their best investments list.

This does not imply that securities such as CDs, T-bills, bonds, and the like are the best performers. As mentioned earlier, they are usually selected for their lack of risk, not their return.

Once you have saved enough to meet your investment goals, whether they be college education for your children, retirement, or otherwise, the shift to government-backed securities is logical. Why leave your money at risk if you don't need to? Obviously your plans need to compensate for inflation, but the ratios should swing decidedly toward the safe side as you get older. Simply put, it is more difficult, if not impossible, for most older people to replace their investment funds; so the older you are, the more conservative you should become in your investing.

7

Strategy for Investing

IT HAS BEEN my observation that anyone who hopes to accomplish any goals, short-term or long, must have a strategy. The strategy may be as simple as that of a counselee I once met, who said, "I'm going to spend what I make and count on the Lord's return before I'm 65." That strategy may or may not work; we'll have to wait and see. But since it depends on events over which we have no control, I don't advise it for most people.

The principle taught in Proverbs 6:6–8 is one more suited to most of our needs: "Go to the ant, O sluggard, observe her ways and be wise, which, having no chief, officer or ruler, prepares her food in the summer, and gathers her provision in the harvest." Since we *don't* know when the Lord will return, and we *do* have specific needs later in life, we are instructed to save some of what we make in our harvest years for use later. Many Christians mistakenly believe that accumulating a surplus is somehow "unspiritual." It may be, if the attitude is one of hoarding. Hoarding means that the *goal* is to create a surplus. In contrast, saving is anticipating a future financial need and preparing for it.

Before discussing strategies for investing, I would like to discuss some biblical justifications for investing. I was once challenged by a dedicated Christian who was convinced that storing assets for the future was contrary to God's will. He said God expects us to take any and all surpluses and put them into His work immediately.

Somehow I knew this was incorrect, but he was a more mature Christian than I was and I respected his opinion, so I decided to do a study on the subject. I found that there is no biblical basis for his statement.

While it is true that God's Word teaches we should share with those in need, and give graciously to do God's work, it also teaches that we are to look ahead, identify future needs, and plan for them. The key is to identify *needs*—not greeds.

The Parable of the Rich Fool in Luke 12:16-21 tells us that once we have "enough" we should not store more. To do so *is* hoarding. But the Parable of the Prodigal Son in Luke 15:11-24 tells of a father who obviously had a surplus that he was storing for his sons. There is no hint of condemnation toward the father in this parable, just as there is no implied condemnation in the previous parable of the farmer's wealth. A survey of God's Word shows clearly that often God promises wealth to those who serve Him. Solomon asked for wisdom instead of riches, so God granted him both. Job was rewarded for his faithfulness with twice his original wealth. Jacob was made to prosper in Laban's employment. The examples go on and on.

If you need further evidence that God does not condemn reasonable saving for the future, consider Abraham, David, and even Barnabas in Acts 4:36-37. It would be very difficult to do God's work without some storage for future needs.

I particularly like the balance taught in Proverbs 11:25: "The generous man will be prosperous, and he who waters will himself be watered"; and in Proverbs 21:20: "There is precious treasure and oil in the dwelling of the wise, but a foolish man swallows it up." So it isn't the surplus that creates the problems. It is the attitude!

It is a sad commentary on self-discipline in America that the average American is worth less at age 65 than he was at 25. The dependence on government programs and acceptance of indulgent lifestyles have deceived most Americans into believing that someone else will take care of them. If God has provided for our future needs by providing a surplus during our harvest years, we shouldn't expect Him to come and bail us out because we wasted it.

There are many who cannot provide totally for the future because they have very little during their working years. But everyone can save something! What they lack later God will provide—if they were faithful with the little they had earlier. Often God will use those who were blessed with large surpluses to help those who have virtually none.

I recall a missionary I met in 1974 who had spent nearly 40 years in Central America, often living on less than $1,000 a year. At age 62, because of health problems and ministry policy, he and his wife returned to the States. He was facing retirement in a highly inflated economy on an annuity of $120 a month. That may have been adequate in 1934 when he began his work, but it would barely pay his utilities 40 years later.

He and his wife had been good stewards of what they had. They just never had much money. The question I asked him was, "If you had the chance to relive your life knowing what you now know, would you return to the mission field?"

He immediately replied, "Absolutely. I believe I was doing what God called me to do."

"Then," I said, "God has the answer. He will not abandon you now."

By 1977 he had turned a hobby, collecting ceramic figurines, into an income of more than $200,000 a year. God had known of his need and had made plans to meet it. But the key was that he had been faithful with the small portion first.

Biblical Reasons for Investing

Motive #1: Giving

I discussed this principle earlier, but I would like to explore it further because it forms the foundation of any strategy. In truth, most of the giving in America is not done by those with the greatest surpluses. In a survey conducted for the National Family Council in 1989, it was shown that those with incomes above $100,000 annually gave about 2 percent of their incomes. Those with incomes between $10,000 and $50,000 gave about 5 percent. The statistics within Christian circles closely match these national averages.

Having said that, let me hasten to add that some Christians with sizable assets do give, and give mightily. For them the ability to make and give money is truly a gift from the Lord (notice what the Apostle Paul says about this gift of giving with liberality in Romans 12:8). For many Christians, making money (investing) is a logical extension of their spiritual gift (giving).

Some Christians rationalize retaining God's portion under the guise that they are saving it for future needs. This ruse can easily be detected because their current giving reflects a stingy spirit. Making more money won't encourage them to give more. Quite the contrary: It is more difficult to give out of more than it is out of less; those who have a million find it harder to give a tenth than those who have a thousand. The commitment to give must exist long before the funds are available.

As you make more money, through investing or laboring, there are more "opportunities" available to spend or reinvest it. I have known many Christians whose stated objectives were to invest more in order to give more. Most of those who reinvested God's portion ultimately lost it or spent it.

I'm sure that over the centuries there have been many Christians who used their talents to make and give money. Perhaps the best known of the twentieth century was R.G. LeTourneau, the inventor of most of the large road grading equipment used today. I would recommend to anyone who desires to see an example of the gift of giving that they read his biography, *Mover of Men and Mountains* (Moody Press, 1979).

To be honest, I know of very few Christians who invest primarily for the purpose of furthering their giving. Most make their money by investing and then feel a conviction to give from the surplus. It is really a shame that more Christians don't understand (and practice) the sowing and reaping principle Jesus taught in Luke 6:38, "Give, and it will be given to you; good measure, pressed down, shaken together, running over, they will pour into your lap. For by your standard of measure it will be measured to you in return." Note in this passage that Christ said *they* (men) will give back to those who give to God.

Of all the people I have personally counseled I have known only one who planned an investment strategy from the very beginning specifically to be able to give more to God's work. She is a widow whose husband operated a very profitable business. During his lifetime they developed a habit of giving large amounts of money to missionaries. After his death she desired to continue to give as they had previously, but since her husband had a buy-sell agreement with his partner she could only give out of the proceeds from the sale of the business. Within a year she realized that it would only be a short time, a few years at most, until she exhausted the funds from the sale and would no longer be able to give at their previous level; so she made a conscious decision to invest her surplus from the sale of the business and give away the profits.

She attended several classes on stock market investing and then set out on a plan to multiply her assets. I believe the Lord honored her heart attitude. She happened upon a small company that was just getting started in the medical field, and invested most of her resources in their stock. Within three years her assets had grown by more than 2,000 percent! She was able to continue her giving goals and, as best I know, continues to do so today.

By the way, she took all but a fraction of the stock and transferred it to a more conservative investment program once it had multiplied. When I asked her why, she said, "There is no sense in taking foolish risks. I have enough to give what we had been giving. Now I'll protect it."

Motive #2: Meeting Future Needs

In 2 Corinthians 12:14 Paul stated an accepted doctrine in his generation: that parents should store up for their children, not the children for their parents. It would seem that we have almost inverted that principle today. Children wonder how they are going to be able to care for their parents in their old age. Some of the problem is culture-related. Today it is considered acceptable to commit older family members to nursing homes, even if they are still able to live useful lives in a family environment. To a large extent this is simply a reflection of our selfish attitudes. We don't want to be inconvenienced by the care of older family, so it's easier to park them in constant care facilities. Obviously this is not true with all the elderly in nursing homes, but all too often it is.

Unfortunately, the net result is a much higher cost of care for aging parents (as well as depriving the younger generation of contact with their elders). I am aware that many exceptions exist. Aging family members with specific problems, such as Alzheimer's disease, need special medical help. But no one will ever convince me that the millions of aging parents now kept in nursing homes in the U.S. are all exceptions. Many, if not most, are indigent and are being supported through public funds. They failed to plan properly themselves and since welfare won't pay to keep them at home it is easier to place them in high-cost care facilities at the taxpayers' expense.

Providing for future needs includes areas such as education, retirement, travel, and possible unemployment. I would like to take a closer look at the first two of these.

The High Cost of Education

We have developed into a society where future success is tied almost directly to education. It is not that higher education in itself is necessary for success, except in the case of specific disciplines such as law or medicine. It is that a college education is perceived as a need and is a criterion for a start in the business world. In other words, as more and more business owners and managers have become college graduates themselves, they have raised the entrance standards for potential managerial level employees to at least a college education.

As a result, most parents now perceive a college education for their children as a necessity of life. With the costs of education rising much faster than the economy as a whole, there are few alternatives except to invest to meet this need (perceived or real) or force both parent and child into long-term debt. The degree of risk an investor must assume is directly proportional to how much surplus is available currently and in the future.

Allow me to illustrate: If the cost of a college education at a state university is presently $50,000, and you have that much to put aside as a lump sum, your goal should be to keep the value of the money growing to match the rising cost of education, plus inflation.

This can be done in a variety of ways: You can prepay the tuition costs at a state university. This guarantees at least that the tuition expense will remain current, regardless of the economy. This also assumes the university will not default on its future contracts. The additional funds needed for room and board need only stay even with the general economy's inflation. Usually this can be accomplished by investing in good quality mutual funds that are widely diverse in their investments.

Other investments that can be used to help defray the cost of a college education are Series EE savings bonds that are tax exempt when used for education; zero coupon bonds, many of which are tax deferred until maturity; and even many retirement accounts, such as IRAs and 401(k)s, that can be utilized for education needs without the normal tax penalties being applied.

Let's look at a more likely scenario. You can put some money aside to help with your children's education, but not enough to pay the entire costs. Then both your investment strategy and your children's expectations must be modified.

Your investment strategy must be more aggressive in order to meet the goal. Instead of investing in savings bonds or zero coupon bonds you must seek out higher risk investments that cannot only stay even with inflation, but grow to meet the need of inadequate savings.

In addition you will probably need to condition your children to attending a good community college for the first two years, and saving toward their own education costs. I personally believe this is a very good idea for Christian parents anyway. Usually when children are involved with paying some of the costs of an education they appreciate it more and apply themselves better. I realize that not every child is the same. Some apply themselves thoroughly even though their parents pay the entire costs. But in my counseling I have found that group to be in the minority. Usually those who pay some of their own costs and manage their own funds understand and appreciate their education more. I rather suspect thousands of Christian young people are in college on their parents' money just to delay making a decision about what they want to do with their lives for four more years.

If you have any doubt about the wisdom of disciplining your children rather than indulging them, just read the following verses sometime—Proverbs 6:20, 10:1, 12:1, 13:1, and 13:18. I find it is much easier to allow God's Word to do the convicting.

Not long ago I had a friend call to say that he had achieved his goal of providing college educations for his children. I had first met him in 1979 when he and his wife came in for budget counseling. They were not overspending, but realized they would never meet their goals for educating their two children on their present course. They were able to put aside about $50 a month toward education, after paying for private secondary schooling. The $600 a year they were saving, even at 10 percent interest a year, would not cover the costs of college educations for two children, ages six and eight.

We discussed several possible moves they could make, including some high-risk investments that might or might not succeed. After two sessions it was clear that high-risk investing was not for them. The thought of having all their children's college money at risk for 8 to 10 years did not fit either of their temperaments.

Since the mother was working primarily to meet the current educational expenses of their children in a private school and to be able to put something aside for college, I asked if they had considered home schooling their children. The mother was a primary school teacher and initially resisted the idea of home schooling. But after reading some literature on the growing home-schooling movement and the high scholastic rating most home schooled children achieved, they decided to try it. With the cost of private schooling removed, they actually netted an additional $50 a month to invest for college. Virtually all the income the wife had been earning had been consumed in education costs, child care, transportation, clothes, etc.

They took her teacher's retirement lump sum of approximately $3,000 and the $100 a month they could save and began to invest it. The investments they chose were tax certificates. Twice each year the county government where they lived auctioned off delinquent taxes in the form of certificates. These certificates paid an average of 18 percent interest (depending on the economy) with virtually no risk. If the taxes and interest were not paid within three years, the tax certificate purchasers owned the property on which taxes were due.

They followed this plan successfully for nearly 15 years without a single default. By the time their first child was ready for college they had accumulated nearly $80,000. They had achieved their education goals without the wife working, and each of their children qualified for full scholarships. Because of the scholarships, their children completed college with nearly $30,000 each to start their own families. This couple matched their personalities to their goals and their investment strategy.

Not long ago a well-known private university in Atlanta announced an innovative method of financing a college education at their institution. All it required was the parents and student to sign a 10-year promissory note with monthly payments of $917 for 120 months (10 years). The idea of parents pledging their home and all other possessions against a college loan of this magnitude is ridiculous. The belief that a college graduate with a bachelor's degree can repay such a loan is the height of assumption, in my opinion.

The Option of Retirement

As I said previously, we seem to cycle from one extreme to another in our society today. Some people seem obsessed with retirement planning; they divert funds from God's work and their families and live like misers most of their lives in order to retire in "comfort."

Others act as if they will remain young and highly employable for the rest of their lives. With few exceptions, this attitude is very naive. Often they will end up living on inadequate income, mostly Social Security, or being totally dependent on their children.

In searching for the biblical principle of retirement I found there were very few references on the subject. In fact there is only one direct reference, and it is found in Numbers 8:25, "But at the age of 50 years they [the Levites] shall retire from service in the work and not work any more." Exactly why a temple priest was required to retire at 50 years of age, or what he did from that point on, is not clear. Taking the totality of Scripture in context we can assume that he had other duties to perform.

I interpret two fundamental points about retirement from God's Word. First, we focus too much on ceasing our work at too early an age. Second, since most of us will not have the same income earning ability at 65 or 70, we need to lay aside some surpluses in our higher income years for use at a later time. Proverbs 6:6-8 describes the prudence of planning for the lean years. And Proverbs 21:20 tells us that a prudent man stores some of what he accumulates.

I believe the best retirement investment that anyone can make is to pay his home off as soon as possible. As noted earlier, with rare exception it is better to use the potential surplus funds that would go into a retirement account to pay off your home mortgage first, and then use the payments that you were making on the mortgage to start a retirement account.

I understand all the arguments about the money in a qualified retirement account being tax deferred, and the interest on a home mortgage being tax deductible. Even so, paying off your home mortgage first still makes more economic sense.

The additional benefit of knowing that your home belongs to you and not some mortgage company is worth it even if it costs more. If you don't believe that, just ask anyone who lost his home in a bad economy. I know hundreds of families who have paid off their homes in lieu of beginning an early retirement plan. Not one that I have ever talked to regretted it.

It is another conviction of mine, having observed many families, that most retirement plans should begin at about age 40. Sooner than that and the average investor sacrifices basic needs. I also doubt that anyone has the insight to look more than 30 years ahead in our current economy and accurately project what will be needed at retirement. But on the other hand, waiting to start a retirement program much beyond 40 usually requires too much risk to meet even reasonable goals.

Without a doubt the vast majority of professionals who have retirement plans would be better off if they simply parked their money in low-risk investments, rather than aim for the highest return. It's that same old basic principle: If you can generate the money to meet your goals, why take risks trying to multiply it?

The fundamental principle in any long-range financial planning is to develop a strategy that will meet your goals and stick to it. To do so successfully requires that some critical factors such as personality, age, and income be factored into your planning. We will look at these in the next chapter.

8
Critical Factors

THERE ARE MANY strategies for investing; no one of them is better or worse than the others. In great part the strategy you select depends on your goals, your age, your income, and your temperament. Each investor must consider all of these or the result will usually be turmoil, frustration, and financial loss.

For instance, I have a close friend who invests in basic metals such as lead, zinc, cobalt, and magnesium. In some cases he simply brokers the metals by locating one party who has a need and another who has a surplus. As a result, he reaps a reward by way of a commission. But there are instances where he is offered a good deal on a load of metals without being able to locate an immediate buyer. Then he must buy the product, store it until he can locate a willing buyer, and hope that the price goes up instead of down in the meantime.

Often he will have hundreds of thousands of dollars, equaling his total net worth, at risk in a particular metal. For him, just as for the commodities trader I discussed earlier, the risk of losing everything must fit his temperament. He has goals for retirement, education, giving, and remaining debt-free, just as we all should. But unless he were able to sleep at night, all the other goals would be meaningless. I can tell you that my basic temperament would not allow me to do the same kind of investing. Certainly anyone would like to reap the financial rewards he is able to achieve, but few people could accept the risks.

On the other hand, I am reminded of a counselee who inherited over a million dollars and was so fearful of losing it that she kept it in a passbook savings account at her local bank. The thought of being such a poor steward of those assets would force me to seek out a higher rate of return if the money were mine. I know that hundreds of missionaries could be sent and thousands of families could be fed out of the increase in her assets just by shifting to T-bills, CDs, or tax certificates with virtually no higher degree of risk.

It is therefore important to remember that strategy involves a great deal more than just achieving specific goals. It involves personality and temperament to a large degree. However, often our personalities and temperaments have flaws that would keep us from achieving God's full potential for our finances. To offset these flaws, God, in His infinite wisdom, has given most of us spouses who mirror ourselves. In other words, they are exact opposites. I have said many times what I believe to be absolutely true: If a husband and wife are similar, one of them is unnecessary. In order to reach the proper balance in any investment strategy it is necessary that spouses communicate regularly about finances. For those who are single through choice, divorce, or a spouse's death, it is important to seek out someone close (who is as opposite as possible) to act as a counselor. One of the ways you can tell when you have found the right person is that he or she is the one individual who never agrees with you.

The Communications Factor

With some exceptions men are the primary risk-takers in the area of investments. Perhaps this is by culture, or perhaps it is by temperament, but no matter the reason it is normally so. For instance, a man often looks at a house as a potential source of capital when needed. A woman looks at a house as her home and rarely is willing to risk it unless there is no other choice.

Men are far more subject to get-rich-quick schemes than are women. In fact, of the several hundred schemes I have personally known about, less than 5 percent were promoted or purchased by women. Perhaps this is because women have been conditioned to listen rather than react, and as a result they are better able to hear the Holy Spirit's voice warning them.

This I do know: I have sat across the table from scores of men who were describing some of the most incredibly stupid investment schemes I had ever heard of, most of which could be eliminated on the basis of common sense. Without any discussion I would often ask the wife, "What do you think about this idea?"

Her response was invariably the same. "I don't know what he's talking about, but I have a real check in my spirit about this."

With no real statistical information the wife usually came to the correct conclusion. It was as if God were saying to her, "Would you please stop this dummy before he loses any more money!"

Interestingly enough, though, if a husband is in financial need because of a bad decision and asks for his wife's help, I find most wives ready and willing to do whatever is necessary, including selling their homes, cars, jewelry, or other prized possessions.

Perhaps the verse that best describes the relationship that a husband and wife should have in all areas, including investing, is found in Genesis 2:24, "For this cause a man shall leave his father and his mother, and shall cleave to his wife; and they shall become one flesh." The closest translation to "one flesh" we have in our generation is "one person." God desires that a husband and wife function as one person, the strengths of one balancing the weaknesses of the other. One of the biggest mistakes any husband can make is to exclude his "helpmate" from the decision process. The same can be said of a wife, but for a wife to exclude her husband from financial decisions is uncommon.

Unfortunately, many wives don't want to be involved in the financial decisions of their husbands. This is very shortsighted on their part and denies the husband the balance God provides through the marriage relationship. It should also be noted that wives outlive their husbands nearly 85 percent of the time, the average age at which a woman is widowed being under 60 years of age. This means that most wives will end up inheriting their husbands' plans, whether they want to or not.

The Age Factor

Age is a very critical factor when making investment decisions. The younger you are, the more risk you can take and still recover if you're wrong. A 25-year-old investor can make some mistakes and still have plenty of time to recover. A 75-year-old investor can ill afford any mistakes, assuming he doesn't have an unlimited supply of money. And as I noted earlier, even $5 billion wasn't enough cushion for the Hunt brothers.

If you do not violate the principles of leverage and surety discussed earlier in this book, there are virtually no situations from which you cannot recover if you are 40 years of age or less. The most you can lose is the money you have at risk. And assuming you didn't borrow it you can only lose what you have, not future earnings. Therefore it would seem reasonable to expect younger investors to be more of the risk-takers, assuming again that they have the temperament to accept some losses.

Several years ago a young man called to ask for counseling. He was interested in investing in commodity option contracts and was trying to do what the Bible admonished in terms of seeking counsel from older Christians.

As you have probably gathered by now, I am not a great advocate of commodities investing since much of it borders on pure gambling. In a conversation over lunch this young man described the research he had done on a particular commodity (wheat) and the prospect of an extremely poor wheat crop in the Soviet Union that year. He was considering buying some options on winter wheat futures. By buying an option his loss would be limited only to the money he had at risk. If the wheat prices went down he could forfeit his option, losing what he had invested to that point but with no contingent liability. If prices went up he could execute his option and sell the wheat or actually resell his option at a profit.

He had saved the money he wanted to risk and had discussed the idea with his wife, who had agreed to support whatever decision he made. They had no children and were renting an apartment. If his "hunch" was right he could make enough money to buy a home for cash, lay aside several thousand dollars for future education needs, and still have several thousand dollars left over.

My question to him was, "If you lost every dime you plan to risk, would you look back with regret?"

He said he had prayed about it and felt he could accept either the loss or gain as the Lord's will.

"What about your wife?" I asked.

"She feels the same way," he replied without hesitation.

"Then go for it," I told him. "If you don't, you may never have this chance again." Upon such opportunities are fortunes made (and lost).

He did purchase the options for winter wheat. That year Russia suffered its largest crop loss in nearly a hundred years. The money he had risked grew by nearly 2,000 percent, at which time he cashed out, paid his tithes and taxes, bought a home for cash, and invested nearly $25,000 in a quality mutual fund for his future children's education. He never repeated the investment risk he took that year, to my knowledge, and settled into a career as a computer programmer. But at 25 he had time to recover, even if he had made a bad guess.

A doctor friend in his mid-thirties had made some poor investments in apartment buildings that created so much stress that they nearly wrecked his health and marriage. He correctly observed the principles of debt and surety by investing in limited partnerships that required only the commitment of his initial investment capital. However, the investments had outstanding mortgage loans. Several of the investments failed due to economic circumstances, creating a huge tax liability for him. Many of the investments he had made through his retirement plan also went sour, causing the IRS to do an audit. They determined that many of the loans and investments he had made violated the "prudent man rule" (taking a risk a prudent man would not take). They disallowed his retirement plan, throwing the previously deferred income into his taxable income. He ended up owing the IRS several hundred thousand dollars in taxes and penalties, plus interest.

A later appeal to the tax court overturned the IRS ruling and required only that he repay the retirement plan the lost earnings, which amounted to about $100,000. He also lost about $30,000 in legal and accounting fees.

Actually, this man was extremely fortunate, because only about 30 percent of tax court decisions go in favor of the taxpayers. By the time his case reached the court he was well into his forties and his income had declined substantially due to competition from HMOs in his area. Remember that anytime you are using tax-deferred money to invest (whether for retirement, government bonds, etc.) you are potentially extending the risk into a later time period. By the time your case works its way through the IRS and the courts, if necessary, you may be well past your youth.

Almost weekly on our call-in radio program, *Money Matters,* someone will share a story of how he risked his life's savings and lost it. Usually these are people who were either retired or approaching retirement and realized that they hadn't accumulated enough assets for retirement. Realistically most people need about 75 to 80 percent of their preretirement income in order to retire. Since they do little investigation about what Social Security benefits will actually pay, they get a real shock at retirement. If they have received a lump sum from their company retirement plan they find themselves eating into the principal each month. This leads them to take risks at an age where the loss of virtually any assets cannot be replaced. Most people in this situation would be far better off to face the reality that they need to supplement their retirement by working, not taking investment risks.

The era of junk bonds in the early to mid-eighties yielded some investments with earnings of more than 20 percent a year. In an economy where CDs and T-bills were yielding 6 to 7 percent, this was just too much temptation for many older investors. Several retirees I know shifted their entire life savings into these high-yield bonds and bond funds. They beat the system for a while and earned double or triple the going conservative interest rates. In spite of any counsel to the contrary, those whom I knew refused to believe they could lose their money. After all, these investments were offered by some of the biggest brokerage firms in the world, and the companies backing the bonds were blue chip with ratings of AA or better.

There was really no way to convince them that the risk was too high. I wrote letters suggesting that they should withdraw the majority of their funds and secure them. I received angry calls and letters from brokers who even threatened lawsuits if I didn't quit maligning their products. I am not an investment analyst, but common sense and logic say you don't get something for nothing. If an investor is promised twice the average return that a normal bond is offering, he should probably assume there is at least twice the risk.

In the late eighties, reality struck home as many companies found themselves stuck with high-interest junk bonds in a declining economy. Most could not even maintain the interest payments. They apparently had assumed the good times would last forever, and had leveraged their companies up to and beyond their limits. Many of these companies simply filed for bankruptcy protection, leaving the junk bond holders with little or nothing. Even those that didn't file for bankruptcy "renegotiated" their bonds to reduce and delay the interest payments.

Not only did many banks, savings and loans, and insurance companies that held these bonds fail, but millions of smaller investors, Christians included, saw their assets dwindle to practically nothing.

I mention the junk bond era not because I believe junk bonds will again be offered to the average investor as a "good deal." They will not be; at least not in this generation. Too many people got burned and remember it too well. But junk bonds simply represent a class of investments that will always be available to the naive investor. These are investments that seem too good to be true, and are the darlings of the investment brokers. In the sixties it was the high tech stocks, in the seventies it was land syndications, in the eighties it was junk bonds and tax shelters. In the nineties it will be something else, and on into the next century it will be still another deal too good to be true.

Just remember, the older you are and the greater your need for excessive returns, the more susceptible you are to these schemes.

The Income Factor

It seems to be a human fallacy that the more income people have at their disposal the less cautious they are with it. Some years ago I did an informal survey of some doctors and business owners I knew to determine how many of them had lost money in a bad investment. I was astounded to discover that 100 percent of those surveyed had made at least one bad investment.

Next I surveyed some middle-income families I had counseled and found out that about 50 percent of them had lost money in a bad investment.

Finally, I surveyed average-income families. Of this group about 10 percent had lost money through a bad investment.

The logical conclusion you could draw is that those in the lower income group had less money to risk so they obviously would have made fewer investments. Not so. The percentage of investments made stayed remarkably constant, regardless of the income. But the kinds of investments they chose and risks they assumed changed drastically depending on their incomes.

My conclusion is that the lower income investors are less willing to assume high risks. The higher income investors willingly accept the greater risks. Probably much of this can be explained by what is called "sweat equity." In other words, the lower the income the more sweat went into the money to be risked.

Perhaps the lesson to be learned from this survey is: Treat all of your money as if you earned it chopping firewood for a living.

9

Where to Go for Advice

ONE OF THE most common questions I am asked is, "Where can I go to get good investment advice?" The answer to that can range all the way from an inexpensive magazine or newsletter to very expensive professional counsel. There is no "right" answer to the question. In large part it depends on the same factors we just discussed: age, income, and temperament.

Budgeting

Perhaps the best way to address the subject of where to go for advice is to start with the basics and work our way up.

The first tier or level in seeking advice is to be able to manage the money you earn in order to create a surplus to invest. In the simplest of terms this is called budgeting. Everyone needs a budget, even those with higher incomes. It is impossible to be a good steward of what God has entrusted to you if you don't manage it well. Obviously those with less income also need budgets or they will never develop a surplus that can be multiplied.

I have written extensively on the subject of budgeting and therefore will not occupy more space in this book to repeat it. For more detailed information refer to *The Financial Planning Workbook* (Moody Press) or *The Complete Financial Guide for Young Couples* (Victor Books), available at most Christian bookstores. Both contain step-by-step instructions as well as the forms necessary to budget one year of income and expenses.

Any good budget should be no more complicated than is absolutely necessary to manage your finances. It must be developed by both the husband and wife together. And it must be fair and balanced, not abusive.

To develop a working budget should take about four hours of planning and no more than 30 minutes per pay period to maintain. Any more than that and it's too complicated. A great many people are now using some form of computerized budgeting system on a home computer; some excellent software programs are available for less than $100. I personally don't use one yet because I can maintain my home budget faster manually. When the systems are advanced enough to pay bills by direct computer access I will probably convert to an automated system.

For those who need personalized help in developing and managing a budget, there are thousands of trained volunteers who provide this counsel in their communities and churches all across the U.S. To locate one in your area, consult the counselor referral section in the Appendix. For those who have debt problems, a national nonprofit organization called the Consumer Credit Counseling Service has affiliate offices in almost every major city in the country.

Remember this principle because it is a fundamental one that I will refer to often as we evaluate various investments later: The best investment you will ever make is debt reduction. Each dollar of credit card debt you reduce is the equivalent of making a guaranteed investment at 18 to 21 percent. You'll have a very difficult time matching that return.

The return for paying off car loans may not be quite as good. They often average only 12 to 14 percent. Try to find a guaranteed investment with an equivalent return.

The return for paying off home mortgage loans may drop as low as 9 percent for some families. That is still a good return with no risk. And remember that if you pay off your home, *you* own it, not a mortgage company. No matter how bad the economy gets no one will be able to force you out of your own home.

Advisors For Entry-Level Investors

Once you have a workable budget and develop a surplus to invest, learn as much as you can before taking any risks. Usually the counselors or advisors available to low-budget investors are commissioned salespeople who make their livings by selling products such as insurance, mutual funds, and annuities. This is not an indictment against these salespeople. In practical truth a professional investment advisor cannot make a living selling financial planning services to this level of investor. The fee-only planner would have to charge several hundred dollars and could do little, if any, follow-up.

So it means that a low-budget investor has three basic options: (1) do your own investing and pay the price of learning as you go; (2) take the advice of the product salesman and hope that he or she sells a good quality product; (3) seek out inexpensive written materials that you can rely on for guidance.

Since the first two alternatives are self-explanatory, I will concentrate on the third: materials.

A variety of good materials is available to help and advise nonprofessional investors. Several of these are listed in the resource section in the Appendix. Usually first-time investors subscribe to too many resources. This often results in confusion and frustration because often one publication will contradict another. The key is to select resources that don't push a particular agenda such as precious metals, insurance, mutual funds, and the like. I personally prefer magazines that don't accept advertising from investment product sales companies. I think it would be very difficult as an editor to be objective if you knew that a sizable portion of your revenue came from a product you were evaluating.

Newsletters are generally a good source of basic advice. There are some 1,700 financial newsletters published in the United States. Some are free; most carry subscription rates of up to several hundred dollars a year. They range all the way from general economic information to detailed analysis of specific investments, such as stocks, bonds, real estate, and mutual funds.

I recommend that low-budget or first-time investors subscribe to newsletters written specifically for them. Again, the key is to verify if the editors have a hidden (or sometimes not so hidden) agenda. It is also crucial to verify the track record of the managing editor since usually that person is the primary advice giver.

One popular newsletter writer I have observed for several years promotes a doom and gloom message (which is easy to sell in a bad economy). He advises his followers to buy guns, gold, and food for the coming collapse, the same basic message he has promoted for nearly 30 years. (He gained great popularity after the run-up in gold prices in the late seventies.) What most of his readers don't know is that his success as an investment advisor came right on the heels of several complete financial failures for him personally. His single success—predicting gold prices would escalate after the ownership of gold was again legalized for Americans—was a one-time fluke. His subsequent success record on investment advice has been about 12 percent. You can do better than that by flipping a coin and save yourself about $300 a year in newsletter costs.

Look for a newsletter that takes the first-time investor through each phase of learning, including *specific* advice about what investments to use at each level of income and assets. While no one source should be used to the exclusion of all others, I recommend newsletters as a good first resource.

A noncommercial magazine which has developed a high level of integrity over the years is *Consumer Reports.* The credibility of the magazine is based on accepting no advertising from any source, and the fact that they purchase all the products they evaluate. Once a year the magazine does an analysis of insurance, mutual funds, and a variety of other financial products. It is well worth the time and cost to invest in these issues and study them carefully before starting an investment program.

A second magazine I recommend is *Money Magazine.* Although more commercial in nature than *Consumer Reports,*

Money has excellent information about mutual funds, insurance investments, and the like.

Beyond these resources I personally don't rely on much that is printed besides the normal daily reports such as *The Wall Street Journal* and *Investor's Daily*. I'm sure there are other sources that many of you use regularly, and I have listed some of the more well-known ones in the Appendix. But with limited time I try to limit myself to only those I can scan quickly.

The Commissioned Salesman

The next tier up in investment advice is using someone who sells a product (or products) and generates a commission (as opposed to charging a fee).

I have to be honest and say that my observations of this type of investment counselor have been mixed. There are many men and women who are very qualified to give good, objective counsel and also earn commissions in the process. But the industry is also full of novices or incompetents who sell only what they have been taught to sell and offer little or no balance in their advice. One way to sort them out is to require several references from others with whom they have worked. I recommend checking with at least five of their clients to verify their track record. It is also important that these people have been clients for at least three years. If they won't provide the references, I suggest that you keep on looking. At the very best, selecting the proper investments can be both frustrating and confusing. What you don't need is a salesman making it worse by giving misinformation.

Unfortunately, many of these salespeople stretch the truth a lot in order to make a sale. They represent their products as high-yield and secure, when in truth many are low-yield and highly risky. Let me use an example: A man who came to me for counsel had been sold an insurance policy as a good investment, as well as lifetime protection for his family. The salesman presented the plan as a guaranteed 9 percent return. The concept behind the policy was that once the premiums had been paid for a period of six years no further contributions would be required and the dividends would compound at 9 percent a year for life. The salesman even presented computer printouts reflecting this return ("With no risk," he said).

Later, the buyer discovered that the returns the salesman quoted were based on the gross earnings of the insurance company. After the service fees, commissions, and administrative expenses were deducted, the actual earnings were less than 6 percent.

The policy would, at best, require 10 years of payments to be fully funded. Unfortunately the company's earnings declined over the next few years and the payment period grew to nearly 15 years. After four years of payments the buyer had virtually no accumulated value in the policy, except the cash values, which belonged to the insurance company and would become loans against the policy if he drew them out.

His "investment advisor" was a new hire who had lost his job in industry and had chosen insurance sales (investment advising) by default. He didn't purposely lie. He simply didn't know enough to discern the truth.

My advice when selecting a commissioned sales person is: Be certain he or she has at least a five-year track record in the industry. I have said this before and have received angry letters from advisors who are new in the field. Their common argument is, "How will we ever get the experience if people won't use us until we're seasoned by at least five years of experience?"

My answer is, "Sell to your family and close friends and be extremely cautious about what you don't know during this learning phase. Then verify the track records of other agents in your company and see if what you have been taught is right. If not, change companies until you find a good one."

Let me repeat again, many good, honest, ethical salespeople are to be found in the financial field. But they are the ones who think more about their clients than they do their own financial needs. A hungry agent will often oversell, pressure, and prod a client. Those who try to put a guilt trip on you to buy from them because they are Christians (or church members) should be avoided with all diligence. If an agent's products and track record will not stand by themselves—stay away. Otherwise you'll probably lose your money as well as a friend.

One last note on this point: Perhaps the worst of these salespeople are the doom-and-gloomers who sell "collapse-proof" investments such as gold and silver. Several investment groups have taken to using the Christian media, particularly radio, to ply their wares. They use guests who speak of a coming worldwide economic disaster (perhaps true) and then tout precious metals as the protector of all real wealth. Too often they quote, or misquote, Old Testament passages such as Haggai 2:8, " 'The silver is Mine, and the gold is Mine,' declares the Lord of hosts," as justification for buying their products. My counsel is: Avoid these "prophets" of doom who actually have in mind their own "profits."

Fee-Plus-Commission Advisors

In addition to advisors who make their incomes exclusively from commission sales, there are a growing number of investment advisors who will work either way—fees or commission sales, or both. Usually these advisors will initially provide counsel for a fixed fee per hour. Then if you elect to buy products from them they will reduce the fee by the commissions they receive.

A prudent investor would do well to remember that a counselor or advisor usually exercises an undue influence over his or her clients. In many instances this means investors end up buying what the advisors recommend, which are usually the products they sell. The question then becomes, is the fee-plus-commission really a ploy to get clients to buy from them while thinking they are receiving objective advice? That totally depends on the character of the advisor, something you will need to discern for yourself. A simple comparison of the value and prices of the products suggested will tell you whether or not the counselor is totally objective. If the investment products they offer are as good as those offered through other agents, then why not buy from them and reduce the fees? But if what they offer is inferior or higher priced, avoid the advice as well as the product.

Fee-Only Investment Advisors

A fee-only advisor is exactly what the name implies. He or she charges a fee, but does not sell any products or accept commissions—usually. I say "usually" because I have found some advisors who advertised themselves as fee-only planners but accepted commissions, known as "finders' fees," from product companies. In my opinion this is blatantly dishonest and I would avoid advisors who do this.

By virtue of the fact that they generate their income from fees, you can expect fee-only advisors to be expensive. Most cater to the upper-income investor and often have a minimum level of net worth for the clients they advise. The fees can range from several hundred dollars for a one-time evaluation to several thousand a year for continuing clients.

In general I have not found fee-only advisors to be any more accurate in their advice than a well-seasoned, fee-plus-commission advisor, although there are exceptions.

The one area where fee-only planners usually excel is in designing long-term investment strategies for their clients. Since follow-up is so essential they also usually do a good job at getting their clients to implement their plans. After all, if you're paying someone $10,000 a year to advise you, you'll usually do what they say.

Fee-only planners run the gamut from conservative to speculative just as do those who earn commissions. You will need to select a planner based on your personality and objectives. But since they do cater to upper-income clients with sizable asset portfolios, the logical perspective should be preservation of capital, rather than speculation.

Of the professional investment advisors I queried about fee versus non-fee planners, the assessments were split nearly down the middle. I have attempted to provide an objective evaluation of both the good and bad sides of fee versus commission advisors. But the single most consistent comment offered by virtually all the advisors I asked was, "Check out their track record carefully."

The bottom line of any investment advisor is not whether you paid their salaries by way of a fee or a commission. It is whether they made you more money than they cost you. A commissioned salesman who makes his clients 12 percent after all commissions, administrative charges, and market fluctuations are taken into account is still better than a fee-only planner who makes his clients 6 percent after all costs.

Remember to ask for at least five local references that you can talk with about your advisor's track record. If you can't get them to share such a list with you, keep on looking.

Christian or Non-Christian Advisors?

Psalm 1:1-2 says, "How blessed is the man who does not walk in the counsel of the wicked, nor stand in the path of sinners, nor sit in the seat of scoffers! But his delight is in the law of the Lord, and in His law he meditates day and night." There is a clear implication here that our primary source of counsel should be from those who know the Lord. Does this imply that we should never take counsel from an unbeliever? I don't think so. I believe the implication is not to rely on secular counsel as our daily source of wisdom. All counsel should be weighed against the wisdom of God's Word and discarded if it fails the test. That includes Christian and non-Christian counsel.

Put in perspective, I would say to any Christian, seek out the best Christian investment counsel available to you. But if it is not adequate, as is too often the case, then seek out the counsel of knowledgeable, ethical nonbelievers. Just be sure to weigh their counsel against the wisdom in God's Word.

Some time back I needed angioplasty surgery on one of the arteries to my heart. I called a cardiologist friend at an excellent hospital in Atlanta and asked who he thought was the best angioplastyst at his hospital. Without hesitation he gave me the name of the cardiologist he would use himself if he were having the same procedure done. As it turned out, the doctor was a Christian also and I felt a great relief when he accepted me as a patient.

But the actual specialist my cardiologist used to perform the delicate procedure was not a Christian. My friend's comment was, "He is the best in the world at this particular procedure. I believe God would want you to have the best."

I agreed, and he did the procedure successfully. The point is, I used Christians as my primary counsel, but used the best technicians to actually perform the procedure. As a Christian you will need to settle this issue of Christian and non-Christian counsel yourself.

Personally I would rather have a competent nonbeliever (as long as our basic values were compatible) than an incompetent believer who would give me bad advice. Let me assure you, I have known several investment advisors who memorized a lot of Scripture but didn't know their trade very well. Proverbs 14:7 applies to Christians and non-Christians alike: "Leave the presence of a fool, or you will not discern words of knowledge."

Where to Find Good Investment Advisors

This is another one of those difficult questions for which there is no absolute answer. Many people call our offices asking if we recommend any particular advisors. Our answer is always a resounding no!

We have trained many financial counselors who help people with their budgets, and teach the biblical principles of handling money, usually within their own churches. If we hear that one of our volunteer counselors is giving investment advice to those they counsel, we remove that person from our recommended list. We are here to advise people how to manage their finances, not where to invest.

But since many people need good investment advice also, I would like to offer some advice on locating a good advisor.

1. *Ask around in your church and Bible studies for references.* Don't hesitate to ask if the advisor has made them money over the years. Also apply the five-year rule (10 if possible). Anyone can guess right one time, and one guess does not establish a track record. If a counselor has not ridden out at least one major recession in his field, in my opinion he is still a novice.

2. *Check his credentials with the National Association of Securities Dealers, if he is a registered broker.* If he has ever had his license suspended or revoked, be very cautious.

3. *Ask several local accountants who do tax returns for people you know.* Often they see the good and the bad of a planner's efforts. Although most will hesitate to give a negative report on someone, most will not hesitate to give a positive report on the good ones. If the accountant uses a financial planner because of how well he or she has done for one of the accountant's clients, that is a very strong recommendation.

Discount Brokers

Over the last decade or so, many discount brokerage firms have been started that will place investment orders for very low commissions. This trend is certain to grow as banks expand further into the investment area. These firms cannot offer investment counsel to their clients. They are restricted to placing the buy or sell orders issued by their clients. Once you have a level of expertise that allows you the freedom to make your own investment decisions, the use of a discount broker can save you a great deal of money when trading.

10

Following Solomon's Advice

THERE IS NO doubt that if I were looking for investment advice I would go to the person who had the best track record with his own money. I have a friend who is particularly good at selecting profitable investments. For several years he has allowed some missionaries to invest some of their meager earnings in many of his ventures. Thus far his success rate has been almost 100 percent. Sometimes the investments only make a little, sometimes a lot. But they have always been on the positive side. Most investors wish they could say as much for those times when they have chosen their own investments. It would be ridiculous for the missionaries who invest with my friend to launch out on their own. After all, he offers proven and tested counsel at no cost.

Few people realize that another investment counselor also does this. The best investor the world has ever known (outside of the Lord, obviously) was King Solomon. The Queen of Sheba noted that everything his hands touched prospered. So it would seem logical that if we could glean some investment advice from him we should be able to improve our percentages too. Fortunately, Solomon talked a great deal about his financial philosophies, as well as many other areas of life. The Lord told Solomon that He would endow him with riches, honor, and wisdom. Over the centuries he has been noted as the wisest man who ever lived (again outside of our Lord).

There are two basic investment principles Solomon discussed in the Book of Ecclesiastes and one in the Book of Proverbs that are worth our attention.

Investment Principle #1: Diversification

Solomon wrote in Ecclesiastes 11:2, "Divide your portion to seven, or even to eight, for you do not know what misfortune may occur on the earth." I interpret this to mean that we should divide our wealth (investment capital) into several parts and not risk it all in one place. This concept was known in prior generations as, "Don't put all your eggs in one basket."

Diversification is essential regardless of your age, income level, time frame, or personality. Obviously those with small amounts of money to invest cannot diversify as well as those with greater resources. But as your savings grow, your diversity should grow too.

It is important to diversify not only into different investments, but also into differing areas of the economy. Usually certain types of investments move inversely as the economy cycles. For example, when interest rates go up, fixed income investments such as current issue bonds go up too, while common stocks trend downward.

When the stock market is doing well and investor confidence is high, generally precious metals are down. Obviously there are always going to be individual exceptions caused by outside circumstances such as war, pestilence, and earthquakes. And there are times when it seems that contrary investments are moving in unison, but these are anomalies, caused in part by the complexities of our manipulated economy. Sometimes contrary investments are actually crossing the same threshold, with one heading up and the other heading down.

And, lest we forget that investing is an art and not a science, it is important to remember that people, their decisions, and their emotions affect the movements of investments. For instance, decisions by the Federal Reserve Board can affect the money supply and interest rates regardless of what is happening in the "real" economy. So short-term rates might be increasing at the same time long-term rates are dropping.

A good example that investing is more art than science can be seen in the great bull market of early 1991. Several thousand "program" traders (those who buy and sell based on computer models) received clear signals that the stock market would decline. This was a thoroughly logical analysis of an economy in recession and a pending war in the Persian Gulf. Thousands of these hearty speculators sold "short," meaning they borrowed stocks at current prices hoping to repay them at a future date with cheaper stocks as the prices fell.

Unfortunately, prices didn't fall. They rose rapidly and steadily for more than three months. Billions of dollars were lost by the program traders whose computers predicted higher oil prices, a sell-off in the stock market, and rising inflation. They missed on all three counts by several months.

But even though such exceptions occasionally occur, over the long run different investments move in opposite cycles. To avoid being wiped out if you need money during one of these cycles, diversity is essential. The principle is simple: Draw from the investments that are cyclically up and hold those that are down, and you won't get wiped out.

I have a friend who retired from dentistry with virtually all of his assets in good rental properties that had served him well for many years. Then, about two years into his retirement, his area of the country experienced a major recession lasting about three years, and many renters defaulted. Unable to live on the declining rental incomes, he was forced to sell some properties at substantial losses to generate income. Three years after he sold some of his rentals at distressed prices, the buyers resold the properties at nearly twice what he had received. He quickly diversified as the housing market in his area recovered.

In our ever changing economy, investors would be wise to diversify even into some foreign assets that are not subject to the swings in the U.S. economy. Certain mutual funds offer this kind of diversity.

When I discuss investment strategies for different ages of life later in this book, I will share some practical investments available to most average investors that offer a reasonable degree of diversity, but don't require a high degree of risk or expertise. Again, my basic philosophy is: I don't want to have to wake up every day wondering what brilliant moves I must make to protect my limited assets. If your goal is to maximize your profits (and risk), while maximizing your stress, you probably need to return this book for a refund and buy one on "no-money-down real estate," or "how to short the market and make a mint." I have known people who have attempted one or all of these. Some are in jail. Some are in hiding. And virtually all of them are dead broke.

In 1977 I met a retired couple who were living on the income from Sears department store stock. The husband had retired from Sears 10 years earlier after working his way up from a shoe clerk to department manager over some 40 years. During the Depression years, Sears had often paid their employees a portion of their incomes in stock, since they lacked the funds to pay in cash. As a result he had accumulated a significant amount of Sears stock, traditionally one of the best stocks in America since the Great Depression.

After retirement he and his wife were able to live quite well off the dividends and an interesting strategy of buying and selling some of his stocks annually. He had developed a strategy that was quite imaginative. Each year in the summer off-sale season, Sears stock would dip in value; then during the Christmas season it would regain its value. Knowing this, he would sell a portion of his stock in the winter, and repurchase it in the spring, often gleaning several thousand dollars profit to augment their income.

Not being emotionally attached to Sears, I suggested that he convert some of his stock and diversify into other areas that were not so single-purposed. But he and his wife had a strong loyalty to the company and forgot the cardinal rule of investing—objectivity. He couldn't bring himself to sell any of the stock permanently. "Besides," he said, "this plan has worked very well for nearly 10

years while many of our friends have lost money in their investments."

There was no way to argue that what he said was anything
but correct. The only argument I had was that nothing is forever,
except the Lord. Diversification does not guarantee success. But it
does reduce the risks long-term.

When discount stores such as K Mart and Wal-Mart entered
the retailing business they forever altered the way chains like Sears
and J.C. Penney do business. Sears stock took some swift and
terrible losses as a result. The last time I saw this couple their
assets had dwindled to less than half of what they were previously,
and both were forced to reenter the job market to supplement
their incomes.

If you select mutual funds as your primary investment vehicle,
they will usually offer a high degree of diversification within a
single fund. For instance, most good funds allow investors to shift
their money from an aggressive growth stock fund to a corporate
bond or government fund without penalty at least once per year. If
you are investing through a company retirement plan into a mutual
fund you will normally have this same election at least once each
year. Some funds even offer their investors the right to shift to
another mutual fund entirely, such as their international fund, with
only a small administrative fee. Obviously, asking about these options is an important part of selecting the right investment for your
needs.

Investment Principle #2: Ethical Investing

The second principle taught by Solomon is found in Ecclesiastes
12:13, "The conclusion, when all has been heard, is: fear God and
keep His commandments, because this applies to every person."
This certainly is good advice for anyone, but it is absolutely essential for Christians. Therefore, the first thought any Christian must
have is, "Is what I am about to do going to be pleasing to the

Lord?" If not, stay away from it—no matter what the potential profit.

Usually this comes under the heading of what is called "ethical" investing in our generation. There are investments that can yield very high rates of return with little or no risk. The difficulty is they prey off the weaknesses of others.

One example of this is a whiskey future. There are companies that specialize in selling whiskey futures, just as others do in real estate or corporate bonds. The concept is simple. When whiskey manufacturers brew their product it needs to be aged. Rather than leave their own money tied up in these barrels of whiskey, they sell (more like lease) them to investors who hold the whiskey for the time required. Once it is properly aged, the whiskey company redeems the futures contract and markets the product. Often a whiskey future will yield from 3 to 5 percent higher return than other "safe" investments. Is it a good investment? No doubt about it. Is it honoring to the Lord? No doubt that it is not.

Similar types of investments can be found in many diverse industries.

Pharmaceutical companies that have holdings in foreign subsidiaries often sell abortives outside the United States to kill unborn children.

Some U.S. drug companies purposely overproduce drugs that are shipped to virtually unregulated countries and eventually make their way back into our country as street drugs.

I once had a friend who owned a considerable investment in Holiday Inns of America stock. The stock had done quite well and appeared to be heading for even higher levels. But after reading an article about Holiday Inns offering pornographic movies in their rooms my friend sold all of his stock and divested himself of any mutual funds that owned more than a fractional interest in the chain. He also wrote the corporate officers expressing his convictions.

One interesting side note about his decision is that shortly after he sold out his stock the law governing long-term capital gains was changed to disallow the 50-percent exclusion for stock held more than six months. If he had waited just one year more his taxes on the sale would have nearly doubled. The moral: It's profitable to listen to the Lord's convictions.

This issue of ethical investing is one that comes up often in our counseling. There are really two diverse opinions that any Christian needs to consider. The first is expressed by Amy Domini and Peter Kinder in their book, *Ethical Investing* (Addison-Wesley, 1984). Basically their perspective is that a Christian (or anyone else) should avoid any company, or mutual fund, that contains even a fractional interest in any product or industry that would be deemed socially unethical.

In principle I agree with their position. The difficulty arises in actually implementing it. If you buy into a mutual fund and observe their stock portfolio from year to year you will find that it changes significantly. The managers buy and sell frequently to take advantage of changing values. Unless the company has a clearly stated policy of what it will or will not invest in, you may find that they were "socially ethical" in one year and not in the next. The way to avoid this conflict is to buy and sell your own stocks, bonds, real estate, etc., and only select companies where the leadership adheres to your same ethical standards, which is virtually impossible. However, there are some mutual fund companies that strive to adhere to Judeo-Christian values. A newsletter called *The Social Investment Forum* tracks these companies on a regular basis. The address is listed in the Appendix.

The alternative opinion to never investing in any fund or company that has even an incidental interest in socially questionable areas is expressed by Austin Pryor, editor of the *Sound Mind Investor* newsletter. He also agrees that a Christian should never invest with any company that is blatantly unethical in its product philosophy. But of investments, such as mutual funds, that have only an incidental interest, he says:

The average investor's interest would represent only 1/1000 of the fund's ownership. And the fund itself may represent only 1/1000 of the company's stock ownership. To divest yourself of the fund's stock does not hurt or influence the company's operations at all.

Instead, Pryor suggests that not buying a particular company's products may be a far more effective and practical way to influence their social ethics. Also he notes that if you own even one share of stock in a company with whose policies you disagree, you have the right to attend the annual stockholders' meetings and voice your opinion in public.

Both of the preceding arguments have validity and I will leave it to you to decide which is the right perspective for you.

In my experience I have found that boycotting a company's products has a much greater effect on their policies than boycotting their stock. I live in a relatively small community where the local convenience store was purchased by a national chain. Almost immediately they installed a rack of pornographic magazines. I took the time to get a comment form from the clerk, who also said she disagreed with the magazines. I wrote the parent company, and within two weeks received a letter of apology from the company president. A week later the magazines were removed. I doubt seriously if they would have responded in the same manner if I had simply threatened not to buy any stock in their company. But again, each of us has to make an individual choice.

Investment Principle #3: Good Counsel

The one last bit of direction I would offer from Solomon is the admonition that good counsel is essential to good planning. I made that point in an earlier chapter, but it is so important I would like to emphasize it one more time. As Proverbs 15:22 says, "Without consultation, plans are frustrated, but with many counselors they succeed."

One of my major frustrations is the contradicting counsel that is offered by investment advisors and financial planners who present themselves as experts. It's no wonder that many people either don't try to invest at all, or they simply park their money in low-interest savings accounts. Often they have listened to bad counsel and lost a lot of money, usually on the advice of another Christian.

Most Christians don't want to give a bad report about another Christian, so even when someone asks for an opinion on the abilities or ethics of another Christian they hedge by saying, "Oh, he's a nice guy."

I have also done this in the past, to the detriment of some friends, and have purposed never to do so again. I will not give a bad report without first confronting the person involved, but I also won't skirt the question and allow someone else to suffer a loss that I could have prevented.

The example that always comes to mind is a Christian who left the insurance business to go into financial planning during the eighties. He passed all the licensing requirements, took the appropriate courses, and even learned the language well. But from the first time we met, through a mutual Christian friend, I knew he was a poor financial planner. He was a likable person, definitely a committed believer, but totally incompetent to give good investment advice.

He had been one of the top salesmen for a major insurance company and was a salesman personified. He made friends of virtually everyone he met, and was so likable they felt compelled to buy from him.

I knew that a friend was considering doing business with him, but rather than tell him my convictions I simply said, "Be sure you check it out with your accountant first." As I look back, that was just a cop-out to avoid what I assumed would be an unpleasant confrontation. Also I thought the accountant would realize the planner was incompetent too. Unfortunately, he didn't, or at least he didn't say so. Not only did my friend invest a sizable amount of money as a result of this planner's advice, but he also introduced the planner to several of his friends.

The investments the planner recommended were truly awful. They were a combination of tax shelters, limited partnerships, and low-quality insurance products. One of the worst was an ostrich ranch where these large, ornery birds were being promoted as the answer to the growing demand for low-fat meats (and an illusionary market for ostrich feathers). After a two-year attempt to create a "McOstrich" franchise the project was abandoned, along with several hundred thousand dollars of investors' money.

My friend, and his former friends, are still paying for this counselor's advice. They ended up owing the IRS taxes and penalties for the tax shelters that failed, including the ostrich ranch. The advisor has gone back to selling insurance and is doing quite well himself. I learned a lesson through this that has stuck with me: When you know the truth, say it (in love).

My counsel is, always use more than one advisor, including your spouse. Tell them to be as honest with you as they would want you to be if the roles were reversed.

11

The Financial Seasons of Life:

Ages 20 to 40

I HAVE OFTEN said that if I could go back and relive my life, I wouldn't. I will gladly trade the youth of 20 for the wisdom of 50 any time. I trust that I will still feel the same way about the youth of 50 when I am 70, assuming the Lord allows me to stay around that long.

What I would like to do in the next three chapters is outline some simple financial goals and strategies for the seasons of our lives. Obviously no one will fit into all the seasons at one time. If you're older than 40 you have passed the first season. If you're between 20 and 40 you won't have reached the next season—and so on. But keep on reading. Even if you are older than 60 you may not have accomplished the goals you should have, or maybe you will be able to help your children to accomplish theirs.

The typical financial logic in our generation says that a young couple should buy a home, usually based on two incomes, open an IRA to shelter some income, and start a savings plan for the children. In addition they are told they need life insurance, disability insurance, liability insurance, and a good attorney for the divorce that about half of them will face before the seventh year of marriage (because of financial troubles). I believe that logic is faulty. There are specific goals that should be met at each phase of life, not simultaneously.

Let's assume that one goal is to own a home (debt-free); a second is to provide adequately for our families in the event of premature death; a third is to have enough surplus to help our children with college expenses; and a fourth is to be able to give at least 20 percent of our income to the Lord's work: all by the age of 40. There can be some lesser financial goals, but if you achieve these major goals you'll be in the 3 percent of Americans who have. From this point on I'll shift from we (general) to you (specific) since this book is for you, and I'm already in the 50-to-60 stage of life myself.

Most people at age 25 are thinking about how to buy their first home, pay off their school debts, and find the "right" job. Few are really interested in what investments have the highest rates of return with the least risk. That's both understandable and normal. So what I would like to do for this group is discuss some ideas that will pay financial dividends later by helping to save money presently. Remember that investing for the future is inversely related to spending during the present.

I would like to begin by working from the smallest to the largest purchases. Attention to the smallest financial details is good training for managing larger amounts of money later.

Insurance

We all need some insurance in our modern society, even if it is just liability insurance for our cars or homes. The better you understand exactly what you need, the better decisions you can make. Each dollar not spent on unnecessary insurance is a dollar that can be saved toward long-term goals such as education, retirement, and elimination of debt.

Deductibles

The higher deductibles you can afford the more you will save on any type of insurance. For instance, if you elect to carry collision insurance on your car the difference between a $100 deductible or a $500 deductible can be as much as half the annual premium. Therefore, if you can absorb the first $500 in repairs you can save $150 a year or more. The key is to buy only what you need, and not be coerced into a more expensive plan than absolutely necessary. The same can be said for deductibles on home insurance, health insurance, and the like.

Combining Policies

Most people don't realize that by consolidating their insurance they can save a considerable amount of money. One company may offer a better rate on car insurance; another may have a better rate on home insurance. But usually one company will write all of your personal property insurance for less than the total of several companies. Also, if you place your property insurance with one company often they will underwrite an "umbrella" liability policy of a million dollars or more for a very small additional cost. You need to ask if this is an option before selecting any company. My insurance company provides me with such a policy and it costs me less than $100 a year extra. This can be an important asset as your financial base grows, especially in our litigating society. One lawsuit, justified or not, can destroy a lifetime of earnings.

I learned with my first home that it is much cheaper to buy my own insurance than to purchase it from the lender. A good homeowner's policy through a reputable company turned out to be less than half the cost of a fire insurance policy sold through the lender. Additionally, a homeowner's policy covers not only the dwelling but contents, liability, jewelry, clothes, and temporary housing.

I also learned that shopping for the best quality insurance at the best price is essential. The cost of insuring personal property will vary by 200 to 300 percent depending on the company you select—so shop. One of the best resources available is the *Consumer Reports* magazine. Each year it evaluates all types of insurance and reports on the assets and liabilities of the country's major insurers. You can normally find a copy of the issue you need at any public library.

Mortgage Insurance

Most mortgage lenders today require a mortgage insurance policy that will pay off the outstanding loan balance if a home buyer dies.

The mortgage lender often sells an insurance policy that costs several times what an equivalent term life policy would cost from a major insurance company. My advice is to buy your own insurance and assign the amount necessary to pay off the mortgage to the lender. The savings can be significant.

Life Insurance

I can remember being approached by insurance salesmen while in college. They tried to convince (scare) me that if I didn't buy right then I might never be insurable again. The truth is only a small fraction of the population is uninsurable, and most are uninsurable from birth because of diabetes, heart abnormality, or some other congenital disease.

Later I learned that the policies many of these agents offered were inferior, overpriced, and usually blatantly deceptive. Often they were high-cost policies that were heavily financed in the front end to make them appear cheaper. Later the costs rose significantly while the protection declined. In short, they were a rip-off.

Life insurance should be used only to provide for those who are dependent on you while you are living. Otherwise it is a waste of money, in my opinion. If you are not married, or have no children, you rarely need life insurance, except for burial expenses. And if you join a memorial society, they will provide burial services at less than the cost of one year's insurance premium (in most cases).

Below the age of 40 it has been my observation that the majority of people who need life insurance are better served with "term" insurance. This is life insurance that accumulates no cash values, pays little or no dividends, and costs a fraction of what a whole life, or cash value, policy costs at the same age. The vast majority of young couples are underinsured and overextended because someone sold them a policy that was too expensive for their needs. A good, annual renewable (to age 100) insurance policy at age 25 to 35 will cost less than one tenth of an equivalent cash value policy at the same age.

If you are disciplined about following the rest of the strategy outlined in this book, your need for life insurance will diminish greatly before the term plan ever reaches the average cost of a typical cash value plan.

A young couple in their twenties can save an average of $15,000 in premiums before the age of 40 by buying term rather than cash value (whole life) insurance. That money, if invested wisely, will grow to nearly $200,000 by age 65. If you are unable to save the premium discounts between the ages of 20 and 40, your insurance strategy will need some change in the next stage of life.

Disability Insurance

Disability insurance, outside of a group plan, is generally very expensive if it is designed to provide for a loss of income for life. The cost is greatly reduced if the length of coverage is reduced. Most younger people would be better off with a plan that provides for three to five years, instead of life. Remember also that Social Security does provide for disability benefits, as does workmen's compensation, if the disability is job-related.

Weighing the benefits of disability insurance is critical since the costs are high. Actual costs can vary by 50 percent or more, depending on the company. If funds are limited, disability insurance should be fairly low on your list of priorities. Again, don't be panicked by horror stories of those who failed to carry a disability policy and were permanently disabled. They are the exception to the rule. I would also add that God can still provide, regardless of anyone's disabilities. I always reflect on Joni Eareckson Tada, a quadriplegic, as an example that anyone can learn to earn a living, regardless of physical handicaps.

Credit Cards

Obviously my advice is don't finance any purchases on your credit cards. The rates are usurious, and the temptation to buy things you don't need and can't afford is amplified by the easy use of credit. If you can't afford to pay cash for consumer items such as food, clothing, vacations, gas, and auto repairs, then do without them. There is no alternative if you ever expect to be financially free. I would refer you to my book, *Debt-Free Living* (Moody Press, 1989) for a complete plan on getting and staying out of debt.

Automobiles

It is usually common for most young couples to finance their first car. Unfortunately, many, if not most, opt to buy a car too expensive for their budget and plunge themselves into debt. Pick a car that fits your budget and don't be swayed by advertising that promotes cheap financing. There is no free lunch, and if a company lowers the interest rates to entice you to buy its new car, it's because the car is overpriced.

The least expensive way to finance a car commercially, especially a used car, is often through a credit union. If you are a member of a credit union, explore this alternative first. If you are not, then look for a car that can be totally paid off in two years or less and shop for a simple-interest loan. Stay away from add-on interest loans because they carry a front-end interest penalty if you want to accelerate the payments.

It is usually best not to finance a car loan through a dealer. When you mix trade-ins, finance charges, credit insurance, and sometimes even life insurance, into the deal, it's difficult to tell what the car actually costs. If you have to finance a car, arrange the loan outside and negotiate with the dealer as if you were paying cash—which you are. The convenience of dealer financing is often very costly.

I believe that Christian parents should help their children with their first home and car, if they can afford to do so. Sometimes it is just a matter of asking parents who have the means if they will help. Just be certain that you treat any family loan with the same respect and discipline you would a bank loan. If the parents want to discount the loan, that is their right, not the borrower's.

Home Loans

One of the best ways to finance a home is by borrowing the funds from a pension or retirement plan. It is possible for anyone to extend a first mortgage loan from their retirement account to a nondependent. I personally know many Christians who have done so to help young couples get into their first homes. The obvious advantage is that there are no discount points, closing costs are minimal, and the loan is backed by the home so the retirement account is protected. Typically the loan is arranged at whatever the prevailing government T-bill rate is, usually 2 to 3 percent less than a commercial loan.

Most home loans today are for 30 years, but just paying an extra $100 a month will retire a $100,000 loan approximately 12 years early and save nearly $140,000 in interest charges that can be used to start a long-term investment program, as mentioned earlier.

A second option is owner financing. This is where the person selling the home becomes the lender. Obviously the home must be debt-free for the owner to be able to do this. This is often the best arrangement for both parties. The buyer can arrange a lower interest rate and avoid the discount point penalties normally required by a commercial lender. The seller benefits through the up-front down payment, the home is collateral for the loan, and the interest rate is higher than the prevailing rates they could earn through a bank deposit.

If financing cannot be arranged through a retirement account or owner financing, shop for the best rate available. Often financing for a shorter period, such as 15 years, can save 1 percent or more in annual interest. On a $100,000 mortgage, 1 percent interest saved amounts to $1,000 the first year.

There are often government programs available for first-time home buyers at preferred interest rates. Since the programs change frequently, you will have to verify them as the need arises.

Investment Goals

It is my strong conviction that becoming debt-free, including the home mortgage, should be the first investment goal for any young couple (or person). Once you have achieved that goal, then, and only then, should you invest in other areas. As I said earlier, the exception to this would be a company retirement account with matching company funds where the proceeds could be withdrawn at some future date to retire a home mortgage.

Let's assume that by the age of 35 you have achieved the goal of becoming debt-free and want to move to the next step, the accumulation of education funds. If the children are within five years of college, at least half of all available funds should be kept in investments that can easily be converted into cash as needed. Normally these will be no-load mutual funds, short-term bonds, or liquid savings plans such as money market funds and CDs.

As the children begin college the investment plan can be temporarily curtailed so that current funds can be used for many of the annual expenses. This is really a matter of matching your available funds and costs. The use of local community colleges or state schools can stretch available funds significantly.

Assuming that you have enough surplus funds to meet the need for college, these funds should be accumulated in relatively low-risk investments. Again the prevailing principle is that no greater risks should be assumed than are necessary to meet your goals.

If the funds are insufficient, then higher risks must be assumed. Under any circumstances, the maximum risks that should be taken with designated college funds are probably good quality growth mutual funds. If you can accumulate only enough funds to help your children attend a local community college, that is better than to risk everything and not be able to send them at all.

Systematic Savings

Perhaps the single most important part of any investment strategy between the ages of 20 and 40 is systematic and regular savings. The temptation, once the home is paid off, is to increase your spending level because the additional funds are available. Most young couples with potential surpluses consume it on bigger houses, cars, boats, motor homes, and vacations. Controlling these indulgences must be a part of your long-term plans.

For instance, if you have a two- or three-step plan to move up in housing, stick to it. After the third move into the home you have agreed will meet your needs, resist the temptation to move up again. Often to do so will delay your getting debt-free well into your fifties, if ever.

As I said earlier, I prefer mutual funds as a savings vehicle for most people because they will normally accept monthly payments of as little as $10, or as much as you can afford.

Obviously, a reasonable cash reserve should be maintained for emergencies such as layoffs, illnesses, additional children, and emergency giving. The normal formula for emergency savings is approximately three months of income, although this will vary according to your profession. A postal worker has less need for a large cash reserve than does a real estate agent by virtue of their respective professions.

If by the age of 40 you have your home debt-free, have saved at least one half of your first two children's college education expenses, and have begun a long-term investment plan, you will have accomplished more than 95 percent of all Americans today. You're ready to move on to phase two.

12

The Financial Seasons of Life:

Ages 40 to 60

IF, AT AGE 40, you have achieved the goals outlined in the previous chapter, you are ready to ascend to the next stage of your financial life. But if you have not been able to become debt-free, including your home, you need to make that your priority. One bit of counsel I would offer is, don't panic or start speculating wildly as a substitute for good, sound planning, even if you're approaching your sixties. God is still able to provide what is needed. Rethink your strategy to accomplish the debt-free goals in this phase and adjust your retirement goals to later in life.

For those who are now facing children's college expenses but have no surpluses to cover them, I would offer some additional counsel: Don't plunge further into debt to send your children to college by taking out a home equity loan, government loan, or the like. Help your children to the extent that you can without taking on more debt. They will need to adjust to attending a local junior or community college, and working their way through college to a large extent. Prior to the easy credit years of the seventies and eighties, that's how most of us made it through college. Let me assure you that it can still be done, and your kids will survive, in spite of their wailing to the contrary. This can be an opportunity for them (and you) to trust the Lord in a visible and objective way. God can still provide for our needs, including the education of our children, despite all the ways we have found to circumvent it.

Some time back I was talking with a long-time friend who was suffering some financial setbacks. He was lamenting the fact that his daughter was being forced to leave the university she had been attending for three years because he was not able to secure a loan to help her financially. When he paused, I responded, "Well, praise the Lord for that."

Unfortunately he didn't see it that way and took offense. He informed me that his daughter was a member of the honor club, the college drama club, the glee club, and several other activities. "For her to leave college would cause her to miss out on one of life's great opportunities," he told me irritatedly.

I assured him that I was not playing the role of one of Job's friends, proclaiming that he was being punished by God. I explained what I believe the Scripture says: To borrow more money (for any reason) when you cannot repay what you have already borrowed is contrary to God's will. As Proverbs 3:28 says, "Do not say to your neighbor, 'Go, and come back, and tomorrow I will give it,' when you have it with you." When you borrow while in debt you risk the existing creditors' positions. Literally you rob them of assets they are owed.

My friend didn't really want to hear anything further, so for the next 30 minutes we ate breakfast in relative silence. It was several weeks before I heard from him again. He called to tell me that his daughter was attending a local college in their city, and loving it. She had been trying to find a way to tell her parents that she did not want to go back to the university she had been attending. The drinking, sex, profanity, and open use of drugs at the school ran contrary to everything she had been taught to believe. She had stuck it out for two years only because she felt that to quit would have let her parents down. She has now graduated from college, is working part-time for a Christian state senator, and is looking forward to attending law school on a full grant-in-aid from a local law firm that wants her on their team when she graduates. Sometimes it is necessary for us to step back and allow God to do His will.

Forty and Aging

By the age of 40 if you have not settled into a lifestyle you sincerely believe is God's plan for your family, you need to do so. Too often these become the indulgent years when couples buy airplanes, motor homes, large boats, second homes, or sports cars. Within reason, some additional spending is possible once education needs are met. But there will never be enough surplus to buy all the grown-up toys that are available today.

There are two general lifestyle strategies I have observed in the 40-to-60 age group. Obviously there are always exceptions to the rule; but these aren't rules, they're observations.

One strategy is for a couple to maximize their living standard by buying the home they always wanted but could never afford while the kids were at home. This strategy means that the majority of their available assets will be sunk in a home, and perhaps a vacation condo. This allows the kids to come back with the grandchildren at holidays and vacations. It also means (for most people) another lifestyle change at retirement. I am not speaking about those who make $100,000 a year or more during this 20-year period. Their choices are broader and often they can have the home they desire and still invest in other assets for retirement. This is not meant to be an indictment or an approval, simply an observation.

If you establish this strategy, then the sale of the home just before retirement is critical because so much of your net worth is invested in it. Such a lifestyle change can be traumatic and, in truth, many couples won't make that decision until they realize that taxes, utilities, maintenance, and insurance consume too much of their income after retirement. Sometimes they are forced to sell their home in a down market and lose a large part of their net worth.

If the majority of your net worth is in your home, you need to be realistic about when (or if) you can retire. If you are forced to retire by company policy you will need to adopt a budget matching your retirement income at least five years early (by age 60) to assess whether or not the home fits your budget. If not, allow enough time to sell it at market value.

The second strategy used by those 40 to 60, planning toward retirement at 65, is to pare down, move into a smaller home, and free more money for investing and traveling during these years. Some friends of ours recently made this move—to the dismay of their children, who didn't want their parents to sell the home they had lived in for more than 20 years. But our friends decided they would take advantage of the one-time capital gains exclusion of $125,000 on their residence, buy a smaller home, and invest the difference.

They also wanted to do some traveling during these years without constantly being tied down to a home that required a great deal of maintenance and upkeep. They purchased a much smaller home on sale from the Resolution Trust Corporation (selling defunct S&L assets) for about $50,000 in cash, bought a summer cottage in the mountains of North Carolina for $40,000, and still had well over $100,000 to invest for retirement. Their overall housing expenses dropped from about $600 a month for utilities, maintenance, and taxes to about $250.

They obviously had to make some sacrifices in terms of lifestyle. Their children could no longer all gather at one time in their parents' home. So now they all go to one of the other children's homes for Christmas, birthdays, and other special occasions. The children can still visit their parents' home, but only one family at a time since they have only one free bedroom and a small study available. Obviously this is a strategy that affects everyone in the family and requires a lot of prayer, but this couple, and many others, believe it will pay financial dividends in the long run.

Insurance Needs

Those in the 40-to-60 age range will quickly discover that the term insurance they bought earlier, at a very low rate, gets progressively more expensive the longer they live. By the age of 50, term insurance begins to get prohibitively expensive, unless the insured is very healthy and can qualify for a reduced rate.

The alternatives available for life insurance narrow down rapidly after age 50. Basically, you can continue to pay the high cost of term (if you can afford it); you can reduce the face value of your policy, thereby reducing the premium; or you can convert the term to whole life (assuming your policy provides that option).

For me, the best option was to reduce my coverage, which reduced my annual costs. That option was available because my need for life insurance had declined. In my case it was because we had our home paid for, our children grown, and were saving some of our earnings regularly. I still needed *some* life insurance in the event that I died before my wife reached 62 and until our investments matured to provide for her income.

Often insurance agents make the argument that life insurance can be used to pay estate taxes, which is true. But since the estate tax laws were changed to allow a surviving spouse to receive unlimited assets, that argument isn't economically logical, in my opinion. The money you leave your children or grandchildren is surplus, not necessity, unless they are totally dependent on you. It doesn't make a lot of economic sense to me to pay an insurance company a profit to leave children something they don't really need anyway. But you may feel differently, which is your right.

I converted a term life insurance policy with a face value of $150,000 to a modified whole life policy at age 49. I did so primarily because of the need for at least that amount for my wife, who was then 46. I selected an option, called a split-dollar plan, that allows the premiums to be paid in lieu of salary and then I pay the income taxes due. There are a thousand ways to arrange life insurance. If you'll find a good independent agent, I'll guarantee that he'll find a way to sell you what you need at a price you can afford.

Risk

The 40-to-60 age period is when you should logically be able to absorb the highest degree of risk. If you're debt-free, have your children's college expenses taken care of, and can afford to take some risk with a portion of your surplus, now's the time. Just make the absolute rule—*no surety!* With no surety the worst that can happen is you lose the money you have at risk. Obviously I'm not suggesting taking foolish risks. But in these years you can look for investments that multiply, as opposed to simply earning interest. The exceptions to this strategy are investors who can earn all the money they will ever need, in which case, as I said before, why take the risk?

Other exceptions are widows, divorcees, disabled people, etc. Remember that risk is not just a factor of age. It relates to temperament, income, and ability to replace the funds that can be lost. For instance, a widow in her early forties with a lump sum from her husband's estate to invest, probably needs to adopt the "60-plus" strategy. She should be primarily concerned with preservation of capital, not growth. I realize that this is repetitive, but it cannot be stressed enough—do not assume a risk above what you can afford to lose, regardless of your age!

Use of Retirement Accounts

If you have access to a retirement account, it is normally a good way to invest for the long term. As I said earlier, there are exceptions. I personally would not invest in a company retirement account where my investment choices were controlled by others and the past track record was poor. I would rather pay the taxes and earn 10 percent on the remainder than invest tax-deferred income in a plan that has lost half of the money entrusted to it.

IRAs are the most flexible retirement accounts available to average-income investors and should be a high priority for those who can qualify to use them. It has been my observation that many people do not understand that IRAs are *not* investments themselves. They are retirement *accounts* that shelter income by deferring the income taxes until the funds are withdrawn. An IRA can contain any type of investment that is available to the general public. For instance, an IRA can contain mutual funds, stocks, bonds, CDs, Treasury bills, and so on. You can also establish IRAs that are "self-directed," meaning that you place the money in a cash account such as a money market fund, then later direct the administrator where you want the money invested. (NOTE: Self-directed IRAs are usually available through selected banks. Most banks charge an annual administration fee that ranges from $10 to $50. Check with your bank about their fees and policies before establishing a self-directed IRA.)

You can also cancel one IRA and transfer the funds into another IRA, provided you do so within the prescribed time frame (presently 60 days), without additional tax consequences. At present such transfers are limited to one a year.

Self-employed people, and those who work for them, have access to several good retirement plans (at the time of this writing) including an HR-10 (Keogh) plan, a Self-Employed Pension plan (SEP), and IRAs. Since a portion of my income is generated from book royalties and constitutes self-employment income, I can shelter a portion of my earning in an SEP each year, even though I also have a portion of my income earned as an employee of a nonprofit organization.

The SEP is flexible and is offered by virtually all investment companies as an option. The funds are invested according to your personal choices and can be transferred if necessary. For instance, I purchased a variable annuity several years back that projected a 9 percent return on investment. Instead it averaged only 6 percent after all administrative charges. So I withdrew the funds from the annuity and reinvested them in a mutual fund. The mutual fund company provided all the forms and handled the transaction at no cost to me. They also provided an 800-number service to answer any questions I might have. The same procedure can be used to transfer funds from an IRA, HR-10, or company plan to any other qualified retirement account.

It is important to note that although the current law restricts any one individual's annual contribution to an IRA to no more than $2,000, that rule does not apply to transfers from another qualified retirement account. So you could have $25,000 in an HR-10 or SEP and still transfer the proceeds into an IRA without incurring a penalty.

The bottom line is, if you can use a tax-deferred retirement plan without sacrificing good investment strategy, do so. A list of the various plans that exist as of this writing are listed in the Appendix.

Plans and Goals

Before developing a plan it is necessary first to define your goals. Your goal may be to retire with 80 percent of your present income at age 62. Someone else may desire to retire on 50 percent of his (or her) income at age 59 and supplement income from another source. Still others may want to continue to work for as long as possible, while storing some reserve in the event they are unable to work at a later time. Whatever your goals, they should be well defined and compatible with God's plan for your life. There is no easy answer to some of these questions. They require a great deal of prayer and communication between spouses.

Let's assume that your goal (at age 40) is to retire at age 62 on at least 70 percent of your present income ($40,000 a year) and work for a nonprofit organization 20 hours a week earning at least an additional 10 percent of your salary. Based on current Social Security benefits, you could expect to receive approximately $15,000 a year in retirement benefits.

That means in 22 years you need to have saved at least $150,000 that could then be invested conservatively to earn $14,000 a year.

Let's also assume that you can realistically save $3,000 a year between now and 62 for a total contribution of $66,000 ($3,000 × 22). You can accomplish your goals easily by investing in one or more good quality mutual funds that average approximately 8 percent real growth a year. The choices for this level of return are plentiful.

For instance, had you invested in one of the 10 leading mutual funds over the last 20 years, your investment of $66,000 would have grown to nearly $200,000. Obviously, nothing guarantees that any investment plan will match past performance; but if you follow the strategy I outlined earlier and switch funds if necessary, you should be able to achieve the needed return.

Remember that the concept of goal-setting is critical and deceptively simple. You need to know what you are trying to accomplish and then select the investments that will achieve those goals with the least risk possible.

I'll use one more example before moving on to the next stage. Let's assume that at age 50 you succeed in becoming debt-free. Now you have $400 a month to invest (after taxes) and your goal is to retire at age 65 on at least 75 percent of your current income of $30,000 a year.

Social Security retirement benefits will be approximately $12,000 per year. Your monthly saving will total $72,000 ($400 × 12 = $4,800 annually × 15 years) at age 65. Your income needs above Social Security would be $10,500 a year. In order to provide that amount from your retirement account it will have to grow to at least $150,000 by age 65.

If you had the entire $72,000 to invest at age 50 that would be no problem. At 8 percent interest your money would double every nine years. Even after taxes it would grow to the needed amount by retirement. But you don't have the entire amount to invest; it's being accumulated incrementally at the rate of $400 a month. So your earnings on the money will need to average about 15 percent a year to meet your goal.

Several investments have earned this amount over the last decade. However, again it is important to note that all earnings are based on past history (since that is all the history we have to go on). You cannot park your money in one or more of these investments and forget it. You will need to watch them and move the funds if necessary. Any investment that averages less than the needed 15 percent over any five-year period would need to be changed.

I would personally use good quality mutual funds to accomplish this goal also, since it is well within the range of growth funds, particularly those specializing in international stocks. These funds have performed well in spite of economic slowdowns in any single country. Funds like Vanguard and Twentieth Century International have averaged nearly 20 percent a year growth over the last 10 years. Hopefully they will in the future. If not, then trade for those that do.

The strategy for those in the 40-to-60 age range is to come out of this stage of life debt-free, goals clearly in mind, and the majority of the needed funds in well-performing investments.

It really doesn't matter whether you select mutual funds, stocks, annuities, real estate, or antique cars, as long as you are on track with your goals. The more funds you have available, the more you can and should diversify. Just keep in mind that once you have met your goals anything else saved is hoarding, not saving. Pray about your goals (husband and wife together). Then stick to them. If inflation, taxes, or your investments change drastically, be ready to make adjustments. Remember that God doesn't hold us accountable for things we cannot control, only for those we can.

13

The Financial Seasons of Life:

Age 60 and Up

FROM AGE 60 on, an investor who has achieved the goals from the previous two stages of life will enter the "preservation" mode. Basically this means that you, the investor, need to concentrate on preserving what you have worked so hard to accumulate.

Obviously if you have not achieved the goals set in the previous stages, you will need to delay your retirement plans and work to become debt-free, accumulate the supplemental funds you and your spouse will need, and adopt a very conservative lifestyle. It is unfortunate that so few Americans establish any realistic financial goals early in life and face the 60-plus years with unrealistic expectations.

The most common mistake most Americans make is to retire without adequate financial preparation. They simply believe that 62 or 65 represents the "mandatory" retirement age, regardless of their situation. Two points need to be made here: First, there is no mandatory retirement age (not biblically). Many people can and do remain gainfully employed long into their seventies and even eighties. Perhaps they cannot work as hard, but they have learned to work a lot smarter.

Second, you cannot take a 50-percent (or more) cut in income and expect to enjoy your retirement years. Unless you have adjusted to the projected retirement income level at least three years prior to retirement, you're fooling yourself.

Often those who retire without adequate preparation find themselves trying to reenter the job market shortly after retiring only to find that they can't earn anywhere near the salary level they left. Many end up taking entry-level jobs at very low wages. They would have been far better off to have stayed at the job they left. Current laws prohibit mandatory retirement, except in age critical professions, such as airline pilot. So retirement is an option, not a requirement.

Let me restate an absolute. If you can't adjust to the projected income you expect to receive after retirement at least three years before that time—stay where you are! Reset your retirement goals to 65, 68, or 80, but don't become a poverty statistic. As Christ said in Luke 14:28–30:

> For which one of you, when he wants to build a tower, does not first sit down and calculate the cost, to see if he has enough to complete it? Otherwise, when he has laid a foundation, and is not able to finish, all who observe it begin to ridicule him, saying, "This man began to build and was not able to finish."

I saw an interesting example of this principle at work a few years back. Phil and Andy, both in their sixties, worked for a wholesale automobile supply company. Andy, the delivery man (called an expeditor), earned about $12,000 a year. Phil, the plant manager, earned about $40,000 a year. Neither had put any significant savings aside, nor had either taken advantage of the company's retirement plan. Phil, the plant manager, obviously lived in a bigger home and drove better cars, and took better vacations during his working career.

At age 62 each elected to take an early retirement option from the company. Andy received a lump sum of about $10,000 from the company; Phil received a lump sum of about $35,000.

By coincidence both men came in for counseling about two years after retirement. Andy had adjusted very well to his Social Security income, in addition to working a part-time delivery job that paid him about $50 a week. In fact, Andy and his wife were actually better off financially than when he had been fully employed. All they needed was some budgeting help to maintain better control of some nonmonthly expenses such as annual insurance, home taxes, and car repairs.

Phil, on the other hand, was in deep financial trouble. He had spent all of his severance bonus and had run up sizable credit card debts. The reason was obvious. He had taken more than a 50-percent cut in income to retire on Social Security alone. The severance bonus buffered him for a little more than a year, but when it ran out his lifestyle crashed in on him. Phil attempted to find work also but could locate only minimum wage jobs.

In reality Andy, the delivery man, was better prepared than his boss. He made nearly a lateral move into retirement because he never had the money to indulge or to accumulate any debt to speak of. Phil took a drastic income reduction and was unable to make the adjustment. The principle is taught clearly in Proverbs 12:9, "Better is he who is lightly esteemed and has a servant, than he who honors himself and lacks bread."

Alternate Income

Before discussing financial strategy for those 60 and older I would like to share an observation: A marketable skill is the most dependable retirement plan anyone can have. As long as you are reasonably healthy, you will never be listed among the impoverished in our society.

This idea is neither new nor original with me. It is a concept that was traditional until the last two generations. Most young men learned a trade while they were at home. Even if they left that trade and went to college or into another business, the skill was still retained. I used this approach to work my way through college long before any banker was crazy enough to lend a college student money.

When I was in high school I knew that my family would not be able financially to help me go to college. So for several summers in high school I worked as an apprentice electrician and attended night classes twice a week to pass the journeyman electrician's license test. By the time I finished high school I had my license and was earning about $3 an hour, while my friends who worked in grocery stores or retail stores were making $1.25 an hour. That trade allowed me to work my way through college at the Cape Canaveral Space Center in Florida, eventually becoming a manager of an experiments station. Although I have not worked at the trade for nearly 25 years now, I still remember the fundamentals and could market that skill to earn a living if necessary. Anyone approaching retirement who has doubts about having enough income can do the same thing. Just sign up for night classes at any good vocational school and learn a trade that suits your abilities; you'll always have an income. If you don't believe it, just try to hire someone to check out your air conditioner (or fix a faucet, or build a closet, or paint your house) and see what it costs.

Retirement Strategy

For those who have met the required criteria for 60-plus—they are debt-free and have enough investment savings for the winter years—it's time to start making some adjustments in strategy. The basic strategy for over 60 is to develop a more conservative long-range outlook. The principal objective now becomes one of protection and conservation, rather than growth.

That does not mean to shift all of your assets into U.S. Treasury bills. Your strategy may be as simple as shifting from high-growth mutual funds to income funds. Usually any mutual fund company offers a wide range of investment pools or mixes, each with a differing objective. By requesting a prospectus, any investor can determine which of the plans best fits the age and strategy needed.

I have chosen to use a tiered system to describe the types of investments used at each stage of life. You will notice a decided shift toward the conservative end of the tier at this point. It doesn't matter whether you elect to use mutual funds, stocks, real estate, or collectibles to build your investment base; you still need to shift strategies with enough of your assets to secure the income you need to live on.

By adopting this more conservative strategy, you will probably miss out on some of the major stock market rallies, as well as some of the better "deals" offered by your brother-in-law who just went to work for the plasma engine dealer. Such is life. If you want to retire with some degree of financial security you will need to make such sacrifices. The whole object from age 60 on is to try to avoid the disasters that can wipe you out totally.

If, after securing the major portion of your assets, you still have funds with which to speculate, that is a decision between you, your spouse, and the Lord.

Remember that the one variable in this age-related strategy is inflation. If inflation is re-ignited by the massive debt spending of our government, you will need to adjust your planning. Inflation can erode your long-term assets just as surely as a bad investment can.

The Tiered Shift

Let's assume that you are approaching 60-plus and have achieved most of your goals through the use of mutual funds and rental real estate. Now you need to make the necessary adjustments to a more conservative posture. The following illustration shows how your funds could have been allocated up to this point. The majority (nearly 80 percent) of the investments were oriented toward some aggressive funds during your forties and fifties. The only funds left in the most conservative tier were those used to pay for college educations as they came due.

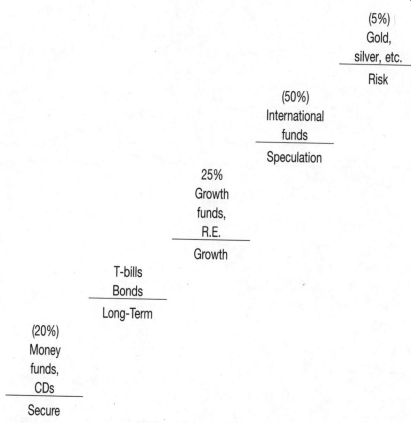

(5%)
Gold,
silver, etc.
Risk

(50%)
International
funds
Speculation

25%
Growth
funds,
R.E.
Growth

T-bills
Bonds
Long-Term

(20%)
Money
funds,
CDs
Secure

Now the shift to the conservative side is necessary. About six months' salary will be maintained in a cash reserve account to meet emergencies. As the regular dividend income is received, it is deposited in this account. Once the account accumulates more than eight months' reserve, it is shifted to a longer term cash reserve account, such as a CD, to earn more interest.

The goal is to maintain a spendable income of approximately $2,500 per month at retirement—including Social Security, investment earnings, and some generated income.

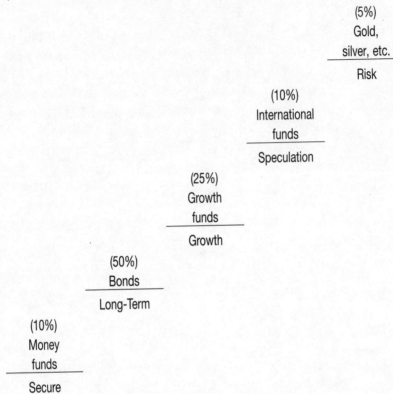

One additional note here: Since earned income can affect your Social Security pension, it is critical to shift as much of the earned income as possible to unearned income. There are several ways to do this. It should be noted that the tax laws change frequently so these options may or may not be available at the time of your retirement. However, the one certainty is that some options will always be available since our elected officials also retire.

Using a Corporation

If you have earned income and can shelter it within a corporate structure, you can avoid some of the earned-income liability. The corporation can provide medical, life, and disability insurance without affecting your Social Security income. It can also retain the earnings or profits and redistribute them as dividends. Obviously, there would be some additional tax considerations. But if the amount of corporate income taxes paid are less than the loss of Social Security due to earned income, you will still benefit.

Also a corporation can offer you a Section 125 plan (often called a Cafeteria Plan) where 100 percent of your salary can be assigned. From this plan you can pay all medical expenses, child care for dependents, dental, eye care, etc. This does not affect your Social Security earnings and is exempt from all taxes.

Before using a corporation to shelter income, it is essential that you consult a good tax accountant. Tax laws do change frequently and only a working professional in the field can advise you properly.

I will use the example of a Christian I'll call Don to demonstrate what can be done with some good planning.

Don was a computer specialist with a large company and elected to accept their early retirement plan at age 62, even though he had not planned to leave the company for several more years. The early retirement package, including a lump-sum settlement, actually provided him with more than the amount he would have earned during the following five years, had he continued to work.

Don had a specific retirement goal: He desired to do volunteer mission work with his church six months of the year and operate a computer consulting company the other six months.

He invested the majority of the lump-sum settlement in conservative bonds and other securities. This provided him with a monthly income of approximately $2,000. In addition, his Social Security provided another $1,200 per month. This amount would have been higher except that Don had been exempt from the system for 10 years earlier in his life.

Don and his wife lived in an extremely high-cost area of the country and desired to remain there as long as possible to work with their church and stay close to their children and grandchildren. In order to do so, Don required an additional $600 per month. So he established a corporation through which he would do his consulting. The company provided him with a supplemental health care plan for Medicare, a company vehicle, and a Section 125 plan to pay for all additional health-related expenses, thus dropping his total monthly expenses by nearly $400. Once a year Don would also receive a dividend check from the company, providing the remaining income he required (on which he had to pay income taxes). Since the dividend was not earned income, his Social Security benefits were not affected.

As the company accumulated retained earnings, Don used some of the funds for the ministry he was involved in, as well as for a cash reserve in times of emergency.

In a matter of months Don had shifted his strategy from a retirement age of 67 to 62 with no reduction in annual income. By January of the next year he and his wife were doing mission work in Central America, helping to evangelize business people in that area—a goal he had established as a part of his strategy nearly 10 years earlier.

Catching the Vision

I trust that by now you have correctly assessed the rationale behind planning for the stages of life. It is to allow you to shift your priorities as you mature.

The first priority of any Christian is to serve the Lord with all of his heart, soul, and mind (Matthew 22:37). To do that effectively requires some ordering of priorities. The beginning stage should be to free ourselves from debt so that our families are secure financially, regardless of what happens in our economy. The second stage is to accumulate a surplus to meet ordinary expenses, such as education, and to set aside some surplus for later. The third stage is to free ourselves to continue to be active and serve others without the pressures of earning and accumulating the needed funds through daily labor.

Retirement therefore is not what most Americans think of as the time to stop all gainful employment. Rather it is the time to shift into a higher gear, free from the pressures of the competitive work world to a large degree. If, for some reason, the Lord allows the entire U.S. economy to fail, including many of our own investments, we will have the assurance of knowing that we were the best possible stewards of the resources He gave us to manage. The worst that can happen to us is to lose some or all of our surpluses and continue to work at whatever level we are capable. Being debt-free makes that strategy a lot more feasible.

One closing thought on the concept of staying active: Several recent studies have shown that many men and women once thought to suffer from irreversible senility recovered much of their earlier abilities by daily exposure to mental and physical stimulation. Some studies even indicated that active older people experience a regeneration of brain activity, once thought to be impossible. It is not surprising that the scientific community is beginning to discover what we Christians already knew: God created us to be productive beings throughout our *entire* lifespan. As the old cliché goes: "Use it or lose it."

14

Evaluating Investments:

The Five-Tier System

I WOULD LIKE to present briefly some of the more common investments available and place them on what I referred to in the previous chapter as the "tiered" system (tiered according to how I rate them for risk and return). I trust this will help you later as you consider which investments are right for your plan. (NOTE: This is an expansion of material I have previously covered in my book *The Complete Financial Guide for Young Couples.)*

I have simply assigned a scale from 0 to 10 that can be applied to each type of investment. Zero represents the least return or the least risk, and 10 represents the highest risk or highest return. Therefore, an investment with an income potential of 0 and a risk factor of 10 would represent the worst possible investment. An investment with an income potential of 10 and a risk of 0 would be the best investment. You can't find those, by the way.

I have also added a third factor: growth. Growth means the ability of an investment to appreciate, such as common stocks. Investments such as bonds have a potential growth factor also. If a bond pays a yield of 10 percent and interest rates drop to 8 percent, the bond value increases, and vice versa.

The investments will be divided into the five basic tiers:

Tier 1. *Secure Income:* Selected because it generates cash with very little risk.

Tier 2. *Long-Term:* Selected for stability of earnings for one-year deposits or longer.

Tier 3. *Growth Investments:* Selected primarily for long-term appreciation.

Tier 4. *Speculative:* A mix between growth and speculation.
Tier 5. *High-Risk:* Selected for their volatility and maximum growth potential.

Remember that the rating for each type of investment is purely my evaluation. It should not be accepted as an absolute. Times and economic conditions constantly change, and the degree of return or risk for most types of investments will change with the economy. When interest rates and inflation are high, real property, residential housing, apartment complexes, or office buildings generally do well. But when interest rates and inflation are down, stocks and bonds generally do well.

Tier 1: Secure Income Investments

Government Securities (Income 5)(Growth 0)(Risk 1)
Treasury bills (T-bills), Government National Mortgage Association bonds (Ginnie Mae), and savings bonds all fall into this category.

Bank Securities (Income 5)(Growth 0)(Risk 3-4)
One advantage of bank investments like savings accounts, certificates of deposit (CDs), and insured money funds is that you can invest with smaller amounts of money. It generally takes $10,000 to $25,000 to purchase a Treasury bill, but you can purchase a CD for as little as $500. The disadvantages are that they offer little or no growth because the payout is fixed and the income is taxable as it is earned.

Be certain that you invest with a bank or savings and loan protected by the FDIC or a credit union insured up to $100,000. If worse comes to worst, the government will print the money to pay what it owes. If you elect to tie up your money long-term and have a choice between a government security or bank note, I recommend the government security, because it is a primary obligation of the government.

Tier 2: Long-Term Income Investments

Municipal Bonds (Income 5)(Growth 0)(Risk 7-8)
These are bonds issued by a local municipality, usually a larger city such as Houston or Hartford. The primary selling feature is that most or all of the income from municipal bonds is exempt from federal income tax (and state income tax in the state where they are issued).

The liabilities of municipal bonds are: (1) they have low yields; (2) they normally require a large initial investment; and (3) they are illiquid, meaning that if you have to sell them, you will normally do so at a loss. With the exception of buying some municipal bonds for diversification, most average investors are better off with government bonds.

Take for example an investor in a 15-percent federal and 3-percent state tax bracket. A $10,000 municipal bond paying 5 percent interest yields $500. A CD paying 9 percent would yield $738 after taxes. The yield on the CD is better and the risk is less.

Mortgages (Income 8)(Growth 0-5)(Risk 3-4)
A mortgage is a contract to lend someone money to buy a home or other real property. The lender (investor) holds the mortgage rights to the property until the loan is totally repaid. Mortgage repurchase agreements are commonly offered by commercial lenders who want to resell loans they have made. The seller normally discounts the mortgage to yield from 1 to 3 percent above the prevailing interest rates. So if current interest rates on CDs are 7 percent, you can earn 8 to 10 percent through repurchased first mortgage loans.

The risk on this type of investment is relatively low because you have real property backing the loan. If a borrower fails to pay, you can foreclose on the property. The key here is the value of the property securing the mortgage. I suggest that any investment in a first mortgage be backed with property valued at two to three times the outstanding loan.

The liabilities of this kind of investment are: (1) they are hard to find—it's usually necessary to know a local attorney or a banker who will handle them; (2) the return on your investment is 100 percent taxable, as ordinary income; (3) there is no growth on your principal, unless interest rates drop, in which case your mortgage might be worth more; and (4) your money will be tied up for a long time, usually from 15 to 20 years.

If you're looking for long-term income, a first mortgage is a good way to invest. If you're selling property that you own debt-free, consider taking a first mortgage for the amount you were going to invest for income purposes. Often you can earn a higher rate of interest with less risk than virtually any other investment.

Second mortgages usually yield a higher return, with an equivalent higher risk. If you lend money on a second mortgage and the borrower defaults, you must assume the first mortgage (if it is in default too) as well as any outstanding property taxes in order to protect your equity. Many states do not allow foreclosure for default on second mortgage loans so, in order to collect, you must file a personal judgment suit against the borrower and have a levy attached to the property. If the property is ever sold, your levy must be paid once the first mortgage loan is satisfied.

Corporate Bonds (Income 6-8)(Growth 0-3)(Risk 5-6)

A corporate bond is a note issued by a corporation to finance its operation. Quality bonds often yield 2 to 3 percent higher interest rates than an equivalent CD or T-bill. The amount of return depends on the rating of the company issuing the bond. Bonds are rated from a low of C to a high of AAA. The higher the grade of the bond, the lower the rate of return, but the risk is lower as well.

In this era of junk bonds and leveraged buyouts, the rating of a company can change quickly. In my opinion, most average investors would be far better off using a bond mutual fund to achieve the long-term income they seek. The returns are slightly lower, but the risks are lessened through diversification in many companies' bonds.

Many investors prefer bonds which generate current income through business operations, such as utility company bonds. In the past, public utility company bonds have been very stable and predictable. However, many utilities have suffered massive debts from nuclear power station construction, making them greater risks. In general, though, most utility bonds are safe investments.

One liability with corporate bonds is that repayment depends on the success of *one* company. If that company defaults, the assets of the entire company can be lost—including your bond money. Another negative is that the income is totally taxable. A bond has little chance for growth unless your rate of return is in excess of the current interest rates.

Insurance Annuity (Income 3-4)(Growth 0)(Risk 5-6)

This investment requires a prescribed amount of money to be paid into the annuity, and then the issuing insurance company promises a monthly income after retirement age.

The advantages of investing in annuities are: (1) the earnings are allowed to accumulate, tax deferred, until you retire; (2) the investment is fairly liquid, so if you have to get your money out, you can, although there is often a penalty; and (3) compared to other tax-sheltered investments, the returns are good.

But be aware that the stated yield of an insurance annuity isn't necessarily what you will receive. Sometimes the percentage given is a gross figure from which sales and administrative costs are deducted. It's best to ask for a net figure to do your comparisons and get all quotes in writing from the agent offering the annuity.

Stock Dividends (Income 4-5)(Growth 0-10)(Risk 6-7)

Common stocks usually pay dividends based on the earnings of the company. One advantage is that stocks can be purchased for relatively small amounts of money. It's possible to invest in a stock paying a dividend of 7 to 8 percent and invest less than $100. This obviously appeals to the small investor. Since the dividend is totally related to the success of the issuing company, I would look for a company that has paid dividends for many years, particularly during economic hard times.

Be aware, though, that just because a corporation has paid dividends for decades doesn't necessarily mean that it can continue to do so. The automobile industry in the early eighties is a good example. Some of the companies that had paid high rates of return for three and four decades had to cut their returns drastically. Most eventually recovered, but the people who depended on the dividends went through some lean times. So, if you plan to invest in stocks for income, you need to assess the degree of risk.

As stated previously, a good quality mutual fund can lessen the risk while achieving the same results. Professional management, together with broad diversification, provide a great advantage.

Money Funds (Income 4-5)(Growth 0)(Risk 2-8)
Money funds are the pooled funds of many people used to purchase short-term securities. These are not true savings accounts, but are short-term mutual funds that pay interest. Shares normally sell for $1 each but can vary, depending on the fund's assets value. Money funds are available through most brokerage firms, savings and loans, and banks; those offered by brokerage firms are not federally insured against losses. The interest rates are normally adjusted monthly.

It is extremely important to verify the rating of any money fund frequently. If the rating drops below an "A," remove your money and select another fund. Also, don't maintain more than $25,000 or 10 percent of your assets (whichever is lower) in any one money fund.

Tier 3: Growth Investments

This tier is in the middle and represents the crossover from conservative to speculative investments. During one cycle of the economy these investments may appear to be conservative, but then during the next cycle they appear to be speculative.

Undeveloped Land (Income 0-2)(Growth 6-7)(Risk 3-4)

During the highly inflationary seventies, farmland and other undeveloped properties were good investments. People speculated in land just as they did in income properties. This drove prices up and, unfortunately, tempted even farmers to speculate.

The eighties saw inflation subside and land prices level out. Consequently, raw land prices also fell. Today an investment in raw land is considered fairly conservative, although there is a risk if the purchase is leveraged. The prospect of the kind of growth seen in the seventies and eighties is considered unlikely, but this scenario can and will change again as the economy changes.

Housing (Income 5-7)(Growth 0-5)(Risk 3-4)

As noted previously, no investment during the last 25 years has been consistently better for the average investor than single-family rental houses. That doesn't mean that residential properties will appreciate the way they did over the last two decades, but I can see no long-range trends away from rental housing in the next decade. In fact, with the Tax Reform Act making multi-family housing less attractive to investors, fewer apartments will probably be built during the nineties. That should place more value on rental housing.

Housing costs are out of the price range of most average young couples, and since they have to live somewhere, most of them are going to rent, at least temporarily.

One advantage of investing in rental housing is that it can be done with a relatively small initial down payment. When investing in rental properties, the most important principle to remember is: no surety. If the house won't stand as collateral for its own mortgage, pass it by.

Rental housing not only generates income but also shelters much of that income through depreciation, interest, and taxes. The 1986 Tax Reform Act placed limits on what can be deducted for tax purposes against ordinary income, and it's entirely possible that future tax changes will affect real property even more. But I still believe rental housing promises good growth through the end of this century, barring an economic catastrophe.

On the other hand, there are several negatives to consider before investing in rental housing. (1) If you don't want to be a landlord, don't buy rental housing. (2) If you aren't able to maintain and manage your own property, many of the benefits decline. (3) It's not always easy to get your money out if you need it.

An option to investing in single-family rental housing is to invest in duplexes and triplexes. If you don't have the money to get into a duplex or triplex by yourself, there are two alternatives. You can invest in limited partnerships offered by individuals who purchase and manage duplexes and triplexes, or you can invest with another person. Since I have discussed both of these options earlier I won't elaborate again. The key factor to keep in mind is: The managing partner has total control. The advantage of owning a duplex or triplex is that your income isn't limited to one renter. In a single-family home, if your renter moves out, you have 100 percent vacancy. But in a duplex you would still have a 50-percent occupancy.

The liabilities with duplexes and triplexes are that they require a bigger investment and more maintenance, and you really do become a landlord.

Remember the three key factors about buying any rental property, whether it is a single-family house, duplex, or triplex: *location, location, location.*

Mutual Funds (Income 6-8)(Growth 4-5)(Risk 4-5)

A mutual fund is an investment pool for many small investors. A group of professional advisors invests for them, usually in the stock or bond markets. There are specialized mutual funds that invest in automobiles, precious metals, utility companies, government securities, and so forth. In fact, you can find a mutual fund for almost any area in which you want to invest.

Mutual funds are valuable for the small investor for several reasons. (1) You can invest with a relatively small amount of money (many mutual funds require as little as $500). (2) Your money is spread over a large area in the economy. (3) The return on the best mutual funds has averaged more than twice the prevailing interest rates for any 10-year period.

I would encourage any potential investor in mutual funds to go to independent sources and check out the fund first. Several sources are listed in the Appendix. Since we are discussing growth mutual funds, it is important to verify the track record and projected earnings of any fund you might select. A prospectus from the mutual fund company will clearly define the "secure" or low-risk funds and the "growth" or speculative funds.

I prefer to use no-load (non-commission) funds, because they allow my money to grow without the service fees or commissions coming out of the initial investment. No-load funds normally do not carry penalties if you decide to withdraw your money.

Tier 4: Speculative Investments

Common Stocks/Mutual Funds (Income 2-8)(Growth 0-7)
(Risk 7-8)
Again, the advantages of common stocks are that you can invest with a relatively small amount of money and potential exists for sizable growth. The liabilities of common stocks are obvious. First, you can suffer a loss as easily as you can make a profit. Second, stocks require buying and selling to maximize their potential and consequently require broker fees. If you expect to make money in common stocks, you're probably going to have to trade them periodically. If you're not willing to do that, it's better to stick with other kinds of investments.

Precious Metals (Income 0)(Growth 0-8)(Risk 8-9)
As mentioned before, precious metals such as gold, silver, or platinum can be purchased either for long-term growth or pure specu-

lation. For long-term growth, buy the metal, put it in a safety deposit box, and hope it appreciates over a period of time. Most people do this primarily as a hedge against a potential calamity in the economy. In an economy as unstable as ours, a small percentage of your assets invested in precious metals can help to balance other assets more vulnerable to inflation. When buying and selling anything, especially precious metals, it's wise to remember what Baruch said: "Buy when they sell. Sell when they buy." Keep a long-term mentality about precious metals—at least those you invest in as a hedge.

Both gold and silver fluctuate with the economy. Gold usually cycles faster and further than silver, primarily because more people trade in it. In general, the cycles of gold run the opposite of the U.S. dollar, so watch the dollar's trends for clues to the price of gold.

Other speculative investments include limited partnerships, syndications, penny stocks, and collectibles. It is virtually impossible to assign a rating to these since they vary so greatly, depending on the investor's expertise. Suffice it to say that the risks are great and so are the potential returns.

The reason that many of these investments are shown in both the speculative and high-risk categories is because they fall into either, depending on what the economy is doing at the time.

Tier 5: High-Risk Investments

These investments should play only a relatively small part (5 to 10 percent at the most) in any investment plan. Their primary value is the potential appreciation; in other words, speculation. Most generate little or no income and are highly volatile.

Gold/Silver (Income 0)(Growth 0–10)(Risk 9–10)

Not only can you invest in precious metals for long-term growth, but you can also invest in gold and silver for short-term speculation. This would be most beneficial in a highly volatile economy where major changes were occurring, such as the oil crisis in the mid-seventies or the run-up in silver prices in the late seventies.

Obviously, such events are difficult to predict and are extremely risky. They are for the investor with a strong heart and cash only. Unless you are a professional investor, this is probably not an area where you want to risk a lot of money.

Oil and Gas (Income 0–8)(Growth 0–10)(Risk 10+)

In the late seventies and early eighties when crude oil prices cycled up, oil and gas investments were the hottest things going. But many people who invested money in oil and gas did not understand the risks involved, and the vast majority lost their investments when the prices fell and marginal wells became unprofitable. A high degree of risk exists, particularly in oil exploration.

In an effort to reduce the risks, many people invested in oil and gas limited partnerships in known gas and oil fields. Not only did they lose their money on these investments, but they also discovered they were liable for environmental damages caused by the wells. This kind of an investment is not only very risky, but usually very expensive. I believe the income potential for oil and gas over the next two decades is excellent, but if you plan to invest in oil and gas, risk only a small portion of your assets and don't let anybody talk you into risking larger amounts.

Commodities Market (Income 0)(Growth 0–10)(Risk 10+)

Commodities speculation requires a relatively small dollar investment and can bring huge returns, primarily through the use of leverage. As noted previously, a $1,000 investment in the commodities market can control $10,000 worth of contracts—or more—for future delivery. If that sounds good, remember this: "A fool and his money are soon parted." Approximately 1 out of every 200 people who invest in the commodities market ever gets *any* money back. That doesn't mean a profit; that means *any* money back. Investing in commodities is probably the closest thing to gambling that most Christians ever try. In fact, it *is* gambling. You can lose everything you own, and even more.

Collectibles (Income 0)(Growth 2-10)(Risk 10+)

Antiques, old automobiles, paintings, figurines, etc., are all collectibles that can be used while you hold them to sell. One of the most important prerequisites to investing in collectibles is *knowledge.* You need to know value before investing. Second, you need to put some time and labor into locating the best places to buy and sell. Third, you must have the capital to wait for just the right buyer. Often novice investors get discouraged and sell out at a loss.

Unless you have a high degree of knowledge in this area, the risk is inordinately high. With most items like antiques, automobiles, figurines, and paintings, you can develop the expertise you need by talking with other people and reading key periodicals. The rate of return on collectibles can easily be 10+, but the risk of loss is just as great.

Precious Gems (Income 0)(Growth 0-4)(Risk 10+)

Diamonds, opals, rubies, sapphires, and other stones can be purchased for relatively small amounts of money. Then they can be mounted into a ring or pendant and worn while you're waiting for them to appreciate. In my opinion, gem investors should consider this their best use. For every person I know who made money in gems, I know a hundred who lost money. As stated earlier, it's almost impossible for a novice to know the true value of a gem, even with a "certified" appraisal. Worst of all, it's very difficult to sell gems at a fair price unless you have your own market. The rule here is to stay with what you know or with someone you thoroughly trust.

Limited Partnerships (Income 0-7)(Growth 0)(Risk 10+)

Limited partnerships are formed to pool investors' money to purchase assets, usually in real properties. The investment is managed by a general partner who has the decision authority for buying and selling. Since your investment in a limited partnership is no better than the property and the management, the key is to know the general partner and his credibility.

A limited partner's liability is normally limited only to the amount of money at risk. Limited partnerships requiring subsequent annual payments or operating loss guarantees, or carrying contingent tax liabilities, should be avoided. Limit your liability to only the money you have at risk.

In the past, limited partnerships in properties, such as apartment complexes, office complexes, or shopping centers, were purchased primarily to shelter ordinary income. However, since 1987 most of these benefits have been gradually eliminated, and the tax write-offs can be used only to shelter passive income. For most investors, the risk is too high and the returns too uncertain.

This basic review of the five major types of investments is by no means exhaustive, but I trust it will provide you with the pointers to get started in an investment strategy once you have your budget under control and develop a surplus.

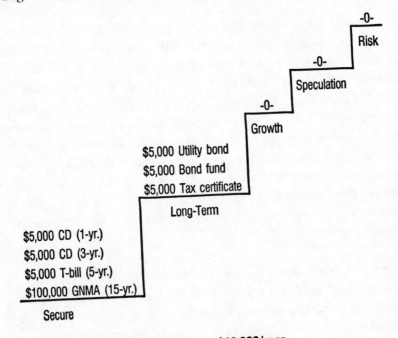

Total Return = $10,000/year

How The Tiered Approach Can Work

Let's walk through five examples of how different investors might tier their investments to meet their goals.

1. *A widow, age 68, with $130,000 in cash to invest.* Her goals are to supplement her Social Security income by $500 a month, and leave her estate to her children upon her death.

As you can see, her strategy is weighed heavily toward the low-risk tiers because she can meet all of her goals without assuming any significant risk. Her investments also provide her with adequate liquidity in the event she needs cash for medical expenses or other emergencies.

In the event that inflation picks up and begins to erode her assets, most of them are renewable in five years or less so she can reinvest at higher interest rates when necessary.

2. *A 36-year-old physician with an income in the $150,000-a-year range.* Goals: To become debt-free (medical school loans, office loans, and home loan), start a college fund for his children, and begin a retirement plan. He has $25,000 a year to invest after making required payments on indebtedness.

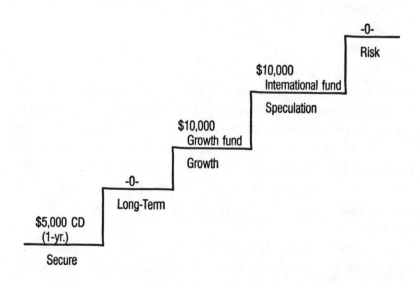

His primary investments are in mutual funds, divided between U.S. growth stocks and international stocks, for his children's eventual education. Other than a normal amount of emergency savings, his investment money is better used in retiring debt at this point in his career. His strategy should change between ages 40 and 60, then again at 60-plus.

3. *A car manufacturer employee with $30,000 to invest at age 62.* Goals: To retire this year on Social Security and company retirement income of approximately $2,000 per month combined, to use his surplus savings for travel and additional spending that his retirement income will not allow.

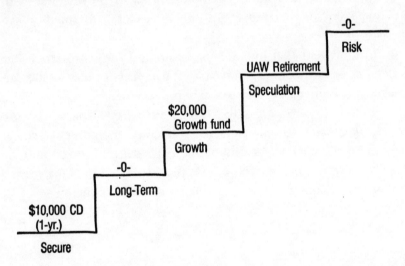

I have mapped this man's retirement account as a part of his investment program because it is, even though he has virtually no control over it. The $30,000 savings is divided into emergency savings and growth income. His risk is slightly higher than would be normal for a 62-year-old with limited assets, but since he does not require the funds to live on, he can maximize the return without too much risk. His average annual yield should be 10 to 12 percent.

4. *A 50-year-old manager of a municipal power company with $100,000 to invest from an inheritance.* Goals: To be debt-

free by 62 and retire to work with his church. He and his wife have no children, owe $60,000 on their home, and have no other debts. He has an additional $800 a month to invest toward his retirement goals.

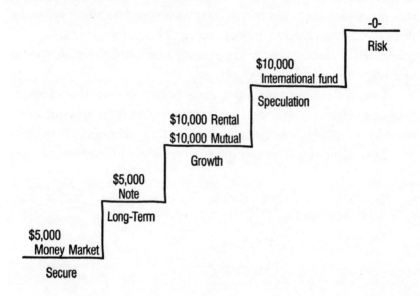

You will notice an obvious absence of $60,000 from this investment plan because they used that sum from the $100,000 inheritance to eliminate their home mortgage. The strategy is to reinvest the mortgage money in good quality mutual funds monthly.

The $40,000 they have to invest is placed in the middle risk/return tiers. They are seeking modest growth without excessive risk. This plan should return approximately 8 to 10 percent a year, providing a savings of approximately $200,000 (including the monthly investments) by age 62.

5. *A 52-year-old executive with $300,000 to invest, and approximately $100,000 per year in surplus income; no debts, college already provided for their children, and no specific retirement plans.* Goals: To multiply their assets to be able to give to missions work in Central America above the $100,000 they presently give.

Since this individual obviously doesn't need the surplus to live on, and since he has the ability to generate a sizable surplus annually, he decided to place most of the funds in the upper tiers for maximum return. He used the fifth tier, but avoided the very high-risk areas like precious metals and commodities. Since adopting this plan, he has earned approximately 25 percent annually on his investments. He has kept his asset level at approximately $200,000 and has given the rest away annually.

I need to make one point clear before closing this chapter. You don't necessarily need to lay out your financial goals in a tier plan. I do this because it makes the examples simpler. The principle is the same whether you diagram or write out your goals: *You*

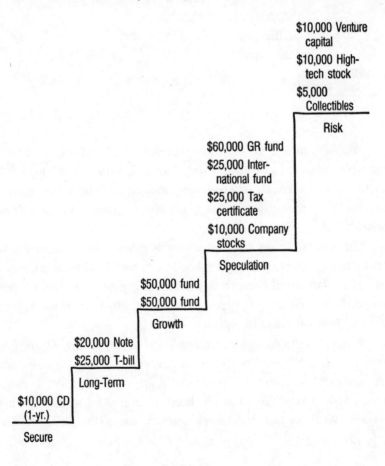

need to make very specific plans if you ever hope to accomplish them. Both spouses need to discuss their long-range goals, and commit them to prayer. Until you do, why should you believe that God will entrust more to you? As Jesus said in Luke 16:10, "He who is faithful in a very little thing is faithful also in much; and he who is unrighteous in a very little thing is unrighteous also in much." Manage well the portion that you now have and God will be able to entrust even more to you.

15

Evaluating Cash Investments

On THE SURFACE, deciding where to put your cash would not seem very complicated. But based on the amount of money still stored in passbook savings accounts I would surmise that many people don't realize there are better ways to invest their cash reserves. For instance, the same bank that pays 6 percent for money saved in a passbook account usually offers a money market account paying 1 to 2 percent more interest with almost exactly the same terms and safety. A phone call is all that is necessary to make the transfer. So why doesn't everyone do it? Most don't know they can.

Even the decision about whether to keep surplus funds in a checking account to qualify for free checking services can often be confusing. If a bank offers free checking for deposits of $1,000 or more and you write at least 40 checks per month at an average cost of 15 cents per check ($6 a month) you would have to earn over 7 percent interest (tax-free) in a savings account to match the earning on your $1,000 in the checking account. Also, many banks now pay interest on checking accounts with more than a $1,000 average monthly balance, so the benefit is increased even more. Some will say, "The amount of money is insignificant." Those who believe that are too rich!

I can assure you that based on the amount of money banks and brokerage firms spend advertising their cash accounts, they don't consider this decision inconsequential. The competition in CDs is fierce. I can also assure you that much of what you see is purposely confusing. I spent a few minutes recently calling several banks about their cash deposits and found that the rates were flexible, depending on who I talked to. The terms for early withdrawal, borrowing against the deposit, and even how the interest was calculated and paid varied from bank to bank.

In the end, I found my best return was a large brokerage firm's money market account in government securities. I beat the banks' best rate by a full percentage point and had no withdrawal restrictions on my (imaginary) funds. So clearly it is best to shop, even when looking for a cash savings account. This is especially true when placing sums of $10,000 or more.

Bank Savings

The majority of American investors still keep their cash reserves in banks. Total cash reserves in banks as of 1991 were nearly twice that of all other consumer accounts at brokerage firms, credit unions, etc. Cash deposit accounts at banks can be broken down into three basic categories:

Passbook Accounts

These are unrestricted accounts that usually pay the minimum amount of interest, while allowing the depositor daily access to the funds. Usually a transaction fee is levied if the account is used more than a few times each month. The only advantage I can see with these accounts is that they will allow deposits as little as $10. Once the minimum amount necessary to qualify for a money market account is reached, the funds should be transferred.

Money Market Accounts

These can go under a variety of titles such as "Golden Passbook," "Ready Cash Account," "Preferred Investors Account," and so on. Usually they offer check writing privileges on amounts of $500 or more, and many banks also offer free cashier's checks, travelers' checks, even special loan rates to depositors. These accounts were established to compete directly with the brokerage firms' accounts that were attracting much of the small depositors' cash in the early eighties. The rates they offer are usually directly related to the brokerage firms' rates. Depositors can withdraw their funds without penalty at any time.

Certificates of Deposit

These are time deposit accounts that can vary from as short as three months to several years. Usually the longer the time and the larger the deposit, the higher the interest rate paid.

Usually there is a penalty for early withdrawal of funds, although the interest can sometimes be withdrawn without penalty. The Certificate of Deposit is probably the best known and most widely used of all the cash accounts, primarily because of the extensive advertising done by banks.

All three types of the aforementioned bank accounts are covered by the Federal Deposit Insurance Corporation (FDIC) up to the prescribed amounts (presently $100,000) in a single bank. As of this writing, accounts in different banks are insured separately. So you could have three deposits of $100,000 each in three different banks and each account be insured to the maximum amount. This is almost certain to be changed in the future to limit the maximum insurance on a combination of all FDIC accounts.

A significant liability of these cash accounts is that any income is taxable as it is earned, unless it is held in a qualified retirement account.

Brokerage Firm Accounts

Most major brokerage firms offer a variety of cash investments, including the resale of most local, state, and federal government loans. Usually brokerage firms are the primary buyers of initial government loan offerings, which are then resold for a small percentage increase on the open market.

Perhaps the most common type of brokerage firm account is the money market fund. These are mutual funds that allow the participants to withdraw their cash as needed. Many money market funds provide check-writing privileges for the investors. Usually shares are offered for $1 apiece and the fund maintains that value. In other words, if you buy into the fund at $1 per share you can get out at $1 per share. Many people who use these funds don't realize that they are mutual funds, not savings accounts. There is no guarantee that the fund will repay dollar for dollar. So far the major funds have always repaid investors at par value, but nothing in the investment world is guaranteed.

Varieties of options exist even within the money market funds. Some funds invest only in short-term government loans, some specialize in business loans, etc. The interest they pay usually directly reflects the risk they take with your investment dollars. When a fund promises a higher than average rate of interest, you can be certain that there is a commensurately higher degree of risk.

If you have any concern about the safety of your funds, you would be better off leaving your cash reserves in an insured account.

Credit Unions

The growth of credit unions in the United States has been significant over the last two decades. These institutions offer savings accounts to their members that usually pay 1 to 2 percent higher rates of interest than other commercial institutions, such as banks. At one time the credit unions were rated as higher risks because they were insured by private underwriters, rather than the FDIC. In light of liabilities assumed by the FDIC over the last two decades, however, the credit unions are probably as good or better risk than FDIC banks, in my opinion.

If you invest with a credit union, be certain the institution is a member of the National Association of Credit Unions, is covered by their approved insurance program, and is fiscally sound.

Insurance Companies

For more than 100 years insurance companies have been used as repositories for long-term savings. In the past the interest paid on cash values in insurance plans was meager but dependable. Throughout the Great Depression of the thirties when hundreds of banks failed, no major insurance company defaulted on its financial obligations, an admirable track record.

However, these are not the thirties, and insurance companies are not as stable as they were in past decades. Because of intense competition for investment dollars, insurance companies have been forced to increase their returns, and to do so they have taken on more risk themselves. Many large insurance companies have seen their ratings fall because of too much debt and too many bad investments (such as junk bonds).

As I said earlier, I believe you should look at insurance as provision in the case of premature death, not as an investment. The cash reserves in your policies can be used as emergency funds, but remember that loans against the policy reduce the death benefit to your dependents. The use of insurance products as investments is discussed in a later chapter.

16

Evaluating Bond Investments

Most AMERICANS INVEST in a bond at one time or another during their lives. It may be a U.S. savings bond offered by their employer, or money from their 401(k) retirement account loaned to their company. Few investors realize that even the cash reserves in their insurance policies are often invested in bonds. Unfortunately the individual investor seldom has a voice in which bonds protect the money in insurance policies; and recently many have lost their savings in over-leveraged corporate bonds, the so-called "junk bonds."

Bonds form the backbone for most long-range financial planning; therefore it is critical to select them carefully, especially in the 60-plus stage of your financial life.

Bonds and Bond Funds

Bonds

Bonds are the primary obligation of the issuer. The issuer can be an individual, a business, or a local, state, or federal government. Most brokerage firms sell bonds (and bond funds) for a small fee. The interest promised on any bond is directly related to three basic factors: the length of deposit, the amount invested, and the rating of the bond issuer.

It is arguable that some corporate bonds are probably safer than many government bonds. A major corporation like IBM may well be more solvent than a municipality like New York or Philadelphia. Actually a company, such as IBM, is probably sounder than the federal government, although the federal government does have the unique ability to print money.

Usually an investment in a specific bond is for a predetermined period of time. Thus the principal invested is not readily available unless the bond is resold. The face value of a bond can fluctuate according to the prevailing interest rates. For instance, if you purchase a bond for $1,000 paying 10 percent interest and the market rate drops to 8 percent, your bond will probably go up in value. If the prevailing market rate climbs to 12 percent, the bond value will probably drop. The actual increase or decrease in value is what makes the bond market volatile. As discussed previously, it is also what tempts the commodities dealers to gamble on the future value of bonds.

Bond Funds

Bond funds represent the best option for the majority of average investors, in my opinion. The diversification they offer helps to lessen the fluctuations in value and risk. Most bond funds also offer the option of buying and selling the shares without the penalty an ordinary bond would carry. It is important to select the bond funds with the same degree of caution that you would a specific bond. The security and dependability of the fund is directly related to where the fund invests its assets. For maximum safety, select the all-government fund. For higher income, select the corporate fund. For maximum income (and risk), funds made up of repurchased junk bonds, Third World debt, etc., are available.

Bonds are rated according to a complex formula that takes into account the company's (or government's) projected ability to repay under the most adverse of circumstances. These ratings from the rating services (see Appendix) change regularly if the risk of the bond issuer changes. The best bonds, and bond funds, carry a AAA rating. The riskiest carry a C rating or less. For the average investor, any bond or bond fund with a rating of less than AA should be considered risky. Most of the financial analysts I spoke with about rating services tended to depend more on the Standard and Poor's service because of the way they gathered the data on the bond issuers. For an interested investor, this information is available by subscribing to one of the bond-related newsletters.

Zero Coupon Bonds

Zero coupon bonds have become increasingly popular with investors over the last several years, particularly for funding education needs. A zero coupon bond is actually a note issued by a company or government agency at a discount. For instance, a 10-year bond with a redemption value of $1,000 may be sold to an investor for $700. No interest or dividends are paid during the period between issue and maturity (hence the term "zero coupon"). A more traditional bond contains interest-bearing coupons that can be clipped and redeemed during the holding period.

Depending on the type of zero coupon bond (or bond fund), the appreciated value of the bond is taxable income to the holder in each year. Hence a $1,000 bond, sold for $700 initially with a three-year maturity, would have taxable income assessed in each of the three years. This can create a tax problem unless the investor has the cash reserves necessary to pay the taxes. Some limited-issue zero coupon bonds are taxable only upon maturity. Usually these pay a slightly lower rate of interest because of this feature. Consult with your bond salesman before purchasing either type of bond. The same ratings apply to zero coupon bonds as with other types of bonds.

Government Bonds

There are three basic types of cash investments marketed directly by the federal government: savings bonds, Treasury bills (T-bills), and Treasury bonds.

SAVINGS BONDS. Savings bonds are loans to the government for a predetermined period of time (usually seven years or longer). They were designed primarily to help fund the U.S. involvement in World War II, and were originally called "war bonds." Since the government hates to stop any program once started, the bond program was continued after the war and retitled "savings bonds."

Since savings bonds are loans made directly to the government, they are considered very secure. Savings bonds have one additional benefit in that the interest earned is not taxed until the bond is redeemed at maturity. Savings bonds, like most time deposits, carry a significant penalty for early redemption.

Savings bonds can be purchased in denominations as small as $25, which makes them available to most smaller investors. In 1990 a Series EE bond was introduced that allows the interest to go untaxed when used for the college education of the investor's dependent (under certain conditions). If you want a more detailed explanation of U.S. savings bonds, refer to the newsletters listed in the Appendix.

TREASURY BILLS. These are also loans made directly to the U.S. government. They can be purchased in small denominations for periods ranging from a few months to several years. The interest they pay depends on prevailing market conditions, but it is usually about 1 percent less than the interest paid on an equivalent bank CD because the federal government is considered a lower risk.

TREASURY BONDS/NOTES. These are usually offered in larger denominations of $25,000 or more, and for periods of up to 30 years. They constitute the government's basic method of financing its long-term debt. The interest rates vary with the prevailing markets, but usually are at least 1 percent lower than equivalent bank CDs and several percentage points lower than the equivalent corporate bonds.

Ginnie Maes

Ginnie Maes are bonds issued by the Government National Mortgage Association, and are actually a composite of mortgage loans guaranteed by the federal government and resold to the public. Ginnie Maes can be purchased in units of $10,000 or more, normally with an average maturity at the time of this writing of about 12 years. Other government agencies also back loan fund bonds, such as the Student Loan Marketing Association (Sallie Maes), and the Federal National Mortgage Association (Fannie Maes); all offer

higher rates of interest with slightly more risk than other government debt.

The single largest negative of bonds like Ginnie Maes is that
the borrowers have the option to prepay their loans at any time.
So although you may purchase a Ginnie Mae bond expecting to
receive your prescribed interest for the term of the bond, if the
interest rates drop and the borrower elects to refinance and thus
pays off your bond, you have no option. You may well find yourself trying to reinvest your funds at substantially lower interest
rates.

Some municipal loan programs for poor and lower income
families are backed by government bond programs such as Ginnie
Mae. These bonds provide tax-exempt income for the investors,
but usually carry a lower rate of interest. Quotes can be obtained
from any bond broker.

Tax Certificates

A little-known and seldom utilized type of bond is a municipal tax
certificate. A tax certificate is actually a lien placed on a taxpayer's
property for delinquent taxes by a municipality (state, county,
city, etc.).

In virtually all municipalities, property taxes are assessed and
payments required annually. If the taxes are not paid within a
prescribed period, a lien is placed on the property, and a tax
certificate is issued that is then sold at public auction.

The buyer (lender) of a tax certificate is legally the lienholder
on the property. If the certificate is not repaid with the accumulated interest before the statute of limitations for tax liens expires
(three years in most states), the lender can foreclose on the property, thereby assuming all the rights of the property owner.

The interest rate assigned to tax certificates is usually significantly higher than the prime interest rate. Keep in mind the rule of
risk and return. The reason the rate is higher is the inherent risk
involved. When you purchase a tax certificate you can acquire no

greater rights than the taxpayer. If there is an outstanding mortgage, you must assume that loan. If the property has a title flaw, you will assume that too. It is important to investigate carefully the collateral backing the certificate you purchase. Information on tax certificates can be obtained from most county tax offices.

Church Bonds

I have included this category of bonds because of their prevalence in the Christian community. These are loans made to a church (normally) to fund a building program. Two significant points need to be made here:

1. *It is my conclusion, based on my study of God's Word, that loans to Christians (and Christian organizations such as a church) should be made without interest.* If you would like to study this topic for yourself, I would direct you to the following Scriptures: Leviticus 25:35-37, Deuteronomy 23:19-20, Nehemiah 5:7-10, and Psalm 15:5. (There are several other references about lending without interest to God's people, but these will give you an overview.) Then you must decide for yourself whether or not you believe this principle is applicable to God's people today; personally, I do.

2. *Church bonds are high-risk loans and should be made only out of surplus funds that you can afford to lose if necessary.* I have counseled many Christians, including retirees and widows, who loaned money to a church bond program that they should not have risked. Several lost their entire savings believing they were helping God's work and He would protect them. As best I can tell from God's Word, He is not in the lending business. When you lend, you're on your own.

Junk Bonds

Junk bonds is a term used to describe many of the bonds that were used to finance leveraged buyouts of companies during the eighties. They are usually collateralized only by the good will of the issuer, and carry much higher than average interest rates.

Since the demise of the junk bond market in the early nineties, few new junk bonds have been issued or offered. However, many previously issued junk bonds are still floating around and are regularly resold to gullible investors. There are even junk bond funds established for the sole purpose of investing in these highly risky ventures. The high returns blind many investors who are foolish enough to think they can "beat the system."

Utility Bonds

The public utility companies throughout the country often finance new construction projects through long-term bonds. Over the last two decades, utility bonds (and stocks) have become the backbone of many investment plans. The advantages they offer are stability and relatively high interest rates.

However, utility bonds are not without risk themselves. Many investors who risked their money with utility companies in the seventies and eighties to build nuclear power facilities got a rude surprise as established utility companies defaulted on payments. Cost overruns and government regulations simply made many of these projects unprofitable. Although utility companies operate under a public utility license, they still must make a profit to repay creditors. Those that don't, can't.

Except for the bonds associated with nuclear power development, utility bonds have been rated among the best investments in America for nearly 70 years. For the average investor, the purchase of a utility bond fund probably makes more sense because the risk can be spread over many utility companies. The evidence of this logic can be seen in the fact that even when individual utility companies were defaulting on bonds attached to nuclear power facilities, the utility bond funds were still paying their investors. It is the simple principle of diversification.

Municipal Bonds

Local municipalities can issue interest-bearing bonds that are exempt from federal income taxes. Many states exempt the interest on bonds issued by municipalities within the state from state income taxes as well.

Because of this tax-exempt feature, municipal bonds are popular with higher income investors. However, it is easy to be beguiled by the promise of tax-free income. If you decide to invest in municipal bonds, or bond funds, you need to verify the rating of the issuing municipality. Several large cities are on the verge of insolvency and are able to pay the interest on existing bonds only by selling more bonds. This is very similar to a pyramid scheme in which only the early participants can get their money back. We have yet to see a major municipality default in our present generation. But I assure you, municipal bond holders during the Depression saw many municipalities default.

Also bear in mind that if your total tax rate is 40 percent, a totally taxable bond yielding 10 percent is the same as a tax-exempt bond yielding 6 percent. It may well be that the 10-percent bond is a better buy when risk is factored in.

17

Evaluating Stocks and Stock Funds

THE PROCESS OF buying and selling stocks is probably the most visible area of investing to the average American. Stock market quotes are given on virtually every news program, and changes in the Dow Jones stock index make every major network's news. In recent years violent swings up and down in the market indexes have almost numbed the average American to what they really indicate. The market no longer reflects the true value of a company's worth. Rather it reflects the current mood of those who buy and sell stocks and bonds. With the advent of the large institutional investors (mutual funds and pension funds), relatively few traders can cause huge swings in the market. As the downturn of the market in October 1987 demonstrated, computer-originated trading can actually cause a market collapse if left unattended by human rationale.

What actually happened that fateful day in October (by most accounts) was that the automated trade programs, designed to minimize losses, were triggered to initiate sell orders by a sudden downturn in the indexes they monitor. These sell orders in turn triggered more trading by other programs and the big sell-off was in progress. By the time anyone realized what was happening and unplugged their computers, the biggest one-day drop in the history of the market had occurred. Subsequent changes in the way these programs function have made similar sell-offs unlikely. But without a doubt, something equivalent will occur in the future as stock market trading gets more sophisticated and volatile.

I say this only to warn you again that trading in stocks (and stock funds to a lesser degree) is highly speculative. Stocks should be used only as growth investments for the preretirement years, or for surplus funds after retirement. The use of mutual funds can help to reduce the risk associated with stock trading, but nothing can eliminate it.

I found in my reading that most secular investment books have some excellent sections and some so totally contrary to God's principles that they negate the worth of the good parts. Consistently, the one area most of them are off base is that of stock speculation. The authors of investment books are commonly stock salesmen (and women) who have made a great deal of money themselves by selling stocks. Just remember, a significant difference exists between investing in stocks and selling them. The broker makes money whether we do or not.

I found two consistent flaws in the advice given by most of the writers who also sell stocks for a living. First, they recommended the use of debt to invest. Second, they use stocks as their primary investments to the exclusion of less risky investments.

Discount Brokers

As stated previously, discount brokerage firms place orders; they do not provide investment advice. When using a discount broker you must know what stocks, bonds, or other investments you want to buy. The broker simply places your order and charges a small fee for the service. Usually the fee is a small percentage of what a standard broker charges.

Probably the most widely known discount firm is Charles Schwab and Associates. This company started the current trend toward a nationwide use of discount brokerage firms in the early seventies. For stock or bond investors who need placement services only, a discount broker, like Schwab, can significantly reduce their trading costs.

The argument for using a discount broker is purely economic. More of your investment dollar goes into the investment. The argument against using a discount broker is that you receive no counsel when investing. In general, the decision to use or not to use discount services should be based on your ability to make investment decisions. If you don't need advice, why pay for it? If you do, the fee should be worth what you pay. The bottom line is, a fee-based broker should make you more than his fees cost you.

Blue Chip Stocks

The so-called "Fortune 500" companies are often referred to as the blue chips (an obvious association with the higher value chips used on the tables in Las Vegas). These are some of the largest companies listed on the stock exchange, and represent the base value of American industry.

If an investor had simply spread his stock investments over the blue chip companies (or the Dow Jones list of companies used to establish the daily index) for the last 10 years, he would have earned approximately 10 percent annually (after inflation) in growth and dividends. There would have been some bad moments when it looked like the market would collapse as it did in the thirties, and nothing says it won't in the future, but overall, stocks were a better than average investment. It is the risk that makes them so volatile for the average investor, and the fact that outside of a balanced mutual fund it is difficult for most people to invest in a wide enough base of companies to lower the risk.

Normally good quality stocks are divided into two broad categories by investment analysts: *growth* and *income.*

Growth stocks are usually associated with newer companies, or emerging technologies. IBM was considered a growth stock in the early fifties. Xerox was a growth company in the sixties. Texas Instruments was a growth company in the seventies. Apple Computers became a growth company in the eighties. In the nineties the growth industry will probably be health-related companies. In the next century environmental companies could very well lead the way.

This does not mean that once a company has been a "growth company" that the stock does not appreciate. IBM is a good example of a company that has seen a steady growth pattern for more than three decades. But compared to the company's early days it would now be considered a stable income company.

Income stocks are selected primarily because of their stable, long-term income through dividends. Good examples of this type of investment would be utility stocks, automobile stocks, defense industry stocks, and the like. Once a company has established a decade-long track record of paying regular dividends, many investors seek them as a means to earn both income (through dividends) and growth (through stock appreciation). Often a company that is noted for its dividend payout will see its stock prices fall rapidly if the dividend is less than projected. On the other hand, a company selected primarily for growth may see its stock appreciate even though the company never declares a dividend.

It is important that you know which category a company's stock fits into when making an investment. There are rating services that provide this information. Some of the better known are listed in the Appendix.

The New York and American Stock Exchanges

Most people know there are two stock exchanges, the New York and American, but don't know what the differences are. Both exchanges serve similar functions, but to vastly different sized companies. Generally the American Exchange offers a sales outlet for smaller, less established companies' stocks; the New York Exchange serves the country's biggest companies.

The exchanges are businesses run on a for-profit basis. They are not governmental agencies, nor are they affiliated with any agency of the government. Both are regulated by the Securities and Exchange Commission, which is an agency of the government, but only to control illegal actions that can adversely affect the public.

Over-the-Counter Stocks

The cost of preparing a company's stock for sale on the national exchanges is prohibitively expensive for many emerging firms. In order for them to have a market for their stocks, the exchanges created the over-the-counter market. Stocks offered on this market are subject to less stringent Securities and Exchange rules as far as capitalization, income, and size are concerned. Basically these are speculative offerings of companies in the growth category. Buyers are presumed to be warned by the very fact that a stock is offered through the over-the-counter market.

Contained within this group of stocks are those often referred to as "penny" stocks. These probably represent the ultimate in risk of any stock regularly traded to the public.

The term *penny stock* refers to the very low price of the stocks, although not necessarily only pennies. When sales in these stocks began, the prices were actually a few pennies; since then the name has stuck. Investors in penny stocks should be advised that the risk is extremely high. These companies come and go regularly, rarely leaving any equity behind. The few that survive can appreciate greatly in value. But very few companies now traded on either exchange started as penny stock companies.

Mutual Funds

As previously discussed, a mutual fund is nothing more than a pooling of investors' money to purchase a cross section of stocks or bonds. Mutual funds gained popularity in the sixties, but really grew in popularity during the seventies. Where originally some 30 funds existed, there are now literally thousands of mutual funds offering wide diversification.

In order to attract investors in a very competitive field, mutual funds now offer a variety of options. One fund may offer investments ranging from growth stocks and blue chips to utilities, government bonds, and municipal bonds. When you invest in the fund you have the option of shifting or spreading your money into one or more of these areas without penalty. Most funds now allow investors to shift their funds within their "family" of investments once or twice a year without penalty. This offers maximum diversification even for small-dollar investors.

Since mutual funds are securities, they are normally sold through registered brokers. The fund company must also publish a prospectus showing the current financial condition of the fund, including administrative costs. Since the returns shown in the prospectus are historical only, it is important either to read the prospectus carefully or to subscribe to a service where a trained mutual fund expert does it for you. Such services are listed in the Appendix.

Past history is a good indication of what a fund has done, but it is not always a good indicator of what it will do in the future. A trained analyst can review a fund's performance and compare it with current management philosophy, cash position, and market position to come up with a reasonable projection of what the fund can do in the future. Never rely on a one-year performance record (and certainly not a one-quarter performance) when selecting a fund. It may well be that the managers guessed right in a given market and cannot duplicate the feat again.

Loaded Versus No-Load Funds

We discussed this aspect of mutual funds earlier, but it is worth repeating one more time. A "loaded" fund is one in which a commission or sales charge is taken out of the funds invested before the fund units are purchased. For example, if you invested $1,000 in a fund whose units sell for $1 a share, and pay a 6-percent "load" or commission, you will own 940 shares.

A "no-load" fund has no commissions or sales charge taken out at the time of purchase, so you would own an additional 60 shares. No-load funds are sold exclusively by the fund company through direct solicitation. Since no commissions are paid, there are no local sales agents.

Whether a fund is a loaded or no-load has no real bearing on its performance. There are no-load funds listed among the top funds, and there are loaded funds in the top group also. It is important to select a good fund, regardless of how the fees are paid.

Given the fact that a good no-load fund can perform as well as a good loaded fund, I personally would rather invest in the no-load fund so that more of my money is working for me from the outset. "Net" return is the most important feature of any investment. It is critical to know how much the fund you select charges in annual administrative fees and commissions. There are many good fund rating services that evaluate net performance. You will find them listed in the Appendix under "Mutual Fund Services."

Market Timing

In recent years a lot has been said about market timing in mutual funds. Market timing means that the funds are shifted from one type of investment to another depending on what's happening in the market. Or more correctly, what someone *thinks* will happen.

For instance, if a major downturn in the stock market is projected, it makes sense to shift from a growth fund to a government bond fund, thus avoiding the loss associated with the market downturn. Conversely, it also makes sense that when the market is projected to turn up again, the funds should be switched back to the growth fund.

During the eighties, dozens, perhaps hundreds, of these market timing services were started. Most evolved into newsletters and phone services that advised mutual fund investors when to switch from one type of fund to another. Some actually assumed the responsibility of switching the funds for investors.

More often than not, these timing services were started by a financial advisor who had gained notoriety by correctly projecting a major market move. Also more often than not, the feat was not repeated and the subsequent timing advice was usually inaccurate.

I asked several top financial advisors who have used these services at one time or the other how well they had done for them. The average was 25 percent right—about half of what flipping a coin would be. For the average investor, the cost of subscribing to such a service rarely is worth the benefit derived from it, in my opinion.

18

Investing in Real Estate

WITHOUT QUESTION, RESIDENTIAL housing has been one of the most profitable areas of investment for most Americans over the last 40 to 50 years. The advent of the consumer credit boom that began after World War II provided the impetus for real estate appreciation, especially residential real estate. Simply put, more families were able to afford better housing through long-term financing.

The difficulty with any debt-financed expansion is that as the debt bubble expands it gets increasingly difficult to keep it inflated. The people who get in at the beginning make real profits since they can resell their expensive homes, move to a less expensive area of the country, and live on the surplus. But as the expansion continues there are fewer less expensive areas to move to and less appreciation in the existing homes. In a worst-case scenario the price of property drops as new buyers cannot manage the increasing monthly payments.

Once investors progress from residential real estate to other forms of real estate, such as commercial, farm land, and multi-family, the picture gets a lot cloudier. Some investors have done exceedingly well in high-growth areas like Florida and California. Others have done quite poorly in areas where the values rise and fall quickly. The oil patch in Texas and Oklahoma is a classic example of this fluctuating market. In these states, investing in real estate is much like investing in stocks; if you hit the right market you can make a lot of money. But if you hit the wrong market you can lose it all—and then some.

What I would like to do is discuss briefly each area of real estate investing and share some insights from others who have done well.

Residential Real Estate

There are no "magical" insights when it comes to investing in residential properties. The old adage in real estate is still true, "There are three important factors to consider when buying rental property—location, location, location."

The primary determinant of resale is where the property is located. Other factors are important, such as physical condition, price, even how a home smells. But these can all be corrected if necessary. Location is fixed and forever. Obviously if you buy for the long term, you also need to consider area trends. A neighborhood that is on the decline can destroy the value of homes in the area. Conversely, a neighborhood on the mend can add great value to the properties.

One major consideration before investing in rental properties is whether or not you have the temperament to be a landlord. If you don't have some maintenance ability, including some mechanical aptitude, I suspect you will not be happy owning rental property. Another factor is temperament. If you don't have the temperament to tell people they must vacate your property if they don't pay their rent, don't be a landlord. That may sound a little harsh, but I'll guarantee you that every landlord is eventually faced with that decision.

The general rule for investing in rental housing is that 11 months of rental income must be able to cover 100 percent of all expenses including payments, taxes, maintenance, and insurance. If it will not, normally it is not a good investment. This formula leaves one month per year that can be used for income, or vacancy.

The long-range strategy for investing in rental property should be to have the property pay off the mortgage before you retire so that the income is available at retirement. A second alternative is to sell the property using owner financing. The mortgage payments then become a steady, dependable source of income after retirement.

In my opinion, the biggest drawback of investing in rental properties today is that virtually no commercial lenders will finance real estate without a personal guarantee on the loan. I would not give a personal endorsement (surety) for any loan. Therefore, unless I could find an owner-financed home, or borrow using only the property as collateral, I would not invest in rental housing (or anything else). When you borrow on surety you potentially risk everything you have accumulated to that point.

Commercial Real Estate

For the vast majority of average investors, commercial real estate is beyond their financial resources, unless they pool their funds with other investors. I have already discussed the use of limited partnerships to do this in chapter 5, so I won't rehash that again. It is sufficient to say that unless you have a large degree of control over a project, you're generally better off pooling your investment money in a mutual fund where professional management is used.

From this point on, I will assume that those who will invest in commercial real estate have the financial ability to do so, and are not numbered among the fainthearted. If these two elements are present (money and courage), a great deal of money can be made in commercial real estate. A review of those who attempted to get rich quick in commercial real estate should be sobering enough to frighten most investors out of the commercial real estate market. I will not attempt to discuss the details of investing in one of Donald Trump's hotels, or investing in multi-story office buildings. If that is your investment strategy, you probably won't be helped by reading this book. I suggest a good book on psychiatry instead!

In reality there are only a few investments in commercial real estate available to average investors. I will briefly discuss some of the more common opportunities.

Storage Buildings

Some of the most profitable investments in commercial properties over the last 20 years have been mini-warehouse storage buildings. These are the small rental buildings used by many people for temporary storage space. The initial investment in these facilities is not insignificant. Often the cost of land, construction, and start-up advertising can run several thousand dollars per unit. But in good locations the storage units will repay all costs in five years or less. The obvious key is selecting the right location and analyzing the market carefully, including the competition.

I have a friend who has invested in mini-warehouse storage for nearly 15 years. All of his units repaid their total costs in six years or less, and now generate substantial cash flow for him. When he started he lacked the resources to buy the land and construct the storage facilities without going deeply into debt, which he had determined not to do. He solved the problem by forming a joint venture with some businessmen who had the funds to risk. He became the manager and part owner of the first several units, while they were basically silent partners. He located the properties, contracted for the construction, rented the units, and collected the monthly payments. For his partners, the storage units became their best investments ever, returning nearly 30 percent a year on their initial investments. As you would imagine he had no lack of willing partners, once the word got out.

Once he was established he was able to build more storage facilities using his own funds. In 15 years he has accumulated nearly $400,000 in paid-up units, generating almost $80,000 a year in income.

Since he lives in a recreational area, he has recently diversified into boat storage units located adjacent to a large nearby lake. The return per dollar invested is nearly twice that of ordinary storage units. It seems that American boat owners are attached to their pleasure crafts. It also seems only fitting that he is able to take some of that recreation money and put it back into the Lord's work.

Time-Share Condominiums

During the late seventies and eighties the concept of building condominium complexes in recreational areas and selling interests to multiple owners was hatched. The idea caught on with investors immediately, and time-shared condos sprung up in Florida (and elsewhere) like cabbage palms.

On the surface the idea was great. Why should vacationers tie up a lot of money in a cramped motel room when, for a small investment, they could own a share in a condo and rent it out when they didn't want to use it?

Difficulties surfaced as more and more units were constructed and the competition for renters grew so fierce that finding them required large advertising budgets and steep discounts. Since the rental agencies were not going to take the losses, the only logical prospects were the absentee owners. Many investors found themselves stuck with a condo they couldn't use, high annual mortgage payments, maintenance fees, and rental costs, not to mention declining income from their units.

When the tax laws changed so that the interest and depreciation could no longer be used to shelter other income, many investors tried to dump their shares, collapsing the resale market. Those who bought in during the collapse stage actually got some very good values for their investments. But overall, time shares have proven to be a very bad investment for the majority of buyers. Unless you really know what you're doing and can manage your own units in an area where you live, my counsel is to avoid them.

Lease-Repurchase Agreements

A popular concept that was developed in the eighties is selling rented office space to investors. I have several counselees who have invested in these situations and have done quite well. The concept is simple. A developer builds an office building and rents it out to qualified tenants. The rented offices are then resold to individual investors who become the owner/landlords. Assuming the tenants are stable and dependable businesses, the arrangement works well for all parties. Often the tenant will sign a lease agreement with an option to buy at a later date. A good office building can yield an average return of 20 percent a year, or more.

The caution here is in qualifying the lease tenant. If the tenant cannot or will not pay the lease, the unit must be rented to another qualified tenant. Often that entails remodeling the offices to suit the next lessee. Unfortunately, the owner has to bear this cost.

As lease-repurchase agreements have grown in many areas of the country, the competition for good tenants has increased and revenues have declined. In short, this investment should be considered only with firsthand knowledge of the tenant. If you can't afford to pay cash for the unit, you should probably avoid this type of investment.

Land Speculation

Virtually everyone in America knows of someone who struck it rich in the land business. Those who don't know someone certainly know someone who said they would have been rich had they just had the sense to invest in land 20 years ago. Tucked in the back of our minds somewhere is this secret desire to be one of those people who owned 10 acres in Kissimmee, Florida before Disney World came to town. I had a friend who owned 30 acres there and profited greatly. But it was purely by chance, not by design.

We both worked at the Kennedy Space Center in Florida, long before Walt Disney ever thought about building his Magic Kingdom in central Florida. My friend got so tired of the stress that he decided to move to a quiet little community—Kissimmee—and start an antique car restoration business. Little did he know at the time he would relocate in the busiest community in America three years later. It worked out okay for him since he sold his property for slightly over $10 million more than his original purchase price of $20,000. Few people are so fortunate, but it is those who receive the publicity.

I heard my father tell the story about owning hundreds of acres in central Florida during the early twenties. He gave it back to the county when he had to start paying taxes on it. After all, who would want to pay taxes on virtually useless swampland?

These stories could be repeated by millions of Americans, and each time the consensus would be, "If I had only known then what I know now." Unfortunately that's true of any investment. Who would have believed in Edison's day that anyone would want a light bulb when there was no cost-effective way to power it? Besides that, gas lights worked just fine. For every one who invested in Edison's invention and prospered there were millions who lost money in ventures (land included) that looked more promising at the time.

With rare exception most people who invest in raw (undeveloped) land show very little return for their investment. Unless they can use the land themselves, the annualized rate of return when they sell is less than 5 percent a year. They would have done far better in a good stock fund over the same period of time.

If you are bound and determined to invest in raw land I would offer these suggestions:

1. *Buy only if you can see a future use for the property that will make it appreciate.* (For example, it's generally safe to buy raw land in a developing community where the property might eventually be going commercial or residential.)

2. *Plan to keep the property until it is totally paid off.* Don't anticipate selling it before a balloon payment comes due. If you can't handle the payments until it is paid off, don't take the risk.

3. *Buy only if the property can be used as total collateral for the loan (no surety).* Usually this will require owner financing, since virtually no commercial lender will lend without a personal endorsement.

4. *Avoid joint ventures or partnerships to buy land.* Often what happens is the other parties can't pay their share and you will either have to pay the entire costs or forfeit your equity. Then not only is their credit rating blemished, but yours is too. As Proverbs 22:1 says, "A good name is to be more desired than great riches, favor is better than silver and gold."

19

Evaluating Collectibles and Precious Metals

INVESTING IN COLLECTIBLES (coins, stamps, cards, antiques, etc.) is clearly more of an art than a science. Often it is a matter of guessing what the other collectors want and finding the good deals before they do. If you can buy the right product at the right price, a profit can be made. But if you guess wrong, you probably made a purchase rather than an investment.

Investing in collectibles is not new. For centuries investors have purchased paintings and other forms of art, as well as furniture, dolls, toys, and books. In our generation the art of collectible investing has been brought to the level of a corporate enterprise. Major auctions are held regularly where anything from autos to baseball cards is offered. This publicized buying frenzy has driven up prices over the last decade, and there would appear to be no slackening in the foreseeable future.

Collectible investing truly is a worldwide market today. Any auction of significance will draw bidders from every part of the globe. If you have the right item at the right time, price is no object to many wealthy industrialists who have apparently run out of places to spend their money.

The real key to making money through collectibles is *expertise.* You must know what you're doing or someone who does will sell you the proverbial "pig in a poke." Before you decide to risk any of your money in collectibles, I would heartily encourage you to focus on one area (cards, stamps, etc.), read all you can about it, practice with "pretend" funds, and then start small.

Even though a collectibles salesperson professes to be a Christian and seems willing to offer you a good deal in his or her area of expertise, you need to know what you're doing. Usually I find that the people who are particularly good at what they do seldom need other investors. It is the people who sell investments for a living who offer the "good deals" to others. Unfortunately, many of them know only what they have been told, and that is just a little bit more than the people to whom they are selling. The more you know yourself, the easier it is to sort out the sheep from the goats.

I have known many people who have invested in collectibles. In general, I would categorize most of them as relatively successful. Usually the pattern was that they got started by buying from a professional. With rare exception they lost money on the "good deals" offered by the professionals. However, often this sparked an interest that developed into a hobby, and later into a business. So you could say the professionals helped launch their investment career in collectibles.

My observation is: Skip the losses and learn what you need to know first. Attend a few shows or auctions, read the best books available, and start small. You will be amazed how simple it is to become an expert in any one area.

Collectibles with Established Markets

Collectibles such as stamps, coins, sports cards, paintings, and antique furniture all have established markets, meaning that they are regularly traded through established outlets. Some are traded through auctions. Others are traded through trade shows. Still others are traded through magazines. Some are bought and sold through all of the above.

Having an established market outlet is a very important consideration for the average investor because often it is much easier to buy a collectible than it is to sell one. You may invest in a fine crystal glassware set that has good potential, but unless you can find a willing and able buyer you may not be able to resell it. The law of supply and demand works in the collectible area just as it does in any other. The more people who regularly buy and sell collectibles, the higher the price can go (normally). The principle of supply and demand is simple: Increase the demand with a limited supply and the price will also increase.

Many excellent books are available on how to understand the area of collectibles. If you will invest a few dollars and a lot of time to study these carefully, you can avoid many of the hard lessons that come with losing money.

Nothing can replace an instinct for finding the good deals. Some people can read all the books ever written on buying and selling collectibles and still not have the knack for evaluating what is a good deal and what is not.

I have a friend who literally eats and sleeps with rare coins. He began collecting when he was about 12 and has been trading them ever since. For entertainment he goes to trade shows and barters coins. For reading material he scours the trade magazines. As a result, he has made a considerable fortune from rare coins.

You may not want to go to that extreme in your investing. But there are two things to remember: *first,* the more you know, the easier making money becomes; *second,* in any investment field there are people, like my friend, with whom you will be competing. He makes a large portion of his money off of novices who buy too high, panic when the market declines, and then want to sell quickly.

Non-Market Collectibles

Many collectibles either have no established market, or a very limited market. Such is the case with semiprecious stones. There is a readily available market to purchase stones like topaz, aquamarines, and amethysts. Unfortunately, that market normally works only in one direction. In other words, the dealers will sell to the consumers, but won't buy from them.

When you invest in collectibles that have no ready market you must either make the market by advertising, selling to friends and family, or through some other means—or else you're stuck with the items and no way to get your money out.

My counsel is to avoid this type of collectible unless you truly know what you're doing and can market them yourself. I know someone who does just that. He shops estate sales, flea markets, garage sales, and any other source for collectibles with unique value. The items he buys may be anything from gems to historical memorabilia. He then ships them to another friend in California who has access to Hollywood celebrities where he sells them at outrageous prices to people who have more money than sense. He has made a market where none existed before, and profits handsomely from it.

Narrow Market Collectibles

This type of collectible includes investment-quality diamonds, works of art, historical documents, and the like. I term them narrow markets because an organized outlet usually exists but access to it is limited to a few select dealers and brokers. As I mentioned in an earlier chapter, when you risk your money in something like an investment-grade diamond you must be careful that you're not paying retail, because when you want to resell, the dealer will rarely pay above wholesale. There are collectors who will pay a fair price for such items, but usually they buy only through established dealers. So the average investor is excluded from access to the collectors except by random chance advertising.

I once counseled with a widow whose husband had invested in rare books for many years and owned a fine collection of original manuscripts by several well-known writers. Unfortunately, when she attempted to sell the collection, the dealers offered her only a fraction of what she knew their collector value was. But without their contacts she was unable to find qualified buyers.

Eventually a Christian friend helped her to market the collection in an ingenious way. He contacted the original publisher of some of the books, who was still in business, and asked if the company would be interested in buying the collection for display. They were, and she received an excellent offer. The remainder of the books was donated to a historical museum and the tax write-offs were enough to shelter most of the profit from the sale. The moral here is that God often intercedes to help widows. Foolish investors may not be so fortunate.

Precious Metals

The ownership of precious metals, particularly gold, has become as much of a controversy as the issue of whether to buy whole life or term insurance. What has created the controversy in precious metals is the radical movement that believes the economy will collapse and gold will be the salvation of all wealth.

In reality there is a lot of truth in that position. It is quite possible that our economy will collapse under the weight of its excessive debt burden. It is also possible that precious metals will appreciate in value greatly during that time. But the fallacy of that theory, in my opinion, is believing that gold or any other precious metal will become the principal means of transacting business. There is simply too little gold available and too much currency in circulation. It is more probable that the whole world's exchange system will become totally electronic, using no currency at all. At that point gold will become just another speculative commodity. Any long-term financial planning should include the purchase of some precious metals, but should never be weighed too heavily in balance with other investments (in my opinion). I would recommend limiting any investment in precious metals to around 5 percent, and certainly no more than 15 percent, of your total investment funds.

Buying and Selling Gold or Silver
I will limit the discussion of precious metals to only gold and silver
since they are the most recognizable and regularly traded of all
precious metals.

Both gold and silver are bought and sold by a variety of agents
throughout the country. Some deal exclusively in precious metals,
but most sell a variety of other investments as well. Because of the
volatility of metals, most brokers have had to offer a variety of
other products to keep their investor base. When the economy is
unstable and metals are in vogue, dealers do quite well. But when
the economy is growing, the metals market often turns down and
most brokers find it difficult to earn a living. This is generally true
with any investment products, but with precious metals the
swings are wider, the peaks are shorter, and the down periods are
longer. When the demand for precious metals is waning, it seems
that gold salesmen use the fear mentality to promote gold as the
panacea for all economic woes. I rather suspect this is more to
drum up business in a down market than a conviction that gold
really is the answer to a potential collapse.

When an investor buys gold or silver through an established
broker, it is very much like buying a diamond through a retailer. In
most instances the metal is being marketed at retail price. When
investors attempt to resell they find that the dealers will offer only
the current wholesale price or less. The difference can often
amount to 15 percent on any given day. Obviously, if the price of
gold or silver increases more than 15 percent (of retail), a profit is
made. But more often than not an investor finds that although the
price has increased, it is less than the difference between wholesale and retail. An even worse situation is to sell when the price
drops below the original purchase price.

Gold and silver can be purchased directly from member brokers of the commodities exchange, as well as from dealers. Usually
the broker requires a minimum purchase of several hundred dollars in the metal. The advantage in using a broker is that he or she
usually charges a fixed rate above the wholesale price. This will

vary per broker, but is normally significantly less than what a local dealer charges.

An alternative method of buying metals is through a discount broker. Discount brokers advertise in most investment magazines, as well as *The Wall Street Journal.* They will usually sell gold and silver for the current "ask" price quoted on the exchange, plus a nominal commission. Be sure if you buy through a discount broker that you take physical delivery of the metal. I have known several investors who opted to allow the broker to warehouse their purchase. Later, when they tried to recover their investment, they discovered the broker had closed shop and disappeared, along with their gold or silver. If you need to store the metal, use a bonded, established warehouse.

Speculation

The general rules of buying and selling precious metals just discussed are oriented toward those who buy gold and silver for the long-term. If you elect to speculate in precious metals by buying them for quick resale, you need to locate a good broker through whom you can buy and sell without paying the "normal" fees. Otherwise the short-term fluctuations will rarely cover the fees paid.

A second option is trading in futures on the commodities exchange. As I mentioned earlier, the only people I have personally known who were able to make money at it are the commodities brokers who live off of gullible amateur speculators. This type of investing is for the strong in heart and weak in mind (in my opinion).

20

Evaluating Insurance

I KNOW OF no investment subject that can generate as much emotion (on the part of salespeople) as that of insurance. For decades the insurance industry held a whole generation of potential investors captive to very low interest rates.

The reason the industry could do so is that people who lived through the Great Depression and saw their savings evaporate in banks, stocks, and virtually every other type of investment often lived off of the cash values in their insurance policies. They developed a well-earned trust of the insurance industry. For many it was the only store of money that survived the Depression. It mattered little that the interest rates they had earned were minuscule when compared to other investments.

After the Depression the insurance industry played off of this theme for decades, promoting the concept that only in insurance is an investor's money totally safe. For millions of Americans this was the gospel according to Prudential, or Metropolitan Life, or whomever.

The industry was quite effective in raising enormous amounts of capital, storing it in insurance policies, and paying about half of the going interest rates to their policy holders.

In the early seventies a new philosophy of insurance emerged: "Buy term and invest the difference." The "term only" salesmen simply showed insurance clients how they could buy inexpensive term insurance, invest their savings in other products, primarily mutual funds, and profit greatly. This message reached a new generation who had not experienced the ravages of the Great

Depression and were looking for earnings, not security. They bought into the concept of "buy term."

At first the insurance industry tried to ignore the "term" people. But as millions of "whole life" policies were dropped and converted over to term, the industry responded quickly. The result was a new generation of "whole life" products, such as universal life, minimum deposit life, and single premium life. These are actually modified whole life plans that offer higher rates of return for the savings portion of the policy.

In addition, the traditional insurance annuities, or retirement plans, were also upgraded to compete with the skyrocketing mutual fund industry.

In order to offer competitive returns to their policyholders, the insurance companies themselves had to become more competitive by investing their surplus capital at higher rates of return. After all, no company can pay out more than what they earn, at least not for long. As a result, many insurance companies now are faced with many high-risk investments—junk bonds, commercial loans, and commercial real estate—in their own portfolios.

It now behooves a prudent investor to evaluate carefully the insurance company that backs the policy he or she owns. An insurance company is a corporation (or an association). As such, the products they sell—life insurance, health insurance, annuities, etc.—are only as secure as the company itself.

In order to evaluate an investment in an insurance product, it is necessary to separate the insurance side from the investment side. A number of methods are commonly used to do this. One is to compare the cost of a term insurance policy with that of a whole life policy, less the "investment" side of the latter. The usual method is to use a 10- to 20-year comparison.

For example: Assume you purchased either a $100,000 annual renewable term policy for 30 years (age 35 to 65), or you purchased a $100,000 adjustable life plan at age 35. The adjustable life policy would cost $600 annually, and at age 65 would have accumulated approximately $10,000 in savings.

The annual renewable policy would cost $200 a year at age 35 and increase to $4,300 a year by age 65. Using the early years' savings on the term insurance to invest in a mutual fund averaging 10 percent annual growth, the net result at age 65 would be a loss of $3,700.

The difference in cost between term and whole life begins to narrow as the age increases, because the annual renewable policy gets progressively more expensive. The only way such a plan will work is to assume you can cancel the annual renewable insurance once your other sources of savings reach $100,000 (or at least reduce the coverage).

The bottom line is: If the total worth of the mutual fund at age 65 is greater than the total worth of the cash value policy, the term is a better investment. If not, the cash value insurance is better. In our example, the latter proved to be better.

This all may sound a little complicated, but any investment advisor or insurance agent with access to a computer can run this comparison for you in a few minutes.

Since I am not trying to sell you anything, I can tell you what I have observed. To date I have not seen any cash value insurance products (universal life, annuities, or other) that would match buying term insurance and investing the difference in a good quality growth mutual fund if the insured was able to shop for a new policy at least every three years. This continually allows for the lowest term rates. But with many of the newer whole life plans, such as adjustable life, the line between insurance and investment tends to blur.

I would also be less than totally honest if I didn't say that only a few people actually buy term and invest the difference. Most buy term and spend the difference. That's okay provided they consciously make that decision, but most simply fail to execute the plans they have made.

Cash Value Policies

The concept behind all cash value insurance policies is basically the same. The policy requires a fixed annual payment that is calculated to amortize the premiums as the insured gets older. By investing the early years' overcharge of premiums the insurance company can offset the costs in later years. Some of the newer plans called "minimum deposit" insurance require a set amount to be paid into the policy either as a lump sum or over the first few years. Then the deposit is invested and the proceeds are used to maintain the annual payments.

Some insurance companies are "stock companies" owned by investors. The policyholders have no ownership interest in the company. Normally stock companies pay lower returns to the policyholders because of the necessity to pay stockholder dividends, unlike "mutual" companies where each policyholder is a pro-rata owner in the company. In a mutual company, profits are distributed to the policyholders in the form of dividends.

Mutual companies were formed to compete directly with the older stock companies. They did so by passing along the profits to their policyholders. This arrangement increased the effective yield of the policies and attracted a large number of participants.

The actual yield to policyholders is often hard to discern because many companies, both mutual and stock, quote their gross yields before all commissions and expenses are taken out. Before investing in any insurance product you need to ask for a detailed analysis of *net* yield over the previous 10 years.

It is also important to remember that most quoted yields in insurance policies are projected only. They can be changed at any time because of prevailing market conditions, increased company expenses, and even investment losses by the company itself. The only dependable rate is the guaranteed rate, which is normally several percentage points lower than the projected rate.

If you decide to invest in an insurance product, you need to know what it will cost if you elect to drop the plan, withdraw your funds, switch plans, or stop paying any further. You also need to know what the annual fees are, including commissions.

One advantage of cash value insurance is that the cash value accumulation is not taxable to the insured. As noted earlier, this is because the cash values are really an overcharge of premiums and don't belong to the policy owner but to the insurance company. More recent policies do transfer ownership of the savings to the policy owners at specific intervals or upon the death of the insured.

Annuities

There are basically two types of annuities: *fixed* and *variable*. The fixed annuities normally are offered as either single premium deferred or regular. Regular annuities are being used less and less because of their inflexibility. Once a payout has begun, the monthly payments cannot be changed.

A single premium deferred annuity operates much like a CD, except that the interest is not taxable until it is paid out (usually at age 59½ or later). The yield is normally higher than an equivalent CD. The deferred annuity is relatively liquid in that you can make penalty-free withdrawals of up to 10 percent a year of the accumulated interest.

I believe the variable annuity offers the most flexibility for investors under age 50. A variable annuity's return is based on its earnings, while a fixed annuity pays a guaranteed amount. Obviously there is a greater risk with a variable annuity. If the managers do well, so do the investors. If the managers do poorly, the investors lose too. But since a fixed annuity cannot be adjusted for inflation, it has little flexibility for younger investors.

I recommend that after age 60 any annuities be converted to a fixed payout. Most variable annuities offer this option.

Questions to Ask About Insurance and Annuities

1. *What year did the company begin operations?* A young company's operating ratios may look good, but keep in mind that a company less than 25 years old hasn't proved itself through a series of business cycles.

Another caution for investing in a young company is that the mortality rates may be inaccurate because it has not had the claims experience needed; that comes only through time.

2. *What is the company's form of corporation?* Insurance companies are under two major categories: mutual companies and stock companies. Mutual companies are owned by the policyholders, who share in the company's profits. Stock companies may direct all their earnings to shareholders or to a parent holding company. Mutual companies have historically been more inclined to provide better products for the consumer than stock companies.

3. *What company assets and insurance are in force?* Bigger isn't always or necessarily better, but a very small company may have difficulty in a period of adverse experience or may lack the expertise needed to handle a large case.

4. *How has the company fared with the rating services?* There are three main rating companies that rate insurance companies and financial institutions:

Moody's Investor's Service Incorporated assigns ratings based on a company's ability to discharge senior policyholders' obligations and claims. The ratings range from AAA (the highest) to C (the lowest). Categories are further divided by numerical modifiers from 1 to 3, with 1 being the highest. Moody's insurance rating is an *opinion* of the insurance company's ability to meet its policy obligations over a long-term period.

Standard and Poor's Corporation assigns each insurance company a rating which is an assessment of the company's ability to meet its obligations under the most adverse circumstances. The ratings range from AAA (the highest) to D (the lowest).

A.M. Best is an independent research service which publishes an annual review of insurance companies. Their overall ratings range from C (the lowest) to A+ (superior), and represent a company's financial solvency. Most consumer advocates recommend purchasing from an A+ rated company.

A.M. Best was started in 1905, Standard and Poor's in 1971, Moody's in 1986. A.M. Best rates over 1,400 U.S. companies; Standard and Poor's rates 110 companies; and Moody's, to this date, had rated 65 companies. It is extremely important to be aware of any changes in ratings. Information on these rating services is available in the Appendix.

5. *What are the company's operating ratios?* When evaluating a company's investment products, you need to be aware of the ratios that can help in determining the success of that company: mortality, net investment yield, lapse ratio, and renewal expense ratio. A company with better results in these areas is more likely to sustain favorable long-term returns.

Net yield is the overall return the company earned on its invested assets. The higher the number, the better the return. If a company says it is paying 10 percent, but you find that the company has only earned an 8 percent investment net yield, chances are it is going to be difficult to pay to the consumer a 10 percent return on that investment product.

Lapse ratio represents the amount of insurance terminated by lapse or surrender. High levels of lapse ratio usually mean increased expenses and may indicate customer dissatisfaction. Lower numbers mean less lapse activity and may indicate greater consumer satisfaction.

Mortality represents the dollar amount of claims the company paid in relation to the amount of insurance in force. A lower number means the company is experiencing better mortality costs and usually is an indication of quality underwriting.

Renewal expense ratio is a ratio of expenses to insurance in force and represents the operating efficiency of a company. A lower number means lower expenses.

Finally, in summary, look at exactly how the client has been treated after he is considered an old client. Many companies feel that old clients should be treated as fairly as new clients, which means that if there are substantial changes in new policies, the old policies are upgraded. This is extremely important because the day after you buy any product, you are an old client.

(NOTE: This information was provided courtesy of J.H. Shoemaker & Co., Inc., Memphis, Tennessee.)

21

Social Security and Estate Planning

SINCE THIS IS a book dealing with investments, not government welfare, I will limit my discussion to the retirement aspects of the Social Security system. If you would like to have more details on the other aspects of the Federal Insurance Contributions Act (FICA), otherwise known as Social Security, refer to the reference materials in the Appendix. The most thorough discussion I have read on this topic is *The Complete and Easy Guide to Social Security and Medicare* by Faustin Jehle. (See Appendix for another resource.)

I decided to include a separate section on Social Security retirement benefits because, like it or not, for the majority of Americans it is a forced "old age pension plan" that requires a substantial contribution from the day most of us go to work until we retire—or die. At present all covered workers are required to "contribute" over 15$\frac{1}{2}$ percent of their wages up to $53,400 a year. It is an absolute certainty that both the percentage and the maximum salary to be taxed will increase during the next decade as more "baby boomers" retire.

Many salaried employees do not realize that the total FICA tax is over 15 percent because the portion an employee must pay is one-half of the total tax. But I assure you that the portion paid by an employer is a part of an employee's salary and directly affects what an employer can pay in total salary.

Social Security does have some good benefits, especially for those people who would never discipline themselves to put anything aside for later years. But actually it is a bad investment, as far as retirement benefits go. For someone who began working in 1960 at age 25, and paid into the system for the next 42 years until age 67 (the retirement age for workers born since 1938), the contributions they made to Social Security (assuming they started at the 50 percent of maximum level and went to 100 percent in 10 years) would yield a retirement income of approximately $20,000 a year. The same amount of investment in an annuity that earned 6 percent (tax deferred) would pay over $60,000 a year at age 67! And the income from the annuity would not be affected by additional outside earnings, as Social Security benefits are.

But since contributions to the system are no longer "voluntary," you do need to understand how the system functions and what you can expect to receive at retirement age. For those workers born before 1938, the retirement age is 65 for 100 percent benefits. Social Security offers the option to retire as early as age 62 (disabled workers are subject to more lenient rules). Those who elect to retire at age 62 have their retirement benefits reduced by 20 percent.

If you retire at any time before age 65, your benefits are reduced by 0.555 times the number of months before retirement age. For instance, if you retire 30 months early, your formula would be $30 \times 0.555 = 16.65\%$. So your benefits would be reduced by 16.65 percent a year.

To take a 20-percent reduction in lifetime benefits by retiring at 62 may sound like a bad option. But since you would receive 36 monthly checks prior to 65 it would take nearly 12 years of earnings at the higher rate to break even. So in great part it depends on your long-range goals.

Get An Audit

Since the earnings you make during your working career directly affect the amount you will earn upon retirement, it is important to calculate what your benefits will be for planning purposes. This is particularly true for those over age 50.

A worker is deemed to be fully "vested" or insured once he has paid into the system for 40 quarters, with some exceptions made for those who came into the system as a result of tax law changes passed in 1984. However, since the government never makes anything simple, there are several exceptions. A quarter for Social Security purposes is also any period in which a worker earns the required amount ($540 as of 1991). So if you were paid $2,160 for any month that year, you earned four quarters worth of credit ($540 × 4 = $2,160), but you cannot accumulate more than four quarters of Social Security benefits in a single year, no matter how much you earned.

The schedule for minimum annual earnings has been increased as the Social Security tax and benefits have increased, so earlier years require less earnings, later years more.

Also, retirement benefits are adjusted for different levels of earnings, so participation in later years can enhance earnings, while nonparticipation will reduce retirement earnings.

If the accuracy of the Social Security Administration equals that of other branches of the federal government, you can expect some errors in your records. Many people have been shocked to find out that their benefits have been miscalculated due to contributions not being allocated to their accounts properly. It is important to audit your Social Security file prior to retirement so that you can clear up any errors if necessary. The Social Security Administration will run a free audit of your file upon request. This form is the "Request for Earnings and Benefits Statement." You can obtain one at no cost by calling your local Social Security office and requesting a copy of Form SSA-7004PC [see Figure 1, p. 217]. Once you fill this out and return it, the audit normally follows in six to eight weeks, and is called the "Personal Earnings and Benefit Record" (Form SSA-700PC).

After you receive the audit of your work record (and your spouse's too), you will need to review it carefully. It will show every year in which you were credited for contributions and how many credits you have earned. It will also provide an estimate of your projected retirement benefits (plus disability and survivor's

SOCIAL SECURITY ADMINISTRATION

Request for Earnings and Benefit Estimate Statement

To receive a free statement of your earnings covered by Social Security and your estimated future benefits, all you need to do is fill out this form. Please print or type your answers. When you have completed the form, fold it and mail it to us.

1. Name shown on your Social Security card:

   First _____ Middle Initial _____ Last _____

2. Your Social Security number as shown on your card:

   ☐☐☐ - ☐☐ - ☐☐☐☐

3. Your date of birth: _____
   Month   Day   Year

4. Other Social Security numbers you may have used:

   ☐☐☐ - ☐☐ - ☐☐☐☐
   ☐☐☐ - ☐☐ - ☐☐☐☐

5. Your Sex: ☐ Male ☐ Female

6. Other names you have used (including a maiden name): _____

7. Show your actual earnings for last year and your estimated earnings for this year. Include only wages and/or net self-employment income subject to Social Security tax.

   A. Last year's actual earnings:

   $ ☐ , ☐☐☐ . 0 0
   Dollars only

   B. This year's estimated earnings:

   $ ☐ , ☐☐☐ . 0 0
   Dollars only

8. Show the age at which you plan to retire: _____

Form SSA-7004-PC-OP1 (6/88) DESTROY PRIOR EDITIONS

9. Below, show an amount which you think best represents your future average yearly earnings between now and when you plan to retire. The amount should be a yearly average, not your total future lifetime earnings. Only show earnings subject to Social Security tax.

   Most people should enter the same amount as this year's estimated earnings (the amount shown in 7B). The reason for this is that we will show your retirement benefit estimate in today's dollars, but adjusted to account for average wage growth in the national economy.

   However, if you expect to earn significantly more or less in the future than what you currently earn because of promotions, a job change, part-time work, or an absence from the work force, enter the amount in today's dollars that will most closely reflect your future average yearly earnings. Do not add in cost-of-living, performance, or scheduled pay increases or bonuses.

   Your future average yearly earnings:

   $ ☐☐☐ , ☐☐☐ . 0 0
   Dollars only

10. Address where you want us to send the statement:

   Name _____

   Street Address (Include Apt. No., P.O. Box, or Rural Route) _____

   City _____ State _____ Zip Code _____

   I am asking for information about my own Social Security record or the record of a person I am authorized to represent. I understand that if I deliberately request information under false pretenses I may be guilty of a federal crime and could be fined and/or imprisoned. I authorize you to send the statement of my earnings and benefit estimates to me or my representative through a contractor.

   Please sign your name (Do not print)

   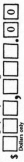

   Date _____ (Area Code) Daytime Telephone No. _____

   ABOUT THE PRIVACY ACT
   Social Security is allowed to collect the facts on this form under Section 205 of the Social Security Act. We need them to quickly identify your record and prepare the earnings statement you asked us for. Giving us these facts is voluntary. However, without them we may not be able to give you an earnings and benefit estimate statement. Neither the Social Security Administration nor its contractor will use the information for any other purpose.

   ☐ SP

Figure 1.

benefits) and the amount by which your benefits would be reduced for early retirement [see Figure 2, p. 219-220]. This is an excellent service provided by the Social Security Administration and you should take advantage of it.

By the way, a 1987 study done by the General Accounting Office (GAO) estimated that as many as 9 million American workers may have errors in their work records. So check it out! If you find that your file has errors, you will need to appeal to the Social Security Administration for correction. Finding the W-2s or similar records for past years may not be simple. If you have not kept them, you will need to appeal to the IRS for copies (good luck).

Survivor Benefits

In doing your retirement planning it is important to factor in the survivor's benefits. I will assume for illustration purposes that the husband was fully insured for maximum benefits and chose to retire at age 65 (67 for those born after 1938). In the event the insured worker dies, the spouse is entitled to only 50 percent of his or her benefits (except in the case of disability or dependent children). Failure to compensate for this reduction can result in financial hardship for the spouse.

The best way to plan around this problem is to store enough assets to provide for you both with only 50 percent of Social Security benefits available. That way the transition will be painless for the surviving spouse. Since your source of income is unearned (as opposed to wages), the additional income will not affect your Social Security benefits under present laws.

Once your budget is established on 50-percent Social Security income, you can reinvest the additional Social Security as a hedge against inflation or premature death or you can give it to the Lord's work.

TABLE FOR ESTIMATING AMOUNTS OF SOCIAL SECURITY BENEFITS

Average Monthly Wage	Old-Age Benefit Age 65	Old-Age Benefit Age 62	Dependent Spouse Age 65	Dependent Spouse Age 62		Average Monthly Wage	Old-Age Benefit Age 65	Old-Age Benefit Age 62	Dependent Spouse Age 65	Dependent Spouse Age 62		Average Monthly Wage	Old-Age Benefit Age 65	Old-Age Benefit Age 62	Dependent Spouse Age 65	Dependent Spouse Age 62
$83	144	115	72	54		609	495	396	248	186		1250	710	568	355	266
92	158	127	79	59		641	517	413	258	194		1275	716	573	358	269
101	172	138	86	65		660	527	421	263	198		1300	722	578	361	271
107	184	147	92	69		685	536	429	268	201		1325	729	583	364	273
122	195	156	105	79		705	544	435	272	204		1350	735	588	367	276
146	210	168	105	79		725	551	441	276	207		1375	741	593	371	278
169	224	179	112	84		745	559	447	280	210		1400	747	597	373	280
193	239	191	119	90		770	567	454	284	213		1425	753	602	376	282
216	253	202	127	95		790	573	459	287	215		1450	759	607	379	285
239	268	215	134	101		810	580	464	290	218		1475	764	612	382	287
258	280	224	140	105		835	588	470	294	221		1500	770	616	385	289
281	294	235	147	110		860	596	477	298	223		1525	775	620	388	291
300	306	245	153	115		885	604	483	302	226		1550	781	625	390	293
323	320	256	160	120		910	611	489	306	229		1575	786	629	393	295
342	331	265	166	124		930	618	494	309	232		1600	792	635	396	297
365	346	277	173	130		955	626	501	313	235		1625	797	638	399	299
389	361	288	180	135		980	634	507	317	238		1650	803	642	401	301

Figure 2.

TABLE FOR ESTIMATING AMOUNTS OF SOCIAL SECURITY BENEFITS

Average Monthly Wage	Old-Age Benefit Age 65	Old-Age Benefit Age 62	Dependent Spouse Age 65	Dependent Spouse Age 62
412	375	300	188	141
436	388	311	194	146
459	402	322	201	151
478	413	330	206	155
501	427	341	213	160
524	440	352	220	165
548	454	363	227	170
563	464	371	232	174
577	473	379	237	178
591	483	387	242	181

Average Monthly Wage	Old-Age Benefit Age 65	Old-Age Benefit Age 62	Dependent Spouse Age 65	Dependent Spouse Age 62
1000	640	512	320	240
1030	648	519	324	243
1050	654	523	327	245
1075	661	529	331	248
1100	669	535	334	251
1125	676	540	338	253
1150	683	546	341	256
1175	690	552	345	259
1200	696	557	348	261
1225	703	562	352	264

Average Monthly Wage	Old-Age Benefit Age 65	Old-Age Benefit Age 62	Dependent Spouse Age 65	Dependent Spouse Age 62
1675	808	647	404	303
1700	814	651	407	305
1725	819	655	410	307
1750	825	660	412	309
1775	830	664	415	311
1800	836	669	418	313
1825	841	673	421	315
1850	847	677	423	318
1875	852	682	426	320
1900	858	686	429	322

Figure 2 (contin.)

Medicare Health Benefits

Perhaps the greatest current benefit of the Social Security program is health care for older Americans. I almost hesitate to comment on this feature because I am totally convinced that, except for retirees before the end of this century, the program will be greatly modified to eliminate many current benefits. Sadly, it is a great idea that is simply too expensive to survive long-term unless the government also goes into the health care business to control costs. And how would you like to go to a government hospital to qualify for Medicare benefits? One thing is for sure, the morbidity rate would lower the number of Social Security retirees drastically!

It is my opinion that the trend in Medicare will be similar to that of the Medicaid program provided by the states. The Medicaid benefit is available by need only, and access to the system is limited to the indigent. If Medicare does evolve in this direction, the very planning that prudent investors do will work against them because it serves to build a strong asset base.

Assuming that Medicare does restructure to provide health care benefits only to the indigent, there is a possible alternative available. You can join with a group of similarly minded people of all ages who can provide the funds necessary to care for the older retirees. These are called "associations" and, in fact, there are at least two in operation now that I know of and more that are sure to develop as health care costs escalate. The concept is simple and is based on the principle taught in 2 Corinthians 8:14-15:

> At this present time your abundance being a supply for their want, that their abundance also may become a supply for your want, that there may be equality; as it is written, "He who gathered much did not have too much, and he who gathered little had no lack."

Virtually every insurance company is founded upon this principle: that there are more healthy people than sick, and the healthy can pool their resources to care for the sick, knowing that when they are ill, others will do the same for them.

Two groups that practice this concept are listed in the Appendix under "Alternate Health Care Services." At the time of this writing the cost of an average family health care insurance plan is about $300 per month nationwide. The cost per family in these associations is only about $110 per month, primarily because the groups are comprised of nondrinkers and nonsmokers, and coverage is limited to major expenses related to hospital stays. Also, since each member has a vested interest in keeping costs down, there is an active effort to monitor and limit all excessive bills.

To my knowledge there is no other health care resource available that will provide as much coverage for so little cost. Normally even a Medicare supplement will cost that much, or more.

Estate Information

Since a portion of anyone's long-range financial planning must be balanced with the inevitability of death, it is important to plan for that eventuality as well. If you do no planning for what happens upon your death, the effects can be devastating on your survivors, especially your spouse. As stewards of the Lord's resources, it is not an option to ignore the inevitable. Indeed, it is the height of selfishness for a provider to ignore the needs of his or her dependents after death.

The minimum planning anyone should do is to have a current, valid will while living. A well-drafted will directs how the assets should be distributed upon the owner's death. Both husband and wife need wills in the event they are killed in a common accident. In larger estates, the tax consequences of estate assets passing from husband to wife to heirs in a concurrent death situation can severely dilute an estate. With no wills, the certainty is that the state is going to assume the worst case situation; that is, to their financial benefit.

A simple will (as of this writing) can cost as little as $100, depending on the attorney involved. The more complex the estate situation, the higher the costs can run. It is always important to locate the most knowledgeable attorney, even at a somewhat higher cost. The only time you need a will is after you die. If the attorney made a mistake, it's too late to correct it then.

Estate Taxes

The current federal estate tax law allows for an unlimited amount of assets to be passed along to a surviving spouse, and approximately $600,000 to other heirs, without incurring any federal estate tax. In larger estates it is important that the ownership and assignment of assets be carefully checked by someone knowledgeable in estate planning. For instance, insurance proceeds that are assigned to a surviving spouse as beneficiary become taxable estate assets upon the death of the second spouse. If the insurance is assigned to a trust with the surviving spouse receiving lifetime income benefits, the tax consequences can be greatly reduced.

The federal estate taxes begin (presently) at 37 percent on estates above $600,000 and go to 55 percent [see Figure 3, p. 224], so they are not inconsequential for larger estates. It would be a shame to allow your hard-earned assets to be allocated to the government when, with a simple will or trust, they could go into God's work.

State Death Taxes

Most states use the federal estate tax codes as their guide for state death taxes, but not all. These exceptions can be disastrous if you don't know about them. Figure 4 (p. 225) shows the taxes per state as of this writing. Obviously these can and do change if state laws change. I would heartily encourage you to contact a good estate planning attorney to verify the tax consequences in your state.

Unified Rate Schedule for Estates and Gift Taxes			
If the Amount Is		Tentative Tax Is	On Excess Amount Over
Over This	But Not Over		
$ 0	$ 10,000	0 plus 18%	$ 0
10,000	20,000	1,800 plus 20%	10,000
20,000	40,000	3,800 plus 22%	20,000
40,000	60,000	8,200 plus 24%	40,000
60,000	80,000	13,000 plus 26%	60,000
80,000	100,000	18,200 plus 28%	80,000
100,000	150,000	23,800 plus 30%	100,000
150,000	250,000	38,800 plus 32%	150,000
250,000	500,000	70,800 plus 34%	250,000
500,000	750,000	155,800 plus 37%	500,000
750,000	1,000,000	248,300 plus 39%	750,000
1,000,000	1,250,000	345,800 plus 41%	1,000,000
1,250,000	1,500,000	448,300 plus 43%	1,250,000
1,500,000	2,000,000	555,800 plus 45%	1,500,000
2,000,000	2,500,000	780,800 plus 49%	2,000,000
2,500,000	3,000,000	1,025,800 plus 53%	2,500,000
3,000,000	10,000,000	1,290,800 plus 55%	3,000,000
10,000,000	21,040,000	5,140,800 plus 60%	10,000,000
21,040,000	....	11,764,800 plus 55%	21,040,000

Figure 3.

Probate Costs

A number of books currently give much attention to how to avoid
probate costs. This in turn has sparked an interest in the use of
trusts to avoid these costs. Many valid reasons exist why someone
would need a trust but, in most instances, probate is not one of
them.

In most states the cost of probating (proving) an in-state will
is nominal. I live in Georgia, where the probate cost is about $50.

State	Death tax ($) On $600,000 estate left to:	
	Spouse	Child
Alabama	None	None
Arizona	None	None
Arkansas	None	None
California	None	None
Colorado	None	None
Connecticut	$0	$37,875
Delaware	0	31,250
Dist. of Columbia	None	None
Florida	None	None
Georgia	None	None
Hawaii	None	None
Idaho	None	None
Illinois	None	None
Indiana	0	24,950
Iowa	0	39,825
Kansas	0	21,750
Kentucky	0	45,370

State	Death tax ($) On $600,000 estate left to:	
	Spouse	Child
Louisiana	$17,050	$17,050
Maine	None	None
Maryland	6,000	6,000
Massachusetts	23,500	55,500
Michigan	0	33,700
Minnesota	None	None
Mississippi	0	1,400
Missouri	None	None
Montana	None	None
Nebraska	0	5,850
Nevada	None	None
New Hampshire	None	None
New Jersey	None	None
New Mexico	None	None
New York	25,500	25,500
North Carolina	0	7,000
North Dakota	None	None

State	Death tax ($) On $600,000 estate left to:	
	Spouse	Child
Ohio	$2,100	$30,100
Oklahoma	0	17,725
Oregon	None	None
Pennsylvania	36,000	36,000
Rhode Island	7,900	12,400
South Carolina	0	33,000
South Dakota	None	None
Tennessee	None	None
Texas	None	None
Utah	None	None
Vermont	None	None
Virginia	None	None
Washington	None	None
West Virginia	None	None
Wisconsin	0	56,250
Wyoming	None	None

Figure 4.

A trust to avoid this expense would cost significantly more, and the ownership of all assets must also be changed to assign them to the trust. I am not trying to discourage anyone from using a trust if their attorney advises, but be certain of the costs and savings first. Obviously the probate cost in some states is more significant. In fact, many elderly people move from high-cost states to those with lower costs just to spare their estate the expense. Check with the court of the ordinary in your community to determine the probate costs in your state.

The Use of Trusts

Several excellent books on wills and trusts are listed in the Appendix, so I won't even attempt to elaborate on this issue, especially since I am not an attorney and would simply be drawing from what I had read in those publications. What I would like to do is at least acquaint you with the basics of using trusts so that you can factor that information into your long-range strategy.

There are two basic types of trusts: living (inter-vivos), and dead (testamentary). These can be further divided into two additional categories: revocable and irrevocable. The first you can change while you are still living. The second you cannot. Obviously a living, revocable trust becomes a testamentary, irrevocable trust upon the death of the person involved.

Assets assigned to a living, revocable trust are still a part of the owner's estate, and the assets assigned to that trust will be subject to estate and death taxes, but not probate costs.

Assets placed in an irrevocable trust are no longer a part of the grantor's (owner's) estate and can avoid estate taxes if the trust is qualified. Obviously they would also avoid probate, since a trust does not require probating.

A testamentary trust is one created by the death of the grantor, usually within a will. The assets are assigned to the trust upon the completion of probate and the trust controls the assets from that point on. It is common for one spouse to create a trust within the couple's will that will provide for the care of the other spouse during his or her lifetime, with the assets going elsewhere upon the death of the surviving spouse. By doing so, a portion of the estate and death taxes can be avoided.

Other Trusts

There is a proliferation of other specialized trusts at the disposal of qualified estate-planning attorneys. Among them are many charitable trusts that provide current tax-saving benefits and allow the ultimate disposition of the assets to go to the qualified charity of your choice. I have known many Christians who have used charitable trusts to provide for their loved ones, save taxes, and fund the Lord's work. Any of the books listed in the Appendix discuss these trusts also.

Questions and Answers

Because of the many questions raised by such a brief discussion of such a complex subject, I thought that a short question-and-answer section would help to clarify some of them. I would always add this disclaimer: I am not an attorney, nor an estate planner. Before acting on any of the information in this section, consult with your own attorney.

Question 1: *Can I draft my own will without having to pay an attorney?*
Answer: Yes, you can in the majority of states. A self-drawn will is called a holographic will. Holographic means that it is a document written totally in the handwriting of the person drafting it. The rules governing holographic wills vary by state, and you must thoroughly understand the laws of your state to ensure your will is probatable (provable) in court.

Question 2: *What if one of my witnesses has died?*
Answer: In order for a will to be probated, the judge may require the will to be verified. If you used only two witnesses and the state

requires a minimum of two, both must be alive and available. It is always best to use three or even four witnesses that you know well. If less than the required minimum are still alive, you will need to amend your will with a codicil to have other witnesses verify it.

Question 3: *Should I keep my will in a safety deposit box?*
Answer: If you do so, you need to be sure that someone else has access to the box. Since a safety deposit box cannot be opened except by court order, the process can be lengthy and expensive in the event of your death. If no one else knows about the box, it may never be recovered. I suggest that you name your spouse as an authorized signatory, as well as your attorney or accountant.

Question 4: *Do I need a new will if I change residences from one state to another?*
Answer: Possibly. You need to have an attorney in the new state review your will to ensure it conforms to that state's laws.

Question 5: *What if I own property in more than one state?*
Answer: Generally, your estate is governed by the state in which you reside at the time of your death. Thus a valid will drawn in your state can control the distribution of assets in another state, even if that state's laws are different.

Question 6: *Do I need a will if my wife and I hold all of our property in joint tenancy?*
Answer: Yes. Joint tenancy means that the surviving tenant or spouse owns the property upon the death of the other tenant, but if there are assets owned outside the joint properties, they would not be covered. In our generation this is common where there may be large settlements due to negligent deaths, such as an automobile accident.

Bear in mind also that some states tax joint property as if the deceased owned it outright, while others tax a proportionate interest in it. You will need to check with an attorney in your state to determine how jointly owned properties are taxed, if at all.

Also, if both of you are killed in a common accident, the last surviving tenant would be declared intestate (without a valid will). The estate would be subject to dual taxation and additional legal costs.

Question 7: *Who can I name as my estate executor?*

Answer: You can name anyone you desire to act as executor of your will and estate. That person's duties are to probate the will and distribute the assets accordingly. You may choose to name more than one person to serve as executor and should always name at least three alternates in the event that one cannot or will not serve.

Unless you stipulate otherwise, many states require an out-of-state executor to post a bond. Some require a bond equal to the value of the estate. Since your estate will have to bear this cost, you may want to waive the requirement to post bond.

Bear in mind that if you use a professional executor, a fee will be charged. This can vary from an hourly fee to a percentage of the estate value. Any such fees should be clearly spelled out in a contract and attached to your will or trust.

Question 8: *What is a trust?*

Answer: A trust is a legal contract to manage someone's assets before and/or after death. There are two basic types of trusts: a "living" trust, known as an inter-vivos trust, and a "testamentary" trust, meaning that it commences upon the death of the person.

Question 9: *What is the advantage of a trust?*

Answer: A trust is not a public document, as is a will, and does not require probate. Thus, a trust ensures a greater measure of privacy. Also, since a trust is not probatable, there are no probate costs associated with assets held in a living trust. Since a testamentary trust is created within a will (normally), the will must first be probated before the trust becomes effective. A testamentary trust therefore does not avoid probate costs on the assets of the assignee.

If the living trust is irrevocable, the assets held in trust are not subject to estate taxes, except to the extent that the assignee retains an interest in them. Literally, the assets are given to trust and become trust property. There may be gift taxes due on assets assigned to a trust for the benefit of others.

Question 10: *Can I draft my own trust?*
Answer: Will and trust "kits" are available in most bookstores today. These purport to explain how to draft your own will or simple trust. While it is legal for a layman to draft a holographic will or trust, I personally don't advise it. Once you are deceased, it's too late to change the will or trust if it doesn't pass the test. As the old saying goes, you can be "penny wise and pound foolish."

Question 11: *How much tax will my estate have to pay?*
Answer: That depends on the value of your estate at death. Through a marital deduction allowance, each spouse can leave the other an unlimited amount of assets. However, assets left to someone other than a spouse are subject to estate (death) taxes. (See the section on federal and state estate taxes earlier in this chapter.)

Question 12: *When are the taxes due?*
Answer: Usually within six months of death, the state will require an appraisal of the estate. The taxes are due and payable at that time, although in practice both the state and federal tax collectors will normally work out a plan to convert the assets necessary to pay the taxes so that the estate doesn't suffer a severe dilution through a forced sale.

Liquidity (cash) in an estate is very important since the taxes must be paid in cash. Otherwise, assets must be sold to satisfy the tax collectors. If the assets cannot be sold through normal market channels, the estate may be auctioned off at a substantial loss.

Question 13: *What if I change my mind after I make a will?*

Answer: You can change your will through the use of a codicil (supplement). The codicil is subject to the same laws of probate, so it is important that it be drafted properly. Attach all codicils to the original will and store them together. Remember that only the original will or codicil is probatable, so protect them carefully.

Appendix

Guide to Appendix Information

(The information and advice provided by these resources do not necessarily represent the opinions of the publisher or the author.)

Guides to Buying Antiques

(1) *Antiques and Collectibles Price Guide*
Katherine Murphy
Dubuque, IA: Babka Publishing Co., 1986

(2) *Emyl Jenkins' Appraisal Book*
Emyl Jenkins
New York, NY: Crown Publishing, Inc., 1989

Asset Management Services

(1) Pryor & Associates
2337 Glen Eagle Drive
Louisville, KY 40222

(2) Winrich Capital Management, Inc.
23702 Birtcher Drive
Lake Forest, CA 92630

Rare Coin Ratings/Appraisals

(1) The American Numismatic Association (ANA)
Certification Service
818 N. Cascade Avenue
Colorado Springs, CO 80903

(2) *A Guide Book of United States Coins*
R.S. Yeoman
Racine, WI: Western Publishing
(published annually)

(3) Professional Coin Grading Service (PCGS)
P.O. Box 9458
Newport Beach, CA 92658

Precious Gems Services

(1) American Gemological Laboratory
7th Floor, Ste. 706
580 Fifth Avenue
New York, NY 10036

(2) United States Gemological Services
No. 237
14801 Yorba Street
Tustin, CA 92780

Gold and Silver Services

(1) The Silver and Gold Report
P.O. Box 109665
Palm Beach Gardens, FL 33401
(subscription fee)

Alternate Health Care Services

(1) The Good Samaritan
P.O. Box 279
Beech Grove, IN 46107
317/894-2000

(2) Brotherhood Newsletter
P.O. Box 29
Barberton, OH 44203
330/848-1411

Insurance Company Rating Services

(1) A.M. Best Company
Ambest Road
Oldwick, NJ 08858-9988

(2) Duff & Phelps, Inc.
Suite 3600
55 E. Monroe Street
Chicago, IL 60603

(3) Moody's Investor Service, Incorporated
99 Church Street
New York, NY 10007-2787

(4) Standard & Poor's Corporation
25 Broadway
New York, NY 10004-1064

Mutual Fund Market Timing

(1) Telephone Switch Newsletter
2100 Main Street
Ste. 300
Huntington Beach, CA 92648
(subscription fee)

Mutual Fund Services

(1) Guide to Mutual Funds
Investment Company Institute
1401 H St. NW
Ste. 1200

Washington, DC 20005
(fees for material)

(2) Income and Safety
    Institute of Econometric Research
    2200 SW 10TH St.
    Deerfield Beach, FL 33442
    (subscription fee)

(3) Mutual Fund Forecaster
    Institute of Econometric Research
    2200 SW 10TH St.
    Deerfield Beach, FL 33442
    (subscription fee)

(4) Mutual Fund Values Newsletter
    Morningstar, Inc.
    225 West Wacker Drive
    Ste. 400
    Chicago, IL 60606
    (subscription fee)

(5) No-Load Fund-X
    235 Montgomery Street
    Ste. 662
    San Francisco, CA 94104
    (subscription fee)

(6) Sound Mind Investing Newsletter
    2337 Glen Eagle Drive
    Louisville, KY 40222
    (subscription fee)

General Financial Newsletter

(1) The Cornerstone Investment Newsletter
Suite 302
297 Herndon Parkway
Herndon, VA 22070
(subscription fee)

Tax-Deferred Retirement Plans

(1) IRA

(2) SEP IRA

(3) SARSEP

(4) 401k

(5) Tax Sheltered Annuity (403-b)

(6) HR-10 (Keogh)

(7) Pension

(8) Profit Sharing
Contact your tax or investment advisor for specific details on
these plans.

Social Security Guide

(1) *What You Should Know about Your Social Security Now*
The Research Institute of America, Inc.
90 5th Avenue

New York, NY 10011
(a free publication)

Stamp Collecting Services

(1) The American Philatelic Society
P.O. Box 8000
State College, PA 16803

(2) The Collector's Club
22 East 35th Street
New York, NY 10016

Stock Services

(1) The Dick Davis Digest
P.O. Box 350630
Fort Lauderdale, FL 33335
(subscription fee)

(2) The Value Line Investment Survey
220 East 42nd St.
New York, NY 10017
(subscription fee)

Resource Materials on Wills and Trusts

(1) *Family Guide to Estate Planning*
Theodore E. Hughes
Scribner

(2) *A Second Start: A Widow's Guide to Financial Survival*
Judith N. Brown/Christina Baldwin
Simon & Schuster

(3) *Plan Your Estate with a Living Trust* and *Nolo's Simple Will Book*
Denis Clifford
Nolo Press

(4) *Thy Will Be Done: A Guide to Wills, Estates, and Taxation for Older People*
Eugene Daly
Prometheus Books

(5) *The Essential Guide to Wills, Estates, Trusts, and Death Taxes*
Alex J. Soled
Scott Foresman, Lifelong Learning Division

Recommended Reading

(1) *Encyclopedia of Investments*
Jack P. Friedmon
Warren, Gorham & Lamont

(2) *One Up on Wall Street: How to Use What You Already Know to Make Money in the Market*
Peter Lynch
Simon & Schuster (hardback); Viking Penguin (paperback)

(3) *Personal Financial Planning*
G. Victor Hallman & Jerry S. Rosenbloom
McGraw-Hill Book Co.

(4) *The Templeton Plan: 21 Steps to Personal Success and Real Happiness*
James Ellison
Harper & Row

(5) *The Thoughtful Christian's Guide to Investing*
Gary Moore
Zondervan Books

(6) *Your Finances in Changing Times*
Larry Burkett
Moody Press

(7) *The Complete Financial Guide for Young Couples*
Larry Burkett
Victor Books

(8) *The Complete Financial Guide for Single Parents*
Larry Burkett
Victor Books

Resource Contributors

(1) Thomas G. Cloud
Cloud & Associates Consulting, Inc.
8735 Dunwoody Place
Suite O
Atlanta, GA 30350

(2) Kenneth Frenke, CFP
1870 Forest Hill Blvd.
Suite 208
West Palm Beach, FL 33406

(3) George M. Hiller, JD, LLM, MBA, CFP
George M. Hiller Companies
3414 Peachtree Road
Suite 1110
Atlanta, GA 30326

(4) Vernon D. "Woody" Laywell
Laywell Financial Resources
306 East Fair Harbor Lane
Houston, TX 77079

(5) Don McAlvany
International Collectors Associates
Bank One
2696 S. Colorado Boulevard
Denver, CO 80222

(6) Dr. James McKeever
P.O. Box 4130
Medford, OR 97501

(7) Austin Pryor
Pryor & Associates
2337 Glen Eagle Drive
Louisville, KY 40222

(8) Robert R. Rhinehart
Merrill Lynch
3500 Piedmont Road, N.E.
Suite 600
Atlanta, GA 30305

(9) Bill Robertson, CLU, CFP, ChFC
William F. Robertson & Associates
1200 Summit Avenue
Suite 516
Fort Worth, TX 76102

(10) James H. Shoemaker, CLU, CFP, ChFC
Shoemaker & Co.
2176 West Street

Suite 110
Germantown, TN 38138

(11) Winrich Capital Management, Inc.
23702 Birtcher Drive
Lake Forest, CA 92630

II

PREPARING
FOR RETIREMENT

This book is dedicated to our Lord, Jesus Christ,
who promises us the only sure retirement plan.

"But seek first His kingdom and His righteousness,
and all these things shall be added to you.
Therefore do not be anxious for tomorrow;
for tomorrow will care for itself.
Each day has enough trouble of its own."

(Matthew 6: 21-34).

Contents

Introduction

RETIREMENT, USUALLY AT 62 to 65, is something that most of us have come to accept as an attainable goal after our working careers. In fact, since the advent of Social Security in the thirties, it has become an assumed right.

In many ways the concept of retirement was good for the economy in the past since it freed positions for younger workers to fill. But the dynamics of the American work force have been altered greatly during the last two decades. Abortions and birth control have decimated the generation that will be entering the marketplace in the twenty-first century.

From 1946 to 1964 approximately seventy million baby boomers were born—thirty million more than would be the norm for our society. As a result, according to statistics from the U.S. Census Bureau, Americans ages 55 to 74 will increase from approximately forty million in 1989 to over seventy million by the year 2010—just when the middle-aged population is in its most rapid decline.

In addition, health care and extended life cycles have driven up the cost of retirement. Simply put, people live longer, collect more benefits, and utilize more expensive life support systems. The demand for more taxes to support the retirees places ever-increasing burdens on those who have not yet attained their "golden years." Consequently, the liabilities to society of retirement now far outweigh the assets.

When the idea of old age pensions was first proposed in 1934, the average life expectancy of a man was approximately 63.

For the designers of Social Security, as well as insurance company annuitants, providing retirement benefits that started at 65 was an economically sound idea. Theoretically, the vast majority of the participants would never live to use their benefits. But because of better health care, fewer work hours, and generally better health habits, the average man's life expectancy today is about 73. (Women generally have a life expectancy of two to three years more than men, although the difference tends to narrow after the age of 70.)

I believe the keys to good planning for the future are found in the timeless wisdom of God's Word. Therefore, the great majority of financial decisions can be made on the basis of God's principles.

So here we are with a retirement concept that was designed to make a worker's "twilight years" more comfortable (Social Security was designed only as a supplement to retirement) in a generation in which the average worker recovers his or her total contributions to the system in five years or less. It is a virtual certainty in the next century that those living on Social Security alone will be relegated to the impoverished class unless some very prudent planning is done before approaching retirement.

As you will learn in this book, there are some very sobering economic problems facing our nation in the twenty-first century that will very likely force the vast majority of retirees back into the work place. Those who are not aware and prepared may end up a part of the homeless explosion in our cities. By no means do I believe this is inevitable. With good financial planning and God's help, the elderly can lead productive and comfortable lives well into their eighties and nineties. But the one phrase we will all have to eliminate from our vocabulary in the next decade is: That can't happen here!

Most of the nation's major financial magazines have carried numerous articles on the failure of insurance companies, banks, and major pension plans during the late eighties and early nineties.

Any current or future retiree would do well to heed the signs of economic decay in our society and not get trapped by a "prosperity forever" mentality. However, it would be equally shortsighted to orient all of your planning toward a "calamity" mind-set.

I believe the keys to good planning for the future are found in the timeless wisdom of God's Word. Therefore, the great majority of financial decisions can be made on the basis of God's principles.

I have spent the last twenty years of my life studying the biblical principles for money management and applying them in my own life. If you will commit to doing likewise, you will discover a biblical absolute: You can rely on God's wisdom, regardless of the economy.

Allow me to use an example. In our generation a great deal of attention is focused on generating quick profits. And, in fact, many people have been able to do so by high-risk speculation in a variety of "investments" from real estate to stocks. But it has been my observation that very few speculators are able to keep what they make. More often than not the same get-rich-quick mentality, which makes money for speculators originally, later causes them to take even greater risks; eventually they lose most of what they make.

This mentality is particularly disastrous at an older age when the losses cannot be recouped. Speculation, in and of itself, is not necessarily wrong but, when taken to extremes, it becomes a get-rich-quick mentality. The wisdom of Solomon still holds true today: *"A man with an evil eye hastens after wealth, and does not know that want will come upon him"* (Proverbs 28:22). Before launching into a discussion on retirement, I want to explain why I wrote this book and what you should expect to gain from reading it.

This book is not meant to be merely an investment guide for retirees (or those approaching retirement), but rather a comprehensive handbook for retirees, present and future. To be sure, if you fail to plan financially, retirement can be a frustrating and fearful time. But the best financial planning in the world done in the nineties may be worthless in the twenty-first century if you don't take into account future health care costs, inflation, the economy, taxes, and so on. Therefore, I will try to help you think through each of these areas and make the best decisions possible as you approach retirement age. But, more important, it is my desire that you understand how to evaluate future changes for yourself and adjust accordingly.

There is an old cliché: *Information without application leads to frustration.* This is usually the case with the families I have counseled who attended seminars, read books, and even sought good counsel, but did nothing as a result of what they learned. More often than not, the reason people do nothing is because they hear so many conflicting viewpoints they become paralyzed by confusion. At some point you must decide to take the plunge and make a decision. In other words, do something!

My advice and observations certainly are not infallible; all too often the opposite is true. But if you will weigh what you read against God's principles found in the Bible, you'll find that I never purposely give advice contrary to that in God's Word. I have spent the last twenty years of my life studying the biblical principles for money management and applying them in my own life. If you will commit to doing likewise, you will discover a biblical absolute: You can rely on God's wisdom, regardless of the economy.

As I try to evaluate what the economy of the twenty-first century will be like, it's almost impossible to comprehend the changes that will take place. There will be as many economic changes from the twentieth to the twenty-first century as there were technological changes from the nineteenth to the twentieth centuries.

My father lived to see the transition from horse-drawn carriages to jet planes. I have seen the transition from vacuum tube radios that weighed thirty pounds to television sets that can be carried in a shirt pocket. Early in the next century we will see the end of all currency in exchange for a worldwide cash-less economy. If the present trend prevails, we will see people living longer, but with steadily declining lifestyles. As America slips from an industrial to a service-oriented economy, there will be fewer jobs at lower salaries; production will migrate to the developing countries that have cheaper labor bases and fewer regulations.

> *My plan in this book is to present a balanced perspective of what you can expect well into the next century and help you to plan accordingly.*

Sometime before the end of this century and the beginning of the next, it seems very likely that we will have a major economic depression, caused by our massive accumulation of debt. If, as I believe, this depression is coupled with runaway inflation caused by our government printing money to cover its deficits, then all the rules for modern-day economics will be rewritten. As I read through the statistics on our economy, and our nation as a whole, my thoughts often go back to 1958—my senior year in high school. Somewhere between my junior and senior year, my interest in history was sparked—a passion that continues even today. I remember that I was reading through a copy of *The Rise and Fall of the Roman Empire* when I thought to myself, *How could those people have been so stupid that they ignored the indicators all around them? Their indulgences finally led to the collapse of their economy and ultimately their civilization.* Well, here we are today, repeating their mistakes on a scale beyond their wildest imaginations.

In reality, the economic decline of America is merely tracking our moral and social decline—all of which can be traced to a single root cause: a denial of God. Any nation that denies the existence of God will ultimately ignore the principles taught in God's Word. When that happens the slide into mediocrity is a virtual certainty. As the Apostle Paul said in Romans 1:28, *"And just as they did not see fit to acknowledge God any longer, God gave them over to a depraved mind, to do those things which are not proper."*

Anyone who attempts to do any realistic retirement planning without taking into account the signs of a rapidly changing economy is being very nearsighted. But, as I said earlier, you cannot do all of your planning based on a "crisis" mentality either. To do so will either drive you into a shell, in which case you'll bury all your assets in the backyard, or it will tempt you to risk everything in get-rich-quick schemes, as you try to "beat the system."

My plan in this book is to present a balanced perspective of what you can expect well into the next century and help you to plan accordingly. For some, my approach may be too conservative—especially those who look (and even hope) for an economic apocalypse.

If an apocalypse does indeed occur, the best financial planning most of us could do would be inadequate. Only the very wealthy or the very poor maintain their relative positions in an economic collapse. I don't expect the entire economy to fail, although a major economic "adjustment" seems inevitable at some point in the future.

Understand that even during the Great Depression in the thirties only 24 percent of American workers were unemployed, and 30 percent of the businesses failed. It is unlikely that the next depression would exceed the last. But if your money is invested in a failed company, the depth and breadth of the problem is pretty much irrelevant. The key to good planning is in being among the surviving 70 percent.

> *This book is meant to be a handbook for the plethora of decisions you must make, such as whether to buy more life insurance, purchase nursing home insurance, use a living trust, or prepay funeral expenses. The critical decisions you will make between now and the year 2000 are important. But, again I emphasize that the best any person can do is give you advice. Only God can give true wisdom.*

I realize that some readers will feel that I present too pessimistic a view of the future. After *The Coming Economic Earthquake*

(Moody Press) was published in 1991, I was severely criticized in articles and reviews written by investment salespeople. Reading between the lines I could see what was happening; many of their clients were coming in and telling them, "I read this book *(The Coming Economic Earthquake)* and I believe it. I think I'll stop my investments for a couple of years while I pay off my debts." Consequently, some investment advisors attacked the book for being too radical.

Personally I don't see a volatile economy as being a negative for financial advisors. In reality, just the opposite should be true. Almost anyone can prosper in a stable, secure economy if they earn enough and save a reasonable percentage of it. But economic survival during a depression and/or inflation requires good counsel and quick reflexes. Good investment advisors can help their clients to diversify as a hedge against both situations.

To plan only for a growing, non-inflationary economy over the next ten years or so, I believe, is very imprudent. If I'm wrong about a depression followed by hyperinflation, the worst that can happen is you'll end up with a diversified retirement portfolio. But if I'm right, and you do nothing to prepare, you can end up on welfare.

The economic scenario I will presume is that both events—depression and inflation—will occur sometime before the end of this decade in rapid succession. This will primarily affect the investment side of retirement planning. Most other decisions will not change radically, irrespective of the economy.

Keep in mind that this book is not an investment guide for those planning retirement. I covered that topic in the book *Investing for the Future* (Victor Books). This book is meant to be a handbook for the plethora of decisions you must make, such as whether to buy more life insurance, purchase nursing home insurance, use a living trust, or prepay funeral expenses. The critical decisions you will make between now and the year 2000 are important. But, again I emphasize that the best any person can do is give you advice. Only God can give true *wisdom.*

I will begin this book with a reminder from Solomon—the world's wisest man: *"How blessed is the man who finds wisdom, and the man who gains understanding. For its profit is better than the profit of silver, and its gain than fine gold"* (Proverbs 3:13-15).

1

The Facts About Retirement

Is retirement itself a biblical principle God established for His people? Since there is so little Scripture dealing with this subject, it would seem logical to make one of two assumptions: Either God forgot to discuss the subject of retirement, or it is not a part of His plan for us. I discovered long ago that God doesn't forget anything; therefore it has to be that our whole perspective of retirement is out of balance.

ACCORDING TO THE Social Security Advisory Council's annual report for 1991, retirement in America is due for some drastic changes by the end of this century. The report points to a shrinking work force and expanding retirement sector as the single greatest problem facing future retirees. The report looked at three future scenarios of income and payments through the Social Security system over the next twenty-five years or so. The present "pay-as-you-go" plan simply won't work, unless workers in the next decade are willing to fork over 40 to 50 percent of their wages to retirees.

When the Old Age Benefit system began in the mid-1930s, there were approximately fourteen contributors for every potential retiree. By 1990 that figure had declined to approximately four workers for every retiree, and by 2010 it is estimated (under the best scenario) to decline to less than a three-to-one ratio. This is due to a number of factors that we will discuss, but suffice it to say that three working taxpayers (especially lower-income taxpayers) cannot adequately support one retiree in any degree of comfort.

Essentially this means that either the majority of Americans must plan for and fund their *own* retirement, which is highly unlikely given the current "spend-as-you-go" mentality, or plan to keep on working. In reality the best alternative probably lies somewhere in between.

Before discussing the details of what decisions must be made to plan for a reasonably comfortable retirement, I would first like to discuss some basic biblical principles that will help to define retirement.

Anyone who has accepted Jesus Christ as Savior has made the decision to live his or her life according to God's directions (to the highest degree possible). In order to do that, a Christian must first learn God's basic principles. These are found in the Bible—God's manual for living.

It is my firm conviction that any advice (regardless of who gives it) that cannot be validated on the basis of God's Word is just an opinion. We all have opinions; some opinions are better than others, depending on the person's level of expertise.

Personally, I believe it is best to start a retirement program at about the age of 40, and only after paying off all loans, including your home mortgage.

For instance, if you want my opinion on which car to buy, I can identify those that get the best gas mileage, require the lowest rate of repairs, and have the highest average resale value. All of these factors are verifiable statistically.

But the decision about which is *the* best car is still just my opinion because, as near as I can tell, God has not detailed in His Word the best car to buy. And since only the Lord can know if you would get a lemon, all I can do is make an educated guess. Also, I would probably recommend that you buy a red car since red cars usually have a better resale value, but you might not like red cars, so you would be dissatisfied.

If the subject under discussion changes to a topic like brain surgery, my best opinion becomes woefully inadequate. A skilled neurosurgeon would be the best source of advice on that topic. However, a visit to any three neurologists will verify that each has a slightly different perspective on what the right course of action should be.

The same principle can be applied to financial advisors, attorneys, accountants, or auto mechanics. If you're totally dependent on someone else's counsel, you can be certain you'll get some bad advice from time to time.

The majority of Americans are constantly inundated with conflicting advice, especially on the topic of retirement. One advisor says to start investing for retirement at a very young age since the money will compound for a longer period of time. Time is a very important factor when compounding is considered. Obviously the longer the money is compounded, the larger it grows. So, why not start your retirement program at age 25? Because it's been my observation that the temptation to take that money out and spend it on indulgences is too great for many people to resist.

Personally, I believe it is best to start a retirement program at about the age of 40, and *only* after paying off *all* loans, including your home mortgage.

So, who should you listen to? your financial advisor? or me? The answer is: neither of us—totally. The best we can do is present the various alternatives as we see them from our limited perspective. The primary counsel you should seek is the Lord's. Only He knows if you will live long enough to accomplish your goals, or if your investments will still be around when you need the money.

From my perspective as a family financial counselor, I have seen a lot of good and bad (mostly bad) financial decisions. I think of all the people I have known who invested in American Motors, Eastern Airlines, Pan American—even the PTL club; their investments are gone, but most of their debts linger on. Based on this observation (with rare exception), I advise people to pay off their debts first since paying off debt is the one *sure* investment available.

But on the other side are those who invested in high-growth companies like IBM and Microsoft and saw their money grow by 1,000 percent. Well, that's why you should seek the *Lord*'s counsel. God's Word teaches that debt should not be the norm for His people. Although the Bible doesn't prohibit borrowing, it does establish some practical guidelines, one of which is: Don't stay in debt long-term. Biblically, the longest debt period for God's people was seven years, or less. That's why I teach the principle of paying off debt before starting a retirement plan.

Most Christians *say* they want God's counsel in their financial decisions. But the majority, if they were totally honest, would admit that they aren't totally committed to following His counsel except in a crisis. And even then they're not really sure they can recognize God's counsel from among the jangle of advice they try to sort through.

By definition, all true Christians believe in the existence of Jesus Christ. Christians also believe that Jesus died for their redemption and He intercedes on their behalf with His Father in heaven. Christians believe that when they die they will go to be with the Lord and will be able to talk with Him. Unfortunately, what most don't believe is that such a dialogue is possible in this life and on this earth.

If Christians really believed it was possible to ask questions of Jesus and receive specific answers in response, they would be living different lifestyles and planning a lot differently (including retirement). I say that not as an indictment against other Christians; I include myself in that same category.

Even when we strive to serve the Lord, the society around us molds us into its image. As a result, it becomes increasingly difficult to separate God's voice from the cacophony of sounds around us. This is due, in large part, to the fact that we have difficulty attuning our minds to God's "frequency."

Allow me to use an example. Not long ago, while flying from Atlanta to Dallas, I found a magazine on psychiatry in the seat pocket in front of me. Since I am prone to read whatever literature I can find (to distract me while flying), I leafed through this magazine, expecting to find nothing of interest. Instead, I discovered a research article on something called RAS (reticular articulation syndrome). Although I was unfamiliar with the terminology, I found that I was totally familiar with the concept. RAS, the writer explained, is the ability to focus one's mind on areas of interest so that all other distractions are virtually eliminated from consciousness.

For instance, RAS is the reason that a mother can hear her child crying in a room of twenty screaming children; she has assimilated her child's voice into her retention pattern. In other words, she has prioritized her mind to distinguish her child's voice from among many others.

Retirement, as we know it, is so new that most current retirees can still remember when practically no one retired. In my grandfather's generation certainly few, if any, ordinary citizens would have seriously considered that they could stop working and play golf at 65 or so.

We all do this in one way or another on a daily basis. I love old cars, and one of my favorite hobbies is restoring these relics of the past, which otherwise would go to the junk heaps. I can usually detect the outline of an early model car even if it's covered with vines and other undergrowth. I can assure you though that my wife, Judy, does not share this passion, even though she tolerates having our garage used as a rescue center for derelict cars. She is more into antiques—like furniture and other uninteresting (to me) stuff.

One summer when we were traveling to North Carolina to visit my mother, I spotted several old cars well back off of the road. Knowing that I had been less than patient some miles back when Judy had wanted to stop and look in an antique store, I didn't even suggest that we stop and look at the cars. Imagine my surprise when she asked, "Did you see that?"

"Sure," I replied. "Would you mind if we go back and take a look?"

She said "Okay" so enthusiastically that I thought I just might have been successful in convincing her that old cars are more important than old furniture. I wheeled the car around and parked as near as I could to the old cars. But when I started to get out she asked, "Why are we stopping here?"

I replied somewhat cautiously, "Because this is where the cars are."

"But I wanted to go there," she said as she pointed to an antique store a little farther down on the other side of the road. She hadn't even noticed the cars I had spotted, and I certainly didn't notice the antique store. Why? Because of our different RAS.

The same basic principle is true today in Christianity. Most of us have our RAS attuned to the world around us and, consequently, we miss the road signs God puts in our paths. God is speaking, but we're on different frequencies. The way we get back onto His wavelength is by reconfirming our vows to follow His path—no matter what the world around us is doing. That is fundamental if we are to settle this issue of retirement planning. The question is: Are you willing to make your decisions according to God's Word, even when it conflicts with all the counsel around you?

Is Retirement Scriptural?

I am convinced that retirement, as we know it in our generation, is not scriptural. I'm not implying that someone who retires at age 62 or 65 is living in sin. There are some instances where retirement is a part of God's plan for a particular individual. But the basic concept of idling the majority of people at such an early age is a modern innovation, *not* a biblical principle.

There is actually only one direct reference to retirement in the Bible: *"This is what applies to the Levites: from twenty-five years old and upward they shall enter to perform service in the work of the tent of meeting. But at the age of fifty years they shall retire from service in the work and not work any more"* (Numbers 8:24-25).

For our present system of retirement to function, two essential elements are required: first, a large class of workers who make sufficient incomes to save a sizeable portion for the

*future; and second, most of these workers must be so dissatis-
fied with their jobs that they're willing to quit at an early
age.*

Exactly why God directed that the priests should retire at 50
is not known. It is possible that they assisted in other functions
but could not perform the ceremonies themselves. So if you're a
Levite priest, according to God's Word your retirement decisions
have been made. If you're not, read on.

Retirement, as we know it, is so new that most current retirees can still remember when practically no one retired. In my
grandfather's generation certainly few, if any, ordinary citizens
would have seriously considered that they could stop working and
play golf at 65 or so.

In the first place, few Americans made enough money to be
able to retire to the golf course. And those who did were so committed to their careers that they had little interest in retirement.

For our present system of retirement to function, two essential elements are required: first, a large class of workers who make
sufficient incomes to save a sizeable portion for the future; and
second, most of these workers must be so dissatisfied with their
jobs that they're willing to quit at an early age.

Such a combination was found in two groups of workers during the fifties: union members and federal employees. As the labor
unions grew in number and strength during the high employment
period after World War II, their collective bargaining eventually
took in long-term benefits, such as retirement. Companies were
more than willing to negotiate for deferred benefits in lieu of current wage increases.

For the first time, retirement became an attainable goal for
blue collar workers. The impact this idea was to have on American
society was incalculable at that time. It would eventually give rise
to a multibillion dollar investment industry in the sixties, and
would doom the Social Security system to failure as the majority of
workers over sixty decided they *could* retire.

Once the retirement "bandwagon" got rolling, millions of additional people joined it. Eventually American workers became convinced that retirement is a basic "right." During the sixties and seventies laws were passed *requiring* workers to retire by age 65. With more and more younger workers coming into the work force, retirement became a logical way to free up jobs. As I said earlier, several factors now have made that same notion illogical—not the least of which is the lack of gainfully employed people to support the Social Security system.

Workers who planned to retire in the sixties, including my father (born in 1902), developed their retirement plans around Social Security and a modest company pension that would allow them a reasonably comfortable lifestyle. They had the best of all benefits: a growing economy, a growing labor force, low interest rates, and low inflation.

Social In-Security

Only three decades earlier, the Great Depression of the thirties had ended any thought of retirement for the average American worker of that day. Instead, for nearly ten years the emphasis for most Americans shifted to basic survival. At the outset of the Great Depression in the early thirties, millions of hard-working older Americans had been wiped out financially by the collapsing economy. Those beyond the age of 50 were often unemployable and yet, outside of finding whatever work they could, they had no means of living. The New Deal established the Old Age Pension Plan, now known as Social Security, as a means to bridge the gap for these workers.

The Roosevelt administration never intended that Social Security would be used as anything but an old age *supplement.* Social Security remained a supplemental income plan until after World War II, when politicians, vying for public favor, began to expand the system to match benefits in the private sector, including workers' disability, survivors' benefits, and more extensive retirement benefits.

Based on much of the material I have read from that era, it's quite possible the enhancement of the Social Security system was motivated by guilt over an ever-expanding federal retirement system. In an economy with nearly full employment, low-cost credit, and worldwide exports, little thought was given to the future costs of funding such a massive system.

By the late sixties, most Americans viewed retirement as a foregone conclusion. At age 65, you retire. In the seventies, the average retirement age had dropped to 62. Unfortunately the assumptions upon which most Americans based their hopes for retirement in the fifties and sixties changed drastically in the seventies and eighties, including Social Security.

But I'm getting ahead of myself. The basic issue I am addressing here is not the Social Security system; nor is it whether individuals can save enough to stop work at 62 and live comfortably. The real issue is: Is retirement itself a biblical principle God established for His people?

Since there is so little Scripture dealing with this subject, it would seem logical to make one of two assumptions: Either God forgot to discuss the subject of retirement, or it is not a part of His plan for us. I discovered long ago that God doesn't forget anything; therefore it has to be that our whole perspective of retirement is out of balance.

Having concluded that retirement (as we know it) is not scriptural, I would like to clarify what I mean. Although retirement is not biblical, it cannot be placed in the same category as objective sins—adultery, lying, stealing. These are expressly prohibited by God.

Retirement is not *prohibited*, it simply is not discussed to any degree. Therefore it is little more than an innovative way for modern society to escape the drudgery of work-place boredom. For some people it is a way to extend their useful years by seeking out new careers, supplemented by a retirement income. And for some, retirement is necessitated for health reasons. But, in general, retirement is not biblically endorsed.

> *Statistics indicate that retirement probably will not be possible for most Americans beyond the end of this century which, at the time of this writing, is less than ten years away. There simply will not be enough active workers to support all the retirees.*

If God's plan for most of us is not retirement, then what is it?

Any logical observer would agree that the vast majority of people who live beyond the age of 70 are not capable of doing the same amount or level of work they were at ages 30, 40, 50, or even 60. The aging process lowers physical stamina, reflexes, and senses (although not necessarily mental faculties).

Often that's true even at a younger age. Just look at professional athletes. Few professional football players are gainfully employed as active athletes beyond the age of 35; none are beyond the age of 50. But since they're not employable as professional athletes, should they automatically conclude that their working careers are over? Hardly so. I know many ex–professional athletes who have started successful careers after retiring from their sports. Frank Gifford, Roger Staubach, Terry Bradshaw, and Fran Tarkenton are just a few. Some, like Jack Kemp, have attained recognition in career fields totally removed from their athletic careers.

The point is, just because they can no longer do what they had been doing doesn't mean they can't do something! The same principle holds true for the rest of us. We may not be able to do the same things at 70 or 80 that we could do at 30 or 40, but we can do something useful and meaningful.

Some good friends, Walt and Ralph Meloon, are walking examples of this truth. For many years Walt and Ralph ran the Correct Craft Boat Company in Orlando, Florida. Now well into their seventies, both men have turned the day-to-day operations of Correct Craft over to their children. But Walt and Ralph have not settled down into their rocking chairs; nor do they spend their days on the golf courses of Florida. They're some of the most active men I know. Often when one or the other is passing through our area he'll stop over to have lunch. Usually they are traveling around the country visiting some of the Correct Craft distributors as ambassadors for the company.

A few years ago the Meloons started a ministry to help business people who are in financial distress and, often, in imminent danger of bankruptcy. They sponsor weekend sessions, called Turn-Around Weekends, where couples can come for advice and counsel. At these sessions both Walt and Ralph spend endless hours counseling with hurting people and sharing their own experiences about when Correct Craft was forced into bankruptcy during the early fifties.

Age has most certainly been a limiting factor for these two men of God, but they have simply found a way to be useful within these limitations. Christian history is full of examples of those who knew the biblical truth about retirement: It begins in eternity.

Remember: God uniquely created each of us, including our endurance and durability and, as a result, not everyone will have the same ability to work at the various stages of life. Consequently, there will be varying degrees of retirement for all of us. The degree to which we slow down is not the fundamental issue here; ceasing all productive activity is.

Statistics indicate that retirement probably will not be possible for most Americans beyond the end of this century which, at the time of this writing, is less than ten years away. There simply will not be enough active workers to support all the retirees.

God has provided a plan for His people to rest and recover during their working lives. As best I can determine, God has not prescribed a time when we should retire. We have arbitrarily decided that at age 62, 65, or some later period, our active working careers should stop.

This leads to some pretty sobering conclusions: Either the majority of workers will continue to stay gainfully employed or society will find a convenient way to lower the costs of maintaining the non-productive ones. If you think euthanasia never can happen in America, just consider what those in their twenties and thirties are now doing to their unwanted offspring. This is the generation that will be in control of our country in the next century.

Sabbaticals

God in His infinite wisdom knew that His creation would need rest and relaxation. The method He chose to provide that rest and relaxation is called a sabbatical—the resting time. The term sabbatical comes from Sabbath, or the day of rest in each week.

In the fifth chapter of Deuteronomy, the Lord told the Jews that they should work six days, but *"the seventh day is a Sabbath . . ."* The meaning behind the Sabbath is twofold: The first is to set apart a day to honor the Lord; the second is to take a day a week to rest and recover. This practice was extended to include a Sabbath year, called the year of remission, described in Deuteronomy 15:1-11.

This is not a book for an in-depth discussion of the Sabbath day. Rather, I want to point out that God has provided a plan for His people to rest and recover *during* their working lives. As best I can determine, God has not prescribed a time when we should retire. We have arbitrarily decided that at age 62, 65, or some later period, our active working careers should stop. Nothing could be further from the truth, and we should begin to adjust to a saner and more reasonable philosophy.

Storing some funds during the most productive years of your life for the later years is both logical and biblical. As Proverbs 6:6 says, *"Go to the ant, O sluggard, observe her ways and be wise, which, having no chief, officer or ruler, prepares her food in the summer, and gathers her provision in the harvest."* Having some reserve allows you to take more frequent sabbaticals later in life or to volunteer your services to ministries without the necessity of being paid. But if you want to live the long, happy, healthy life that God has prescribed for you, don't retire!

Now, having stated my case against traditional retirement, I will rest it there and assume that you'll decide this issue before the Lord. From this point on, I'll conclude that the decision is yours.

The remainder of this book is dedicated to covering the decisions you'll be facing as the aging process continues. The only alternatives to the aging process are either the Lord's Second Coming, in which case nothing further is needed, or death, in which case retirement is not an issue.

2

Retirement Realities

One of the realities of retirement is that retirees become prospects for virtually every would-be financial advisor around—Christian and non-Christian alike. With the current lax rules on who can qualify as an investment advisor, it is prudent for retirees to learn enough so that they are not totally dependent on the counsel of others.

As I SAID in the last chapter, I will presume from this point that you have determined that at least some form of retirement, total or partial, is right for you, and therefore my function is to answer as many retirement questions as possible.

I would like to digress slightly and outline my personal philosophy on retirement. In doing so I hope to answer some of the expected questions that may arise from this book by those who earn their living selling retirement-oriented investments. I want to make it clear that I have thoroughly thought out my personal retirement goals. If the Lord allows me to retain my mental faculties and reasonably good health, I hope to continue working throughout my lifetime.

However, two considerations tend to shape my future economic decisions. First, there are no guarantees that I can continue to work at my current pace all of my life; so I may be forced to modify my traveling, teaching, and writing schedules. Second, I love to write more than any other thing I do and, therefore, I hope to be able to continue that work regardless of my age. Only the loss of my mental faculties would cause me to abandon that plan.

For the majority of retirees, inflation is the most disastrous of all the circumstances they may face.

Because of what God has allowed me to do, I realize that I can develop a retirement plan that is significantly different than most. As long as people read books and a few are willing to buy those I write, my income can be generated through my labor rather than through investments. This is critically important because my need for retirement income through investments is less than for most others, and I don't have to do nearly as much long-term planning to cope with future inflation.

For the majority of retirees, inflation is the most disastrous of all the circumstances they may face. In a depressed economy, those living on fixed incomes may actually do better, since some prices tend to fall (assuming the retirees' source of income is dependable during that time). But inflation will eat the heart out of any retirement plan at a time when the retiree has little or no flexibility. I will address some methods to counter this problem in a later chapter.

Philosophically, I believe the first phase of any long-term financial goal should be to own your home *debt-free.* I am amazed how few people in our generation feel that owning their homes debt-free is important today. The practical truth is that having a debt-free home is better than earning the income to make the payments. No investment income is absolutely guaranteed, but mortgage payments are. The average mortgage payment in my area of the country is about $700 to $800 a month. For those who can itemize their deductions for tax purposes, this translates to approximately $500 to $600 in net costs. To earn that much through investments at an average rate of 10 percent would require at least $50,000 to $60,000 in investment capital and with no guarantees that the investments would be there in a bad economy.

My wife and I paid our home mortgage off in 1988, and I can say honestly that I have never regretted that decision; nor am I ever tempted to look at our home as "idle capital."

The second part of my financial philosophy is to put aside the equivalent of my previous house payment in a tax-sheltered plan each month. Because I am self-employed, I have the use of an SEP-IRA (Simplified Employee Pension-Individual Retirement Account) which allows me to put 15 percent of my net income (including the deductible contribution) into an SEP plan if I desire. I personally never put that much aside because my long-term goals don't require it. I believe the funds can be put to better use in God's work today.

I do not presume that my plan is the best for everyone. My goal is that, by age 65 (more or less), my long-term investments will provide approximately one-third of my annual income needs.

The third phase of my planning is to put approximately 10 percent of my net income into long-range investments—after taxes. It is my opinion that assets stored in qualified retirement accounts are extremely vulnerable to the whims and wishes of the politicians. As I have reviewed the needs of the Social Security system, I simply cannot see enough tax dollars available to keep the system solvent into the next century. I also believe the Social Security system is a "sacred cow" within political circles and will be maintained at all costs (except possibly for high-income retirees).

As I have reviewed the rising costs of Social Security and the declining sources of revenue, I've concluded that additional funding will be absolutely necessary. It's my *opinion* that private retirement accounts for middle and upper income workers are the most likely source of those funds. I realize that presently this isn't being debated in Washington, and most of the experts I talked with consider it highly unlikely that private retirement funds will be used to support the Social Security system. *I do not.*

In the quest for social program funds, nothing is beyond our politicians. They have broken existing contracts before, and I believe they will do so again. Therefore, my counsel to those saving for retirement in the twenty-first century is: Don't put your total retirement savings in a tax-sheltered plan—ever!

In order to be balanced about this particular aspect of long-term financial planning, I would ask anyone who does not share my particular perspective on this topic to reserve judgment until you finish this entire book, including the discussion on Social Security. Then put yourself in the place of politicians who have made impossible promises to future retirees, and decide what you would do if you had to make the decisions. If the government can remove the U.S. currency from the gold standard (which it did), confiscate private property for failure to pay taxes (which it does), and steal Social Security trust funds that are clearly earmarked for retirees (which it is doing), I doubt that anything is beyond possibility.

The point that needs to be emphasized is that nothing *is certain in the area of long-term financial planning.*

In discussing the realities of retirement, it is important to note that many decisions other than investment decisions can dramatically affect your plans. For instance, I recently received a letter from a widow whose husband had retired from a major company two years earlier. She said that one of his options at retirement was either a single-life annuity with a higher monthly income, or a two-life annuity with a lower income. The two-life annuity would continue to pay her in the event of her husband's death. Since the two-life option had a lower monthly payout, her husband opted for the single-life plan. He died unexpectedly two years later, the annuity income ceased, and she was left with nothing but a small Social Security income to live on. As a result, she was forced to return to the job market in her mid-sixties in order to meet her minimum needs. As the old cliché says, he was penny wise and pound foolish.

In counseling many retirees I found that many seemingly non-investment decisions drastically altered their retirement plans.

Bill, an airline pilot, retired from a major airline company at age 60 with a pension income of nearly $40,000 a year in 1975. Forty thousand dollars a year was a fantastic retirement income in the mid-seventies. Because he had attained his retirement goal, Bill decided to cancel all of his personal life insurance, except a small burial policy. He had selected the two-life retirement benefit from the airlines so that his wife would receive his pension in the event something happened to him, so he felt his need for life insurance was negligible.

Unfortunately, in the late eighties, the airline went bankrupt and left much of the pension plan unfunded. Without a source of income from the parent company, the pension plan was forced to reduce the payout to its retirees. In Bill's case, this trimmed his retirement income by nearly one-half. The income was still adequate, provided Bill supplemented it by working part-time. Less than a year later Bill was diagnosed with terminal cancer and died within a few months. His wife was left with no insurance, a sizeable medical bill (since the company's medical plan was also eliminated), and not enough income to live on as Bill had planned. He had not anticipated the complete failure of the parent company and the retirement account as well.

The point that needs to be emphasized is that *nothing* is certain in the area of long-term financial planning. Bill assumed that since he was retired from a major corporation he was set for life. The decision to cancel his life insurance was made without considering the total consequences. Obviously it's not possible to foresee every possible scenario for the future, but the basic principles of long-term financial planning don't change all that much from one individual to another. Once you understand the basics, the decisions become easier. Just bear in mind the two rules of Murphy's Law: "Anything that can go wrong will go wrong" and "Murphy was an optimist."

In both of the previous examples, two basic principles were ignored: Wives outlive their husbands most of the time; and, there should always be a fall-back plan if your total retirement income is invested in one area.

In the early 1980s a couple came to see me with a difficult situation. The husband, Ted, had retired from a computer company at age 62 and elected to take his retirement savings in a lump sum rather than a monthly annuity. With over $200,000 in hand, Ted set out to invest the money to supplement his Social Security income.

A Christian investment advisor in his church knew about his recent retirement and offered to help invest the money. With the best of intentions, and some very bad strategies, this man talked Ted into investing in the commodities market.[1] He convinced Ted that by investing in futures options he would be able to limit his liability while maximizing his return.

Ted was no dummy, but all of his business experience had been in selling computers and business equipment. Besides, the advisor was a Christian and had shown Ted some remarkable graphs demonstrating what (profit) he had made personally using the same strategy.

Let me pause for a moment to make a comment: I have seen many Christian financial advisors who, with the best of intentions, gave bad advice. Too often the investors placed unrealistic confidence in them because they were Christians. It's been my observation that Christians can give some pretty bad counsel. So be careful.

Ted began his retirement investing by risking initially only a small portion of his savings. In the first year, his average return was over 100 percent on the money invested. Gradually Ted increased his stake until he had nearly $150,000 at risk. What Ted didn't know was that his advisor had shifted his strategy from options, which limited Ted's exposure only to the money invested, to actual futures contracts, in which the profits were potentially enormous but so were the proportionate risks.

Obviously for a retiree like Ted, with virtually no experience, risking retirement money in options was illogical enough. But gambling on commodity futures would be illogical for a 30-year-old with a $200,000 annual income. I've discussed the idea of commodities investing with Mark Ritchie, one of the major brokers on the Chicago Board of Trade. He estimates the odds of an amateur investor getting his money back (no profit) at 200-to-1. That doesn't make any sense—except for the broker.

---

[1] For a discussion of commodity future options, see *Investing for the Future.*

You can probably guess the ultimate outcome in this case: A major shift in the commodities market caused the investments to plummet. The broker handling the contracts made a call to Ted's advisor for more collateral to cover the contracts (bought on margin), and Ted got a rude awakening.

Ted described a call he received one Friday morning from his investment advisor.

"Ted, we have a problem."

"What kind of problem?" Ted asked guardedly.

For several months Ted had known that something was wrong, although he didn't know exactly what. Several times in previous weeks the advisor had called to pressure Ted into increasing his investment—each time telling him about a great "opportunity" that couldn't wait. Each call resulted in Ted's risking several thousand dollars more. Initially Ted and his wife, June, had set a limit on what they would invest in any one area, but the profits from the option trading looked so good that Ted had continued to increase his percentage—without telling June.

At the insistence of his advisor, Ted had actually signed a limited power of attorney authorizing him to buy and sell in Ted's name. At the time, Ted had a check in his spirit about signing a power of attorney, but he had been assured that the document was necessary if they were to act swiftly on the opportunities available.

"It's for your protection," the advisor had counseled Ted as they ate lunch. "If something happened to me and all the contracts were in my name alone you'd have a terrible time getting your money out."

So, in spite of his better judgment, Ted signed the document, which was the equivalent of authorizing withdrawals from his savings account.

Ted decided not to mention it to June since she was already upset about the amount Ted was investing. Ted knew he was risking too much money in something she didn't understand. When he thought about it, which he tried not to do too often, Ted wasn't sure he understood it either.

Ted's attention returned to the call. "You'll need to put up some more money," he heard the advisor say.

"How much more money?" Ted asked with a tinge of alarm in his voice, "and why?"

"I'll need at least $50,000 today," the advisor stammered, trying his best to sound authoritative.

"Fifty thousand!" Ted shouted into the phone. "I don't have $50,000 now. All my money is tied up in these options. How could you need that much?"

"The broker who handles our trading has made more margin calls," his advisor replied defensively, trying to shift the blame to the broker.

"What exactly is a margin call?" Ted asked. "I thought you said I was only liable for the money I had at risk."

"Didn't you read the reports I sent you each month? They clearly showed that I shifted most of your account into commodities futures."

"I didn't understand one thing those papers said," Ted replied angrily. "If you'll remember, I asked you about them and you said not to worry—that you'd take care of all the details."

"I don't remember saying that," the advisor replied nervously. "But the bottom line is, you'll need to wire some money to the trading account immediately or the broker will sell your contracts and charge you for the losses."

The net result of Ted's trading was that he lost virtually all of the money he and his wife had worked so long to accumulate. Fortunately for Ted and June, the commodity brokerage firm decided not to sue for the contract deficiencies, which amounted to more than $30,000. The financial advisor eventually lost his securities license but, unfortunately, Ted was unable to recover any of his money since the man declared bankruptcy.

This situation was obviously traumatic for Ted and June. She felt that Ted had deceived her, or at least ignored her by not keeping her informed about what he was doing. In the period before I saw them, they also had accumulated several thousand dollars of credit card debt. Typical of many young (and older) couples in this situation, they supported themselves by using credit cards until that source ran out as well.

Fortunately for Ted and June, they had raised four godly children who stepped in to help. The children paid off the credit card debts, with the agreement that their parents would go for counseling. Over the next few months Ted began receiving his Social Security pension, and he was able to find a part-time job in a retail computer store. Their income stabilized at about $1,000 a month, or approximately one-third of Ted's pre-retirement income. They made the adjustment, but the lifestyle they had planned for all those years was modified drastically.

One of the realities of retirement is that retirees become prospects for virtually every would-be financial advisor around—Christian and non-Christian alike. With the current lax rules on who can qualify as an investment advisor, it is prudent for retirees to learn enough so that they are not totally dependent on the counsel of others. Even giving Ted's advisor the benefit of the doubt about his motives, his expertise and judgment were deficient.

Anyone can be duped by a slick salesperson. This is especially true when the salesperson presents himself or herself as a Christian and therefore is presumed to be ethical and honest. Unfortunately, as I said earlier, this is not always a logical presumption.

3
Future Problems

Nothing in our economy happens in a vacuum. Each time a major player in the economy fails, the ripple effect is felt throughout the system.

IT SEEMS PROBABLE that we have seen the zenith of the American economy. I don't mean that all future generations will live in poverty; probably they won't. But future workers and retirees will face an increasingly difficult economy in which there will be fewer jobs at lower wages.

Many workers in the next century will discover that the social programs of the twentieth century came with a high price tag: future jobs. From the 1970s on, the politicians who engineered the entitlement programs lacked the courage to tell the American people the true cost of re-engineering our society. Instead they borrowed from future generations and stripped the economy of investment capital that would otherwise have gone into creating more jobs.

When the working people of the next century are asked to increase their "contributions" to support the baby boomers, the price simply will be too high. Consequently those people born after 1940 had better plan to expect less entitlements or the "me" generation of the sixties and seventies will probably seek out some creative ways to reduce their overhead.

Keep in mind that those who will be in control of our country in the next two decades have been raised on a steady diet of permissiveness, selfishness, and indulgence. If they won't tolerate the inconvenience of their own children, why would they tolerate the inconvenience of high costs for the elderly?

By the turn of the century, environmental restrictions will force thousands of other companies to close or relocate.

It seems obvious that the U.S. economy is shifting from an industrial base to a service industry base; and practically speaking, the service industries—fast foods, car repairs, computer services—don't pay the same wages as automobile manufacturing and steel production.

The United States may recapture isolated segments of lost markets, but our cost of labor, lower productivity, and lack of available capital make a large-scale recovery of these basic industries almost impossible. The international investors get much better rates of return in developing countries, such as China, India, and Mexico, where the rules are more lax and the laws favor the company rather than the workers. Also the extremely high cost of litigation in America discourages new industries from starting here.

This can be evidenced by the demise of the private aircraft industry in the U.S. After leading the world in aviation technology and development for eighty years, the U.S. now has *no* private airplane manufacturers. Unlimited litigation, government regulation, and luxury taxes have eliminated more than 1,175,000 high-paying American jobs.

By the turn of the century, environmental restrictions will force thousand of other companies to close or relocate—many of them right across the border into Mexico, where the pollution will flow into the U.S. while the jobs flow into Mexico. Perhaps we'll see Americans sneaking across the border to find work in Mexico in the next century.

This is not to say that our country cannot reverse these trends. But it would seem unlikely, given the current mentality of our politicians and the reluctance of the social and environmental liberals to make the compromises necessary.

For those who will be facing retirement age in the twenty-first century, this is not just an academic discussion on the economy. The statistical facts are that more Americans are living longer and the employed ranks are growing slimmer.

As the graph below indicates, by the time today's children reach middle age, nearly 20 percent of the population will be over

The Narrowing Population Gap

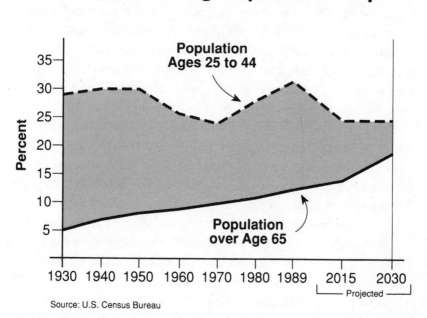

Source: U.S. Census Bureau

the age of 65; only 25 percent will be in the primary wage earners group (25-44).

When the shift to a nonindustrial base is factored into the next century, retirees will face some real challenges.

The Pension Benefit Guaranty Corporation (PBGC)

It is likely that many private retirement programs will fail during the decade of the nineties as the companies behind them either fail or withdraw from the U.S. work place. The PBGC is the federal agency that insures the private pension plans of approximately forty million Americans. The PBGC operates much like any other government insurance agency in that it has far fewer assets than liabilities—overwhelmingly so.

It should be noted that federal insurance plans—FDIC, FSLIC, FHA, VA, and the PBGC—were never meant to be total-cost insurers (meaning that they would guarantee all the liabilities of the funds they represent). It was assumed that the U.S. economy would be viable and growing and, at best, a few banks, savings and loans, or major companies might fail, necessitating these agencies to help only a fraction of the groups they insure. Instead we have seen a time-delayed "crash" of sorts in our economy. Big companies such as LTV, Eastern Airlines, and Pan American went bankrupt, leaving millions of dollars in unfunded pension liabilities. In addition, the collapse of the S&L industry burdened taxpayers with billions of dollars in unfunded depositor liabilities.

Nothing in our economy happens in a vacuum. Each time a major player in the economy fails, the ripple effect is felt throughout the system. With the federal government attempting to play the role of protector and trying to guarantee that no American loses any investment money, the unfunded liabilities continue to pile up. The real question is: What happens if several of these contingent liabilities fall due at the same time? It would seem that no one really wants to answer that question today. Considering the direction of our economy, it's a legitimate question that will either be addressed now, or later; and for retirees, later is not good enough.

I would like to focus attention on the PBGC briefly because it represents the typical problem retirees will be facing. The PBGC is little more than a government "shell game." On the surface the system looks sound enough. The agency was established as a fail-safe for pensioners whose retirement plans might go "belly up" because of company failures. It was recognized that many private pension plans were (and are) woefully underfunded. Quite often a parent company funds an employees' retirement account on a "pay-as-you-go" concept. As long as the company remains profitable, there is no problem. But once the company begins to lose money, the pension plan represents a significant cash drain. If the company files for bankruptcy protection, the drain is removed, but so is the employees' retirement income.

Too often individuals tend to think the problems are so big that they can do nothing about them. I assure you that is not

*true. Just one person who has the correct facts and is willing
to take on the establishment can make the difference.*

In 1974 Congress created the PBGC to cover this contingency—well before the huge trade deficits of the late eighties and
while the annual federal deficit was a mere $70 billion or so.

As of 1992 the total liabilities of the private pension system
are about $900 billion; the assets total about $1.3 trillion. So it
would seem the system is secure and adequately funded. But, if
you will recall, the same assessment was made of the Savings and
Loan industry in the early eighties. Unfortunately, whether it is
banks or pension plans, the assets are often overvalued and, once
the slide starts, the remaining assets lose much of their value
quickly. As in the case of the S&Ls (an industry that boasted a total
net worth of $600 billion as late as 1983), the failed "thrifts"
actually had a combined deficit of some $500 billion once the
collapse began.

In looking at the viability of any insurance program, it is
important to look at the worst case scenario, not the best. Remember what Murphy's law says: If anything can go wrong, it will.

Granted, the overall pension system is solvent at this time;
however, it is not possible to rob from the well-funded plans to
give to the underfunded plans—according to existing law. (If that
law were changed, the underfunded pension plans would quickly
deplete the well-funded ones.) Consequently the PBGC has to be
reviewed as if the underfunded plans will fail, leaving the agency
to pick up the deficits. This is very revealing.

In 1990 the agency's single-employer pension plan had a total
deficit of approximately $1.9 billion. By 1991 the *deficit* had in-
creased to $2.5 billion—an increase of 32 percent.

But even this trend pales in comparison with the underfunded liabilities of major companies. In 1990 company pension plans were underfunded by approximately $30 billion. By the
end of 1991 the deficit had risen to $40 billion. According to the
General Accounting Office, even this amount is significantly understated. The failed plans taken over by the PBGC in 1991 had their

assets overstated by between 20 and 40 percent, while the liabilities were understated by some 37 percent. Logically, one can assume the same would be true of plans that have not yet failed.

Basically this means that the $70 billion line of credit issued to the PBGC by Congress could be depleted easily if the economy suffers any significant setbacks over the next ten years, as many economists expect it will.

From my review of the information released on the PBGC, the danger lies more in the next decade than in the present one. There are adequate reserves and loans that can be tapped to continue the system under normal conditions. It is the abnormal conditions that future retirees should be most concerned about. Those who are dependent on company-funded retirement accounts should get information on how their funds are invested and whether or not the company is allowed to "borrow" the funds for current expenses.

Because so many plans are underfunded, new laws now require that companies set aside reserves for future retirees. However, this condition often is satisfied by purchasing an insurance company annuity to cover the future liabilities. In the wake of recent insurance company failures, it would be prudent to verify the rating of the insurance company issuing the annuity.

Too often individuals tend to think the problems are so big that they can do nothing about them. I assure you that is not true. Just one person who has the correct facts and is willing to take on the establishment can make the difference. If you find your company plan is underfunded, you need to start a campaign to get it corrected—now. That means writing the company officials, calling and writing your elected representatives, and educating others who will be affected.

The most important action any of us can take is to pray. The Lord tells us in Matthew 6:31: *"Do not be anxious then, saying, 'What shall we eat?' or 'What shall we drink?' or 'With what shall we clothe ourselves?' "* And then in verse 34: *"Therefore do not be anxious for tomorrow; for tomorrow will take care for itself. Each day has enough trouble of its own."*

I interpret these passages to say that we are to trust God in the midst of chaos. But does this mean that we are to do nothing to help avoid a calamity? In Proverbs 27:12 God's Word also says: *"A prudent man sees evil and hides himself, the naive proceed and pay the penalty."* I believe this means that we should try to avoid being part of the problem—if at all possible.

The Problem of Health Insurance

The ever increasing cost of medical care has to be one of the primary concerns of any older person, especially a retiree. Since the implementation of Medicare in 1965, most older Americans have had their basic medical expenses insured through that system. But there are approximately six million people over the age of 65 who are not covered by any type of health plan. Some can qualify for Medicaid, the state-run medical supplement plan, but others cannot meet the qualifications because of income or other factors. Medicaid and Medicare provisions are discussed in Chapter 7 so I won't spend time discussing them here.

One observation that must be made, however, is that both Medicare and Medicaid *will* be reformed in some fashion over the next few years. Any discussion of these programs will have to be updated periodically as the laws are revised.

The cost of maintaining these programs in their current form will be impossible as more baby boomers approach retirement age and the economy adjusts downward to a service-oriented system. Again I repeat: I don't expect those who are already in the system to be dropped (except perhaps the higher-income retirees).

The political climate in our country makes changes to existing retirees' benefits almost sacred. Certainly our politicians are aware of the voting power of older Americans, and the fact that they do vote in greater numbers than any other age group makes them an imposing political group. Perhaps the one change that will be adopted is to remove the automatic cost of living adjustments that force the annual deficits ever higher.

I have heard it said that once the government decides to manage the health care system it will conform to government norms: Your local doctor's office will have the courtesy of the IRS, the efficiency of the Post Office, and the cost of the Pentagon.

The fact is, a health care system which cannot be supported financially but also cannot be changed spells disaster. To adequately fund the Medicare portion of Social Security will require massive influxes of new tax dollars. If the current trend in costs is not controlled, the health insurance funds will run out near the end of this decade. The following is a quote from the 1991 "Annual Report of the Medicare Board of Trustees."

> There are currently over four covered workers supporting each HI [Hospital Insurance] enrollee. This ratio will begin to decline rapidly early in the next century. By the middle of that century, there will be only about two covered workers supporting each enrollee. Not only are the anticipated reserves and financing of the HI program inadequate to offset this demographic change, but under all but the most optimistic assumptions, the trust fund is projected to become exhausted even before the major demographic shift begins to occur. Exhaustion of the fund is projected to occur shortly after the turn of the century under the intermediate assumptions, and could occur as early as 2001 if the pessimistic assumptions are realized.

This virtually assures those not already in the system that fundamental changes will be made before they qualify for benefits. It is anybody's guess what changes will be made, but almost certainly some form of national health care will be implemented.

The obvious question has to be: If we already can't afford the smaller system (Medicare/Medicaid), how will we be able to afford a larger scale system? The answer is: We won't be able to, but we'll do it anyway. This added cost may well drive the last nails into our economic coffin. I have heard it said that once the government decides to manage the health care system it will conform to government norms: Your local doctor's office will have the courtesy of the IRS, the efficiency of the Post Office, and the cost of the Pentagon.

Alternative Choices

Until the actual changes are made to our health care system, it is impossible for me to comment on them. But as of this time there are some viable alternatives for those who are not covered under Medicare and expect to retire in the next few years. If you are covered and have questions about supplemental insurance coverage, that will be discussed in Chapter 8.

Major Medical Plans

Retirees with good health can usually qualify for individual health insurance. Normally the cost of a full coverage policy is prohibitively expensive for most retirees. However, policies that pay primarily for major expenses, called major medical plans, are generally less expensive. That does not mean they are cheap; no health plan is cheap anymore. But the savings can range from 50 to 60 percent when compared with a full coverage plan.

The purpose of a major medical plan is to protect your assets from a catastrophic expense that would either deplete your savings or put you in debt for years. A single major health expense, such as a heart by-pass operation or cancer surgery, can easily do this.

Selecting both the policy and the issuing company is very important. Buying the cheapest plan may be "penny wise and pound foolish." The first priority is to have a company that will pay off when you have the need. Selecting a policy based only on the initial cost can lead to a bad experience when that need arises. Some companies thrive on litigation and find it less costly to retain attorneys than to pay legitimate claims.

Some good advice for any potential retiree is, buy quality in health care providers, not initial costs; and always check the rating of your provider with the recognized rating services.

One couple I met in Atlanta discovered the hard way that there's a lot more to medical insurance than just the monthly premiums.

Roger and Nancy had lived most of their thirty years of marriage with virtually no medical expenses. When the 1990 recession began, Roger was a professional architect for a large commercial construction firm. His company was hit very hard by the downturn and, eventually, Roger realized that his position would be eliminated. Rather than wait for the inevitable, Roger accepted a voluntary early retirement from the company. He felt that he could easily earn a living until he was 62, at which time he would qualify for both Social Security and a pension from his company's 401(k) retirement plan. He had the option of continuing the company's health care insurance under the COBRA Act for eighteen months. But after reviewing the costs he and Nancy determined it would be better to purchase their own policy at a much lower premium.

They contacted an insurance agent within their church and viewed an array of policies. Each policy offered different benefits, and most were so confusing that Roger and Nancy scarcely understood the exclusions, much less the actual coverage. Eventually they decided just to tell the agent what coverage they wanted and what they could afford. Essentially they wanted a major medical plan that would protect them against potentially catastrophic medical bills.

The agent suggested a $1,000 deductible plan that would pay 80 percent of any hospital-related bills. He narrowed the choices down to two companies with about the same benefits, but the premiums of one company were less than half of the other.

When Roger questioned the difference in costs, the agent replied, "The smaller company is trying to buy into the market, so they're giving some very low rates up front."

"But won't they raise the rates later?" Nancy asked.

"Probably so," the agent agreed, "but we can lock in the lower rates for three years, and even then they won't be able to increase them much," he added. "If they do we'll just shop around for another company."

Obviously Roger should have questioned the wisdom of that advice. The logical questions he should have asked were: "What would the policy rates be if either of us were no longer insurable?" and "How long has this company been in the health insurance business?" But since Roger had always been a part of a group insurance plan, he didn't really know the right questions to ask; so he chose the cheaper policy.

A few months after Roger left his job, Nancy began to experience some dizzy spells. After repeated visits to her own doctor and several specialists, she was diagnosed with a rare blood disorder that required extensive hospitalization.

The medical bills for three months of care came to nearly $230,000. Their deductible and co-insurance costs were nearly $45,000. The sum was staggering but, since they had saved diligently most of their lives, it was at least manageable. Roger had been doing some consulting work, and he felt they could pay their portion off in less than two years.

But when the hospital and doctors began sending notices that the insurance company had not paid on any claims, Roger contacted the company in California. He had a sinking feeling when the operator responded, "The number you are calling is no longer in service."

Frantically Roger contacted his agent, who then contacted the state of California's insurance commissioner's office.

"The company has declared bankruptcy," the polite woman in the commissioner's office told him. "They have nearly $3 million in unpaid claims. You can file with the bankruptcy court but our investigation shows that the company has virtually no assets."

The trustee's report later verified that the company had no viable assets to cover its liabilities. The company had been in financial trouble even when Roger was evaluating their policy. Although the information was not disseminated widely, several insurance company rating services had listed them on their "problem" circular. Had the agent taken the time to verify some of these sources, he could have advised Roger and Nancy better. But he didn't.

Roger quickly learned that his obligations to the doctors and hospital were not contingent on his contract with the now-defunct insurance company. He still owed the health providers, irrespective of whether or not the insurance company paid him.

The state of California had a pooled fund to help cover the deficits of failed insurance companies, but the claims from within the state took priority. Once all the other debts were settled, Roger still owed a great deal more than he could ever hope to pay on a retirement income. Also, by that time Nancy was no longer insurable, and the bills continued to pile up.

Fortunately for Roger he was still relatively young and had a marketable skill that allowed him to reenter the work force. He was able to secure a job with a commercial construction company that provided group health insurance, so Nancy was covered once again. His retirement plans were put on hold for several years, but at least he was able to salvage some of his life savings.

Some retirees are not so fortunate. Some good advice for any potential retiree is, buy quality in health care providers, not initial costs; and always check the rating of your provider with the recognized rating services. Most of them can be found in your local library (see the Appendix for a listing of these services).

A Biblical Alternative

Outside of Medicare, Medicaid, or national health insurance, there are very few alternatives available for those approaching retirement age. However, for some, the alternative may be a biblically based plan, such as the Brotherhood Newsletter or the Good Sa-

maritan Fund. When I first heard about these plans, I was skepti-
cal. I have seen just about every kind of scam imaginable being
promoted in the name of Christ—everything from engines that
supposedly run on water to miracle healing gloves. So naturally I
was more than a little cautious.

As I began to investigate the idea of Christians pooling their
funds to provide health care for one another, I was impressed by
the soundness of the concept.

In 2 Corinthians 8:14–15 the apostle Paul said: *"At the present
time your abundance being a supply for their want, that their
abundance also may become a supply for your want, that there
may be equality; as it is written, 'He who gathered much did not
have too much, and he who gathered little had no lack.' "* This is
the principle upon which all the insurance companies in the
world are built. It basically means that in any large group there will
always be more healthy people than sick and more people living
than dying. In insurance terms the principle is called actuarial
probabilities: It is probable that more will be paid into a group
plan than will be consumed.

The founder of the Brotherhood Newsletter, Bruce Haw-
thorn, took the passage in Corinthians literally and established a
plan whereby Christians would band together and pay each others' medical bills. The principle is deceptively simple: If the group
is large enough and most of the people in the group are healthy
(on the average), they should be able to pay the costs of caring for
those who are ill.

Each month the Brotherhood receives the medical bills from
its members, spreads them across the entire group, and each
member mails a small amount to the person assigned to him or
her.

For example, let's assume that I join the group and agree to
voluntarily send a gift of up to $50 a month to any other member
who has a medical bill. If one member has a bill of $500, it would
take ten members, each mailing $50, to cover that expense. Later,
if I incur an expense of $500, ten members would do the same

for me. As long as most of the members are well, the system works.

The same principle applies to all insurance companies. The only difference is that the insurance companies keep the surplus (their profit) and absorb the losses, if there are any. In truth, most insurance companies rarely take losses on their health coverage premiums since any losses in one year are passed along in the way of higher premiums the next year. The losses incurred by most insurance companies are in their investment portfolios, not in their benefits plans.

As of the date of this writing, the Brotherhood Newsletter has approximately 12,000 members, making it the largest self-help plan in the world (that I know of). The system seems to be functioning well and all the bills to date have been paid.

There is no guarantee that this plan, or a similarly structured plan called the Good Samaritan Plan, will withstand the assaults by insurance companies or by state insurance commissioners. The insurance business is highly competitive, and their legal departments are well funded. Most do not welcome any new competitors, especially Christian ones. Both the Brotherhood and Good Samaritan plans are regularly involved in defensive actions in various states.

There are restrictions in joining both the Brotherhood and the Good Samaritan Plan that limit their applicability to many people. To join, members must be Christians, nondrinkers, nonsmokers, and attend church regularly. Additionally, some pre-existing conditions are excluded from coverage, just as there would be in a qualifying health plan. But for those who can qualify and have no other affordable coverage, the plans represent an idea whose time has come. In an era when individual health policies can cost hundreds of dollars a month, these plans represent a viable alternative (see the Appendix for details on how to contact the Brotherhood Newsletter or Good Samaritan Plan).

Note: The author has no affiliation with either the Brotherhood Newsletter or the Good Samaritan Plan. Nor does the author give any endorsement of these plans in the future. All the information presented here was provided by the Brotherhood Newsletter and the Good Samaritan Plan without certified financial reports. The reader should rely on independent counsel before deciding on any health insurance provider.

4

When to Start a Retirement Plan

*A prudent man looks ahead and sees the problem and tries
to avoid it, while the naive proceed without caution and pay
the penalty (a paraphrase of Proverbs 27:12).*

As I MENTIONED previously, one theory of retirement planning is to start at the earliest possible age. The logic behind this
thinking is twofold: First, the younger you are, the more time you
have to save for retirement; and, obviously, the more time you
have, the more your savings will compound. The second reason
for starting early is that it develops a habit of regular savings—a
habit most Americans sorely need.

I can't fault the logic of starting a savings plan early. It's both
biblical and practical. In Proverbs 21:20 we are told, *"There is
precious oil and treasure in the dwelling of the wise, but a foolish man swallows it up."* Simply put, this means that wise people
save a part of their earnings.

When it comes to *retirement* savings, though, I see two difficulties with the philosophy of starting at a young age.

First, it's very difficult to determine what will be a good investment in thirty years or so. Of course you can invest in areas
that will allow you to shift your strategy as the economy changes.
But for most average investors, that rarely works out. Either they
shift too soon or too late. Usually by the time word of a problem in
the market reaches the general public, the parade has already
passed (so to speak).

The second problem is what I call the "communications"
factor in marriage. Usually husbands and wives have totally different perspectives on the use of surplus funds in their early years—
at least where retirement is concerned. The husband may see retirement planning as a noble and achievable goal, but his wife is

generally more interested in houses and furniture during these years. Until some of the more basic goals are achieved, any attempt to start a retirement plan is usually met with something less than enthusiasm by the wife. In no way am I trying to imply that saving money isn't important during these early years. It is. But other than a savings account for basic emergencies (four to six months of income), I believe the primary savings should be in debt reduction—not retirement planning.

Strategies

In *Investing for the Future,* I discussed the strategies of investing according to the seasons of life, so I won't elaborate here; but I feel the necessity to at least explain the concept for those who have not read that book. If you look at age in terms of the seasons of life, it will help develop some realistic goals for what you want to accomplish financially prior to retirement.

> *There is no trick to good financial planning. It is simply a matter of establishing priorities and sticking to them.*

This discussion would be much simpler if I were addressing either a group of college seniors or a group of retirees (individuals who are all about the same age and on somewhat equal footing financially). Unfortunately, that is not the case. I know some readers will be in the 20 to 40 year old range, and others will be in the 60 to 80 age group. Still others probably are somewhere between those two. Some of you have stored sizeable amounts of money already, while others are approaching their retirement years with little or nothing in savings.

According to the Social Security Administration, less than 2 percent of all 60-year-old adults in America are financially secure. They can support themselves (including Social Security) with an income the equivalent of the average American family ($28,000/ year). According to the same source, approximately 60 percent of all 65-year-old retirees still have mortgages on their homes. The average length of their mortgages is eighteen years. That's pretty optimistic for a 65-year-old. It's also pretty alarming for their economic future.

The Spring Season—Ages 20 to 40

During these early years most young families are concerned with building careers and families. Their financial goals should revolve around having adequate life insurance, buying debt-free automobiles, starting college funds for their children, and paying off their home mortgages. Assuming that each of these areas are kept in balance, any couple can be debt-free (mortgage included) by age 40, provided they make this a high priority.

Summer Season—Ages 40 to 60

Once the car(s) and home(s) are debt-free, there should be sufficient funds available to pay for most of their children's college expenses from freed monthly income—provided the money is not diverted into indulgences like bigger homes, boats, vacations, and such.

One point should be made: There is no trick to good financial planning. It is simply a matter of establishing priorities and sticking to them. A short-term indulgence, such as a new car every four or five years, translates into tens of thousands of dollars consumed that cannot be recovered.

Good financial planning does not exclude all new cars or better homes forever. It simply means prioritizing goals. As Proverbs 28:22 says: *"A man with an evil eye hastens after wealth, and does not know that want will come upon him."* Unfortunately this concept is not taught much anymore, particularly in a society that depends on debt-ridden consumers.

Debt retirement is one of the few absolutely guaranteed investments you can make in this or any other economy.

Some time ago I had the privilege of interviewing Sir John Templeton, founder of the multi-billion dollar Templeton Mutual Funds Company. I asked Mr. Templeton, "To what do you attribute your great success?"

His reply was, "The Lord and disciplined saving." He went on to describe how he and his wife had saved 50 percent of their meager earnings early in their married life. They once furnished an apartment for $25 by buying at auctions and second-hand stores. He limited his lifestyle early in his life in order to accomplish greater goals later, which he did.

Mr. Templeton also shared that he avoided the use of debt to the highest degree possible throughout his career. The only loan he ever had was a $10,000 note to help capitalize his investment company. He drove used cars, lived in rented apartments, and rarely ate out until his income was well established.

Not everyone has been gifted with the abilities of John Templeton, but anyone can apply basic financial principles to his finances—especially that of saving to make purchases, rather than continually going into debt.

The 40 to 60 season should be the time for paying off all outstanding debts, including your home. I realize this counsel will often run contrary to the advice of other financial counselors; but bear in mind that those counselors don't have to make your mortgage payments if you hit a financial setback. Debt retirement is one of the few absolutely guaranteed investments you can make in this or any other economy. During a bad economy you may not be able to find your investment advisors, or even the companies you invest with, but the certainty is, you won't have any difficulty locating your mortgage company.

Too often in our generation people are looking to the government to meet their needs in the "fall" years of their lives.

One of the greatest temptations most Americans face at this stage of life is lifestyle adjustment. Usually this is the time when incomes have peaked and expenses have declined. The children are gone, or leaving, and most of the college expenses are behind. This is the single greatest opportunity to develop the surpluses to invest (or give), but unfortunately most Americans use the potential surpluses to buy motor homes, take more expensive vacations, buy bigger houses, and generally indulge themselves. The result is clearly seen in the next season of life.

The Fall Season: Age 60 Plus

By age 60 most Americans could be debt-free and have some significant surpluses available for retirement. It is a statistical fact however that relatively few do. Too often in our generation people are looking to the government to meet their needs in the "fall" years of their lives. When the government proves unable to do so (as they ultimately must), many will be facing some harsh realities, not the least of which will be returning to the job market with decreased capacities and outdated skills.

If you're in this situation beyond the age of 60, there is not much I can say or do in this book that will help you. There is no easy fix for the lack of financial discipline discussed so thoroughly in God's Word. Perhaps Proverbs 13:18 best describes this principle, *"Poverty and shame will come to him who neglects discipline."*

Obviously one word of encouragement I can offer is that God forgives our transgressions, including our lack of discipline. He also promises not to forsake us, even in the financial area. But nowhere in God's Word does He promise to restore the wasted years or the squandered resources. All too often a reduced living standard is the consequence of earlier wrong decisions.

The 60-plus season is the time to begin shifting from the accumulation to the conservation mode. This generally holds true for the majority of people, although there will always be some exceptions, such as Harland Sanders of Kentucky Fried Chicken. For most people over the age of 60, the funds earned at an earlier age cannot be replaced if lost, so *caution* is the key term.

I wish that I could require every 40-year-old in America to counsel with a few retirees who have done the wrong things financially and are suffering with their consequences. Perhaps it would shock some of the younger group into using more common sense. Suffice it to say that a prudent man looks ahead and sees the problem and tries to avoid it, while the naive proceed without caution and pay the penalty (a paraphrase of Proverbs 27:12).

Those who are 60 and older need to adopt a balanced, conservative investment policy. That does not mean no risks; but it certainly does mean no foolish risks.

A retiree, whom I'll call Jack, had been a successful salesman most of his working career. He took an early retirement at age 59 with the idea that he would play golf, start a garden, and putter around in the yard when he needed to fill in some time.

What Jack failed to take into account was that rarely does a 59-year-old man just shut down his work motivation, as he was attempting to do. Within six months he was bored out of his mind and looking for something to do.

Unfortunately Jack had always made most of the financial decisions in his family, with little or no input from his wife. When he was working he was able to cover his remarkably consistent string of mistakes by generating more income. Most of his losses went undetected by his wife, although she had a strong suspicion that several investments had gone sour—especially when Jack worked harder for a while.

Jack met an energetic young businessman in the swap shop newspaper business during a Saturday golf game. He shared with Jack his great idea for developing a new business: a computerized swap shop.

The basic concept was very good. He would combine all the neighborhood swap shop newsletters and merge them into one computerized system, thereby matching buyers and sellers from all areas of the city. All he lacked, he said, was adequate capital to develop the computer software.

Jack recognized the potential in the younger man's idea and provided the initial $25,000 in funding. Had his investment been limited to no more than the original $25,000, Jack could have sustained that loss without doing irreparable harm to his retirement income. But, as you might guess, the investment grew as the idea developed, until Jack had nearly $300,000 invested—virtually all the capital he had saved.

The need for additional funding didn't arise the first week. It developed as the idea developed, and Jack supplied progressively more money to protect the money he had already loaned.

In this case, the idea really was good and the potential business quite viable. But the amount of capital it would have taken to develop the software and buy the necessary equipment was at least twice what Jack was able to provide. When his money ran out Jack was left with little more than a distant hope that he would ever get even a portion of his investment back. The one thing he was left with was a very hurt and angry wife who felt she had been betrayed by her husband of thirty years.

Jack went back to work, which was probably the best thing for him at that time anyway. His guilt over having lost the money and having alienated his wife helped him get his priorities in order. I met them because Jack had committed to live on a budget for the first time in his life, and he committed also to include his wife in every decision he made from that point on.

Fortunately, in Jack's case, he later recovered nearly $100,000 of his money when a large company purchased the idea that had been developed. He and his wife decided to reinvest $25,000 in the company that took over the project. During the next several years that investment also grew to nearly $100,000.

When to Invest?

I would like to stop here and once again address the issue of when to start a retirement program. As you might guess, it is very difficult to start an effective retirement plan after the age of 60. Colonel Sanders was 66 when he started his first Kentucky Fried Chicken franchise (now known as KFC), and he has become a positive role model for older Americans. It would be naive to think that every retiree might follow in his tracks. Most people simply lack the time and income to develop a significant surplus beyond the age of 60—but some could.

> *I want to emphasize that the one sure investment that anyone can make is to give to the Lord's work. God said that an investment in His kingdom will return one hundredfold. That's a 10,000 percent return!*

I previously stated that my advice to young investors (ages 20 to 40) is to concentrate on debt reduction. So the majority of actual pre-retirement planning will be relegated to the 40 to 60 age range for two reasons: One, that's the age when the income is greatest and some risks can be assumed; and two, that's the biggest group of Americans alive today. I seriously doubt that it is possible to look ahead twenty years and develop any realistic financial plans, given our current economic situation. But as noted previously, if you wait too long time will eliminate your options, so you need to start now, trust the Lord for wisdom, and stay flexible.

If our economy fails during the next ten years, your best efforts probably will be futile; but those options are in the Lord's hands, not ours. We are directed to do the best we can with what we have, including our limited knowledge of the future.

I want to emphasize that the one *sure* investment that anyone can make is to give to the Lord's work. God said that an investment in His kingdom will return one hundredfold. That's a 10,000 percent return! My suggestion is to ask the Lord to reinvest the dividends for you and allow you to collect them in heaven. Then you will have an eternity to enjoy the fruits of your labors.

5

Who Should Retire?

Some time ago I read a study done by Harvard University on 200 of their 65-year-old male graduates, 100 of whom retired and another 100 who did not. At age 75, seven out of eight of the retirees had died, while seven out of eight of the non-retirees were still alive and well.

THE OPTION OF early retirement is being offered to more and more older employees as companies attempt to pare down their work forces. Many companies offer lucrative bonuses to entice higher-paid employees to retire early because it reduces their fixed overhead—a good option for many bloated companies. But is early retirement a good deal for the retirees? The answer is: It depends.

Temperament

Temperament is a vital factor to consider when you're facing a retirement decision. Some people seem able to adjust to retirement better than others. Usually these are the Type B personalities. Type B people are those who generally are more laid back or easygoing individuals. The Type A personalities (like me) are more aggressive, and they are more project oriented. Adjusting to retirement is often traumatic for the Type A.

If you're not familiar with the terms "Type A" and "Type B" personalities, let me explain. A Type B personality is often characterized as a "people person," and a Type A as a "task person." A Type B personality seems able to adapt to a slower pace more readily than a Type A because the latter needs new challenges regularly (I should know).

It is much better to determine which description best fits you before you retire, rather than later.

If the wife of a husband about to retire dreads the day when he will sit around the house telling her how to clean more efficiently, he's probably a Type A.

Allow me to make a few non-scientific comparisons about these two personalities. But first I'll preface my statements with one observation: No one is an either/or personality; we are all a mixture of several types. But for simplicity's sake, I will limit my discussion to the primary characteristics.

I also realize that any thorough analysis would cover more than just two types of personalities. In our counseling ministry we use a simple test that measures four basic personality types. Even so, it is my opinion that most of us can be classified as either basically a Type A or Type B. For example, my doctor tends to qualify everything he tells me with the statement, "I know that as a Type A you always question everything, so here's some research data on . . . (whatever the topic is).

Type A Personality

Those who question if they are Type A personalities have only to ask their spouses to find out. If the wife of a husband about to retire dreads the day when he will sit around the house telling her how to clean more efficiently, he's probably a Type A.

All of the traits that make Type A personalities good leaders in the work place tend to work against them in retirement.

Retirement can be a death sentence for the Type A personalities. As I said, they are task-oriented, performance-driven people and without challenges they tend to depress easily. Even worse, without goals they tend to become more introverted and easily irritated, even with those they love the most.

Following are a few of the more common Type A personality characteristics.

- They seek immediate challenges and results.
- They make decisions easily, even if they're the wrong ones.
- They hate the status quo and require a variety of different tasks regularly.
- They tend to assume authority easily.
- They like to manage a variety of tasks simultaneously.
- They thrive on problems.

All of the traits that make Type A personalities good leaders in the work place tend to work against them in retirement. Unless they have very specific (and realistic) goals at retirement that include staying active in some type of work, the result is often too much internal stress and usually health problems. Rarely will a Type A person marry another Type A. If they do, the relationship is often described as "hammers and knives at short distances."

My wife is a Type B, and the differences in our personalities never cease to amaze me. Usually I find myself envious of her ability to relax and adjust quickly. Not me. It takes me three or four days after starting a vacation before I can relax, and when I drive, I find myself setting personal goals to see how quickly I can get from one place to another. Stopping just to "look" is anathema to a Type A. We must be taught to relax.

When I walk it is always for exercise, and I compete against the clock. My wife loves to stroll, while I charge ahead. Recently we walked my daily exercise route together. Along the way she pointed out a variety of flowers and even a lake that I had never noticed, even though I walk the same route every day. When I walk I'm not out to look at the scenery; I'm there to *walk!* The next day, when I walked alone, I found it enlightening to notice that there were trees, bushes, and even flowers along my path.

It has been suggested that Type A personalities are actually insecure people who are constantly striving to prove they're worthy. As a Type A myself, I suspect this is true to varying degrees for most of us. By personality a Type A is both competitive and rarely content unless involved in a project. Obviously this characteristic should be controlled under the influence of the Holy Spirit, but the underlying personality is always there.

It is important for those with Type A personalities to recognize why God has designed them this way. They are the "movers and shakers"—the "planners and dreamers," if you will. But, as I said, retirement for a Type A is traumatic, and sometimes fatal. Don't make your retirement plans based on what someone else has done. The person you're attempting to emulate may have the personality to adjust to a life of trivia and little real productivity. You may not!

Type A Personality Test

The following is a condensed self-test for a Type A personality. If many or most of these definitions fit your personality (or your spouse's) you should NEVER plan to withdraw totally from the work place.

1. Tend to make quick decisions, and influence others to follow.

    Yes _____   No _____

2. Tend to interrupt others who drag out an explanation.

    Yes _____   No _____

3. More project-oriented than people-oriented.

    Yes _____   No _____

4. Tend to work on several projects at one time (often over-committing myself).

    Yes _____   No _____

5. Would rather be a "quarterback" than a lineman.

    Yes _____   No _____

6. Tend to feel depressed if not successful regularly.

    Yes _____   No _____

7. Tend to be the problem solver of the family or business.

    Yes _____   No _____

8. Will run a stop light at 2:00 A.M. rather than wait for the light to change.

    Yes _____   No _____

9. Will drive out of the way to avoid stop lights, even if the route is longer.

   Yes _____   No _____

10. Will rarely stop on family trips (even to use the rest room).

   Yes _____   No _____

11. An early riser, and a late nighter.

   Yes _____   No _____

12. Will rarely read an instruction manual before attempting a project.

   Yes _____   No _____

13. Have a poor sense of direction, but hesitate to ask others for directions (a sign of weakness).

   Yes _____   No _____

14. Tend to have mood swings apparent to others, but seldom recognize them.

   Yes _____   No _____

15. Very sensitive, but with a gruff exterior.

   Yes _____   No _____

If you answered ten or more of these questions *yes,* you are most certainly a Type A. You need to stay active at any age. Retirement can be a change of careers, perhaps even a phasedown time, but traditional retirement will traumatize you.

Some time ago I read a study done by Harvard University on 200 of their 65 year old male graduates, 100 of whom retired and another 100 who did not. At age 75, seven out of eight of the retirees had died, while seven out of eight of the non-retirees were still alive and well. After eliminating outside factors, such as illness, the conclusion the researchers reached was: Most died of terminal boredom.

Type B Personality

I have often admired Type B personalities because they seem to be able to stop and smell the flowers (so to speak) more than Type A personalities do. But the very characteristics that help them to adjust to daily routines and control their stress often work against them in a crisis situation.

> *The ability to accept circumstances that cannot be changed is an admirable trait. The acceptance of circumstances that could be changed through some personal effort is slothfulness.*

Let me share an example: Some time ago I spoke at a large church where the pastor was clearly a Type A. That evening we had dinner with one of the church deacons, who was clearly a Type B. Both the pastor and the deacon had gone through heart-bypass surgery in the previous five years. The Type A pastor was obviously watching his diet carefully and described in detail his regular exercise routine. Not only was he counting calories but could estimate the amount of fat in each item on the menu.

The Type B deacon, however, was oblivious to anything but the most basic understanding of the fat content of the food he ordered, and even the warnings of his pastor did not dissuade him from eating what he wanted.

When the pastor counseled him on the need to watch his diet and control his cholesterol intake he retorted, "Why? If I have another problem I can always have another bypass."

This fundamental attitude difference explains a lot about the adaptability of a Type A and a Type B. The Type A is a competitor, highly motivated by a challenge, including heart disease. The Type B will adjust to most situations and treat many difficulties as inevitable.

Unfortunately, in the case of retirement this often translates into doing little or no preparation and then living at or near the poverty level. The ability to accept circumstances that cannot be changed is an admirable trait. The acceptance of circumstances that could be changed through some personal effort is slothfulness.

Following is a brief self-evaluation for a Type B personality.

1. Tend to put off major tasks rather than spend the time planning.

     Yes _____   No _____

2. Motivated to a high degree by the appreciation of others.

     Yes _____   No _____

3. Generally a good listener.

     Yes _____   No _____

4. Tend to be too compliant with people who abuse me.

     Yes _____   No _____

5. Find contentment in minor tasks such as yard work, home maintenance, or similar tasks.

     Yes _____   No _____

6. Will work at the pace of others around me rather than risk offending them.

     Yes _____   No _____

7. Adapt well to modern retirement, but often lose contact with lifetime goals.

     Yes _____   No _____

8. Usually accept the idea that most things really can't be changed by me.

     Yes _____   No _____

9. Tend to be more complacent financially; will have unpaid debts at retirement.

     Yes _____   No _____

10. More family oriented.

     Yes _____   No _____

If you answered at least seven out of the ten questions affirmatively, you qualify as a Type B. The primary negative of this personality is the tendency to procrastinate and lean on the counsel of others too much.

Again, I look at the difference in my wife and me in this regard. She accepts implicitly the counsel of her doctor because he represents an authority figure. On the other hand, I require statistical proof of any diagnosis and will evaluate other resources and studies on my own before agreeing to any procedure. The negative aspect of this is that I'll delay going to my doctor until all else fails, while my wife will seek counsel much sooner.

For each personality type, any retirement planning must entail some realistic self-evaluation. The Type A must realize that any period of time without goals and achievements will usually lead to frustration and discontentment. For these people, leaving one phase of life can only be successful if specific goals are established for the next. To think that a task-motivated individual will be satisfied with working in the yard and playing golf twice a week is foolish. Perhaps volunteering with a non-profit organization is a good alternative, provided there is at least some degree of control over the tasks.

I recall a friend who found out about retirement the hard way after retiring from the military as a field grade officer. Initially he and his wife bought a motor home to travel the country "smelling all the roses" he had missed in twenty-three years of traveling throughout the world in the armed services. According to his wife, their leisurely travel lasted about four months, and then he became more and more restless.

His next project was to buy a home in Florida and take up golf seriously. So for about six months he attacked the game, practicing his putting and drives for up to four hours a day. Then when he hit the links with some of the other retirees, he discovered it bored him terribly.

Next he sold the home in Florida and moved to North Carolina, where he took up painting, and for the next few months he attended art classes and studied the masters. But after ten or twelve paintings (pretty good ones), he decided that too was boring and their home in the Carolinas was too much work. So he sold that home and headed for Bible college.

I could go on with his story for at least five more ventures. Finally he decided that he needed to go back to work, so he volunteered as the facility manager at a church in Georgia. This lasted for about a year and a half—until his ideas conflicted with the senior pastor's. Then he found himself being ignored more and more frequently.

This led to a feeling of low self-esteem and bouts of depression. He began to doubt his abilities and self-worth and, for the first time in his life, he found himself unable to get out of bed in the mornings. Fortunately his wife recognized the symptoms of growing depression and started calling friends they had known throughout the years.

One friend's wife related that her husband had gone through the same experience after he retired a few years earlier. "The answer for my husband," she said, "was in volunteering with a ministry that helps provide housing for the inner-city poor. The group is totally run by volunteers so there is no conflict with the founder or other leaders. My husband is able to use his military training to plan and develop an entire project himself, so he is the developer, someone else is the fund raiser, and other volunteers man the construction crews. He feels he is really contributing, and God is allowing him to use the abilities he has developed over the years to help others."

After some wise counsel from his wife, my friend found an organization that needed a first-class administrator to help schedule relief materials to their volunteer groups all over the world. He has been there for nearly ten years and plans to be there until the Lord takes him home. When he needs to, he can take off several weeks at a time to relax and travel. Since he needed to train someone to replace him in the interim, he scouted out an old Army buddy who was fed up with playing golf down in Florida and they now share the responsibilities.

> *For you Type B personalities, . . . think out your retirement years carefully and start laying something aside before you retire, rather than trying to figure it out after you retire.*

One of my most vivid examples of a classic Type B personality is Andrew, a retired fire chief from Florida.

Andrew had worked up through the ranks of his town's fire department to become the fire chief—by default. He was simply the only remaining candidate after all the others had quit in frustration because the town's mayor constantly meddled in the fire chief's business. That didn't bother Andrew at all. His personality was such that he wanted the mayor (or someone) to give him direction. At age 62 he retired, and no amount of pressure from the mayor could change his mind. Andrew had the notion that a man 62 should be able to lay back and enjoy the fruits of his labor, regardless of how small they were.

When Andrew retired he had a small pension from the public service commission, plus his Social Security of about $300 a month. This left him and his wife with a monthly shortfall of about $300 to $400, depending on some of their variable expenses. To meet this need Andrew instructed his wife (ten years his junior) that she would just have to go to work.

She had never worked during their married life and was ill-prepared for the modern work place. After several weeks of disappointment and discouragement in looking for work, she finally got a job in a small diner. Day after day she would walk to work and, after ten to twelve hours of waiting tables, would return to find Andrew awaiting his supper.

It would be easy to judge Andrew for his selfish attitude and obvious irresponsibility but, in reality, Andrew was a product of a system that convinced him to retire with little or no preparation. After having met with him several times at the request of his children, I can attest that he was a classic Type B personality. The Andrews of our society aren't particularly worried about today— or tomorrow. Type B personalities seem to get by pretty well themselves, but those who live around them are often forced to pick up the slack.

Summary

For those who fit in the Type A category, the best counsel I can give is: Don't ever stop working entirely. You can slow down (and probably should) but retirement is often the first step into an early grave. Instead, plan for each phase of your life, including 65 and older. Then get involved with something that will provide the goals and rewards you need to feel that you are a productive member of society.

Most Type A personalities would be better off staying with the organization they served during their most productive years; but since many organizations require younger employees, it is sometimes necessary to step down and assume a less visible role. If your ego won't allow you to do that, you need an ego adjustment. As Proverbs 16:19 says: *"It is better to be of a humble spirit with the lowly, than to divide the spoil with the proud."*

When you approach your sixties, begin transferring some of your responsibilities to a younger person. You may find a new niche in the organization that will allow you more free time and a much longer career. The concept is entirely biblical. Jewish fathers began transferring responsibilities to their sons as they grew older so they could guide them and help ease the transfer over to the next generation.

For you Type B personalities, my best counsel is to listen to your wives who, in most marriages, are probably Type A personalities. Think out your retirement years carefully and start laying something aside before you retire, rather than trying to figure it out after you retire.

Although the temperament of Type B personalities allows them to make the transition to retirement more easily, the admonition from the Lord to remain productive still applies. Too often Type B personalities' lack of financial discipline makes them vulnerable to get-rich-quick schemes in an attempt to strike it rich. As Proverbs 23:4-5 implies: Those who attempt to get rich quickly usually end up getting poor even more quickly.

Besides, if the Lord still has work for you to do in this lifetime and you stop too early, you may find yourself working for some overbearing Type A in heaven—for the rest of eternity!

6

Retirement Options

I don't think I can overemphasize the need to diversify your retirement funds.

Early Retirement

THE OPTION OF taking early retirement can be enticing, particularly in a recession when your job may seem to be in jeopardy. But is early retirement a good idea? Let's first take a look at the early retirement option of Social Security.

Social Security offers the potential retiree the option of retiring at age 62 with reduced benefits, or continuing to work until age 65 and draw full benefits. Since this is not the chapter on Social Security benefits, I will not discuss the tests for qualifying here.

If a retiree elects to begin receiving benefits at age 62, the retirement benefits are reduced by .555 percent for each month of payout before the age of 65. For example: Let's assume you retire at age 62 (36 months before full entitlement). Multiply 36 × .555 to get the reduction in benefits. In this case it would be 19.98 percent, so your monthly check from Social Security would be reduced by 19.98 percent when compared to what it would have been at age 65. However, it should be noted that once the early retirement election is made, it is irrevocable.

For example: Assuming that your benefits at age 65 would be $900 a month and you retired the month you turned 62, your monthly benefit would be $720.18 ($900 × 80.02 percent).

Is this early income option a financially sound idea, outside of all other considerations? To evaluate this we need to look at all the options.

Option #1: Income from Social Security

For the sake of discussion, I will assume our retiree has qualified for the maximum retirement benefit of approximately $1,500 per month at age 65 ($1,500 × 19.98 percent = $299.70). So the retirement check is reduced by approximately $300 a month. Or another way to say it: At $1,200 a month he receives $43,200 in benefits over the next three years.

> *When a company offers an employee an early retirement option, it is usually to reduce the company's overhead. That . . . should tell you something.*

Ignoring all other factors, such as the interest this money could earn, the time value of money, and inflation, it would take approximately 144 months (12 years) at full benefits beyond the age of 62 before the income paid during the first three years would be matched. In other words, you would have to be at least 74 years of age before any real loss occurred. Financially speaking, early retirement is a good deal under the present Social Security system.

Remember, as of 1983, those who were born after 1938 do not reach full retirement at age 65. The retirement age is gradually extended to age 67, depending on the year in which you were born. The early retirement benefits for these people will be reduced depending on what their actual maximum benefit age is. For example: Since I was born in March, 1939, my maximum benefit age is 65 years and 4 months. For someone born in 1940, it would be 65 years and 6 months.

Also bear in mind that earned income in excess of $7,080 (1991) for those under the age of 65 will reduce the monthly benefit by $1 for every $3 in "excess" income (the government's definition, not mine).

Option #2: Company's Early Retirement

When a company offers an employee an early retirement option, it is usually to reduce the company's overhead. That in itself should tell you something: The benefits after retirement will be significantly less than when the retiree was fully employed.

If the retiree can take the retirement pay and move on to another job where the combination of earned income and retirement pay is greater than what he or she was making previously, it's a sound financial decision; but often that's not the case.

All too often the decision is made because it sounds like a good deal. But when the actual figures are compiled, the net result is a loss in pay. Obviously if the decision is a part of a larger plan in which other funds are available, and a subsequent career is already planned, the decision is not purely financial.

I recall a friend who had worked for the same company since graduating from high school. During that time he'd earned a college degree, and he had worked his way up in the company to head one of their major divisions. Then in the mid-eighties when the merger mania was striking corporate America, his company was absorbed through a hostile takeover. The acquisition company offered him the choice of either taking an early retirement or taking his chances in the new corporate environment.

My friend called to ask for counsel since the retirement option would reduce his income by nearly 50 percent; in addition, he really liked the job he had. I suggested that he pay to have a background check done on the principals of the takeover company through one of the companies that specialize in this area, which he did. The results were pretty conclusive: The group acquiring his company were merger specialists, noted for acquiring sound companies, stripping them of their ready assets, and then cutting them in smaller pieces for resale.

My advice was to get out while he could and take a lump sum if at all possible, which he did. The company was more than willing to give him the lump sum since he settled for less than the total of the company's contributions to his retirement plan. This allowed the company access to the residual in his account.

Within two years the takeover group had stripped the company of all the available assets, including the employees' retirement accounts. In order to gain access to the retirement funds they purchased an annuity from an affiliated insurance company. The long and the short of it was, the insurance company was just another shell owned by the same group and it filed for bankruptcy within the next five years too.

Had my friend stayed with the company, he would have been out of a job and probably would have lost the majority of his retirement benefits as well. After leaving the company, he advised many of the other employees to do the same. Most chose not to do so for the sake of their current income. Only a very few retained their jobs when the company was dissected for resale.

My friend took his lump sum and invested it (through an IRA) in high quality mutual funds. He then took his experience and used it to form a consulting company to help other takeover victims determine their best options. That work has supported him comfortably into his normal retirement age. He now works full time for the Nature Conservancy, looking for land that can be donated in trust for the benefit of future generations. For him, early retirement was a great benefit, but not for all.

A man I'll call Phil worked as the chief financial officer for a foreign furniture manufacturing company based in the U.S. The owners sold out to a Canadian company, who then changed much of the top management, including Phil's boss, the administrative vice president. His new boss quickly became his worst nightmare.

He harassed Phil about the financial reports and tried to force him to "enhance" the reports to make it easier for the company to raise capital, which Phil flatly refused to do. From that point on, Phil's life on the job was miserable.

The asset [of a fixed annuity] is the guaranteed payout, which helps budget planning after retirement. The liability is . . . its inability to adjust to inflation.

Slightly more than a year after the acquisition, Phil suffered a heart attack and underwent bypass surgery. While he was recuperating, his boss took the opportunity to replace Phil with a financial officer more to his own liking. Phil still had a job, but he had no day-to-day functions. At 55 Phil was offered the "opportunity" to take early retirement. He took it.

Unfortunately, Phil made two fundamental mistakes in his retirement decision: He decided to leave his retirement funds in the company, and he accepted a monthly annuity since the benefit was higher than he could get elsewhere. After retiring, Phil retreated into a shell and withdrew from any active involvement in the business world.

When Phil had been in charge of the financial department, the employees' retirement account had been transferred to a professional investment firm, which had recommended greater diversification of the assets. Over the last ten years that Phil had worked with the company, the annual growth of the retirement account had been in excess of 15 percent under their management.

But when the new leadership took over the company, the decision was made to shift more of the retirement funds back into the parent company's stock to help finance growth internally. To insure the solvency of the plan, a high yield annuity was purchased from an insurance company in California.

At the same time all of this was occurring, Phil's health was steadily declining. Instead of exercising as he was instructed to do, he lapsed into a state of anxiety and depression—often staying in his home for days. Although Phil was a Type B personality, which is usually able to adapt, his sense of self-worth was greatly diminished. That, along with the normal post-operative depression often associated with bypass surgery, crippled him emotionally.

The best thing Phil could have done was to take his wife's advice to "go find something to do, even if it's working in a hardware store." Instead, he continued to withdraw into self-pity and depression.

In 1987 the company suffered some significant financial set-backs, and in 1988 the owners filed for bankruptcy protection. It was clear by then that the retirement fund was depleted, so the insurance company began making the annuity payments.

In 1990 the insurance company backing the plan also filed for bankruptcy protection, citing huge losses in their own junk bond portfolio. And although the state in which Phil lived had an insurance trust fund, the payout was only a fraction of the promised benefits.

But Phil never lived to see the collapse of his retirement plans because in 1989 he died of a massive heart attack. His widow told me, "Phil made a decision to die without even realizing it when he withdrew from the business world. There was just too much of himself tied up in his work to quit," she said. Once Phil left the daily routine he had loved, he simply went downhill. It is unfortunate that the same thing can be said of many early retirees (perhaps even most who are forced to retire).

Option #3: Annuity Versus a Lump Sum Payout

When most employees retire from a company, they are offered a variety of choices for their retirement income. Basically the options can be reduced to two: a monthly annuity or a lump sum payout. I would like to discuss these two simple, but overwhelmingly critical, choices.

The Annuity: Probably this is the least common option accepted by most retirees during the last ten years because of all the negative publicity about underfunded retirement accounts. To some extent the trend away from company-provided annuities has been good because so many of the plans have been poorly managed, especially benefit plans operated by government agencies. At least with their own money in hand, retirees are able to control their own destinies—for better or worse.

Normally I advise those who are not in substantial company ownership positions to avoid the annuity option when retiring and, more specifically, the variable annuity.

Usually with a retirement plan annuity two options are given: a fixed annuity or a variable annuity. A fixed annuity means that the plan pays a fixed amount of money per month for the rest of the annuitant's life. The payout is guaranteed, irrespective of how much the plan makes or loses on its investments or what the prevailing inflation rate is.

You can probably recognize the asset and liability of a fixed annuity. The asset is the guaranteed payout, which helps budget planning after retirement. The liability is primarily its inability to adjust to inflation. The decision to receive a fixed payout must be made prior to the first month of retirement and is irrevocable.

The monthly payout from a variable annuity is adjusted, based on the actual earnings of the insurance company backing the annuity. Again, the assets and liabilities are obvious: Since the payout is adjusted according to earnings it can be a good inflation hedge, especially since inflation is a fact of life in America.

The liability is that the plan may actually lose money through bad investments, in which case your income will suffer accordingly. Even in a well-managed retirement plan, usually the investment decisions rest with the company's management, so you have little or no control over how the assets are invested. Ownership and management changeovers can adversely affect the way the plan is managed.

One of the most important decisions you will make involves the choice of a single- or two-life annuity.

Normally I advise those who are not in substantial company ownership positions to avoid the annuity option when retiring and, more specifically, the variable annuity. The exception to this rule is where the retirement account is managed by an independent group with no direct link to the parent company or organization.

If you are considering leaving your retirement funds in a company account, you need to get professional help in evaluating the way the fund is run, how it is invested, and what authority the company has in future changes to the management. The guiding rule is: When in doubt, don't!

Even if your fund is guaranteed by a major insurance company, you need to check it out carefully before deciding on your choice of an annuity or lump sum payout. An insurance company is just that: a company. Any company can fail, no matter how large it is. In my opinion, having all of your assets with a single company is too risky when looking at the future. Unless your particular plan is covered by the Pension Benefits Guaranty Corporation, an agency of the U.S. government, I suggest removing your portion if you can. You can verify if your plan is covered by contacting the office of the PBGC, 2020 K St. NW, Washington, DC 20006-1860 - 202/778-8800.

As I mentioned previously, one of the most important decisions you will make involves the choice of a single- or two-life annuity. If you elect the single-life plan the payout will be higher each month, but if you die the benefits cease. Perhaps if you are a widow or widower this may not seem important at this time, but you always need to consider the future. You may get remarried, and the option to leave your annuity to your spouse would be very important. In my opinion, it is extremely rare to have a single-life plan be more beneficial in the long run. The one possible exception is when a life insurance policy can be purchased to provide for the surviving spouse at less cost per month than the two-life annuity option would be.

My advice to any recent retiree is to place your retirement funds in CDs or government securities for at least one year while you make the emotional and psychological adjustment to your new way of life.

Lump Sum Option: The lump sum option is exactly what it sounds like: an option to receive your accumulated benefits in one lump sum. You then must seek out your own investments to generate the income needed.

If the funds are being distributed from a qualified pension or profit sharing plan, the proceeds must be rolled over into another tax-deferred plan within sixty days to avoid paying the taxes and premature withdrawal penalties.

For the vast majority of retirees, the best option is to roll the proceeds over into an Individual Retirement Account. If you have an existing IRA, the funds can be transferred to that account or you can establish a new IRA just for that purpose. Failure to transfer the funds into another retirement account within sixty days of the disbursement will result in severe tax consequences, so this step is very important. You will owe a 10 percent surtax on the entire amount withdrawn, plus the federal and state income taxes. The entire taxable amount will be lumped on top of your income in the year of withdrawal, and can easily push your total income into the highest tax bracket. So, don't procrastinate!

There is a lot of misunderstanding about the use of IRAs. An IRA is not an investment itself. It is merely a legal entity that allows the funds to be held tax-deferred. You can have an IRA with a mutual fund company, a stock brokerage firm, a bank, an insurance company, or any of dozens of other authorized institutions.

For a new retiree, one of the best options is to establish a self-directed IRA at a local bank to hold the funds temporarily. A self-directed IRA means that, although the funds may be temporarily deposited in the bank, you reserve the right to redirect them at any time in the future. So upon proper notice you can tell the bank to forward the funds to a mutual fund company, insurance company, or any other authorized agency. This provides a way to satisfy the legal requirement of rolling the funds into a qualified retirement account while giving you the option later of investing the money elsewhere.

My advice to any recent retiree is to place your retirement funds in CDs or government securities for at least one year while you make the emotional and psychological adjustment to your new way of life. Use that time to learn what you need to know about retirement investing. Under no circumstances make any financial decisions under duress, especially those based on "hot tips." As Proverbs 24:3-4 says, *"By wisdom a house is built, and by understanding it is established; and by knowledge the rooms are filled with all precious and pleasant riches."*

Diversification

I don't think I can overemphasize the need to *diversify* your retirement funds. I will discuss some of the more practical ways to do this later, but at this point I would like to discuss the dangers of leaving your funds in one company's stock.

Many retirees have worked for the same company for many years—some for their entire lives. As a result, the majority of their retirement funds have been invested in their company's stock. This may or may not have been the best investment over the years, but often it was the only option provided or the company promoted it by offering matching funds in its own stock. However, after retirement the idea of leaving the majority of your assets in a single company's stock, no matter what company it is, makes no real sense.

Any company can fail, and many long-time companies do fail regularly. The economy shifts, and their area of expertise can fade. The company founder (who may have been the driving force behind the company's success) can die, and the whole nature of the company can change.

I don't care how successful your investment in a company's stock has been prior to retirement, the risk is just too great when you no longer have the income flexibility you did in earlier years.

I don't advise that you immediately go and sell all the stock you were issued. Timing in the sale of stock is often critical but, as time and the market make it possible, the ratio of one company's stock to the rest of your assets should be reduced to a level where if it dropped by 50 percent you could still maintain your lifestyle. Even then you should keep a close watch on the company and convert more if there is any significant downward trend.

I recall vividly a friend who had worked for Rich's Department Stores most of his adult life. He literally had grown up with the company as it expanded from one store in Atlanta to a sizeable chain of stores. The bulk of his net worth was held in Rich's stock, which had grown from a total investment of perhaps $25,000 to more than $600,000.

After retiring in 1980, he continued to hold the majority of his retirement income in Rich's stock, despite all of my efforts to persuade him to convert at least half of it. With the country on a "roll" in the mid-eighties, his stock continued to grow and the dividends grew accordingly. My counsel looked pretty weak then.

In 1986 Rich's sold out to the Federated Department Stores chain—a large national chain that included prestigious stores such as Bloomingdales and Macys. Unfortunately, much of Federated's expansion was accomplished with junk bond sales and, in 1990, the chain was in serious financial trouble. By 1991 they had filed for bankruptcy protection. My friend lost more than half of his total asset base before his stock could be sold—a very harsh lesson on the need to diversify.

The advice Solomon offered three thousand years ago is still just as sound today: *"Divide your portion to seven, or even to eight, for you do not know what misfortune may occur on the earth"* (Ecclesiastes 11:2).

7

Insurance Decisions

There is no substitute for knowledge when shopping for insurance; you need to know what you're looking for and what you're willing and able to afford. The principle in insurance is: Don't pay someone else to provide what you can provide for yourself.

This is not a discussion on whether term insurance is better than whole life, or whether a single premium plan is preferable to monthly payments. That type of information has been fully discussed in many other publications, several of which are referenced in the Appendix. Instead, what I would like to discuss is the need for insurance after retirement and some logical alternatives to the ever-rising costs.

A counselee I'll call Scott came to see me shortly after he retired from the Martin Marietta company, where he had worked as a technician for nearly thirty years.

During that time he had invested regularly in the company's employee benefits plan, into which he put 5 percent of his salary, and the company matched it with an additional 2.5 percent. During his working years this fund had grown to just over $200,000 in value. Scott elected to take his retirement as a lump sum, which he put into an IRA and invested it in CDs. That obviously was not the last word in investment planning, but it was an easily workable short-term solution.

Throughout Scott's working career his employer had provided his health insurance, life insurance, and disability insurance. A case could be made that he would no longer need the disability insurance since he would be retiring, but what about the health and life?

Scott's wife was three years younger than him, and although she worked full-time, her income would cover less than half of her actual monthly expenses in the event of Scott's death. Even after she could qualify for retirement on her own, they would not be able to live totally on retirement benefits. Scott would have to earn some income to supplement their savings and Social Security. But the immediate need was for some life insurance to bridge the gap between the time he retired and his wife turned 62.

Those whose total insurance needs are covered by a company plan should consider carrying another policy on their own.

I calculated that Scott would need approximately $100,000 in life insurance to adequately provide for his wife if he died. After further discussion I learned that Scott had suffered a heart attack several years earlier, and although he had no reoccurrence, he was still rated a high risk for insurance purposes. He also told me he was a mild diabetic and required periodic treatment, which certainly eliminated any chance that he would qualify for life insurance. The vast majority of companies exclude pre-existing diabetics and heart patients from their list of acceptable clients. I realized that additional life insurance was not possible.

We also examined the possibility of continuing the company-provided life insurance and found that it was not an option either. Since we had explored every life insurance alternative available and came up empty, I moved on to the next area: health insurance.

Some life insurance on Scott would have been nice, but the greater and more immediate need was for health insurance since Scott would not qualify for Medicare coverage until age 65.

We explored the prospect of getting Scott covered under his wife's company policy since it also offered a group insurance plan. Unfortunately, she lost the option to cover Scott's pre-existing conditions because he wasn't covered during the first thirty days of her employment. So that alternative was out too.

It is a certainty that health care and the related costs will undergo some significant changes in the next few years.

The last possibility was that Scott could continue his company health insurance under the Comprehensive Omnibus Budget Reconciliation Act (COBRA). Under this law an employee is allowed to continue the company health insurance plan for up to eighteen months (thirty-six months in some instances) after leaving the company.

Fortunately for Scott, he was still within the option period and could continue the coverage at the employer's group insurance rate. The real shocker came when Scott heard the cost: $425 a month!

It was fortunate for Scott that they were able to obtain this coverage until he could qualify for Medicare because within a year after retirement his diabetes flared up, causing a greater problem that resulted in drug bills of nearly $500 a month, plus the doctor and hospital bills.

Scott's problems with life and health insurance could have been resolved with some preplanning. Those whose total insurance needs are covered by a company plan should consider carrying another policy on their own. Obviously, few people can afford two health policies, but Scott could have been added to his wife's plan for less than $25 a month initially. His history of diabetes would indicate the need for this precaution. The bottom line is: Think ahead. Usually once you retire it's too late to do much planning. As Proverbs 22:3 says: *"The prudent sees the evil and hides himself, but the naive go on, and are punished for it."*

Health Insurance

Of all the potential problems facing retirees in the future, nothing looms larger than medical expenses. With the average cost of a five-day hospital bill at approximately $6,000 for relatively minor problems, these expenses can quickly plunge a retiree into long-term debt.

As I said earlier, it is a certainty that health care and the related costs will undergo some significant changes in the next few years. I wish it were possible to predict exactly what those changes will be; it would make writing this book much easier. At present, however, no one has even the slightest idea what direction health care provision will take.

The cost of providing health insurance as a retirement benefit is too expensive for most companies to justify, especially if the retiree has access to Medicare.

The possibilities range all the way from total socialization of the medical industry to requiring insurance companies to accept all applicants. In my opinion, either of these probably would raise the cost of insurance and lower the caliber of service. But most certainly, some reform must be made in Medicare.

Medicare is any insurance provider's worst nightmare; it is also any government's nightmare. Just think of the problems from the side of the insurer which, in this case, is the American taxpayer.

First, the system is designed to insure the highest risk group in America: the aged.

Second, women are a higher risk group for health care than men are—particularly older women—and a high percentage of the people on Medicare are women. *Note:* The reason older women are a higher risk group than men is because men tend not to use health services as frequently. However the high death rate among men before the age of 65 indicates that men should see a doctor more regularly.

Third, the Medicare program is administered by the least efficient sector of our economy: the federal government.

Fourth, if individuals tend to treat an insurance company's money as less precious than their own (which they do), they absolutely will devalue health care funds provided by the government.

All of these factors point to some very severe changes in the Medicare system before the turn of the century. I would like to project what I believe the minimum changes will be.

*Investing in a Medicare supplemental insurance plan would
be wise, even for those who have these costs paid through a
company-provided plan right now.*

Medicare will be lumped into some form of national health
care plan where only authorized doctors and hospitals will participate. This will greatly curtail services as well as costs. It may well
be that government health maintenance organizations (HMOs) will
be created to treat the indigent and the aged, while private doctors and hospitals will operate on the current free market system.
The model for this already exists in the form of V.A. hospitals. As
one of our more lucid politicians said recently: "When you step
through the door of a state-run facility, you will be facing a cadre
of government bureaucrats pretending to be health care providers."

I can only guess at the direction retirees' health care will take
because of the current impasse in Washington. One side stands
firmly committed to a government-orchestrated plan. The other
side is just as committed to a private-sector-run plan. I have therefore concluded that, in typical government fashion, we will have
both. Only time will tell if this is a valid assumption.

It would also seem probable that many restrictions, or caps,
will be placed on the Medicare plan, regardless of whether it is
public or private. There is simply no way the Social Security system can absorb the increases that an aging population will bring.
Let's pray that our society doesn't seek the less costly remedy
called euthanasia.

Company Health Plans

Many former executives have their health insurance benefits continued into the retirement years. There is no question that this is a
great benefit in our present economy, in which the cost of health
care is rising faster than almost any other commodity. There is also
little doubt that many companies will be trying to drop this bene-

fit, especially if the company is involved in a merger or buyout. Quite simply the cost of providing health insurance as a retirement benefit is too expensive for most companies to justify, especially if the retiree has access to Medicare.

Recently bankruptcy judges have tended to side with the companies that drop the health care benefits for retirees, even where a contract for these benefits exists.

I bring this up only because the few people who have this benefit should take a realistic view of the future. The trend in American business is generally down, and the trend in long-term retirement benefits is definitely down. Investing in a Medicare supplemental insurance plan would be wise, even for those who have these costs paid through a company-provided plan right now. You may not be able to qualify for the supplement later.

Supplemental Insurance (Medigap Insurance)

Medicare is divided into two basic elements: Part A—hospitalization, and Part B—medical. Since both plans have specific stop limits and deductible amounts that the Medicare patient must absorb, many retirees have found it prudent to purchase a supplemental insurance policy to help cover these expenses. These plans are generally known as *medigap* policies. Since retirees are a large potential market for unscrupulous sales people, many worthless policies have been sold. Discerning the good from the bad is extremely important to your pocketbook.

A thorough review of the limitations of Medicare is vital to selecting the right supplemental policy.

There is no substitute for knowledge when shopping for insurance; you need to know what you're looking for and what you're willing and able to afford. The principle in insurance is: Don't pay someone else to provide what you can provide for yourself.

Covering every out-of-pocket cost is going to be very expensive—and unnecessary. What you want is a policy that will cover the major expenses that can wreck your finances at a time when you can least afford it. Since Medicare Part A and Part B cover most normal expenses, you want a policy that will cover the abnormal. For example, you may want the 20 percent deductible of Part B covered by a supplemental policy that will reimburse you on an 80/20 basis. In other words, it will pay 80 percent of the 20 percent not covered by Medicare. So your actual out-of-pocket costs are about 4 percent of what Medicare won't pay. Also, since Part A limits the number of days in the hospital that Medicare will pay, your policy should pick up that expense after Medicare stops. A single day in the hospital often runs upwards of $500. In intensive care the cost can be $2,000 a day or more. That will put a dent in most any retiree's budget.

A thorough review of the limitations of Medicare is vital to selecting the right supplemental policy. I will summarize these shortly. If you have further questions, I would recommend you purchase a copy of Faustin Jehle's book, *The Complete and Easy Guide to Social Security and Medicare.* I believe it is the most complete and comprehensive book available on this subject.

There are several critical factors in selecting the right supplemental insurance policy, in addition to what coverage the plan offers. The best coverage in the world is useless if the company won't pay off when the need arises.

1. Always check with one or more of the insurance company rating services listed in the Appendix. Normally this is as simple as going to your local public library and looking at a current report. Some of the services will verify the rating of a company by telephone for a fee.

   Verifying a company's rating over the previous three or four years is also important. A company that has been downgraded several times usually reflects a history of losses. A lower-rated company's policies may be cheaper, but its longevity may be in question.

2. Take the time to write the state insurance commissioner's office in the insurance company's home state. Ask about complaints against the company—especially failure to pay claims.

3. Carefully review the contract and particularly your right to renew in the event of claims. Sometimes low-dollar companies reserve the right to cancel your policy for excessive claims. If they have this right, your policy can be canceled at the time when you need it most.

Also verify the renewal premium clause. If the company can increase your premiums based on use, it can price you out of the market. *Note:* Although most states have specific limits on what the increases can be, this is a very difficult area to enforce. It has been my observation that by the time you get someone in the insurance commissioner's office to respond, it's too little too late.

The following is a brief summary of what Medicare A&B do not cover (at the present time). Be certain that your medigap insurance policy addresses these areas. What you don't want is a policy that only covers things like elephants falling out of trees on you.

- Medicare has a 20 percent deductible charge for hospitalization after 20 days of in-patient care.
- Medicare will not presently pay any in-hospital costs after 100 days of care.
- Medicare will not pay for nursing home care in "nonskilled nursing home facilities." Medicare pays only for skilled nursing home care. Nearly 80 percent of all nursing homes do not qualify as skilled care units.
- In-home nursing care is excluded by Medicare.
- Blood transfusions beyond the initial three pints are excluded. This is very important in operations such as bypass surgery.

- The 20 percent deductible under Medicare Plan B for doctors and medicines, as well as routine services, such as immunizations and ear and eye exams, are not covered under Medicare.

Obviously you may not wish to provide insurance for all of these excluded expenses. Total-coverage policies can often run hundreds of dollars a month. But this list will at least aid you in evaluating the various policies offered by different companies.

Note: It is illegal for anyone to knowingly sell you more than one medigap insurance policy. Usually these policies are mutually exclusive and will not pay for the same expenses. Salespeople who knowingly violate this law are subject to a $25,000 fine.

Nursing Home Insurance

With long-term care now costing from $30,000 to $60,000 a year, older persons (especially retirees) must consider how the cost of nursing home care would be funded for themselves or their loved ones. The requirement under Medicare is that the facility be a skilled care unit in order to qualify for benefits. As previously noted, only about 20 percent of all nursing care facilities in the U.S. meet this requirement.

Long-term-care insurance is not for everyone. Something less than 15 percent of all retirees require a full-care facility at any time during their lives.

Medicaid, the state-run health care plan, will pay for nursing home care only in the case of indigent people. This requires that a patient's own assets (other than a home) be exhausted before the state will step in. In recent years these rules have been relaxed to allow the spouse to retain one half of the assets up to a specified amount (usually $60,000). But this exclusion varies state by state. Even under the best of circumstances this leaves very little in the way of long-term financial security for older people.

A word of spiritual admonition: Many people, Christians included, try to avoid the legal restrictions placed on Medicaid patients by transferring assets so that a family member appears to be indigent, and thus qualifies. This is unethical, as well as often illegal, not to mention very unscriptural.

There are companies that now specialize in aiding older people and their families in doing this. Remember, although the government may never detect the fraud, the Lord already has. Honesty in our society today often is deemed "not getting caught." Honesty in God's sight is doing what is right when no one else will ever know. As Joshua said, *"Choose for yourselves today whom you will serve . . . but as for me and my house, we will serve the Lord"* (24:15).

The most common ethical alternative to Medicaid at present is the purchase of an insurance policy that will pay the costs of nursing home care. Since this type of policy is relatively new, there are only a few *major* companies offering them, and the opportunity for fraud and abuse is considerable.

Long-term-care insurance is not for everyone. Something less than 15 percent of all retirees require a full-care facility at any time during their lives. With much attention focused on the financial plight of the few who need such care, it is easy to overreact. A great deal of counsel and prayer should go into this decision.

The costs of long-term-care policies are understandably expensive. The insurance companies are taking on enormous risks and ever-escalating costs. Insurance companies are in the business to make a profit, so they simply calculate the expected costs and price the policies to cover costs, plus a reasonable profit.

> *You should select a company that has been in the health care business for at least twenty years.*

As would be expected, the premiums on long-term-care policies increase with the age of the insured. A typical policy can cost $1,800 a year for a 65-year-old person, $2,500 for a 70-year-old, and

$4,400 for a 75-year-old, according to a 1992 report from the Seniors' Health Cooperative.

Retirees with total assets of $50,000 or less would quickly consume their asset base in annual premiums. The cumulative cost of long-term-care insurance between the ages of 65 and 75 would be something just over $30,000. Since the probability of nursing home care really begins after the age of 75, the cost of most nursing home policies escalates rapidly beyond this age. To presently provide coverage for a couple to age 75 would cost in excess of $60,000, with no assurance that the costs would not run twice that, due to inflation in the nursing home industry.

Since the Spousal Impoverishment legislation allows the non-confined spouse to retain ownership of the home, car, and other personal assets, as well as up to $62,000 in cash, the use of total-care insurance for couples with modest assets does not seem logical.

If your asset base is in excess of $100,000, excluding your home, you may want to consider this insurance. If so, there are some basic elements you will want to look for in a policy.

1. *Company stability.* Just as I mentioned earlier, if the company isn't around when you need it, you wasted your money; so verify the quality of the issuing company.

2. *Time in the business.* You should select a company that has been in the health care business for at least twenty years. Many new companies jump into a growing industry, only to withdraw later because they did not anticipate the costs. Go with a company that has been writing health care policies—especially long-term health care—for at least two decades; there aren't many. You'll find a list of some of the older companies in the Appendix.

3. *Coverage.* The policy should pay at least 80 percent of the average daily cost of a nursing home facility. *Note:* Often you can negotiate with a facility to accept the amount provided by the insurance policy as payment in full.

4. *Provisions.* The policy should have an automatic inflation provision to cover the increasing costs while the insured is in the care facility. Otherwise, just the inflating costs can consume all of your assets, which is precisely what you bought the policy to avoid.

5. *Payment plans.* Always take the waiver-of-premium option in a long-term-care policy. You don't want to be stuck with continuing payments that may escalate rapidly with no choice but to pay them, as would be the case if you or your spouse were in a nursing home.

Summary

Long-term-care insurance is not for everyone, just as disability insurance is not for everyone. The vast majority of retirees will not need to be confined to a nursing home. For those with limited assets, the cost of protection outweighs the risk of asset depletion. For those with discretionary assets of more than $100,000, and certainly for those with assets in excess of $200,000, the cost of an insurance policy may be justified when weighed against the cost of nursing home care for several years. But pray about this decision and ask God for His wisdom. Remember what the apostle James said in James 1:5: *"But if any of you lacks wisdom, let him ask of God, who gives to all men generously and without reproach, and it will be given to him."*

> *[Those] who are not yet in their retirement years . . . need to consider carefully the need for life insurance . . . and prepare while [they're] still young.*

Life Insurance

It is not uncommon for people approaching retirement age to suddenly realize that after they retire they will still need some life insurance. If you're still healthy, the situation is not so critical. However, if you have any pre-existing conditions, you'll probably either be rated in a higher risk category or denied coverage altogether. Unfortunately, there is very little that can be done if you are not insurable, so I'll concentrate on the options available to those who are.

For those who are not yet in their retirement years, I would counsel that you need to consider carefully the need for life insurance in your sixties and seventies (or older) and prepare while you're still young.

Term or Whole Life

No insurance, term or whole life, is going to be inexpensive for people in their sixties or older. All insurance companies operate from actuarial tables that predict the probabilities of death, and it is a fact that the older we get, the closer to death we get.

> *No one insurance plan fits every person or situation, regardless of what any whole life or term salesperson says.*

Those who purchased whole life insurance in their younger years are paying less for it in their later years only because they have paid for a longer period of time. Meanwhile the insurance companies have had the use of their excess premiums for that period of time. But for those who are in need of additional coverage, the decision is: Should you buy term or whole life beyond the age of 60?

The same general principles apply at 60 plus that applied at age 30.

Term insurance (at any age) initially is cheaper than policies that build cash reserves. Quite simply, term is cheaper because you "rent" the coverage based on your current age. The cash value policy must average the cost per year over your total life expectancy.

Let me use a simplistic example. Let's assume a 65 year old man wants to buy a $10,000 whole life policy and his life expectancy is nine years. The insurance company estimates what it can earn on his premiums for the next nine years and prices the policy accordingly. For the sake of discussion, let's assume the total premium is $8,000, or $800 a year.

But since the risk goes up as the insured ages, this person might be able to buy a one year (annual) term policy at age 65 for $400. The next year, however, the rate would increase to reflect his increased age and might cost $450; the next year it would be $500, and so on until, by age 70, he would be paying $1,500 a year. **(The amounts used are illustrative, not actual.)**

If the need for insurance is temporary, such as providing a bridge policy until his wife is 65 (in three years), then the term plan would serve his needs best. If the need for insurance exists for the rest of his life, he would be better served with the whole life plan. No one insurance plan fits every person or situation, regardless of what any whole life or term salesperson says.

In order to buy the correct policy you must first determine your needs. Then contact at least two independent agents who sell both term and whole life and have them present the cost breakdown of their best products. Personally I would also check the annual insurance edition of *Consumer Reports* magazine to verify which companies are rated the best in terms of cost and financial solvency. And as previously recommended, verify the rating of any company you plan to use through one of the national rating services listed in the Appendix.

Television Policies

I'm often asked about the value of life insurance policies sold by celebrities on television. In large part, these are middle-of-the-road term policies. They are neither better nor worse than many products sold by local agents; they are only marketed better.

One principle you always need to bear in mind is: There is no free lunch when it comes to buying insurance. Many of these plans advertise "You can't be turned down—for any reason." The way the company can offer this guarantee is by requiring a two-year exclusion period during which the policy will not pay (this eliminates most terminally ill clients). The policies are usually higher in cost than those available through a local agent, and they either escalate in cost or decline in face value. In general, you will do better with a local agent.

Cancer Policies

The threat of cancer, and its related medical costs, has given rise to special insurance policies commonly called cancer policies. These policies are normally sold as riders (or supplemental plans) to your normal health insurance plan, including Medicare. Normally they are very specific in their coverage and, in fact, this is perhaps their greatest limitation.

> *As a general rule, those facing retirement do not need disability insurance since their incomes will be independent of a regular job [though they may need a] disability policy to provide some "gap" coverage until [they] qualify for Social Security benefits.*

There is not just one type of cancer, but rather many varieties—all the way from leukemia to epidermal melanoma (skin cancer). If you elect to purchase a cancer policy you need to be sure that the wording in your contract is broad enough to cover any type of cancer treatment.

Virtually no insurance policy will provide for treatments not approved by the American Medical Association (AMA). This includes a variety of herbal and vitamin therapies used in other countries, generally by non-licensed practitioners.

In general, the insurance agents I consulted advise against cancer policies, except in instances where clients have a high incidence of cancer in their immediate families. Obviously the insurance companies also realize their exposure is higher in such cases, so they will either charge a higher fee or deny coverage based on family history.

Disability Insurance

As a general rule, those facing retirement do not need disability insurance since their incomes will be independent of a regular job.

However, in one of the earlier examples the wage earner had the need for a disability policy to provide some "gap" coverage until he could qualify for Social Security benefits.

If you feel the need for disability insurance, a few simple rules may help you make the right choice.

1. Look for a plan that satisfies your precise need. If you only need coverage for three or four years, the policy should be a term plan with a fixed cost per year.

2. Most disability policies will exclude pre-existing conditions for at least one to two years (except for non-qualifying group plans). This is usually true even if your pre-existing condition occurred several years earlier. So be certain what is covered and what is excluded before you pay your first premium. There is absolutely no substitute for reading and understanding the policy. The insurance company is bound only by the terms of your written contract, not by what your agent tells you.

3. Check the quality of your policy (and company) with an independent source. I usually recommend the annual insurance report from *Consumer Reports* magazine. Most public libraries will have a copy on file.

Other Insurance Needs

Your need for home, auto, and other types of insurance do not normally change as a result of retirement, unless your lifestyle changes drastically. Therefore your coverage also will not change significantly. About the only recommendation I can make is to investigate alternative sources of insurance, such as the American Association of Retired Persons (AARP), or the Government Employees' Insurance Company (GEICO). GEICO is one of several preferred companies for auto, home, and life insurance. Both are listed in the Appendix.

*Be certain that you carry adequate liability limits on all of
your home and auto policies.*

These are available to you before retirement, but if you are
retired, often the rates will drop accordingly. Most retirees are
better risks because they stay at home more, and are not involved
in rush hour traffic on a daily basis. One additional bit of information is necessary: Because you are facing retirement, your attitude
needs to be one of preservation of capital. A major lawsuit can
strip you of assets at a time when they cannot be replaced. Be
certain that you carry adequate liability limits on all of your home
and auto policies. I would suggest also that you carry an umbrella
policy that will extend your liability limits to $1 million or more. If
you use the same company for both your home and auto insurance, you can usually purchase an umbrella policy for a very reasonable fee in most areas of the country. Failure to carry adequate
liability insurance in our litigating society is "penny wise and
pound foolish," in my opinion.

Alternatives to Insurance

For those who cannot acquire insurance, or cannot afford it, there
are ways to reduce some of the after-death costs—specifically
burial expenses. With the cost of a basic funeral running $4,000 to
$6,000, it is good stewardship to plan ahead. Too often even Chris-
tians avoid planning in this area because they don't want to face
the realities of dying. As best I know, dying is not an option for any
of us, and planning can greatly reduce the financial and emotional
burden on your loved ones.

There are two alternatives to costly funeral expenses for most
of us: joining a memorial society, or prepaying the funeral expenses.

The Memorial Society is a nationwide, nonprofit organization
that specializes in low-cost funeral arrangements. I belong to the
Georgia Memorial Society chapter, which is a part of the national

group. By joining the society and prepaying a small fee ($25) I am then guaranteed a greatly reduced funeral at participating funeral homes. At present the cost of a funeral through the society is approximately $600. You can contact one of the Society's affiliates in your state by looking under "Memorial Societies" in your telephone business directory.

There are some restrictions associated with this type of service, including transportation and the cost of caskets. But for those who don't desire an elaborate funeral, it is an excellent option.

A national service, such as the Memorial Society, simply prearranges for basic burial costs at a reduced rate. You can prearrange funeral and burial services with most local funeral homes, if you desire. By doing so in advance the costs are usually greatly reduced. The average cost in a pre-arranged funeral is often half of what it would be if contracted immediately after death. You might logically ask, "Why not join the Memorial Society and further reduce the costs?" The reason is the Memorial Society has a limited number of participating funeral homes. You may choose to use one closer to your residence.

One significant benefit of pre-arranged funerals is that family members are saved the emotional grief of dealing with these issues immediately after the death of a loved one.

If you elect to prearrange for a funeral, be sure that the funds are kept in an escrow account by the funeral home. I have counseled many couples who prepaid for such expenses, only to discover that the funeral home spent the money and later went out of business—in which case the clients lost their money.

Use of a Cafeteria Plan

If you decide to work part time after retirement, either for another company or for yourself, there is an opportunity worth investigating: the 125 plan (often called a Cafeteria Plan).

A Section 125 (IRS code identification) allows employees to have a portion of their incomes (up to 100 percent) directed to a tax exempt fund in which the proceeds can be used to pay for medical, dental, optical, and other related expenses.

This means that if you work for a company (your own or otherwise), you can designate up to *100 percent* of your income into an account excluded from federal, state, and FICA taxes, provided those funds are used only to pay for medical expenses. These funds will not affect your qualification for Social Security benefits since they will not be reported as earned income.

If you decide to start your own corporation after retiring, you can establish a 125 plan of your own. I recommend that you contact an advisory group specializing in these plans to assist in the details. The paperwork is relatively uncomplicated and well within the capabilities of most people to administer with little help. A company that handles these accounts is provided in the Appendix.

The only prohibition on the use of 125 funds is that *all* allocated funds must be used each year or they revert to the parent company. That will not represent a problem if you also own the company; if you don't, you'll need to be sure you allocated approximately what you know you will be able to utilize.

I know several retirees who utilize the 125 plan to pay for virtually all of their non-reimbursed medical expenses. One of my neighbors works ten hours a week for a company and assigns all of his income to the 125 account. It's a good deal for both sides since he uses the funds to pay for all of his and his wife's medical expenses, and the company doesn't have to pay FICA or workers' compensation on his wages.

8

Reducing Overhead in Retirement

Retirees are a formidable group, and many more services are opening up to meet their needs. Usually these are volunteer organizations manned by the older people who want to stay active—a concept I heartily support (as does God's Word).

DURING THE SIXTIES and seventies most Americans thought of retirees as the old people who are no longer a part of the system, but that's no longer true. Americans over age 60 are now the largest voting block in the nation, representing nearly one out of every four registered voters. They also dominate the thinking of most politicians in our country simply because, unlike many others, they *do* vote.

Many industries now specifically target their products to this group of older Americans. They may not be the biggest buyers of durable goods such as refrigerators, washing machines, or sports cars (like the younger generations are) but they dominate the travel, health, and investment industry's lists of top clients.

In many ways older Americans today are doing a disservice to the younger generations. They have more time and often more money to support the causes that benefit them directly. Too often this means placing more of the financial burden on the working group of younger Americans to support programs aimed solely at helping retirees, such as Medicare. I don't mean to imply that retirees shouldn't have adequate health care provided, but they must also consider the economic impact these programs have on our economy and be willing to bear a larger portion of the costs themselves. Some can't, but many can.

As our economy runs out of options to fund programs for retirees, we will almost certainly see changes like "means testing" applied to Medicare and perhaps to retirement benefits. Many retirees argue that they paid for their benefits in their working careers but, for many, the benefits of programs like Medicare didn't even exist when they were contributing.

Be that as it may, retirees are a formidable group, and many more services are opening up to meet their needs. Usually these are volunteer organizations manned by the older people who want to stay active—a concept I heartily support (as does God's Word).

The physical needs of older people are important, but the spiritual needs are absolutely critical!

I would like to mention a few organizations that operate on a national level to help older people. Some of the services are oriented to those who lack the resources to pay for the help they need. Others are available to anyone.

Meals on Wheels

Not long ago my own mother suffered a broken pelvis as a result of a fall. Since she was unable to take care of herself for a period of time, a group in her community known as Meals on Wheels brought her hot meals daily. They provided enough so that my stepfather could save some from the noon meal for their evening meal. This, along with the help my sister provided in the evenings, kept her well fed (malnutrition is one of the biggest problems with shut-ins).

If we had been paying for the service that Meals on Wheels provided, it would have cost several hundred dollars a month. Since we could pay something, we donated the cost of the food and gas for the vehicles to help someone else. All of the labor involved in Meals on Wheels is provided by volunteers who take turns helping those who cannot help themselves.

There are many such service organizations available in almost every community. I heartily encourage you to make contact with them, support them financially, and donate some time if you can. (See "Programs for Older People" in the Appendix.)

Church Help

I wish that more older Christians would get involved in the lives of retirees outside of their own churches. The ministry that can be accomplished by showing concern for the physical needs of retirees is demonstrable in any church that takes the time to do it.

The physical needs of older people are important, but the spiritual needs are absolutely critical! When we help someone in the name of the Lord, it often opens the door to sharing the message of salvation. That will last for an eternity. Too often we are so busy in the church we neglect the opportunity to reach the unsaved. In Matthew 25 the Lord equated meeting physical needs with spiritual commitment. His words are a strong admonition to help others in need. *"And the King will answer and say to them, 'Truly I say to you, to the extent that you did it to one of these brothers of Mine, even the least of them, you did it to Me'"* (Matthew 25:40).

I have been to a church in the Northeast that takes James's instructions as a command, *"If a brother or sister is without clothing and in need of daily food, and one of you says to them, 'Go in peace, be warmed and be filled,' and yet you do not give them what is necessary for their body, what use is that?"* (James 2:15-16). If I understand correctly what this says, we are to be involved in the physical needs of those around us; this church I mentioned does just that.

Several years ago the pastor was confronted with a situation that ultimately led to a new church ministry. A woman from his congregation had been preparing meals for some elderly people living near her home. She had learned of their needs from her daughter, who worked at the county health clinic.

Too often we think that any program, to be effective, somehow has to be linked to government aid or at least done on a large scale.

Often friends would bring these older people to the clinic for treatment. The most common ailment the doctors at the clinic had to deal with was malnutrition. Usually those who were malnourished lived by themselves and either lacked the funds to buy adequate food, or they lacked the physical ability to prepare it. The county had no facility to provide meals for shut-ins. This lady took it upon herself to begin a home food service, providing meals at least once a day for six older people.

She came to the pastor after her ministry had grown to the point that she could no longer do it out of her home—both in time and costs. She asked the pastor if she could use the church's kitchen facility during the week when it was idle. The pastor not only agreed, he also preached a sermon on the principle of being a servant to others and challenged his congregation to get involved.

As a result of this rather meager beginning, this church has developed a county-wide program to help older retirees in their community. They minister to more than 100 elderly shut-ins every day.

The church has one group that prepares and delivers the food; another provides in-home health services for those who are injured or bedridden. Another group does home cleaning and minor repair work. The purpose is to help meet the physical needs of these neighbors, but the greater goal is to meet their spiritual needs as well.

Too often we think that any program, to be effective, somehow has to be linked to government aid or at least done on a large scale. That simply is not so. Virtually every program from the Salvation Army to the Red Cross was begun by the efforts of one person. Get involved in your own community.

The American Association of Retired Persons (AARP)

Most Americans are familiar with the AARP. If you have stayed in a motel in the last ten years, you've probably been asked if you are a member of the AARP. If you're more than 50, the motel usually offers a reduced rate. The same is true of many restaurants and other establishments.

The AARP was founded in 1963 by retired teacher Dr. Ethel Percy Andrus in Los Angeles and now has over thirty-one million members. The political clout of the AARP members can be felt in any legislation affecting older people that comes up before the Congress. I guess the term "older" is relative anymore since the AARP accepts anyone 50 or older for membership.

The list of products and services available to AARP members fills a sixty-four page catalog the association publishes. The benefits range from information on housing and automobiles to preparing income taxes. There are some 3,600 chapters of the AARP around the country, utilizing nearly 500,000 volunteers to do everything from election campaigning to seminars on how to budget in retirement (a good idea).

In selecting the insurance plan you need for health, life, or nursing homes, the AARP has an assortment of informative brochures for little or no cost. After having reviewed much of the information the association provides, I found the services to be extremely helpful and reasonably priced.

The balance on the other side is that too often the AARP seeks an agenda contrary to the best interests of the younger generation. Unless the costs of Social Security and Medicare can be brought under control, the workers of the early twenty-first century will be paying 40 percent or more of their incomes to support it.

Obviously few people, young or old, want to see the system modified to the point that current retirees are put out of the system, but some compromise is necessary. There is absolutely no way that the automatic cost-of-living increases can be maintained without destroying the financial lives of young families.

I say this to encourage you to take a reasonable stand as a current or prospective retiree. Think about the well-being of the entire country, not just retirees.

County Services

A system of local community help exists outside of Medicare and Medicaid that has been around a lot longer than either of those programs. In some communities it is called community services and includes health clinics that administer minimal health services, transportation for those who cannot drive themselves, and even emergency help for bedridden patients.

In our community the county operates a fleet of vans that pick up and deliver older people to the doctor, library, grocery stores, and other locations where they can help themselves. They administer flu shots for the elderly (and young), as well as help to organize retirees to speak to public schools as experts on a variety of topics.

A check of the yellow pages in your area will help you to locate these services. If you don't presently have a need for the help they offer, perhaps you will be able to help them do their jobs by volunteering some time.

The Advantage of Location

Just as it is easier to rent a boat in an area with lots of water, so too it's easier to locate retirement services in an area with lots of retirees. The principle is really pretty simple: If you need help after retirement, go to a place that has plenty of retirees—such as Arizona, California, or Florida.

Having grown up in Florida, I can attest to the fact that many of the services offered are geared to retirees and their lower incomes. Obviously there are exceptions, such as West Palm Beach where the more wealthy retirees locate. In these areas it is actually harder to live on a modest retirement income because the wealthier retirees have so much to spend that they bid up the services (as well as the tax base and property values). But as you move up the state into areas such as Sarasota, Bradenton, and Leesburg, you'll find more modest income retirees.

If your lifestyle allows you to relocate, or live in a non-income-tax state for at least six months a year, it can save you some money.

In these areas it is possible to live on less because the services are oriented to lower incomes; and when you locate around people of like means, the pressure to compete is lessened somewhat. For instance, although it's not fashionable to live in a mobile home in West Palm Beach, in Leesburg it's both fashionable and normal; the community abounds with them. For retirees who have sold their more expensive homes in other areas, buying a mobile home and investing the residual can greatly enhance their retirement years. And, contrary to popular opinion, mobile homes do not attract tornadoes. It's just that when a park is hit by a tornado the damage is severe and attracts a lot of media attention.

Many states have purposely tried to attract retirees through lower state taxes, including income, real estate, and inheritance taxes. Since the tax base in an area can be of great importance to retirees who can live wherever they want, I would like to focus on this subject for a moment.

Income taxes. At present there are eight states that have no personal income tax: Florida, Tennessee, Alaska, Nevada, South Dakota, Texas, Washington, and Wyoming. If you live in a state that does assess state income taxes, you know what an overhead this can be on a fixed income.

The legalities of establishing residency in any state normally requires living there six months and a day, plus being a registered voter in that state. If your lifestyle allows you to relocate, or live in a non-income-tax state for at least six months a year, it can save you some money.

State Inheritance Taxes. An additional consideration is the tax a state levies on your assets at death. In general, most states allow the same exemptions the federal tax codes provide, so estates of

$600,000 or less are exempt. But the states that don't make this allowance can take a sizeable portion of your estate assets. The following chart shows how the various states treat assets upon the owner's death.

As you can see, choosing the state of residence in which you plan to live out your life can be of benefit to your heirs. At present, the states of Massachusetts, Louisiana, New York, Ohio, Pennsylvania, and Rhode Island are the worst for estate taxes since they also tax the spouse's portion of the estate.

> *If you use a buying club properly . . . it can save you a great deal of money on products you normally buy.*

In addition to inheritance taxes, many states also have fees for probating a will that can run into the thousands of dollars. Check with the office of the Probate Court in your county to verify what the costs are where you live. Good estate planning can help to reduce or eliminate these expenses. You will find more information on this topic in the chapter on estate planning.

Buying Clubs

One great advantage a retiree has over most people who work full-time jobs is time! If you'll take advantage of this asset you can extract some significant savings. Ordinarily I don't recommend buying clubs because the majority of people who join them do so impulsively. Most of them end up ordering things they wouldn't buy ordinarily and, although they actually do save money on the purchases they make, it still costs them more in the long run. The majority of people who join a buying club stop using it within a few months and, consequently, they waste the money they spent on membership fees.

If you use a buying club properly, however, it can save you a great deal of money on products you normally buy. The club that I have investigated and feel is of good quality is listed in the Appen-

State Inheritance Taxes

State	Death tax ($) On $600,000 estate left to: Spouse	Child	State	Death tax ($) On $600,000 estate left to: Spouse	Child
Alabama	None	None	Montana	0	0
Arizona	None	None	Nebraska	0	5,850
Arkansas	None	None	Nevada	None	None
California	None	None	New Hampshire	0	0
Colorado	None	None	New Jersey	0	0
Connecticut	$0	$37,875	New Mexico	None	None
Delaware	0	31,250	New York	25,500	25,500
Dist. of Columbia	None	None	North Carolina	0	7,000
Florida	None	None	North Dakota	None	None
Georgia	None	None	Ohio	$2,100	$30,100
Hawaii	None	None	Oklahoma	0	17,725
Idaho	None	None	Oregon	None	None
Illinois	None	None	Pennsylvania	36,000	36,000
Indiana	0	24,950	Rhode Island	7,900	12,400
Iowa	0	39,825	South Carolina	0	33,000
Kansas	0	21,750	South Dakota	0	41,250
Kentucky	0	45,370	Tennessee	0	0
Louisiana	$17,050	$17,050	Texas	None	None
Maine	None	None	Utah	None	None
Maryland	6,000	6,000	Vermont	None	None
Massachusetts	23,500	55,500	Virginia	None	None
Michigan	0	33,700	Washington	None	None
Minnesota	None	None	West Virginia	None	None
Mississippi	0	1,400	Wisconsin	0	56,250
Missouri	None	None	Wyoming	None	None

dix. This is by no means a complete list, and I'm sure I probably have left out someone's good plan, but I can only comment on plans I know. I could not possibly check out all the plans in existence.

The one feature most of the newer buying clubs offer, which I believe makes them viable, is the ability to ship products directly to your home via one of the parcel services. By utilizing home delivery you can buy nonperishable food goods, garden supplies, household supplies, and other items. If you happen to wear a standard clothing size, you may even find it worthwhile to purchase your clothes this way.

Not only are the prices generally lower from a good buying club but, as of this date, the items purchased out of state are not subject to state sales taxes.

If you're an average-income retiree, a buying club should be able to save you as much as 35 percent on your cost of food, clothes, medicines, household goods, and the like. This translates to about $2,500 a year in savings. Obviously this also means that discipline must be applied to all spending or the savings can quickly be consumed in unnecessary purchases. In other words, you have to live on a *budget* to exact any real savings from a buying club, or any other cost savings idea.

Bartering

An extension of using your best asset (time) is to barter your time for someone else's goods or services. Most Americans do not engage in bartering simply because working Americans have more money than time. This lack of time and availability of money have given rise to the fast food business and to prepared foods. Although these are convenient, they come at a high cost because the buyers are paying others for their labor. As a retiree you can reverse this trend to your own advantage.

I need to emphasize something here: Bartering is *not* an unrealistic concept suitable only for big companies. Few people realize how much bartering takes place naturally in our economy. In the past I have traded counseling services for dental work and books for advertising space. In the business world, such transactions are done regularly. I have a friend who races cars for a living. He regularly trades his promotional abilities for automobiles and other necessities. These are all taxable transactions but usually the taxes amount to less than 40 percent of the value of the products.

As a retiree, you have the time to seek out barters that will benefit both you and the other party. For example, let's assume that your dentist has a child who needs tutoring in math and you're a retired math teacher. The two needs make a perfect match.

Or suppose you visit your friendly family physician and notice that his office could use some painting or redecorating. If you have the time and talent, a deal can be struck that will benefit you both.

I know a retired painter who virtually never pays cash for any dental, medical, or legal work. He simply offers his services to the practitioners who usually have more money than time and are desperate for anyone reliable to do some work around their homes and offices. Ask your dentist or doctor if you don't believe it.

I also know a retiree who offers to baby-sit for her dentist in exchange for his services. Not only does she save the money she would otherwise have to pay for dental care, but she gets about twice the equivalent hourly baby-sitting rate she would if the dentist were having to pay in cash also. Everyone benefits from bartering.

My stepfather took up golf after retiring and became an ardent golf fan. But since he is a retired Navy chief living on a modest retirement income in Florida, the cost of golfing very often is beyond his budget. He has found a way to reduce the costs by offering his services to some pro shops in exchange for green's fees on slack days. It has turned out to be a good arrangement for both since he is a good salesman, and he makes friends quickly.

I particularly like bartering because both parties feel like they get a good deal. In cash transactions, often people will feel cheated; especially if they discover they paid too much, or charged too little. But in a barter situation, you get what you want and the other person gets what he or she wants. So usually both are happy.

I don't generally recommend joining a barter club, however. These clubs exchange goods and services between various groups of people and take a percentage of each transaction. So if you wanted to exchange your time (say painting) you would receive credits that could be used to buy other goods or services you need.

In theory this sounds great; but in practice, most of the barter clubs don't have a wide enough membership to provide the normal products and services most people want. So you end up giving more than you get. Even worse, most of the barter clubs I have known about have gone out of business, leaving many people with nothing to show for their efforts.

If you decide to try bartering, which I heartily recommend, consult with a good accountant in your area about the taxability of the exchanges. As of this date the IRS generally treats any barter as taxable. Remember that your relationship to the Lord is far more important than the small amount of tax that you might save by cheating. As Isaiah 59:2 says, *"But your iniquities have made a separation between you and your God, and your sins have hidden His face from you, so that He does not hear."*

9
Where to Retire

Take at least one year after retiring before you make any relocation decisions.

In THE LAST chapter I discussed briefly some thoughts about where to retire, but I decided that this issue is important enough to warrant more attention.

If you have a choice of where to relocate after retirement, it is important to think through your decision very carefully. I have known many retirees over the years who chose to relocate for a variety of reasons. Some made the right decisions about relocating and loved it. Others made the wrong decisions and lived to regret it, as well as spending a lot of money to correct their errors. There are several important factors involved in deciding where to live after retirement. Some are purely financial and thus quantitative; those I can help you with. But others are emotional and thus qualitative; these require a time of dedicated prayer and are outside of my circle of influence. Whatever you do, don't act hastily or you'll almost certainly live to regret it.

There are three big DON'Ts when it comes to the decision about where to live after retirement.

1. *Don't act out of emotion.* The same mentality that tempts people on vacation to buy into a time-share condo they'll probably never use causes many retirees to rush to Florida, Colorado, or Arizona. It's called *impulse.*
2. *Don't make a hasty decision.* Making quick decisions about anything will get you in trouble most of the time; you can't really trust your feelings. The feeling you get when visiting friends in Florida may make their lives seem idyllic. And per-

haps (in a very few instances) life is ideal for them in Florida. But that does not mean the southern climate will suit your temperament. Take at least one year after retiring before you make any relocation decisions.

3. *Don't think you can escape from the real world.* The pace in most retirement communities is decidedly slower than in most other areas. Usually time is counted on a daily basis rather than hourly. For many people this suits their personalities and they adapt well. But for many new retirees this can often seem like stepping into a geriatric care center. You'll also find that people living in retirement communities have the same problems as everyone else.

Maintaining a Second Home

It's possible that if you have lived all of your life in a cold climate, you long for the warm rays of the Florida sun. But along with the climate comes a proliferation of insect life, bland seasons, and high air conditioning bills. If you're used to a change of season in the fall, as many northerners are, you may find the climate in Florida or Arizona too much of the same all year long.

For some people the balance has been found by maintaining homes in different areas. But for most retirees that is unrealistic for their budgets. Many retirees I have counseled who tried maintaining multiple residences in spite of their limited finances ended up in trouble, and then they couldn't enjoy either place.

The average cost of maintaining a second home, even one that is totally debt-free, is not less than $3,000 a year, and can often run twice that in many areas. If the property is worth $50,000, the loss of earnings on that money makes the real cost more like $10,000 a year!

Relocation is not just a financial decision; it is also an emotional decision.

If you feel that you would like to retire in another state, take at least one year to evaluate it carefully. The rent you pay for a year may be the best money you will ever spend—especially when compared to the cost of moving your belongings across several states and then moving them back again.

Family Ties

If you live close to your children and grandchildren, it's important to assess the emotional effects of moving several states away, even if the lower living costs justify it. I have known many retirees who moved to a state that offered better retirement benefits, only to sell out in a year or two and move back to their home state. Relocation is not just a financial decision; it is also an emotional decision that both husband and wife must pray about before reaching any conclusions.

Employment

If after retiring you decide to relocate in an area saturated with retirees and you need to earn some part-time income, you may find yourself in competition with a lot of other retirees. Usually the job market in these areas is pretty slim. In most instances your best opportunity for employment lies much closer to home.

Most people spend the majority of their lives building relationships in the area where they live and work. These can be essential after retiring if you need extra income. If you have a skill or trade that is marketable anywhere, location probably won't affect you. But in the next decade a retiree who needs to work part time will be the norm, not the exception, in my opinion. So think about how and where you might work and investigate the possibilities thoroughly before selecting a new location.

Other Taxes

I mentioned earlier that several states have no personal income taxes, but there are other taxes to consider, not the least of which are real estate taxes. If you decide to move to another state, carefully study the property tax rates—both county and city. In addition, you need to be conscious of recent trends (especially growth trends) where you locate.

Usually in retirement areas the older people have enough political clout to keep real estate taxes down. Increasingly high taxes can make it virtually impossible for a retiree to maintain a reasonable standard of living.

One of the major issues of the nineties will be safety and security for older Americans.

I have a friend who relocated from Ohio to Gwinett County, Georgia, after selling his business. He chose the North Georgia area because of its moderate but seasonal climate and relatively mild winters (compared to Ohio at least). He also liked the somewhat rural atmosphere, low home prices, and low property taxes.

After selling his home in Ohio, he and his wife were able to purchase an equivalent home in Lawrenceville, Georgia, for about half of what they sold their home for, leaving them more money to invest for retirement income.

What they didn't know in 1976 was that Gwinett County would become the fastest growing county in the U.S. by 1980. As a result of this growth, county services were greatly strained and property taxes had to be increased dramatically. Within five years of moving to Georgia, his property taxes were increased by more than 800 percent! Granted, his property value went up as well, but since he had no intention of selling, this was of small consolation.

Had he chosen a more developed area with many more retirees, they might have banded together to help control the escalation in taxes; unfortunately there were too few retirees in his area to influence the local politicians.

In 1983 he was forced to sell his home and relocate again to another small town—Clayton, Georgia—where he now lives. Since the 1986 Tax Reform Act shut down much of the real estate development in Georgia, he hopes to remain where he is for a long while. If his taxes continue to increase as the state's need for more revenue seems to dictate, he may once again be forced to relocate. "If so," he says, "next time I'll flock in with some other old 'buzzards' who can pressure the politicians not to tax us out of our homes" (an important consideration).

Keep Your Options Open

If you have not yet retired, you need to give some careful consideration to where you intend to spend your retirement years. As you have the opportunity to travel and talk with others, ask some questions pertinent to your future decision:

- What is the weather like?
- What about utility rates?
- What about hospital accessibility and rates?
- What about the availability of geriatric physicians?
- What about real estate taxes?
- What about income taxes?
- What about personal property taxes?
- What about the crime rate?

A negative response on any two or more of these issues should cause you to reevaluate that area as your future retirement location.

One of the major issues of the nineties will be safety and security for older Americans. Crime in the major metropolitan areas is getting worse all the time, and there would appear to be no slackening in sight (short of a spiritual revival). Any retiree would be wise to take this into consideration—especially in areas where major industries are shutting down. God may be calling you to minister in these areas, in which case you should stay there, by all means. But otherwise it may be to your advantage (and safety) to move to a more rural area.

The number of organizations dedicated to improving the overall quality of life for older people has grown from a few to many dozens. A list providing an overview of some of these groups is in the Appendix.

10

Investment Ideas for Retirees

The key to any successful investment strategy is twofold: Be knowledgeable enough to make the most of your own decisions, and diversify to the highest degree possible with the funds you have available.

SINCE I HAVE written a book specifically on investing *(Investing for the Future,* Victor Books, 1992), I pondered how much investment information to include in this book on retirement. I decided that if I didn't include any information here then those who bought this book might feel they were slighted, since investing is such an important part of retirement decisions. But, on the other hand, if I occupied too much space in this book, those who bought *Investing for the Future* would feel like they had paid for the same information twice.

I resolved my dilemma by rereading the investment book. I realized that when I wrote it I had not covered thoroughly the area of retirees' investing, since the book was meant to cover people from 20 to 60 plus years of age. Had I attempted to discuss retirees' investing, that book would have been closer to 400 pages in length instead of 260 pages.

What I will try to do here is concentrate only on the 60-plus age group investment strategy. If you're in a younger age range, I would encourage you to get a copy of the earlier book and review the strategy that fits your age range and long-term objectives.

In that earlier work I outlined three basic seasons of life:

1. 20 to 40 years of age
   For this age group the strategy should be to determine a reasonable lifestyle and control spending to free a monthly surplus.

2. 40 to 60 years of age

The strategy in this age range should be to retire all debts, including the home mortgage, and invest in high growth areas.

3. 60 years of age and older

The strategy for this age group is to settle on a retirement lifestyle and preserve assets in reasonably secure investments.

Now to expand this last group further, I would like to discuss investment strategy for three asset groups: $10,000 to $50,000; $50,000 to $100,000; $100,000 or more to invest.

Modest Investment Resources: $10,000 to $50,000

To those who have struggled to save during their working careers, $50,000 or even $15,000 may not seem modest but, in investment terms, it is. Anyone beyond the age of 60 needs to develop a more conservative philosophy about investing, but those with limited assets must go beyond conservative; they must be cautious!

If all of your income needs are provided through retirement annuities, your cash surplus is probably available for traveling—or whatever you desire. But since this is usually not the case, the income from your savings will need to be maximized, while assuming the least risk possible.

Mutual Funds

The key to any successful investment strategy is twofold: Be knowledgeable enough to make the most of your own decisions, and diversify to the highest degree possible with the funds you have available.

With $50,000 or less I normally recommend investing primarily in balanced mutual funds. These funds will provide the highest degree of diversification and expert management while yielding the highest return (normally). Obviously, if you already have some other investments, such as rental properties that have done well for you, it would be wise to keep them. Basically I'm referring to new investments made after age 60.

You must be able to adjust according to what the economy is doing at any given time.

Within most mutual fund companies there are a variety of "families" or different kinds of funds from which to choose. These range from funds made up of government securities to utility company stocks (and bonds), common stocks, municipal bonds, and any number of other products—depending on the specialty of the mutual fund company.

Usually you can switch between any of the funds offered by a company with little or no cost involved. I believe this is an essential prerequisite to selecting a fund because no investment can be stagnant and survive in the coming economy, in my opinion. You must be able to adjust according to what the economy is doing at any given time.

For instance, an inflationary cycle can easily erode the value of a long-term bond fund since interest rates on long-term bonds are locked in for years at a time. If the current interest rates rise (as they would in an inflationary period), the value of the bond fund declines. At that time it would be advantageous to be able to switch over to a good stock fund. But in cycles where the market is overvalued, stocks and stock funds can lose much of their equity, so a bond fund can help protect your assets. The ability to switch funds in these instances is essential.

If we hit an economic cycle in which the economy is severely depressed and we also have hyperinflation (due to our government printing money to pay its bills, as I believe it will), then the ability to shift a portion of your assets into high-growth funds may be the difference between saving your money or seeing it destroyed through inflation.

If you're interested in reasonable growth and maximum security, I would recommend government-backed mutual funds.

For those in this asset range I recommend that you stay with the less aggressive (and less risky) funds. The most aggressive are often called *growth* or *speculative;* the less risky are commonly called *balanced.* A balanced fund means that it has a mix of many companies' stocks and has a portion of its assets in short-term bonds, as well as in stocks.

There are obviously many relatively secure investments that yield a good rate of return. Most of them require an acquired expertise that many people are not willing to achieve. For the majority of people, mutual funds simply represent a good investment that requires only a limited expertise—basically knowing which funds perform well.

Normally I recommend *no-load* mutual funds (those that have no up-front commissions) because these provide the least dilution of your initial investment capital. The reason no-load funds do not have a load (or up-front charge) is because they are not sold through commissioned sales people. They generally are sold only through direct sales with the parent company.

The disadvantage of no-load funds is that if you have a question there is no one who can assist you face to face. You must always talk to an agent by telephone. For many people this represents no problem. For others, and particularly some older people, they want to have a real live person explain the investment thoroughly, in which case the fee is justified. In general, any good fund held for seven years or longer will perform well, whether it is a load or no-load fund.

It would be very difficult in this book to advise you on any specific mutual fund companies since they often cycle up and cycle down. Instead, I will limit my specific recommendation to the sources that evaluate mutual funds: newsletters. For an average investor, one of the best resources is a monthly newsletter written by those who regularly track mutual fund companies' performances.

One of the best mutual fund newsletters I have found (at present) is "Sound Mind Investing." However, as you might surmise, I can attest only to its usefulness today and trust it will remain so in the future.

You will find a listing of several mutual fund newsletters in the Appendix. The type of investor to which they are aimed is noted. If you're going to do any investing in mutual funds, I heartily recommend that you subscribe to at least one of these publications and learn enough to make the majority of your own decisions. The small amount you will spend on a good newsletter can be your best investment over the long run.

Government Securities

The question that retirees ask most is: Should I have all my money in secure investments? Usually the secure investments they are referring to are securities backed by the U.S. government, such as T-bills, CDs, or savings in an FDIC-insured bank.

I would certainly recommend that any funds you have in a ready asset account be in an insured institution. This would include money you need for emergencies or normal operating expenses. But to squirrel your major assets away in a fixed earnings account out of fear is poor stewardship. The certainty is that inflation will strip them of their value just as surely as a burglar can strip your home; neither announces their entrance.

Those who have large amounts of excess investment capital (more than they need to live on) can afford the luxury of very conservative investments; but those with marginal assets (or less) cannot afford the risk of inflation which, in my opinion, is the greatest risk any retiree faces in the next decade. In other words, Ross Perot can afford to park his money in T-bills because even if inflation erodes 75 percent of its value he still has several hundred million dollars left.

If you're interested in reasonable growth and maximum security, I would recommend government-backed mutual funds. These are funds that invest only in government securities, such as Ginnie Maes. See the Appendix for information on these funds.

Tax Certificates

In most counties throughout America, local governments offer tax certificates when property owners fail to pay their real estate taxes. These certificates are actually liens against the owner's property until the taxes are paid in full, with interest.

> *Perhaps no better investment can be made after retirement than developing an income-producing business.*

Investors can bid on these tax certificates at auction and, after paying the taxes due, hold them as an investment. The interest rates are usually considerably higher than those available through other secured investments. The risk is that if the taxes aren't paid by the predetermined period (usually three to five years) you own the property. So you need to do a property evaluation before bidding on any certificates. Even so, in a severe economic downturn, such as we had in 1991, the fair market value of many properties actually dropped below the tax lien value, in which case the investors had to hold the properties for appreciation. If you need the income on a monthly basis, however, this would not be the best investment for you. Often the property owners will delay paying the certificates until the last possible date. This is particularly true with real estate developers who are short on cash in a downturn.

You can get more specific information on tax certificates in your area by calling your local county tax commissioner's office.

Personal Loans and Second Mortgages

I have a friend in Atlanta who manages investments for several retired people, including several widows. Obviously he is very cautious with their money. Over the years he has developed a good steady source of income for them by investing in personal loans and second mortgages.

The principle is simple: He acts as a coordinator for the lenders and qualifies all the borrowers thoroughly, ensuring that each has a good credit history and adequate collateral. Then he actually drafts the loan agreements and collects the payments, for which he receives a small percentage.

This strategy is done on a small scale, and only the best risks are assumed. Still there are risks associated with this type of investing, as with any investment. To date he has not had a single borrower default, but that is always a possibility in the future.

In most areas of the country there are attorneys who handle transactions like this for lenders. The best way to find someone who does this is to ask in your church. Just be certain that this person has a long track record (at least ten years) and a virtually unblemished record. And limit this portion of your portfolio to no more than 15 percent of the total.

Home Business

Perhaps no better investment can be made after retirement than developing an income-producing business. This does not mean lending money to your brother-in-law to start a car wash. Find something that you can do and risk a small portion of your assets in yourself.

An example would be to invest in a direct sales business such as Amway, Mary Kaye, Successful Living, or any other proven company. Quite obviously this is not an area for everyone. You must have the ability and desire to sell to others and be able to organize and train others—if you want the business to expand. But for those who can do this, it will return their investment thousands of times and has the ability to adjust to inflation too.

There is no doubt that many of the direct sales plans have been misused and been presented as "get-rich-quick" plans. But the fact that one group abuses the concept does not mean the idea is wrong. Just keep your priorities straight and these businesses can be of great advantage to you as an investment. Also use reasonable caution and don't go overboard by investing too much too soon. Start small and use your profits, not retirement savings, to expand.

If getting into a direct sales company doesn't appeal to you, look at other possibilities. For a small investment you can go to a vocational technical school and study computer science or television repair—or, learn how to be a plumber, electrician, woodworker, painter, mechanic, or something you would enjoy doing. Then, with a nominal investment in some tools or equipment, you may find an excellent part-time career in retirement.

Be sure you check out the licensing requirements in your community before investing your time and money. But many occupations such as painting, minor plumbing (faucet repairs), or secretarial assistance usually have no special requirements.

Rental Properties

One of the most common questions I am asked is, "Is rental property a good investment?" The obvious answer is "It depends."

There are definite assets and liabilities in owning rental property. The assets are diversification, appreciation, and allowing the rental income to pay off the properties. The liabilities (especially for retirees) are high maintenance costs, area deterioration and, most of all, the headaches of being a landlord.

If you don't understand an investment, pass it by, no matter how good the deal sounds.

In past years rental properties did well for investors through appreciation. But the high growth periods for real estate probably are gone for the foreseeable future. In fact we are witnessing some significant devaluation in many areas. Rental property can be profitable if it's totally debt-free, but the problems associated with maintaining rental units are many and, unless you're a real "fix-it" type, I would recommend you avoid investing in rental properties after retirement.

If you do decide to invest in a rental property, be sure it is in a good location, qualify your renters just as you would a potential buyer, and study the rules (laws) of renting in your state.

Other Investments

There are obviously other conservative investments that can be used to bolster your retirement income. In virtually every case the risk is directly related to your knowledge about that particular investment. It is very difficult for someone to talk you into making a bad investment if you know what you're doing. So stay with what you know. If you don't understand an investment, pass it by, no matter how good the deal sounds and no matter how many other Christians are involved. The most consistent error I have witnessed with those whom I have counseled is investing because Christians were involved. Believe me, Christians can make as many bad decisions as anyone else and sometimes more.

$50,000 to $100,000 in Investment Assets

A word of caution is necessary if you fit into this group. All too often those who have saved retirement funds through a payroll deduction plan, and then receive it as a lump sum, look at it as inexhaustible. Not only is it exhaustible, but it will evaporate so quickly it will startle you unless you're extremely careful and manage your funds carefully.

There are no "no risk" investments.

If you have never managed a large sum of money, my advice is to park the funds in a good safe place for at least one full year. Only invest your money after first investing your time and effort to know what you're doing when you do invest.

As with the first group, the vast majority of the funds you have will need to be invested for income unless your income needs are satisfied totally through a pension plan and/or Social Security, which is rarely the case.

In reality there is little difference in the investment strategy of someone with $100,000 and someone with $50,000, except that in the latter case less risk can be assumed. No one wants to lose *any* money. But to lose 20 or 30 percent of your asset base is one thing; to lose 50 to 75 percent is quite another.

With $100,000 to invest you should be able to generate between $8,000 and $10,000 a year income without assuming any unrealistic risks. If you attempt to earn more, it will almost always require too much risk, so set realistic goals. Also bear in mind that most people exaggerate when they mention their own return on investments.

The one thing you should be able to achieve with more resources is greater diversification. If you will set a limit of say $10,000 per investment (maximum), the risk will then be spread into ten different areas. Even a loss of 50 percent in any one investment would only dilute your assets by 5 percent. The same requirement for flexibility exists as with a lower asset base. You simply won't have enough assets to park them in fixed earnings investments like CDs or T-bills and leave them there indefinitely. If you do, you'll find your income steadily declining in relation to the cost of living. Inflation, not depression, is your biggest enemy, and you need to protect against it diligently. In my opinion, that can be accomplished best through the use of good quality mutual funds.

Just as the three most critical factors in real estate investing are location, location, and location, the three most important factors in mutual fund investing are quality, quality, and quality! Don't risk your hard earned and virtually irreplaceable savings in new ventures. Stay with those who have at least a twenty-year proven track record of growth in good times and in bad.

The advantage you have with greater assets is greater diversification, even within mutual funds. You can diversify through several different companies and in such widely spread areas as utility companies, blue-chip companies, municipal bond funds, government funds, international funds, precious metal funds, and so on.

Since this chapter is discussing only investment strategy, rather than specific investments, I won't elaborate further. In the next chapter I'll try to share more about where to find the best investments to meet your goals.

One word of caution: There are no "no risk" investments—not even the FDIC is risk free. You must settle on how much risk you are willing to assume and then *stay flexible!* What works in one economic cycle can fail in the next. You can't just park your money and forget it. If you do, you probably *can* forget it because it will be gone!

$100,000 Plus in Investment Assets

The strategy for those with greater assets should shift somewhat. Retirees with lesser amounts to invest are forced by economic reality to take greater risks to stay even with inflation if they need to live off their earnings. But those with more funds to invest should develop a two-tier strategy.

The first tier is to secure the income you need. Let's assume for illustration purposes that you need $20,000 a year above what either a pension or Social Security will provide. (*Note:* this presumes that Social Security retirement benefits will still be available to this income group.)

If the retiree in our illustration has $300,000 available, the first $200,000 or so should be invested primarily in secure, income-producing investments, such as utility company bonds, government bonds, or high quality corporate bonds. The same goals usually can be accomplished through high quality mutual funds that specialize in these investments, if you don't feel competent enough to make the selections yourself.

The additional $100,000 can be invested in areas that will have greater growth potential and can help to offset inflation, much like the earlier examples. The more surplus funds available, the more diversification and growth that can be achieved.

For those with amounts in excess of $500,000 to invest, I would suggest acquiring some international investments and precious metal funds that can help to offset the economic trends in the U.S. Again I would recommend good quality mutual funds for those who lack the experience and expertise to make these kinds of choices.

Retirees with assets in excess of several hundred thousand dollars almost certainly are going to see their Social Security benefits either reduced or at least the cost of living increases curtailed. Due to the voting power of older Americans, I would guess that the latter is more likely. It is extremely important, if and when this occurs, to keep your other assets in inflation-hedged investments. I know it seems that I am harping on this issue but I feel that I would be doing you a disservice if I didn't. You only need to read about the inflation cycle in other countries to realize how devastating it can be to those on retirement incomes, even with large surpluses. Too often retirees become paralyzed with the fear of losing their security, and they get even more conservative.

Obviously God is our resource, and He will provide for His people who are willing to trust Him. My function is to help you understand that we're a part of God's plan, not just observers of it. Use your mind to help avoid some of the pitfalls, if at all possible. If you have done all you reasonably can, God will still provide. But too often it's a Christian cop-out to declare, "We're just supposed to trust the Lord." Certainly we are, while doing all we can to help solve the problems. Remember the lesson taught in Proverbs 24:33-34, *"A little sleep, a little slumber, a little folding of the hands to rest, then your poverty will come as a robber, and your want like an armed man."*

An Inflationary Cycle

The following is a discussion with a businessman from Argentina. In the early 1980s Argentina suffered from a massive wave of hyperinflation. At one point prices on some items were rising 100 percent per *day*. Over an eight-year period Argentina saw an inflation rate of approximately 600,000 percent! There were intelligent, well-educated people living in Argentina—just as there are in our country now. Most of them never considered the effects of inflation on their lifestyles until it was too late. I pray we won't make the same mistakes. I have taken the liberty of paraphrasing the details of what he told me.

My parents were average, working-class people who paid their taxes, went to church, and accepted government as an unapproachable aristocracy. They rarely went out to eat and only dreamed of owning their own home one day.

When the government of Argentina first began to borrow money from the International Bank (The International Monetary Fund) in the early seventies, most Argentineans thought little about it. There were promises of prosperity and new roads, but there had been similar promises in the past, and all the average citizens saw were more taxes and a few roads leading to the politicians' land.

This time it was different. The amount of money Argentina was able to borrow started new projects: dams that employed thousands to build, roads across the countryside, public buildings that employed more Argentineans. But the greatest thing of all was that taxes didn't go up; instead they actually went down—unheard of in a South American country.

There seemed to be a newfound prosperity in Argentina. People who had never been able to save anything were suddenly able to find jobs paying twice what they had made before, working for the government. The government became the employer of preference for anyone seeking to get ahead.

The very politicians who were once looked upon as parasites became the heroes of the average working class. No one seemed to notice or care that Argentina was spending money it didn't have; prosperity abounded everywhere. The thought was, the rich nations of the world would not let us borrow unless they were sure we could pay it back. After all, they didn't get to be rich by being stupid, did they?

As the annual deficit figures continued to rise, some academic people began to say that Argentina was spending its way into poverty. But in general they were ignored as alarmists and terribly old fashioned.

When the debt to the World Bank reached $10 billion, the dooms-dayers predicted that the economy would go up in flames or something equally catastrophic; but that didn't happen either. Sure, the interest payments on the debt were large, but the government simply borrowed more money to cover the payments each year. Prosperity abounded and Argentina was "hooked on credit." The total debt soared past $10 billion and on into $20 billion, then $30 billion, then $40 billion. At each step along the way, the more conservative politicians and academicians shouted alarms, but the country was on a roll and the people were experiencing more prosperity than they had ever dreamed possible. Politicians who even thought about reducing the debt and spending were voted out and more progressive people were voted in.

In Argentina the thought of becoming another world economic power was being seriously discussed. Even my own normally conservative parents were borrowing heavily against the steadily increasing values of their new home and their small bakery business to speculate in land syndications. Taxes began to rise as some of the foreign credit dried up and most Argentineans complained; but prosperity was still the byword, so they paid the higher taxes and counted on economic growth to make up the difference.

The international loans, which had originally been meant to help Argentina develop its natural resources, instead went to government buildings, public assistance (welfare), and more bureaucrats to administer the programs. Roads were built primarily to create new jobs, not to develop new industry. The primary locations were those in the most influential politicians' districts.

Many of Argentina's citizens became direct beneficiaries of the new prosperity. In other words, they accepted government welfare not to work. My own parents sold their little business for a highly inflated price, and my father took a position with the government as an economic advisor.

Eventually, he retired with a comfortable pension and spent most of his time helping to put land deals together for friends and family. Everybody believed that the prosperity was unending; and it was, as long as the money held out.

Then, the plug was pulled. The World Bank was no longer willing to lend Argentina any more money. The debt to Central and South American countries substantially exceeded their total net worth, and there was no realistic way they would ever be able to repay their obligations.

Suddenly Argentina was unable to pay even the interest on its debt. But worst of all, the politicians could not continue the expansion that the Argentineans had grown to expect. Faced with the very real prospect of an internal rebellion, they took the only course that weak-willed officials could: They began to print the money they needed to pay the bills.

At first it seemed that once again the politicians had discovered the golden goose. The prosperity continued, and the borrowing stopped. But in many papers, warnings were sounded by those who had lived through the inflationary times in Germany and later in Brazil. But, with virtually no other choice, the printed money continued to flow.

The Argentine astral was devalued on the world exchange by more than 50 percent. The prices on virtually everything in the cities doubled overnight. Angry citizens demanded that the government do something, so price controls were instituted for food and fuel. The net result was that the supply of food and fuel (outside of the black market) dried up. No thinking merchant was going to sell his merchandise at discounted prices knowing that he would pay a premium to restock what he needed.

I can remember my father telling my mother not to worry. "Our future is secure," he promised her. "Our money is in land, and they don't make that anymore." But neither my parents nor anyone else could have foreseen the disaster that was about to overtake them: *hyperinflation.*

In the six months following the initial printing of money, Argentina's currency was devalued by more than 600 percent! Life for the average citizen became a struggle just to buy food and keep the utilities on. Four months later, keeping the utilities on became inconsequential as the cost of food escalated by some 6,000 percent. The entire life savings of most Argentineans was spent in less than six months, and then they had to sell every possession just to stay alive.

My own parents saw their fragile empire crumble as the cost of living soared beyond their ability to pay for even the basic necessities of life. Their land was repossessed, their home sold at auction to a banking cartel, along with several hundred others, and their government pension would not pay the tax on the food they needed. Life in Argentina became the worst nightmare the alarmists had predicted.

In 1989 the people of Argentina elected a dictator to reestablish control over the runaway economy. Only through stern price controls, backed up by stiff prison sentences, has the government been able to bring inflation under control. The currency has changed three times since the new government took over, and the middle class no longer exists.

Retirees in Argentina are no longer concerned about how to stop work. They are primarily concerned with how to find jobs that will allow them to live with some dignity. Most fear the growing trend in society toward disposing of the aged and the ill on the basis of economic necessity. Few retirees voice opposition to programs eliminating their benefits. They fear being eliminated themselves even more.

11

Where to Invest

Risk is not necessarily bad, as long as you know what the probable risks are and can afford to assume them. The less you know about the investments you make, the harder it is to assess this risk.

I FIND IT very difficult to discuss specific investments because even as I am writing the economy is changing. At present interest rates are down, inflation is down, land values are down, and the stock market is up. But that could change tomorrow and, to some degree, it certainly will by this time next year. Also our politicians may change the tax laws to enhance certain types of investments while devaluing others. I hope you can see why investment specifics are so difficult.

But, I personally don't like books that purport to be "how to" books but talk only in generalities, so I will try to avoid doing the same. Sometimes an author must talk in generalities because the potential audience for the material is too broad to be specific; and to some extent, this is true with a book on retirement. Some readers may only be thinking about retirement; others are already there. It is this last group that I would like address.

I will repeat (less I be misquoted later), that no one, NO ONE, has a good grasp on what will happen in our economy between now and the end of this decade. There are so many divergent ideas on how to fix our economy one can only guess at what changes, if any, will actually be made.

If the current trend in our government toward more spending and greater debt accumulation continues unabated, we will run out of money during the latter part of this decade. More than likely, I will revise this book about 1996 or so. By that time the deficits may well be running a trillion dollars or so a year, and interest on the debt will consume approximately 80 percent of all income taxes collected. Average Americans may be paying one-half of their incomes in direct taxes, and considerably more in hidden taxes on gasoline, utilities, and some form of value-added tax.

The investments that might normally work in a sane economy won't work in such an insane period as this, and if my analysis holds true, you'll need a survival-mode investment strategy. Until we really see whether or not fundamental changes will be made in our economy, the best I can do is help you to "hedge" and to stay as flexible as possible. This strategy is not possible without being specific.

Some investment advisors will disagree with my analysis of the economy and the specific advice I offer in this chapter. That's okay. Everyone has a right to disagree. The best I can do is tell you what I see and let you make up your own mind. The one thing I can say is that I personally have done many of the things I recommend and, thus far, they have worked for me, even with limited resources.

If you have more than $500,000 in investable assets you need more specific advice than I can give you in this type of book. I would suggest that you refer to *Investing for the Future* and read it thoroughly. Then subscribe to several of the newsletters listed in the Appendix. In addition you need a good, professional investment advisor to help you make your decisions.

I believe that professional financial advice can be of great service to those with lesser assets. Unfortunately, they can seldom afford it, in which case written advice is an inexpensive substitute.

Before discussing some ways to generate income during retirement, I would like to lay out what I see as a typical portfolio for those who have limited assets but need good diversification.

Let's assume you're just about to retire and your company offers either an annuity for $1,300 a month for the rest of your life or a cash settlement of $150,000—the amount you have vested in the company benefit plan. Which should you take?

The specifics are as follows:

1. The annuity represents a 10.4 percent return on the amount you have in the account. This certainly is not a bad rate of return. In fact, you would have a difficult time finding an insurance company annuity that would match it.
2. You discover that the annuity initially offered is a single-life plan and would pay nothing to your widow if you predecease her. Taking a two-life annuity would drop the monthly payout to $1,100 a month—a yield of 8.8 percent, which is still okay but not great.
3. You also learn that the annuity payout is fixed—meaning that it cannot be changed once you accept it.

With all of the above facts in hand you decide to take the lump sum. Now that you have $150,000, what do you do with it?

Investment Plan

Go to your bank and establish a *self-directed IRA.* You simply want a place to park the money until you decide where to invest it. You have 60 days to reinvest the funds in a tax deferred plan (IRA) or you'll have to pay the taxes and the early withdrawal penalty of 10 percent.

If your bank offers a self-directed IRA, you will need only to transfer the funds into one of their IRA money market accounts. Otherwise you would need to shop for a bank that has a self-directed IRA. All that is necessary to redirect the funds to the IRA is to fill out the transfer forms provided by the bank and they can be transferred that day.

We'll assume that some time passes, during which you do the appropriate study recommended in *Investing for the Future.* You probably have had several "hot tips" from friends and family, as well as loan requests from cash-poor relatives. I will assume you turned them all down and now you're ready to make some investments.

I believe that inflation is a higher risk to any retiree than virtually any other scenario (other than a loan to your brother-in-law).

After thorough investigation you decide to invest some of the retirement funds as follows:

a. $25,000 in a short term corporate bond fund paying 8 percent per year.

b. $25,000 in a high quality utility bond fund paying 8.6 percent per year.

c. $25,000 in "A" rated municipal bonds paying 6 percent per year (tax free).

d. $25,000 in a second mortgage repurchased from a local mortgage company paying 12 percent per year.

e. $25,000 in a growth mutual fund averaging 15 percent per year appreciation.

f. $25,000 will be kept in a U.S. government securities fund. The fund pays 7 percent per year and is totally accessible on a daily basis.

The net result of this strategy is an income of $8,900 a year in earnings from the taxable funds, another $1,500 from the tax-free fund, and approximately $3,750 in annual appreciation from the growth mutual fund. So you could realistically expect to have somewhere between $10,500 and $15,000 a year available to spend (depending on whether or not you sold some of the growth mutual fund shares to increase your earnings).

By varying the strategy we could either have earned more income (at a higher resultant risk) or taken virtually no risk by parking the money in CDs or T-bills.

As you already know, I believe that inflation is a higher risk to any retiree than virtually any other scenario (other than a loan to your brother-in-law); therefore, I would opt for a plan that will flex for inflation. In this case, any of the mutual funds could be shifted into more aggressive funds that can help to cope with some inflation.

The one great difficulty in any long-term financial plan is implementing it. I can show any number of ways to increase income or reduce expenses, but if you don't actually do something as a result, it's a waste of time. And it is an unfortunate fact of life that the majority of people implement very little of what they hear. To be fair though, I realize that most people want to do financial planning but they get paralyzed by all the options.

The plan just presented can be accomplished through any number of good quality mutual fund companies. A list of some of the best-rated companies is provided in the Appendix. I personally have invested with several of them over the years and have found their services to be excellent. I usually select only non-loaded mutual funds because I don't need the personal help that a local agent can provide.

But I have to be honest and say that some of the companies (mutual funds) I placed money in ten years ago are not performing as well as they once did. After carefully checking each of them I discovered that only one out of ten still matched its performance from five years earlier. I decided to find out why because, using a strategy known as *dollar-cost averaging,* I had been told that over a long period (seven to ten years) the funds would cycle down and then back up. By continuing to invest in both high and low periods (dollar-cost averaging), my return overall should stay constant.

The analogy is rather like flipping a coin. Sometimes you'll hit a succession of heads, sometimes you'll hit a succession of tails, but overall they will average out fifty-fifty—only mine didn't.

Recently a friend and I were discussing this very issue, and I found what he said very enlightening. It seems that any individual mutual fund company will do well with their strategy during one phase of the economy and poorly during another.

For example: One fund I invested in selected only quality companies that had an excellent price-to-earnings ratios. In other words, the stock prices were low compared to the companies' annual earnings. Therefore it was logical to expect the stock

prices to increase, thereby generating a profit for their investors—
in this case my mutual fund company. Since the fund manager
traded companies based on their (stock) price-to-earnings ratio, he
was able to generate gains and increase the value of the fund. If
you need money from this type of mutual fund you have to sell
some of your shares, which should be higher in value than what
you paid.

> *What is needed is a fund so broad and diverse that you can
> take advantage of any market trend.*

As I looked at the trend lines from the various funds, they
were still appreciating, but most were down from their peaks of
several years earlier. In other words, the funds were still profitable,
they just weren't *as* profitable.

As my friend explained it, the problem is in the basic philosophy of the fund managers themselves. They had originally found a
method that worked better than any other: in this case, price/
earnings ratios, which were the rage with investors in the early
eighties. Fund managers who used this selection process were
very successful. But as time went by, the market shifted to other
dynamics, such as high tech stocks. During the late eighties, investors didn't really care about price/earnings as much as they did the
growth potential of companies. So the highest earners were in the
high-tech companies.

By the early nineties the trend shifted to health-care-oriented
companies and, although the high tech companies and companies
with low price/earnings ratios stocks still appreciated, they didn't
appreciate as much as before.

"How then," I asked my friend, "do you solve that basically
unsolvable problem? The very thing that makes a good fund manager profitable in one phase eventually makes him unprofitable—
or at least less profitable."

He responded, "There are two basic ways: One, you can fire
the fund manager as soon as you see some other method working
better than his; or two, you can seek out a mutual fund company

so big and diverse that your investment is spread across the entire gamut of growth strategies, as well as different areas of the economy."

My response was that the first idea is rather hard on fund managers. I think it would be hard to develop much loyalty, knowing that they were going to be fired as soon as someone else did a little better in their investment philosophy.

He agreed and said studies also show that the cycles tend to repeat from time to time, so you just might need him again.

I agreed that the second idea was a good one, but for anyone smaller than IBM I assume that kind of diversification is almost impossible.

"Not really," he replied. "What is needed is a fund so broad and diverse that you can take advantage of any market trend. Certainly you won't maximize your return the way you might if all your money were in the yearly winner, but overall you'll do better and with less risk."

This concept piqued my interest since I'm a great believer in lowering risk wherever feasible—especially if you don't have to sacrifice too much return.

He shared how his financial firm had contracted with one of the largest money management companies in the world to place investor assets in their mutual funds. This company, the Frank Russell Company, then takes the money it manages and spreads it over many well-managed mutual funds (at present there are thirty-six) to take maximum advantage of the talents of the many mutual fund managers. The progression of lowering risk and increasing profits is shown in the diagrams below.

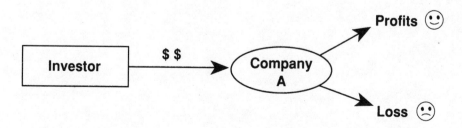

First, if you invest in one company you may make a profit. But if that company does poorly, you lose.

Then, you decide to invest in five companies to spread the risk.

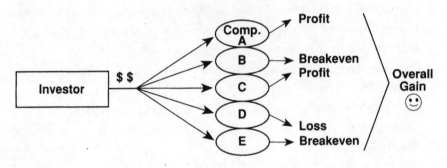

The potential profits may be smaller, but the risk is substantially lower, especially if you diversify by different industries too.

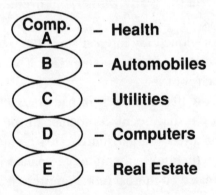

Since that is basically what a mutual fund company does for you, it is simpler to buy a mutual fund and let someone else manage the money.

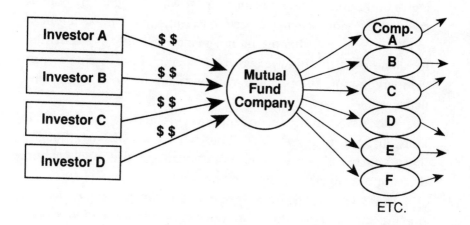

By pooling your money with a larger money manager, he then diversifies even more by allowing you to invest in many mutual fund companies.

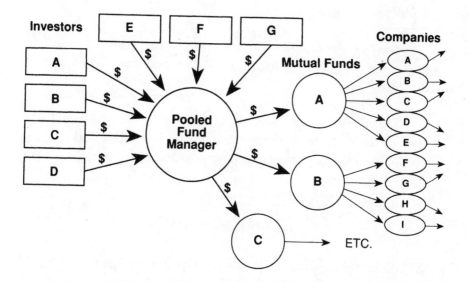

Obviously both the money manager and the fund managers have to make money too. So if you pool your funds there will be a fee for the manager. So I asked, "How much does all this cost, and how much money does someone have to invest?" It was interesting to find out that the total annual cost was no higher by pooling through the money manager than by using a good no-load mutual fund. The reason is that the money manager simply negotiated his fee along with the fund managers' fee, since he was able to provide large amounts of capital with virtually no cost to the fund managers.

The answer to the second question (about how much a single individual had to invest) was about what I would have thought: $50,000. This is because the money manager was pooling hundreds of individuals' funds together.

To my knowledge there is only one company now doing this pooling and then investing with one of the top three money managers in the country. There are probably others that I have not heard of yet. I have listed this firm in the Appendix (see Asset Management Services) for those who, like myself, are looking for maximum diversification with no additional costs. It would seem foolish not to investigate it.[1]

> *Few retirees should seriously consider an insurance plan, other than an annuity, in which to invest their retirement funds.*

I trust the trend in financial planning will continue to be toward the individual planner acting as a counselor and steering his or her clients toward the best possible investments with the least possible risk.

Insurance Products

As I mentioned earlier, I try to avoid repeating information already available in other publications, but some overlap is unavoidable. There are a few investments that virtually every retiree will have questions about and insurance is one of them.

---

[1] The author does not attest to the profitability of the money manager or the fund companies. Investors must carefully evaluate this for themselves.

Separate from the death benefit side of life insurance is the investment benefit, or dividends of a cash value insurance policy. When an insurance company charges an amount in excess of the current premium, as they do in cash value insurance, that money can be invested and income earned on it. Since all insurance companies are competing for customers, they attract additional customers by returning a portion of what they earn (or expect to earn) in the form of dividends. In some of the newer policies issued since mutual fund companies came into existence, the returns are competitive with good quality mutual funds.

However, in my opinion, few retirees should seriously consider an insurance plan, other than an annuity, in which to invest their retirement funds. The cost of insurance consumes too much of their premiums. Basically there is not enough left over to invest and make a reasonable return. So the discussion here is not whether you should buy a cash value insurance policy as an investment after retirement; generally it is a poor investment. The question is: Should you keep a cash value policy already in force, or should you cancel it or at least draw out the cash portion and invest it elsewhere?

These decisions are really statistical ones. If the interest being earned within the insurance policy is equal to or greater than what can be earned in a relatively safe investment (CD, T-bill, or government securities), then there is really no profit in withdrawing it.

Generally, it has been my experience that if the insurance policy was issued before 1980 the earnings will be significantly below that of a good mutual fund. Obviously there are some individual exceptions, but insurance companies did not get competitive with their whole life plans until the mutual fund industry began to eat into their investment funds (around the early eighties).

Most insurance policies have a guaranteed return and an estimated return. With rare exception, the amount advertised is the estimated rate of return. More often than not, the figures an agent uses in promoting the policies are gross earnings, not net (the actual amount you are credited).

Gross earnings is the amount the company expects to earn before commissions and other fees are deducted.

Net earnings is what will actually accumulate to your account each year. This will be higher than the guaranteed amount but lower than gross earnings. Since these amounts can vary annually, you need to verify the actual figures in order to make your decision. Usually the insurance company will provide reports stating the net earnings figure each year. If you keep these reports they will provide the information you need.

The *guaranteed* rate is what the company must pay, irrespective of what their investments do. This is normally 3 to 5 percent per year, depending on the issue date of the policy.

If you have a question about the earnings on your life insurance policy, you should have your agent request a printout of these annual reports.

Your options in withdrawing the funds from a life insurance policy are twofold. You can cancel the policy, in which case the insurance company will surrender the net cash reserves and whatever earnings belong to you. (Of course this also cancels your life insurance.)

The second option is to borrow the cash reserves out of the policy. Usually the interest rate you will pay is about 2 percent more than the policy is paying you (may vary by company). In this case your insurance policy stays in force, but the death benefit will be reduced by the amount of the loan plus accumulated interest. Many people don't understand that they do not have to repay the loan or the interest. As long as the loan plus accumulated interest is less than the death benefit, the policy will remain in effect. Once the cumulative total exceeds the death benefit, the policy is canceled and the loans are canceled as well.

Annuities

Since I have already covered the use of annuities as a source of retirement income, I will not elaborate again. Just remember: If

you decide to use an annuity as a retirement investment, you need
to verify the stability of the issuing insurance company at least
once a year. The resources to do so are available in most public
libraries (Rating Services listed in the Appendix).

If the insurance company is downgraded significantly, you
may want to shift your annuity to another company. This is usually
possible as long as the issuing company is still solvent. Any agent
for the company of choice can usually do this for you.

In the event your insurance company fails, there is still a possibility of recovering some or all of your annuity. Check with your
state insurance commissioner's office to see if your state has an
insurance company pool fund to cover failed carriers. If not,
you're probably limited to filing for recovery in the bankruptcy
court.

Rental Properties

I will exclude from this discussion any mention of commercial real
estate or undeveloped land. These investments normally are suitable for higher income investors, with a high degree of expertise
in real estate. For the majority of retirees, there are simpler, less
risky ways of generating the income needed.

*Under no circumstances should a retiree accept surety for
any investment.*

As I said in the previous chapter, a debt-free single-family
home or a multi-family dwelling, such as a duplex or triplex, is
often a good source of retirement income for many people. There
are obvious risks, the greatest of which is non-paying or destructive tenants but, in general, the risks are usually more mental than
financial.

There is an old cliché in real estate that describes the three
most important factors in buying rental property: location, location, location. This is fundamentally true. The ability to attract

good tenants is primarily dictated by the location of your rental property; and good tenants are the key to any successful investment in rental property.

It is my opinion that the best use of rental properties is to buy them while you're still employed and use the rent from tenants to pay off the loans before retirement. However, since that isn't an option for current retirees, it is important to review whether or not rental properties are as good an investment as other options. There are basic rules to apply when making these decisions.

Allow no *surety*. Surety means taking on a contingent (future) liability. In other words, you have committed yourself to a debt without an absolutely certain way to repay it. In the case of rental property, the asset itself doesn't always cover the liability.

If you buy a rental home and finance it through a normal commercial lender, such as a bank, almost never will the lender accept the property as total collateral for the loan. This means that if for any reason you are unable to pay the loan as required, the lender has the right to recover the property, sell it, and sue you for any deficiency. That is surety according to Proverbs 22:26-27: *"Do not be among those who give pledges, among those who become sureties for debts. If you have nothing with which to pay, why should he take your bed from under you?"*

Under no circumstances should a retiree accept surety for any investment, whether it is a rental home or a gold mine in the Yukon. The last thing you want after working all those years is to have a creditor step in and seize your other assets when you can least afford it. The bottom line is: Don't take the risk.

Surety goes beyond just signing a note with a contingency agreement. For anyone in retirement it is critical to understand all contingencies. Often investments that seemingly have no contingencies can come back to haunt you—especially those involving the IRS.

A retiree I'll call Willard came to see me in the late eighties with a sad tale about surety and contingent liabilities. It seems that Willard had bought several limited partnership shares in various rental properties from a Christian investment advisor in his church. At the time, the properties looked like good investments since real estate, and particularly rental properties, were selling well and the income from the properties, along with the tax deductions, yielded nearly 20 percent return per year. Also the fact that the investments were in limited partnerships appealed to Willard because his financial liability was limited only to the money he invested. In other words, he had no financial responsibility to the partnership beyond his initial investment. However, the properties themselves had large outstanding mortgages on them which, in Willard's case, created a contingent liability of its own.

For nearly four years the properties did very well—not only paying the existing loans but returning some net income to the partners. Then in 1986 the Tax Reform Act changed the laws regarding passive loss write-offs against earned income, and partnerships in real estate took a tumble. Investors with sizeable incomes, such as doctors, pilots, business people, and others could no longer use passive losses, such as depreciation, to reduce their tax liabilities on earned income, as the previous tax laws allowed.

As new rental properties came on the market, many were repossessed by lenders since thousands of limited partnerships failed. The lenders, desperate to fill empty properties, slashed rents. Unfortunately many older properties like those Willard had an interest in became increasingly difficult to rent. Within a few months, several of the partnerships Willard was involved with failed.

Willard lost his investment in these properties which, in itself, was a severe financial setback, but over the next few months he also learned a costly lesson in tax law. Not only did the IRS come after the partners for recapture of much of the depreciation they had claimed on the rentals, but they also assessed them for "phantom income." According to the tax codes, when a debt is forgiven (in this case the loans on the properties), income is generated to the owners, including the limited partners.

Willard's tax bill for his share of the partnership's recapture came to nearly $40,000—a tremendous sum for someone living on $25,000 a year. He was able to pay the taxes only by selling off other assets. His income took a substantial cut. Not only did he lose the income from the partnerships, he lost the income from the additional $40,000 that went to taxes as well.

The moral to this story is simple: Know what the contingent liabilities are—all of them!

The obvious question any potential real estate investor must ask at this point is: Can you ever buy real estate without a contingent liability on the loan? Usually the answer is: only if the property is financed by a private individual.

The only way to avoid the contingent liability to the IRS is to ensure that you don't allow mortgaged property to go back to the lender unless you have the resources to pay the taxes if necessary. In other words, any mortgaged rental properties should be a very small portion of your retirement portfolio.

Since bad tenants can turn a good investment sour quickly, you should always qualify your renters, just as if they were borrowing money from you. Do a credit check on them once they have met any other criteria you set (children, pets). You can purchase credit information from agencies such as TRW and Equifax (listed in the Appendix) for a modest sum. The $50 or so you will invest in a credit check may well save you several hundred dollars in uncollected rents. You should also require references from other landlords, and it is well worth the cost of a phone call to check at least two of them.

Note: Often people are reluctant to provide negative information on former tenants because they fear retaliation (or even a potential lawsuit) if they do. But if you ask, "Would you be willing to accept them as tenants again?" most people will give you a straight yes or no. A no is usually the sign not to accept them as tenants yourself.

One last note about rental properties: If you don't have the temperament to evict a non-paying tenant, then you probably should not invest in rental units. Eventually you will have to evict a non-paying tenant. That, plus the work and time associated with maintaining a rental, is why I will never become a landlord, if I can help it.

The best strategy for rental properties I ever heard is that used by a friend in Atlanta. He prices his homes well below the current rental market so he can be very selective of his tenants. His tenant turnover rate is nearly zero and he has maintained some renters for more than ten years. This arrangement is truly a win-win situation for both sides.

Government Securities

As I mentioned earlier, many retirees need absolute security in their investments since the money they have cannot be replaced and they don't have the temperament to take risks. Usually government securities represent the best overall investment for them.

There are four basic government notes of credit sold to the public: Treasury bills (T-bills), Treasury bonds (T-bonds), and savings bonds. The first two can be purchased through any regional Federal Reserve bank. Savings bonds can be purchased through virtually any bank.

T-bills are generally short term loans made to the U.S. government. The minimum purchase is $10,000, with multiples of $5,000 thereafter. The maturity on these notes is ninety days, one hundred eighty days, or one year, and the average interest rate is usually slightly less than that of the same size and duration CD.

T-bonds are usually issued in $1,000 units or more and have a maturity of seven to twenty-five years. The interest rates are higher due to the longer maturation period.

EE savings bonds are issued in denominations of $25 or more, with maturation periods of seven years or more. Unlike the T-notes and T-bonds, savings bonds and T-bills accumulate the interest and pay the face amount (principle and interest) upon redemption. It is of interest to note that the method by which savings bonds accumulate interest is not uniform, and if you cash them in between distribution periods (normally every six months), you will lose the undistributed interest. In other words, if you cash them in one day before the interest is distributed, you may forfeit six months of earnings.

There is a company, The Savings Bond Informer, that will evaluate U.S. savings bonds for you and advise on when to cash them in (see the Appendix for more information).

There are other government-backed investments available through most national stock and bond brokerage firms. These are government-backed loans issued by agencies such as the Government National Mortgage Association (GNMA)—hence the name Ginnie Mae. Ginnie Maes can be purchased in amounts of $25,000 or more with average maturity dates of about twelve years.

> *In my opinion most retirees would be better served by investing in a mutual fund that invests primarily in government securities, rather than buying the securities directly.*

There are also bonds issued by other government mortgage groups that can be purchased through brokers. These include the Student Loan Marketing Association (Sallie Maes), and the Federal National Mortgage Association (Fannie Maes). These bonds normally pay a higher rate of interest than T-bills and T-bonds.

Fannie Maes are not backed by the federal government, but it seems highly improbable that the government would permit a default on Fannie Mae obligations.

The negative side of government-issued loans is that the borrowers have the right to prepay their loans at any time. So a high interest note may be retired by refinancing it during a low interest period. You would then receive your principal back to reinvest.

Government-Backed Mutual Funds

In my opinion most retirees would be better served by investing in a mutual fund that invests primarily in government securities, rather than buying the securities directly. This provides much more flexibility and since the mutual fund manages thousands of bonds and notes, it tends to level out the fluctuations during economic cycles. Be certain when you invest in a government-backed mutual fund that the fund actually owns the investments (as opposed to repurchasing them from a bank or other holder). Just ask the broker to ensure that the fund is a primary owner of the government notes.

Let me clarify something. I am not an advocate of lending the government any more money. If I had my way, I would try to convince all Americans to cut off the government's credit to force them to live on what they can raise in taxes and fees. However, since one purpose of this book is to explore the alternatives available to retirees, I have tried to cover the topic of government-backed investments in a reasonably unbiased fashion. Investors need to decide for themselves how they feel about our government heaping more debt upon our children and grandchildren. Personally I think it is the height of selfishness. We spend the money now; they pay later.

Where to Store Ready Cash

One of the most common questions asked is: Where should I put the money I need for emergencies or normal living expenses?

The options are limited since the money has to be available quickly: a checking account at a local bank, a savings account at the bank, a money market account at a bank, or a money market mutual fund at a stock brokerage firm. Or, if you belong to a credit union, that's another available option.

Exactly where to store the money is difficult to determine precisely. But there are some rules to follow:

1. Always keep any sizeable amount of funds ($5,000 or more) in an insured account (FDIC or equivalent).
2. Seek the highest rate of return with no greater degree of risk. This will normally be a money market account, as opposed to a savings account with your local bank. If you don't mind

the fact that most of the money market mutual funds with large brokerage firms are not insured, these often pay a slightly higher rate of interest. Personally I consider them as safe as the FDIC.

3. Diversify if you have more than $25,000 to store in any account. I realize the FDIC insures accounts up to $100,000, but the more diversified you are, the safer your assets are going to be. Plus, if you have $100,000, it should be invested more wisely than it would be in a money market mutual fund.

Risk and Return

Before concluding this brief description of possible investments for retirees, I want to comment on the most important principle of investing: The more return you seek on your money, the greater the risk you will assume.

I believe some risk is both necessary and prudent (especially in light of future inflationary periods), but the rules never change about risk and return. Anytime you seek to increase your rate of return you must, by virtue of our free market system, assume some more risk.

Risk is not necessarily bad, as long as you know what the probable risks are and can afford to assume them. The less you know about the investments you make, the harder it is to assess this risk. Conversely, the more you know, the easier it is. As Proverbs 24:3-4 says, *"By wisdom a house is built, and by understanding it is established; and by knowledge the rooms are filled with all precious and pleasant riches."*

There are many excellent resources available in the way of books, magazines, and newsletters, all of which can be purchased for less than $100. When you're considering investing thousands or tens of thousands of irreplaceable dollars, it is worth the time and cost to do some studying. Some of those I use are listed in the Appendix. I encourage you to check them out for yourself.

12

Untapped Income Sources

The Lord can give you wisdom in this area of additional income. Take the time to pray and ask for His guidance. "Trust in the Lord with all your heart, and do not lean on your own understanding. In all your ways acknowledge Him, and he will make your paths straight" (Proverbs 3:5–6).

MARY WORTH WAS a widow living on a small pension from a department store chain where she had worked most of her life. She also qualified for minimum Social Security benefits, which automatically qualified her for Medicare. Even so, Mary essentially lived in poverty, as many elderly do today.

Just the ordinary deductible amounts required by Medicare created financial burdens for Mary; she rarely had ten dollars extra to spare in any given month.

I met Mary after her pastor called and asked if I would be willing to meet with her to discuss her financial needs. He knew she probably was doing without some basic necessities, but she rarely mentioned her personal problems. Actually it was one of the other women in Mary's Methodist women's group who approached the pastor. She had visited Mary while she was recovering from minor surgery and discovered that Mary had little or nothing left to buy food with after paying on her doctor bills.

Since the church had no permanent benevolence funds, the pastor had offered to help her out of his own funds, but she refused his offer. The pastor shared that when he offered to help, Mary said, "You need your money, Pastor. The Bible says that a workman is worthy of his hire." She insisted that she was doing fine and that her needs were being met.

The pastor asked her to at least see a Christian financial counselor. It just happened that she listened to our daily radio broadcasts, so when he suggested that I might be able to help she agreed.

Mary was a thoroughly delightful person. At 73 she was as alert and active as anyone I had ever met. She had a warm spirit and a love for the Lord that permeated everything she did. She was involved with a group that regularly visited several local nursing homes, and she had consistently attended a women's Bible study for nearly thirty years, often taking other women who needed the fellowship.

I asked her, "Mary, how much income do you have monthly?"

"I have enough to get by," she replied.

Having been through this procedure many times, I responded, "If I'm going to help you I need to know exactly what your financial situation is. How do you know that the Lord didn't send me to see you for just such a time as this?"

It was clear that Mary had some financial problems she was not going to be able to handle by herself.

Mary immediately recognized the passage I had paraphrased from the book of Esther where Mordecai asked his cousin, *"And who knows whether you have not attained royalty for such a time as this?"* (Esther 4:14). She said, "Maybe you're right. I have been praying that God would help me pay my bills."

She told me that she had a total income of $412 a month, out of which she tithed, paid her utilities, bought her food, paid her property taxes and insurance, and made payments on her medical bills. The sum left over each month was zero.

In talking with Mary later, I learned that she owed nearly $3,000 in medical bills, on which she paid $20 a month. To most families, that $20 represents little more than a couple of trips to McDonald's. To Mary it represented a major portion of her food money.

Mary had stopped driving her car because she could no longer afford to repair it or pay the insurance on it. When she had a doctor's appointment, she took a cab to the bus station and rode the bus from there. When she visited the nursing homes, she rode with one of the other women; but she was always careful to give them some money for gas.

Mary had no close family; she was the youngest of six sisters, all of whom had died. The only assets that had sustained her in previous years were from a very small inheritance left her by one of her sisters and the home she had inherited from another sister. Mary's husband had died after they had been married only three years (nearly fifty years earlier), and she had never remarried.

It was clear that Mary had some financial problems she was not going to be able to handle by herself. I calculated that if she sold her home, she would probably net $80,000 after all the fees were paid. Invested securely, that amount of money could earn $7,000 to $9,000 a year. For Mary, that would be a fortune. After paying rent of perhaps $4,000, she would still have approximately $300 a month to live on. Even if she used $3,000 of the money to pay off her medical bills, she would still have enough left to net $250 a month or more. Since I had done this analysis between counseling sessions, I was excited to share my idea with Mary. When she came in the next week, I explained my plan. But then we hit a snag: Mary didn't want to sell her home.

One of the last wishes of her sister (who left her the home they had been living in together) was that Mary would keep the home as long as she lived. She had told Mary many times that she should *not* sell her home. She loved Mary and was fearful that someone might trick her out of her property. To Mary a promise was a promise—period. The issue of selling the home was settled. She had given her word.

I met with Mary several more times over the next few weeks, and by that time the women of her church had taken up some money to help meet her basic needs. Since Mary would not accept their money, they used it to buy groceries and other necessities for her. They even went to the drugstore where she had her prescriptions filled and set up an account in her name, which they paid.

This resolved the immediate problem of her basic needs, but it didn't solve the long-term problem of transportation, home repairs, and perhaps a periodic trip or vacation someplace. Mary never even considered traveling since she had so few resources. But she confessed one day that, if she had been able, she would have traveled with some of the other women from time to time.

Without exception, when I teach or counsel, I claim a promise that the Lord made in James 1:5, *"But if any of you lack wisdom, let him ask of God, who gives to all men generously and without reproach, and it will be given to him."* So I started asking God to give me wisdom about how to help this dear lady. He did so one day while I was reading the *Wall Street Journal,* of all things. The answer He gave is one that can be of potential benefit to many retirees.

Reverse Mortgages

The *Wall Street Journal* article discussed the concept of an older person selling his or her home through what was termed a *reverse mortgage.* The way a reverse mortgage works is the buyer commits to paying a monthly annuity to the seller (homeowner), based on the homeowner's age. When the homeowner dies, the house belongs to the buyer. Any residual value above the annuity payout already received becomes a part of the decedent's estate.

For example, if the home is appraised at $100,000, the reverse mortgage lender might pay $75,000 for the home (based on life expectancy). If the homeowner lives longer than expected and collects more than the projected $75,000, the lender loses.

If the homeowner dies sooner than projected, the difference between the actual amount paid and the actuarial value of the home ($75,000) is paid to the estate after the home is sold. So if the homeowner received $50,000, the lender would owe the estate $25,000 after the sale of the home.

In Mary's case, her home appraised for $105,000 and the reverse mortgage lender was willing to pay $68,000, based on her life expectancy. This translated into a $500-a-month annuity for life. As I explained to Mary, it was a win-win situation. She retained a life estate (the right of occupancy for life) and also got paid a monthly income. This arrangement satisfied her sister's request and her own need. She agreed to do it.

The real benefit of a reverse mortgage is that the seller retains the right to live in the home for life while living on the accumulated equity.

A reverse mortgage is not for everyone. In Mary's case, she had no immediate heirs to whom she wanted to leave her home, and she was not threatened by the fact that someone was buying her home while she lived there.

The income (in Mary's case) was not taxable since it was actually a loan against the value of her property.

In 1990 the Housing and Urban Development Commission (HUD) initiated a loan guarantee program designed to encourage more lenders to make reverse mortgages available. The loans are guaranteed by the Federal Housing Authority (FHA) and therefore make reverse mortgage loans much more accessible.

The AARP has a brochure available which explains the details of home reverse mortgages. Just write to: Home Made Money, AARP Equity Conversion Service, 601 E St NW, Washington, DC 20049.

The Shared Annuity Concept

A woman I'll call Naomi was a 73-year-old widow who had recently lost her husband. Because his pension stopped after he died, her total income was reduced by nearly 40 percent. She was left with only one real asset: her home, worth approximately $200,000, for which they had paid $28,000 in 1959.

She could have sold her home but she had no desire to move at such a late stage in her life, and there were no lenders offering reverse mortgages in her area of the country. Her home was located not far from a major university that sent out information periodically on their shared annuity program, which they promoted to nearby residents.

Naomi saw one of the school's brochures and asked my opinion about it. I told her it looked like a good idea and then made contact with the university's financial services office on her behalf. The arrangement that was ultimately made turned out to be a great deal for Naomi and the university.

Naomi entered into a contractual agreement with the school for a life annuity in exchange for donating her home to the university. The terms of her agreement allowed her to live in the home for the rest of her life, and she also received an annuity of $8,000 a year for life. In addition she also received a sizeable tax deduction for the remainder value of her home. This is the residual value of the home the school receives, based on her life expectancy.

> *During the eighties a unique business developed to help terminally ill patients generate income from their life insurance while they are still living.*

Although Naomi was still responsible for maintaining the home and paying the real estate taxes, she netted nearly $5,000 a year in spendable income. The home will become the property of the university when she dies.

Obviously this is not a plan for everyone either. Naomi had no close heirs to whom she would have left her home, so that was not a consideration. Unfortunately she was not in a tax bracket (basically zero) where the deductions would help her financially. But, for higher income people, the tax incentives also can be of great value.

Life Insurance Buyouts

During the eighties a unique business developed to help terminally ill patients generate income from their life insurance while they are still living. This concept, called *living benefits,* has been an effective way for many terminally ill people to live out their lives in relative comfort: They sell their life insurance proceeds while they're living.

Recently some insurance companies (about 100 nationwide, as of this writing) also offer a similar benefit to their policyholders who are not terminally ill. The concept is simple: the company will buy out the policy by offering an annuity instead of a death benefit. So instead of having a life insurance policy, you convert to a life annuity. Obviously the company is doing this to lower their costs, but if you don't have a need for the life insurance, this can be a good source of additional income.

As of this date, the monthly proceeds from such an annuity are considered to be earned income and, as such, subject to income taxes. Depending on other earned income, this could also affect your Social Security income.

In the event the insured dies prior to the total annuity value being paid out, the remainder will go to the designated beneficiaries.

A call to your insurance company's customer relations representative will determine if your company offers this option presently. I rather suspect that as more companies provide this option, others will adopt it also. Just be certain that your need for life insurance has been satisfied before converting your policy.

Charitable Trusts

Generally speaking, the type of trusts I will address here are most beneficial to those who have significant retirement income, since some of the benefits are tax deductions. However, if you need more current income and have already made the decision to give a portion of your estate to your church or other charitable organization, these trusts can be of great benefit to you and the ministry.

There are a myriad of charitable trusts available from virtually every major charitable organization in the country. In most cases, if you're serious about establishing a trust with a specific organization, they will provide all of the legal advice to do so. Some will even have the legal documents drafted at no cost to the donor.

If you are interested in more specific details than you find here, write the organization and request information. I have listed in the Appendix a few of the larger Christian organizations that offer these services. When you write, ask for their brochures on "charitable trusts."

Charitable Remainder Unitrust

This is one of the most common types of charitable trusts available today, and it is also the most flexible. Virtually any asset of value can be placed in a charitable remainder unitrust, with several options for receiving a lifetime income. I would like to use a practical example.

Bob was a 68 year old widower and a long-time supporter of a major evangelistic ministry. He owned a tract of commercial property he had purchased nearly thirty years earlier at a fraction of its current value. Bob had been approached by several developers about buying the property, but he had held out, thinking that one day it would be a prime prospect for a small shopping center.

Although Bob had an adequate retirement income, he had a need for a small amount more and also a desire to see his primary asset used to benefit the Lord's work after his death. After reading a letter from the planned giving department of the evangelistic organization, he contacted them asking for their counsel. The next time one of their field representatives was in the area he contacted Bob. After briefing him on the benefits of a charitable trust, Bob indicated that he was interested, if the details could be worked out. The first step was to arrange for the property to be appraised.

The appraisal came back at nearly $500,000—a surprise to even Bob. The ultimate arrangement worked to the benefit of the ministry, Bob, and the Lord's work.

If Bob had sold the property for $500,000, the taxable proceeds would have been $475,000 in capital gains (the sales price less the $25,000 he paid for the property). Obviously that would have placed him in the maximum tax bracket. His total tax rate would have jumped to approximately 40 percent (federal and state). So he would have paid nearly $190,000 in income taxes.

Instead, by donating the property to the charitable organization, he received a charitable tax deduction of approximately $260,000 (the remainder value of the property at his death) and a lifetime annuity of $2,500 a month. The tax deduction then could be used to offset much of his regular income, plus the annuity income for up to seven years. In addition, he avoided any capital gains tax on the transaction.

The amounts of the immediate deduction, as well as the monthly annuity, are variable—depending on the value of the assets assigned to a trust, the age of the donor, and whether it is a one- or two-life annuity. More recent transactions such as this may also be subject to the alternative minimum tax rules imposed by the 1986 Tax Reform Act. For specific details you will need to contact either the charitable organization or a qualified estate planning advisor.

In the case of a charitable remainder unitrust, the annuity is dependent on the amount of money actually available in the trust. Unlike an annuity where the income is guaranteed for the life of the annuitant, irrespective of the income from the asset, this type of trust limits the liability of the charity to the funds available. Obviously this is a negative for the donor but I personally believe it is an asset since, as Christians, we would not want a ministry to be saddled with an obligation beyond the funds committed to them. However, you must also be certain that the organization you choose to handle your trust is capable and well managed. Generally this will limit you to using larger organizations. If you desire, you also can name more than one organization as beneficiary in a charitable trust.

Charitable Gift Annuities

Just as you can purchase an annuity through an insurance company, you can also purchase an annuity through many charitable organizations. The advantage is that a large portion of the profit accrued through the annuity then goes to the charity.

Usually the charity will actually purchase an annuity through an insurance company themselves, thereby limiting their contingent liability for future payments. If you decide to use a charitable gift annuity, just be certain that the insurance company underwriting the contract is a quality company.

Unprofitable Projects

Since many older Americans are in need of extra income, they become prime targets for scam artists selling everything from government surplus food to condominiums in Florida. Most of these scams follow very similar patterns.

The basic premise is that a company wants to use you as a test customer. This usually involves the sale of home repairs, equipment, or even encyclopedias. The salespeople call to make contact and offer to have their company put siding on your house, replace your roof, or place a set of encyclopedias in your home to use for demonstration purposes.

The salespeople assure you that this will cost you absolutely nothing. In fact, they say you will be able to generate income simply by making your home available as required. The promised rewards are often in the hundreds of dollars a month. Sound too good to be true? Well, that's because it is.

The hook in this bait is that you have to sign a good faith contract insuring the value of the product if any unreasonable damage occurs. More often than not there is also some substantial deposit required at the very last minute.

Almost before the salesperson is out the door, the contract is sold to a third party—usually a shell company owned by the first group. Then the billing starts thirty days later, along with some legal-sounding warnings about what can happen if the payments are not made. So, instead of this being an income-generating product, it becomes a cash drain for unnecessary work done. If this has already happened to you, contact your state consumer affairs department, as well as the state attorney general's office, and file a formal complaint. You also need to hire an attorney to represent you and go to court to cancel the contract.

Since many older Americans are in need of extra income, they become prime targets for scam artists.

There are many other scams aimed at retired people, including the sale of government assets, drug confiscation sales, and so on. The common thread that runs through virtually all of these is the necessity to pay something up front for the service or information. I have investigated dozens of these get-rich-quick schemes and, to date, I have found none that are worthwhile (to put it mildly).

Unless you decide to get into direct marketing sales through reputable companies such as Amway, Mary Kaye Cosmetics, Shaklee, Successful Living, or several others that have been around long enough to prove their validity, very likely you will end up losing some of your money—and some of your friends as well.

I have a retired friend, James Acton, who came up with a relatively simply way to supplement his retirement income. James has always been interested in cars and, periodically, has sold one or two used cars when the opportunity has presented itself. He knows that when people have cars to sell they usually don't know exactly how to go about it.

Since knowledge and need make for opportunity, James began a small business by taking cars on consignment and selling them. After he had sold a few cars for friends, he decided to advertise his service through his church's bulletin board. Several people responded to the notice, and James settled on three good cars with which to start his home enterprise. He simply parked the cars on the vacant lot next to his home with "For Sale" signs in the windows. He then interfaced with the perspective buyers.

When a buyer was serious about a car, James put him in direct contact with the owner, who then completed the transaction. For James's part, he received a $150 commission. For the last several years he has sold between two and three cars a month for other people, with an average investment of not more than two hours per car. Since his reputation has grown, James now has both buyers and sellers calling him regularly. Because he's very selective about the cars (and people) he will interface for, people know they can trust what he says. James is not a used car salesman. He merely puts willing buyers and sellers together.

James took some of his spare time and turned it into a very profitable venture, without paying anyone franchise fees or up-front costs. He did have to secure the proper permits and a city license, but the total annual cost for his business is less than $100.

The Lord can give you wisdom in this area of additional income. Take the time to pray and ask for *His* guidance. *"Trust in the Lord with all your heart, and do not lean on your own understanding. In all your ways acknowledge Him, and he will make your paths straight"* (Proverbs 3:5-6).

13
Social Security Benefits

For those already on Social Security retirement, I believe we will sacrifice to maintain their incomes. But for those facing retirement beyond this decade, it is difficult to envision where the funds will come from.

THERE NEVER HAS been a social welfare program on the scale of the Social Security system. Retirement, Medicare, and disability payments now consume in excess of 40 percent of the total U.S. government's spending. Some people may take offense at my use of the term "social welfare," but that's exactly what Social Security is (as declared by the Supreme Court).

Until 1986 the Social Security system was funded on a pay-as-you-go basis—meaning that current contributions were sufficient only to cover current expenditures. In the mid-eighties the special committee appointed by President Reagan determined that when the "baby boomers" born after World War II began to reach retirement age, the system would not be capable of pay-as-you-go funding. The reason was determined to be twofold. First, there would be a huge influx of retirees—all from approximately the same time period. Second, there would be a steady decline in the number of active workers to replace them.

More recent figures from the Social Security Board of Trustees show the problem to be far more acute than was assessed by the previous panel.

The 1991 Social Security Board of Trustees' Report reflects several converging factors that will drastically affect the system. I will attempt to summarize some of the more pertinent ones. If you require more verification I would encourage you to secure a copy of this report. Contact your regional Social Security office or write to: The Social Security Administration, 300 North Greene St., Baltimore, MD 21201 and ask for a copy of the 1991 Social Security Board of Trustee's Report on Social Security and Medicare.

There are many more potential retirees in the first decade of the next century than the present system can handle.

You may also want to request a copy of the Board of Trustee's Report on Social Security Trust Funds. However, the truth is: There aren't any. Each year the government takes the surpluses, spends them in the general revenue budget, and then substitutes worthless (in my opinion) IOUs for the actual funds. I question that a government that already has issued over $4 trillion in IOUs can ever repay the Social Security Trust.

For those already on Social Security retirement, I believe we will sacrifice to maintain their incomes. But for those facing retirement beyond this decade, it is difficult to envision where the funds will come from. We are facing what appears to be some unsolvable contingencies.

Contingencies

1. There are many more potential retirees in the first decade of the next century than the present system can handle. When the Social Security system began, there were approximately fourteen workers for every retiree (over the succeeding ten years). As of 1992, there are approximately four workers per retiree, and in the year 2000 it is estimated there may be only two active workers per retiree.

2. Even with a ratio of only two workers per retiree in the next decade, there is an additional problem. The American population is shifting more than at any time in the last century. Due to abortion and birth control, fewer children are being born per family unit in the U.S., and the gap is being filled by immigrants—a population base that contributes less to the

tax system than native-born Americans do. (Generally it requires one entire generation before immigrants are fully assimilated into our population and can hope to achieve the same income levels.)

3. The entire economy of the U.S. seems to be shifting toward more service-related jobs, as compared to manufacturing jobs. This tends to create more jobs but at lower overall wages. Thus the income per active worker is actually less in terms of real contribution. As the graph below indicates, real income is steadily declining.

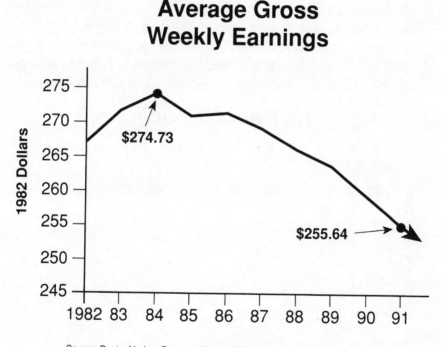

Average Gross Weekly Earnings

Source: Dept. of Labor, Bureau of Labor Statistics

4. The cost of health care is exceeding the average annual inflation rate by 200 to 300 percent. This cost, when factored into the Medicare system, will result in either much higher contributions on the part of wage earners (estimated to be between 26 and 32 percent according to the Board of

Trustee's report), or higher costs to the Medicare recipients (dollar amount not available).

The cost of AIDS to the Medicare system is almost impossible to calculate. The average cost of caring for symptomatic AIDS patients is estimated to be somewhere between $125,000 and $250,000 (depending on the source of information) during a two-year period. The CDC estimates there are one to one and one-half million Americans now infected with the HIV virus. Most of them are expected to develop symptoms by the year 2000, assuming that no cure is found.

As I said previously, the Social Security Trust funds considered necessary for those who will be retiring beyond the year 2000 have been "borrowed" by the U.S. government. In their place, U.S. Treasury bills have been substituted. There is realistically little hope that these funds can ever be repaid since, in fact,

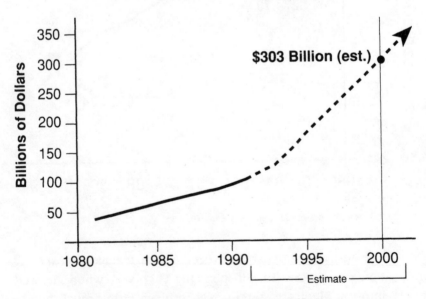

The Cost of Medicare

$303 Billion (est.)

Billions of Dollars

Sources: Dept. of the Treasury, Office of Management and Budget,
Health Care Financing Administration

they are part of the systematic overspending by our government. I personally believe it is naive to think that somehow our government will stop its foolish spending just before the need for these funds arrives.

I can see no real alternatives that would allow the baby boomers to enter the system. Social Security simply cannot absorb the costs of these retirees.

I could go on enumerating the various problems facing the Social Security system in the next decade and on into the next century, but I hope you see the picture the way it really is. If you have any doubts about the accuracy of my comments, please secure a copy of the reports yourself. If you can draw any different conclusions I would be happy to hear from you. I would also recommend that you get a copy of *Social Insecurity,* by Dorcas Hardy. As past commissioner of the Social Security Administration, certainly Mrs. Hardy should know if the system is solvent or not.

Will Social Security Fail?

It is my considered opinion that the Social Security system itself will not fail for those who are recipients prior to the turn of the century. It will be supported at all costs by politicians anxious to avoid the voting wrath of the current retirees.

However, I can see no real alternatives that would allow the baby boomers to enter the system. Social Security simply cannot absorb the costs of these retirees. So if you're one of those people born after 1939, in my opinion you had better do some planning on your own.

In addition to prohibiting the baby boomers from retiring on Social Security, other changes still must be made if the system is to remain solvent (exclusive of any economic disaster). First, the automatic cost of living increases certainly will have to be curtailed, if not totally eliminated. Second, the benefits will probably be means-tested (those who have the resources will be required to pay more and receive less). Third, some method to fund the system, in addition to direct taxes, will have to be found.

It is on this last point that I would like to dwell for just a moment.

In a book I wrote in 1991, *The Coming Economic Earthquake,* I made a passing comment about an idea I believe will be used to help keep the Social Security system solvent when more tax increases are not politically feasible. This idea raised such a furor that I have tried to think it through again. And having done so, I am even more convinced it is too logical to ignore. So I would like to share my opinion about how Social Security can (and perhaps will) be funded when the crisis hits.

At present there is about $2.5 trillion in private retirement accounts of all kinds. Of this amount, much of it is held by individuals making more than $50,000 a year. Does that give you any ideas? It does me.

The possibility of private retirement accounts being "absorbed" to pay for future Social Security benefits seems too plausible to ignore, especially for higher income people and those not yet retired. The precedent already exists in the way the government is absorbing the Social Security trust funds to fund the current budget deficits.

At present the Treasury issues T-bills, which are then substituted for the funds in trust. No matter how you look at it, this is a transfer of dollars for IOUs, and virtually no one is objecting. A similar process can easily be applied to retirement accounts, when and if necessary.

If you think this is too farfetched and that our politicians would never allow this to happen, then you probably are justified in doing nothing further. But if you also believe this is a possibility, then you would be better off not placing all of your retirement funds in a tax deferred plan, even if the current tax laws allow you to do so.

I personally believe that no more than one half of what you are allowed (by law) should be tax deferred. It is my observation that any time the government allows you a tax break, they tend to think of that money as *theirs*. It would be better to pay the taxes on a portion of your long-term investment money and then invest with after-tax dollars than to run the risk of winding up with nothing but empty promises. As I said previously, this is my own opinion, which you may decide is or is not valid for yourself. Personally I would rather pay some taxes and keep my money than save some taxes and potentially lose it all.

Benefits

The Social Security system is very complex. It has a variety of benefits from retirement pensions to disability, each somewhat intertwined. Those who qualify for disability receive different benefits from those who do not. Widows and widowers who qualify on their spouses' incomes receive different benefits from those who earned the income personally. Those who retire at one age receive different benefits from those who retire later. And on it goes.

> *The earnings you make during your working career directly affect the amount you will earn upon retirement.*

In this section I would like to break down the basic qualifications and benefits and then point you to more complete information, if you have a specific question about your own benefits.

It would be great if the Social Security Administration published a chart of earnings and benefits so retirees could just look up their total earnings, draw a line over to the benefits side, and see how much they would have at retirement, but it just can't be done.

The table on the next page is about as close as one can get but, even so, you need to understand that it will yield only a general idea of your benefits.

The only accurate way to determine exactly what your future benefits will be is to obtain an audit of your Social Security account.

A Social Security Audit

Since the earnings you make during your working career directly affect the amount you will earn upon retirement, it is important to calculate what your benefits will be for planning purposes. This is particularly true for those over age 50.

A worker is deemed to be fully "vested" or insured once he or she has paid into the system for forty quarters, with some exceptions made for those who came into the system as a result of tax law changes passed in 1984. However, since the government never makes anything simple, there are several exceptions.

A quarter for Social Security purposes is any period in which a worker earns the required amount ($540 as of 1991). So if you were paid $2,160 for any month that year, you earned four quarters worth of credit ($540 × 4 = $2,160), but you cannot accumulate more than four quarters of Social Security benefits in a single year, no matter how much you earned.

The schedule for minimum annual earnings has been increased as the Social Security tax and benefits have increased, so earlier years require less earnings, later years more.

Also, retirement benefits are adjusted for different levels of earnings, so participation in later years can enhance earnings, while nonparticipation will reduce retirement earnings.

If the accuracy of the Social Security Administration equals that of other branches of the federal government, you can expect some errors in your records. Many people have been shocked to find out that their benefits have been miscalculated due to contributions not being allocated to their accounts properly. It is ex-

Table for Estimating Amounts of Social Security Benefits

Average Monthly Wage	Old-Age Benefit Age 65	Old-Age Benefit Age 62	Dependent Spouse Age 65	Dependent Spouse Age 62	Average Monthly Wage	Old-Age Benefit Age 65	Old-Age Benefit Age 62	Dependent Spouse Age 65	Dependent Spouse Age 62
$83	144	115	72	54	930	618	494	309	232
92	1158	127	79	59	955	626	501	313	235
101	172	138	86	65	980	634	507	317	238
107	184	147	92	69	1000	640	512	320	240
122	195	156	105	79	1030	648	519	324	243
146	210	168	105	79	1050	654	523	327	245
169	224	179	112	84	1075	661	529	331	248
193	239	191	119	90	1100	669	535	334	251
216	253	202	127	95	1125	676	540	338	253
239	268	215	134	101	1150	683	546	341	256
258	280	224	140	105	1175	690	552	345	259
281	294	235	147	110	1200	696	557	348	261
300	306	245	153	115	1225	703	562	352	264
323	320	256	160	120	1250	710	568	355	266
342	331	265	166	124	1275	716	573	358	269
365	346	277	173	130	1300	722	578	361	271
389	361	288	180	135	1325	729	583	364	273
412	375	300	188	141	1350	735	588	367	276
436	388	311	194	146	1375	741	593	371	278
459	402	322	201	151	1400	747	597	373	280
478	413	330	206	155	1425	753	602	376	282
501	427	341	213	160	1450	759	607	379	285
524	440	352	220	165	1475	764	612	382	287
548	454	363	227	170	1500	770	616	385	289
563	464	371	232	174	1525	775	620	388	291
577	473	379	237	178	1550	781	625	390	293
591	483	387	242	181	1575	786	629	393	295
609	495	396	248	186	1600	792	635	396	297
641	517	413	258	194	1625	797	638	399	299
660	527	421	263	198	1650	803	642	401	301
685	536	429	268	201	1675	808	647	404	303
705	544	435	272	204	1700	814	651	407	305
725	551	441	276	207	1725	819	655	410	307
745	559	447	280	210	1750	825	660	412	309
770	567	454	284	213	1775	830	664	415	311
790	573	459	287	215	1800	836	669	418	313
810	580	464	290	218	1825	841	673	421	315
835	588	470	294	221	1850	847	677	423	318
860	596	477	298	223	1875	852	682	426	320
885	604	483	302	226	1900	858	686	429	322
910	611	489	306	229					

tremely important to audit your Social Security file prior to retire-ment so you can clear up any errors if necessary. The Social Security Administration will run a free audit of your file upon request. This form is the "Request for Earnings and Benefits Statement." You can obtain one at no cost by calling your local Social Security office and requesting a copy of Form SSA-7004PC. Once you fill it out and return it, the audit normally follows in six to eight weeks and is called the "Personal Earnings and Benefit Record" (Form SSA-700PC).

After you receive the audit of your work record (and your spouse's too), you will need to review it carefully. It will show every year in which you were credited for contributions and how many credits you have earned. It will also provide an estimate of your projected retirement benefits (plus disability and survivor's benefits) and the amount by which your benefits would be reduced for early retirement. This is an excellent service provided by the Social Security Administration, and you should take advantage of it.

What If There Is an Error?

If you don't have the hard record data (primarily tax records) to back up your claims, you can still appeal through the same process. Hopefully the IRS will still have your past tax forms and will provide them upon request, although personally I have not seen many positive examples in this area.

If your appeal is denied, you should obtain legal representation if the disputed amount justifies the additional expense. Your next step is an appeal for an administrative hearing, and you will probably need someone familiar with the process and rules of evidence within the Social Security Administration.

If your internal appeal is denied (usually a one- to two-year procedure), you can still appeal to the Social Security Appeals Council in Washington, D.C. This group hears appeals based on the written evidence supplied to the Social Security Administration. It is rare for the Appeals Council to overturn a previous ruling within the administration, but you cannot appeal to the federal courts without a ruling from the Appeals Council.

The last appeal step is in the federal district court. This process is usually very expensive and should not be taken without the counsel of a competent attorney who specializes in Social Security Administration law.

By the way, a 1987 study done by the General Accounting Office (GAO) estimated that as many as nine million American workers may have errors in their work records. So check it out! If you find that your file has errors, you will need to appeal to the Social Security Administration for correction. Finding the W-2s or similar records to use in correcting the errors may not be simple. If you have not kept them, you will need to appeal to the IRS for copies.

Recently I had my own account audited through Social Security; it reflected a four-year gap in "contributions" paid into the system. Fortunately I keep all of my past income tax statements so I'm pretty certain that the records can be corrected. It has only been recently that the Social Security Administration has allowed these records to be corrected beyond the statute of limitations (seven years). How long this option will remain is impossible to tell. But I would recommend that anyone not already drawing benefits request an audit immediately.

One additional factor that can affect some retirees is that illegal aliens are using Social Security numbers of U.S. citizens to draw benefits—including, and especially, disability benefits. No one really knows the extent of this fraud, but recently I talked with someone who had this happen to him.

Bill Reece was planning for his retirement from the John Deere Company after nearly thirty years of employment. The company was restructuring and offered Bill an early retirement option at age 63. Since he had plans to join a mission group that worked in Latin America, he willingly accepted. Then his nightmare began.

Bill applied for Social Security early retirement and received a notice that there was a problem with his account. After several weeks of frustration with the regional Social Security office, Bill learned that someone had been drawing disability benefits based on his Social Security record.

Bill proved to the satisfaction of the local office that he was the real William Reece who had opened the original account and had been diligently paying into it for more than forty years. But it wasn't that simple.

When the other party had applied for disability benefits, dutifully accompanied by notarized doctors' statements to that effect, the account had been transferred to the disability claims division, and the address changed. When Bill's subsequent contributions had been sent in by his employer, they apparently went into what one agent called "the La-La Land Account."

Since the government never returns any funds that can otherwise be kept for spending, the system is designed to accumulate contributions, regardless of whether the accounts balance or not. One would reasonably think the accounting system would balance all income against all applied benefits—not so, apparently.

What this meant to Bill was that since the time that someone else qualified for disability using his contributions record, none of his subsequent contributions were credited to his account. For all intents, Bill had lost nearly eight years of contributions, and since the loss involved was the last eight years of his earnings, the difference in retirement benefits was significant.

Fortunately, in Bill's case the discrepancy was recent enough that he had the tax records to correct his account. But even now he will periodically receive a bill from the Social Security Administration demanding repayment of funds he never used from the disability side—the price you pay for computers I guess.

Entitlement Qualifications

Your Social Security entitlement is based on whether or not you have paid in enough quarters. These credits are earned by quarterly contributions to the Social Security system, based on your earnings. They are calculated on the amount you pay if you are self-employed or the amount you and your employer pay if you are an employee.

Any worker who has paid in at least the minimum for forty quarters is qualified for Social Security old age (retirement) benefits. In some cases you may actually need fewer quarters. But since that exception applies only to those who would have reached retirement age prior to 1991, I will assume if it applies to you, you already know it.

Early Retirement

Since I covered this topic in an early chapter, I won't repeat it, except to give you the formula for calculating early retirement (from age 62 to maximum retirement age). You will lose 0.555 percent of your benefits for each month you draw benefits prior to your maximum retirement age.

For example: If you chose to retire at age 62 and you would be fully qualified at age 65, you would lose 13.333 percent of your maximum benefits (0.555×36 months).

Widows and Widowers

The widow or widower of a fully vested worker is entitled to 100 percent of what a retired worker was receiving. Although the spouse of a deceased worker may also qualify for benefits on his or her own work history, the total benefits cannot be greater than the maximum the surviving spouse would have received either under the deceased spouse's benefits, or his or her own work record. In other words, you can't draw more than 100 percent benefits—no matter what.

Widows or widowers who apply for their deceased spouses' benefits at age 60 (earliest age, excluding a disabled child or spouse) will have their benefits reduced by 0.475 percent of the benefit for each month prior to age 65. For example, a widow receiving benefits at age 60 would receive only 71.5 percent of her husband's benefits.

A divorced spouse who lived with an insured worker for ten years or more is entitled to benefits under the worker's plan, beginning at age 62.

The benefits for the divorced spouse are 50 percent of the entitled worker's benefits at age 65. If the divorced spouse takes early retirement, the benefits are reduced by .722 percent for every month prior to age 65.

Disability

A disabled spouse is entitled to benefits based on the worker's contribution record. This is a rather complicated formula, depending on the age of the disabled spouse. Basically the disabled spouse can start drawing benefits as young as age 50, with the benefits subject to the same rules for early retirement—a reduction of .475 percent per month prior to age 65, plus an additional reduction of .179 per month prior to age 60. Plus, the disabled spouse must be legally disabled at least five months before drawing benefits (if that doesn't confuse you, you must work for Social Security).

Employees of Not-for-Profit

In 1984 the tax laws were changed to require all members of non-profit organizations to contribute to Social Security. (*Note:* ordained or licensed pastors are the exception to this rule.) As a result of this forced inclusion into the system, the rules for employees of non-profits were changed.

If you were at least 55 years of age on January 1, 1984, the following table indicates if you are fully vested in the system.

Age on January 1, 1984	Quarters of Coverage
60 or over	6
59	8
58	12
57	16
55 or 56	20

Other Income

If you have worked outside the continental United States or were previously exempt from Social Security through a state or local government exclusion, you will need to have an audit of your contribution record done to determine your exact benefits available.

How to Apply for Benefits

For those who have obtained an audit of their Social Security records and know they are correct, the next step is to apply for benefits. You will need to apply through your local Social Security office. They will provide you with all the necessary forms (see the list below). You can have the forms mailed to your home or office by calling ahead.

The most important aspect of qualifying for benefits is to have all the records necessary.

Form SSA-1 F6   —Application for Retirement Insurance Benefits

Form SSA-2 F6   —Application for Wife's or Husband's Insurance Benefits

Form SSA-10BK   —Application for Widow's or Widower's Insurance Benefits

Form SSA-4BK   —Application for Child's Insurance Bene-
                  fits
Form SSA-5 F6   —Application for Mother's or Father's In-
                  surance Benefits
Form SSA-8 F4   —Application for Lump-Sum Death Pay-
                  ment

You should apply for benefits at least three months prior to retirement. Retroactive payments can be made for only six months after qualifying for benefits, so don't delay too long or you will lose them.

You need to set up a Social Security file at home and place one copy of all your information in it. Remember to write down the names and job titles of everyone with whom you make contact. This will make future contacts much easier.

Many people have a tendency to brush aside suggestions like this but, as a counselor, I can tell you: In the event of a problem, good records are invaluable. In the event of a death they are absolutely imperative. So write it all down, and file it.

The most important aspect of qualifying for benefits is to have all the records necessary. You will need two proofs of your age (birth certificate, marriage license, Armed Services record, Bible entries—almost anything that the Social Security Administration will accept).

Let me assure you, [Medicare] is a good buy in today's economy of medicine.

If you are qualifying under someone else's benefits, i.e., a divorced or deceased spouse, you will need to provide notarized copies of the legal documents.

If you are qualifying for Medicare benefits, remember that you *must apply* to receive any benefits even though you will automatically be eligible at age 65. Also you do not have to be receiving Social Security retirement benefits to draw Medicare benefits.

Medicare Part A

Even if you do not qualify for Social Security retirement benefits, you still can apply for voluntary enrollment in the Medicare system. As of January 1992, the cost is $177 per month for Medicare Part A benefits. Let me assure you, this is a good buy in today's economy of medicine.

Medicare Part A hospital insurance includes five categories of covered services: hospitalization, post-hospital skilled nursing facility care, post-hospital home health care, hospice care, and blood. Specific kinds of care and supplies under these general categories include the following items:

1. semiprivate room
2. meals
3. regular nursing services
4. operating and recovery room services
5. anesthesia services
6. intensive care and coronary care
7. drugs furnished by the hospital
8. laboratory tests
9. diagnostic X-rays
10. some medical supplies and appliances
11. rehabilitation services
12. preparatory services for kidney transplants
13. psychiatric care in a hospital for special cases
14. home health visits from an approved agency
15. physical therapy
16. speech therapy
17. medical social service
18. blood transfusions

Medicare Part B

You will automatically be eligible for Medicare Part B if you qualify for Medicare Part A (by eligibility or enrollment option). However you do not have to take the Part B coverage even if you are taking Medicare Part A.

If you are 65 you can qualify for Medicare Part B even if you don't qualify for Part A for any reason.

Medicare Part B is a fee-based system that, as of this date, costs $29.90 per month. Medical Insurance benefits cover the following general categories of services: doctor bills and other medical expenses and supplies, outpatient hospital treatment, home health care, and blood. Medical Insurance helps pay for some services and supplies that are not covered by Hospital Insurance. Under certain conditions and limitations, Medicare B also covers the following specific kinds of care and supplies:

1. ambulance transportation
2. artificial limbs and eyes
3. chiropractor's treatment for subluxation of the spine
4. oral surgery (not including ordinary dental care)
5. diagnostic testing prior to hospital stay
6. durable medical equipment, such as wheelchairs or oxygen equipment for use in the home
7. home dialysis equipment, supplies, and periodic support services
8. home and office services of independent physical therapists
9. independent laboratory tests
10. optometrist's services for fitting corrective lenses after cataract surgery
11. outpatient maintenance dialysis
12. outpatient physical therapy and speech pathology services
13. outpatient psychiatric services
14. podiatrist's services

15. surgical dressings, splints, casts, braces, and colostomy supplies
16. training for home dialysis
17. X-rays and radiation treatments
18. pap smear examinations (one every three years)
19. AIDS or AIDS-related complex, provided disability requirements are met[2]

I reiterate: This is a good value by any measure. The equivalent commercial coverage would probably cost more than $100 a month and, in some cases, such as pre-existing conditions, other coverage may not be available at any price.

Earned Versus Unearned Income

Social Security retirement benefits are calculated on the basis of what the Social Security Administration considers *earned income*—money you were paid for doing a job. If you work for someone else, your *gross* wages—everything you earn before anything is deducted—are counted as earned income. If you are self-employed, the calculations are made on your *net* income—what's left after expenses are deducted. Some other sources of income are considered *unearned*, are not included in your income calculation for Social Security purposes, and do not affect the amount of your benefits. (Though these exempt categories are not counted in calculating benefits, many of them are subject to federal taxation.)

Earned Income

The money you earn for your work counts toward your benefits. If you are employed, your employer or employers report your work, deduct your Social Security taxes, and file a W-2 form. You should

---

[2] From *The Complete & Easy Guide to Social Security & Medicare, 1991 Edition,* by Faustin F. Jehle, Fraser Publishing Company. Used by permission.

get a copy of the W-2 form from each employer early in the year following the year in which you worked. If you are a self-employed person, you pay your own Social Security taxes when you complete your quarterly income tax returns and send them in.

Items Counted as Earned Income

When you count your earned income, you should include any of the following items. These items are considered earned income, and count toward getting retirement benefits.

1. Wages
2. Cash tips of $20 or more a month
3. Wages in kind—room and board unless you are a household (domestic) worker or a farm worker or you perform services that are not in the course of your employer's trade or business
4. Bonuses
5. Commissions
6. Fees
7. Vacation pay
8. Pay in lieu of (instead of) vacation
9. Severance pay
10. Sick pay

Items Not Counted as Earned Income

The following items are *not* considered earned income. They do not count toward credits for retirement benefits. If you are already receiving retirement benefits, these exempt earnings do not affect those benefits.

1. Dividends
2. Savings bank interest
3. Bond interest

4. Income from Social Security benefits
5. Veterans Administration benefits
6. Pension/retirement plan income
7. Annuities
8. Sale of capital assets
9. Gifts
10. Inheritances
11. Rental income
12. Royalties received after you are age 65 from patents or copyrights granted before the year in which you became 65
13. Retirement payments from a partnership under a written agreement
14. Income from a limited partnership—that income is deemed an investment
15. Income from self-employment received in any year after the year in which you become entitled to retirement benefits, as long as that income is not gained from services rendered after the date of retirement
16. Jury fees
17. Wages or other income accrued for services rendered in years prior to the year in which you become entitled to retirement benefits, as long as that income is not gained from services rendered in the years of retirement

Delayed Retirement Credit for Work After 65

If you continue working after 65, and if you do not collect retirement benefits, you will receive a DRC (Delayed Retirement Credit). This is additional credit toward your Social Security benefits when you do retire. The following additional credits apply.

1. If you turned 65 in 1981 or earlier, your benefit would be increased 1 percent for each year you continue to work after age 65 and up to age 70.

2. If you turned 64 in 1982 or later, the credit is increased to 3 percent a year for each additional year you delay retirement.
3. Beginning in 1990, DRC will increase an additional 1/2 of 1 percent every other year for workers reaching 66 after 2008. The DRC applies only to the worker's personal benefit, not to dependents. It does apply, however, to the widow's or widower's benefit.

The Only Forms You Need for Reporting Income

If you are employed after age 65, you must send to the Social Security Administration your income and tax statements: Social Security Form (SSA-7770 F6) and IRS Form W-2.

Excess Earnings

If you were *over* 70 years of age for the entire year of 1983, or any year thereafter, you can earn income of any amount without affecting your benefits.

If you are *under* 70 years of age and earned over the exempt amount, benefits are affected. Here are the 1991 figures.

1991	*Annual*	*Monthly*
65 or over	$9,720	$810
Under 65	7,080	590

If you earn more than the exempt amount, then $1 in benefits is withheld for each $3 you earn over the exempt amount while you are 65 to 69.

Your Social Security Income

You should be aware of the following rules and procedures concerning your income.

1. *Separate checks:* A husband and wife who are living together may receive one check made out to both of them, but separate checks will be sent if requested.

2. *Overpayments, mispayments:* Overpayments will be withheld from the next checks. If there is a conflict between what Social Security says you should repay and your figures, take your records to your local Social Security office.

3. *For your protection:* You should know that Social Security checks cannot be assigned for payment to someone else and are not subject to levy, garnishment, or attachment, except in very restricted situations, such as collection of federal taxes or by court order to child support or alimony.

4. *Delivery to a representative:* If you fill out a form at your Social Security office, your checks, made out in your name, will be mailed to anyone you designate. You still have to endorse and cash or deposit them.

5. *Direct deposit to a bank:* You can have your check sent directly to your bank for automatic deposit.

Note: Before you decide to use direct deposit, check on your bank's policies. Some banks charge for this service. Other banks will not and may offer other special help, such as notifying you when your check arrives. You should also make sure that the bank will forward any communications to you the bank receives from the Social Security Administration.

14

Military, Ministers, and Missionaries

If you have worked the required number of quarters in a job where Social Security taxes were withheld, you can qualify for some level of benefits.

Military Retirees

THOSE WHO RETIRE from the military have a special set of conditions unlike virtually any other group. They are usually retired at a much younger age than other career fields (average age 42) and have benefits unique to only military retirees. The use of military commissaries, military health care facilities, and the opportunity to start a second career in their forties make these retirees truly unique.

In my opinion we will see many of the benefits for military retirees curtailed in future years as government revenues are stretched thinner. There is no logic to retiring so many people at the peak of their work career. Military retirement is a good deal for those who are already in it, but there is simply no way the country can afford the system. It was designed around the needs of military personnel who fought for their country during extended periods of war. These benefits were but small payments by a grateful nation to its soldiers, and rightly so. But the need is past and, in my opinion, the costs are simply too high.

Your eligibility for CHAMPUS ends the day you qualify for Medicare Part A—regardless of whether you apply for Medicare or not.

I don't want to demean anyone living on military retirement. You paid the price and the nation has a contractual agreement with you that it should keep. But be aware: In our situational ethic society, vows are a thing to be kept only when convenient. As the economy continues to run down, it will eventually be seen as an option, not a contract.

CHAMPUS Coverage

The Civilian Health and Medical Program of the U.S. (CHAMPUS) covers the health care needs of military retirees and their dependents until the retiree qualifies for Medicare Part A, at which time the retiree and his or her dependents are no longer eligible for CHAMPUS.

This is an important factor since your eligibility for CHAMPUS ends the day you *qualify* for Medicare Part A—regardless of whether you apply for Medicare or not. So you can have an inadvertent gap in coverage if you do not file for Medicare benefits.

CHAMPUS is a comprehensive medical benefits plan that in many ways is very similar to Medicare Parts A and B, except that CHAMPUS users are eligible for treatment in military hospitals where available.

There is no annual fee for CHAMPUS, although there is a 25 percent deductible charge on usual and ordinary services, such as doctor visits and hospital care. I won't attempt to cover all the various aspects of CHAMPUS. You can obtain a copy of the CHAMPUS handbook from any military hospital or by writing CHAMPUS, Aurora, CO 80045-6900.

One last note of caution: If you are eligible for Medicare Part A at age 65, you *must* file for it since your CHAMPUS coverage stops at midnight the day you turn 65. If you are not eligible for Medicare, you must get a disallowance notice from the local Social Security Administration office to ensure that your CHAMPUS will continue.

Social Security credits toward retirement benefits may be received for military service in any of the Armed Forces.

If you are a retired reservist, you can qualify for CHAMPUS coverage at age 60. But the same rules regarding Medicare apply to you at age 65, so be sure to apply for Medicare if you qualify.

Veterans

If you became employed after leaving military service and you paid Social Security taxes on the maximum earnings, the information below may not be pertinent to your benefits. However this information may be important if you did not work on a regular basis or if you worked very little, either because of illness or because of lack of technical skills. This information also may be important to your spouse or children.

Farmers, household (domestic) workers, and self-employed non-regular workers who have had military service also may need this information. Their military service credits may be important to them and their families in applying for Social Security benefits.

Entitlement to Credits

Social Security credits toward retirement benefits may be received for military service in any of the Armed Forces.

If you were in active military service between 1940 and 1956, you are entitled to one quarter of Social Security coverage for each calendar quarter you were in active service, if your discharge was under conditions other than dishonorable. Dishonorable discharge entitles you to no credits.

For each month you were in active service you are credited $160, even though no Social Security taxes were paid during the period 1940 to 1956. These wage credits are not payable as a separate benefit. They are used, if needed, to establish insured status or to increase your benefit. No determination as to the use of military service wage credits can be made until an application for benefits is filed.

After January 1, 1957, Social Security taxes were withheld. You are required to prove your period of active service during any time from 1940 to the date of leaving the service in order for you to obtain all the credits to which you are entitled.

Proof Requirements

Proof of your age at the time of entering military service, your date of birth, and the record of your military service are essential to any claim for credits. You should request a certified copy of your military record from the Armed Forces.

Armed Forces Disability Benefits

If you are receiving military retirement pay from the Armed Forces because of disability, and not based on length of service, you are entitled also to credits for Social Security benefits covering the same time period. This is very important to veterans of the Korean conflict and Vietnam. You may be entitled to Social Security disability benefits *in addition* to your Armed Forces disability retirement benefits.

Restrictions on Work Credits

If you get credit toward military retirement benefits for military service from any of the Armed Forces, the Social Security Administration will not give you any work credits toward Social Security benefits covering the same time period. Exceptions are noted as follows.

Exceptions

If the benefit is paid by the Veterans Administration, the Social Security Administration will give you credits.

If you are a "length of service" retiree from the Armed Forces and rendered active duty service between 1951 and 1956 and were on active duty service after 1956, you can receive credits for Social Security for each quarter during such period if another federal agency also is not using this same period of time to compute an annuity.

If you are a widower, you can get credit for certain military service. Under certain circumstances widowers are permitted to waive the right to a civil service survivor's annuity and receive credit (not otherwise possible) for military service prior to 1957 for purposes of determining eligibility for, and the amount of, Social Security survivors' benefits. Under former law, only widows were allowed to exercise this option. The new law is effective and, with respect to monthly benefits, payable for months after the month of enactment.

For individual assistance contact the Retiree Affairs office in the Personnel Section at the nearest military base or the Military Personnel Center for the specific branch of service from which the person retired. These are trained specialists who will help with the details of military retirement pay and CHAMPUS insurance without fee.

Access to military records is restricted to the veteran himself or herself, next of kin if the veteran is deceased, federal officers for official purposes, or those with release authorization signed by the veteran or his or her next of kin. The form that must be submitted for this information is Request Pertaining to Military Records, #180; it gives all the addresses of the records depositories for the different services. To obtain this form, write to: National Personnel Records Center, 9700 Page Blvd, St. Louis, MO 63132.[3]

---

[3] Information adapted from *The Complete & Easy Guide to Social Security & Medicare, 1991 Edition,* by Faustin Jehle, Fraser Publishing Company. Used by permission.

Ministers and Missionaries

Prior to 1984, employees of non-profit organizations were exempt from Social Security if the organization they worked for elected not to be covered. The 1984 Tax Act brought these organizations under the Social Security Act, as well as all of their employees.

In 1986 the law was modified again to allow religious organizations (and some religious orders) to be exempt from the system if they so elected, but all employees are still required to contribute to the Social Security system. Effectively the organization is exempt, but the employees are not. Somehow this seems to make sense in Washington, if nowhere else.

In addition, ministers of the gospel are allowed to opt out of Social Security on grounds of religious conviction. In other words, they have to object to government-sponsored welfare.

As a result of these law changes and previous exemptions, there are many retired pastors and their families who are not covered by Social Security benefits today.

Although the wages earned by a pastor may have been exempt from Social Security, any wages earned through other sources of income (royalties or other jobs) were, and still are, subject to Social Security taxes.

If you have worked the required number of quarters in a job where Social Security taxes were withheld, you can qualify for some level of benefits.

One note of admonishment: if you opted out of the Social Security system for conscientious reasons, you need to test your motives for seeking coverage later. If the decision was one of economic convenience, the motive was wrong. Literally once you signed Form 4361, asking to be removed from the Social Security system, you made a vow and you should keep that vow, irrespective of any financial gain. Even though the income you earned from other sources was subject to Social Security taxes (a circumstance you could not control) that in no way negates your vow.

If I could encourage active pastors and missionaries in the area of housing, it would be to purchase a home well in advance of retirement.

Remember what Solomon said about vows we make, *"When you make a vow to God, do not be late in paying it, for He takes no delight in fools. Pay what you vow! It is better that you should not vow than that you should vow and not pay"* (Ecclesiastes 5:4–5).

Retired Ministers' and Missionaries' Housing

The availability of church-provided housing was a blessing to many ministers and missionaries during their working careers, but it can be become a source of financial frustration after retirement. Often they are thrust into an overpriced housing market with far less income than even the average retiree who either owns a home or is at least buying one from a less expensive time period.

If I could encourage active pastors and missionaries in the area of housing, it would be to purchase a home well in advance of retirement. Even a rental home will normally maintain pace with the average inflation rate.

If you are retired and do not own a home, I would offer some advice and some encouragement.

First, the advice. Try to purchase a home, condo, or mobile home that is within your budget (described in the next chapter). If you cannot buy a home within your budget (no more than 40 percent of your income after tithe and taxes), you're better off renting.

Now the word of encouragement. If you have been serving the Lord in your career to the best of your ability, God has obligated Himself to meet your needs (as opposed to wants and desires). Pray diligently, share your needs with other believers, and claim God's promise: *"Offer to God a sacrifice of thanksgiving, and pay your vows to the Most High; and call upon Me in the day of trouble; I shall rescue you, and you will honor Me"* (Psalm 50:14-15).

God can and does answer the prayers of His faithful servants. I recently witnessed two practical examples of God's provision. A dear Christian brother who pastored a church in Arkansas recently retired with a very small pension to supplement his Social Security. In his last years in the small church he and his wife purchased a modest home that stretched their budget to the limit. After retirement it was woefully beyond their budget.

They struggled to keep the house for nearly two years after retiring, while sacrificing virtually all other necessities. Even with both of them working part time they were constantly strapped to make the payments and pay the taxes and upkeep.

At their request I reviewed their budget, and my advice was painfully simple: Sell your home. You can't afford it. After praying and seeking other counsel, they put the home up for sale. It sold quickly and they netted about $20,000, which they were able to keep by using their one-time housing exemption.

But there they were with $20,000, a limited income, and facing a rental market that was more expensive than their past mortgage payment. Then one day, before they had even moved from their home, the pastor received a call from a member of a church he had pastored for several years in another state.

"Pastor," the caller said, "we heard that you had retired and several of us you ministered to when you were here got together and decided we'd like to do something for you and your wife."

While telling me about it the pastor could hardly contain himself. This church, which knew absolutely nothing about his plight, had taken up a collection of $40,000. With his $20,000 and the gift of $40,000, he and his wife purchased a very nice, double-wide mobile home on a beautiful lot—for cash.

God knew his need long before he retired and planned adequately for it. And, by the way, my friend continues to minister as a volunteer counselor to this day.

Recently an ex-pastor I know moved to a western state where ultimately he and his wife would like to retire. They had long desired to buy a home, but they could never afford to do so. One night, a few weeks before they were to relocate, he sat up in bed, shook his wife awake, and said, "I just remembered that I had an annuity with our church in Ohio."

His wife grunted, "That was thirty years ago. We haven't talked to anyone there in twenty years."

He went back to sleep, but the next day he called the church and talked to the treasurer, asking if he knew anything about the ancient annuity.

"No," he replied, "but I'll call the previous treasurer and ask if he does."

The next day the treasurer called back and reported, "Your annuity is still in force and you have a little more than $40,000 accumulated. Where would you like to have it sent?"

God does care about the needs of His people, and as the old cliché goes, "Seldom early, but never late."

15

A Retiree's Budget

Manage what you have, trust that God is true to His Word and, in response to your stewardship, He will supply what is needed later.

As IMPORTANT AS making the right investment decisions is, there is nothing more important to a retiree than learning to live on a budget. The errors in spending that you may have made while fully employed were probably nuisances. But those you make while living on a retirement income can easily become disasters of the first magnitude.

Recently I counseled with a couple who learned a hard lesson about budgeting. The husband had retired the previous year from IBM where he had accepted early retirement as a part of the company's cost reduction moves. He had received his retirement of $275,000 as a lump sum, and with this much money available to supplement his Social Security income at age 62, the couple assumed they would have no financial problems.

The wife, Anne, said, "I guess we should have realized that we couldn't do the same things we had done when Ben was working, but we didn't realize how difficult it would be to decrease our spending level. Our spending has declined some, but not in the same ratio as our income. For the first time in our lives, we're going into debt every month."

You must agree together to live on a budget in which every expense for the entire year is allocated and funded.

They had come in to ask if they should take some of their retirement savings and pay off their credit card debts to save on the interest they were paying. This is a common question with a simple answer, and I told them *they should, but not until some prerequisites are met first.*

1. The cause of the overspending must first be corrected or else the consolidation (which is the equivalent of what they were proposing) will be temporary at best.
2. There must be an absolute commitment to no more credit card debt (or any other consumer debt). There are three basic rules for using a credit card that are absolutes for retirees.

    a. Never use credit cards except as a temporary substitute for cash.

    b. Pay the balance off every month—no matter what!

    c. The first month you find that you cannot pay off the credit cards out of allocated income, destroy them and vow to use them no more—period! Credit cards are not the problem; the misuse of them is.
3. You must agree *together* to live on a budget in which every expense for the entire year is allocated and funded. Of necessity, this will restrict your financial freedom, just as living within your means always does, but the end result will be well worth it.

For retirees who have never tried budgeting before, it will not be an easy task, but it is necessary. For those who have regularly gotten into financial trouble, even while working full time, it is absolutely crucial. For others, it is good stewardship of your God-given resources. As Proverbs 27:23-24 says, *"Know well the condition of your flocks, and pay attention to your herds; for riches are not forever, nor does a crown endure to all generations."*

A budget should not be drudgery; it should be both simple and freeing.

After doing financial counseling for about twenty years, I can say with some degree of certainty that usually at least one half of a couple does *not* like to budget. Some people argue that a budget is too confining; others say they think too much planning shows a lack of faith; still others are more honest and admit, "I just don't like to do it."

I also know that more often than not it is the husband who does not want to budget. And since more women buy and read books than men do, I assume the majority of my readers are women. If you're the budgeter, you need to do a good selling job on the need to budget. (The same can be said for the husband of a non-conforming wife.)

There are some good ways to approach the subject of budgeting with a spouse, but there are some guaranteed losers. Examples are:

You really need this.
You're always spending more than we make.
Larry Burkett says you need to learn to live on a budget.
Are you going to live on a budget or not?
I can't believe you're so stupid with money!

All of these are sure to stir up strife and detract from the basic principle: God wants us to be good stewards of what He has given us to manage. Try to approach the subject from the perspective of God's Word and good common sense. A budget should not be drudgery; it should be both simple and freeing. I can absolutely assure you that it can be because I have seen many people freed as a result of living on a good budget.

What Is a Budget?

First, a budget will not solve your financial problems. The most any budget can do is to help you establish *self-discipline*. If there is no desire for self-discipline, the best budget in the world is doomed to failure.

Also, if there is not a commitment on the part of *both* husband and wife to work together, no financial plan will work.

Rather than take up space discussing how to deal with an uncooperative spouse, I'll point you to an earlier book entitled *Debt-Free Living,* in which this topic is discussed and alternatives are presented. In truth, though, there is no magical formula. Unless both husband and wife are willing to work together, there is no way to budget effectively.

> *The purpose of any budget, short range or long range, is to balance income and outgo.*

The "one size fits all" strategy does not apply to a budget. To be effective, any budget must be adapted to each family's needs. For instance, if you have $3,000 a month to budget, your need to control spending is probably down to the $20 to $50 per month level; but someone living on $800 a month needs to control spending down to $5 a month. Obviously one could argue that both income levels need to control spending down to $1 per month but, in practical truth, any attempt to do so will usually result in frustration and, ultimately, no budget at all.

Budgeting Basics

Before presenting the details of a budget, I would like to discuss the *concept* of budgeting. If you can first understand how a good budget works, the process of applying it to your own finances is simple.

The purpose of any budget, short range or long range, is to balance income and outgo. The larger the income, the more surplus that can be generated if expenses are held constant. Perhaps that's too simplistic for some, but you would be amazed how complicated some people try to make the budgeting process.

The less complicated a budget can be made, the more useful it is. Usually in any family at least one person is a "detailist" (a perfectionist) who wants infinite detail and, consequently, tries to account for everything, down to the last penny. For the majority of people this is unnecessary. To maintain a budget that will account for 98 percent of all spending should normally take one hour per month (maximum). To account for the other 2 percent will take at least an additional two to three hours of bookkeeping.

Too often the other side is the "generalist"—someone who wants to spend one hour per *year* keeping records. This type of person normally maintains a checking account that is so out of balance it requires $500 in reserve just to ensure that no checks bounce. The budget (if it can be so termed) consists of juggling accounts to pay the totally unexpected bills, such as annual insurance premiums, property tax bills, or late notices on the unpaid utilities. If this plan works at all, it is only because the generalist makes enough money to be sloppy and gets away with it. That won't work well for those in retirement.

Most other people are somewhere in between the detailist and the generalist. They keep their checking accounts "kind of" in balance—meaning they usually have to make an adjusting entry after two months of imbalance, because by then they're sure the bank statement is accurate. And although they're rarely late on any payments, there is usually a nagging feeling that there are unplanned expenses looming out there somewhere.

When I began doing financial counseling several years ago, it was obvious that I needed a way to communicate some simple budgeting concepts to people who had never really grasped the concept of how to maintain their checkbooks properly. I visited most of the local bookstores searching for good materials. What I found were so-called budget books written by accountants—primarily *for* accountants. If most of the people I was counseling could have understood those budget books, they wouldn't have needed my help in the first place. So I went back to the basics and designed a budget system for non-budgeters.

Think of a budget the way our parents or grandparents did before there were checking accounts. Often the money to pay bills, buy food, and replace worn clothing was kept in jars—usually hidden away somewhere in the kitchen.

I have a friend in her eighties who budgets this way. She has a note on the outside of each of her budget jars, which details how much she should reserve out of every Social Security check. One jar contains her monthly allocation for food; one is for utilities; another is for rent; another for tithe, and so on. She has developed a basic budget, and for her, it works: She knows the average monthly amount each budget category needs and, after payments are made, her jars tell her if she has any money left over.

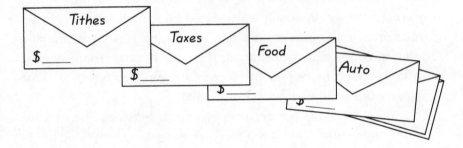

There are some obvious improvements she could make to her budget, such as allocations for non-monthly expenses—medical expenses, car repairs, and travel. But these are just refinements of the basic concept and are simple to make after the basics of budgeting are understood.

Many times in working with families I have actually used an envelope budgeting system to get them started. I normally use at least twelve envelopes to cover the major categories.

On the outside of each envelope I write how much should be put in per pay period. This is done to help balance income and outgo, since normally they are not perfectly matched by pay period. It may be necessary to shift some expenses, such as food and car repairs, to the second pay period since the mortgage or rent payments normally fall in the first pay period.

Some expenses don't fall due every month, but it is essential to allocate some funds to these expenses. Those who don't are often fooled into thinking they have extra money at the end of a month, when actually what they have are bills that haven't come due. For instance, you don't have to buy tires for your car every month, but eventually you must, so some allocation each month for tire replacement lessens the burden when they finally wear out.

Another such expense is dental care. Dental bills don't occur every month for most people, but eventually most people need some dental work. If your average cost for dental care is $600 a year, common sense says that $50 a month should be put in reserve for this eventual need. So within the budget's medical expense envelope, a portion of the cash reserve would be "dental work."

If in any single month you have a special need, such as an abnormally expensive car repair, it is possible to borrow from another envelope, such as the "medical expenses" if there is a surplus. But by doing so you make a conscious decision to postpone your medical or dental care.

All any budget can do is make you *think* about your spending and evaluate the consequences that any one spending decision has on all the others. If you find yourself robbing envelopes regularly, you either need to increase your income or reduce your expenses.

Obviously most Americans, including retirees, are not going to keep their household money in jars or envelopes; nor should they. But the same basic concept can be carried over to a checking account.

Instead of looking at the funds in your checking account as a lump sum, look at the total amount divided into smaller amounts that belong to the different budget categories—just like the jars or envelopes. But instead of jars or envelopes we'll use account sheets. These account sheets will show how much of the total in checking should be allocated per category.

Now instead of looking in your checkbook ledger to see how much money you have left each month, you look at the account sheet for the category of spending.

Let's assume in this case you need to buy some clothes. Based on the checkbook balance, you might be tempted to spend up to $670.

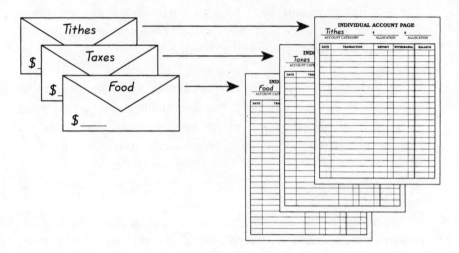

CHECKBOOK LEDGER

DATE	CK. #	TRANSACTION	DEPOSIT	WITHDRAWAL	BALANCE
4-22	1232	Bargain Shoes		32 89	1081 66
4-23	1233	PD Grocery		74 20	1007 46
4-24	1234	Power Co.		165 50	841 96
4-25	1235	MCI		24 54	817 42
4-25	1236	Dr. Smith		45 00	772 42
4-26	1237	PD Grocery		12 94	759 48
4-26	1238	Sears		14 48	745 00
4-27	1239	Hank's Gym		65 00	680 00
4-28	1240	Post Office		10 00	670 00

INDIVIDUAL ACCOUNT PAGE

Clothing
ACCOUNT CATEGORY

$ _____
ALLOCATION

$ _____
ALLOCATION

DATE	TRANSACTION	DEPOSIT	WITHDRAWAL	BALANCE
4-17	Bargain Shoes		32 89	444 34
4-17	Joe's Fashions		64 20	380 14
4-17	Sears		47 50	332 64
4-20	Walmart		48 54	284 10
4-22	Macys		30 98	253 12
4-22	Bargain Shoes		23 64	229 48
4-26	Sears		14 48	215 00

However, a quick look at your clothing account sheet shows you actually have saved $215 for clothes.

If you decide to spend more than what your clothing account balance shows, you'll need to transfer some funds from another category. By deciding to spend more than is budgeted for clothes, you make a decision that will result in lower spending elsewhere (or else you'll live to regret spending too much on clothing).

I hope this brief explanation of how a budget works is clear because living on a budget is both biblical (good stewardship) and practical (regardless of your income).

I have often heard people say, "Why, I just don't make enough money to budget." That's nonsense. We all make enough money to budget—some more, some less. The Lord said in Luke 16:10, *"He who is faithful in a very little thing is faithful also in much; and he who is unrighteous in a very little thing is unrighteous also in much."*

Manage what you have, trust that God is true to His Word and, in response to your stewardship, He will supply what is needed later.

I have provided some sample pages from the *Financial Planning Workbook*, published by Moody Press. This is the basic information I use in all of my budget counseling. Moody also offers the *Financial Planning Organizer*, which contains a notebook, divider tabs, and all the forms necessary to develop a budget for at least one full year. You can find a copy in your local Christian bookstore, or you can write to Moody Press, 820 N. LaSalle Blvd., Chicago, IL 60610-3284.

For you detailists, we also offer a computerized version of the budget system that will balance your checkbook, as well as maintain your budget *to the penny every month,* without you having to invest the extra hours to do it. This computer program is also available at your local bookstore or from Moody Press.

Variable Expense Planning

Plan for those expenses that are not paid on a regular monthly basis by estimating the yearly cost and determining the monthly amount needed to be set aside for that expense. A helpful formula is to allow the previous year's expense and add 5 percent.

	Estimated Cost	Per Month
1. **VACATION**	$ _____ ÷ 12 = $ _____	
2. **DENTIST**	$ _____ ÷ 12 = $ _____	
3. **DOCTOR**	$ _____ ÷ 12 = $ _____	
4. **AUTOMOBILE**	$ _____ ÷ 12 = $ _____	
5. **ANNUAL INSURANCE**	$ _____ ÷ 12 = $ _____	
(Life)	($ _____ ÷ 12 = $ _____)	
(Health)	($ _____ ÷ 12 = $ _____)	
(Auto)	($ _____ ÷ 12 = $ _____)	
(Home)	($ _____ ÷ 12 = $ _____)	
6. **CLOTHING**	$ _____ ÷ 12 = $ _____	
7. **INVESTMENTS**	$ _____ ÷ 12 = $ _____	
8. **OTHER**	$ _____ ÷ 12 = $ _____	
	$ _____ ÷ 12 = $ _____	

Monthly Income and Expenses

GROSS INCOME PER MONTH _____
  Salary _____
  Interest _____
  Dividends _____
  Other _____

LESS:
  1. **Tithe** _____

  2. **Tax** (Est. - Incl. Fed., State, FICA) _____

  NET SPENDABLE INCOME _____

  3. **Housing** _____
  Mortgage (rent) _____
  Insurance _____
  Taxes _____
  Electricity _____
  Gas _____
  Water _____
  Sanitation _____
  Telephone _____
  Maintenance _____
  Other _____

  4. **Food** _____

  5. **Automobile(s)** _____
  Payments _____
  Gas & Oil _____
  Insurance _____
  License/Taxes _____
  Maint./Repair/Replace _____

  6. **Insurance** _____
  Life _____
  Medical _____
  Other _____

  7. **Debts** _____
  Credit Card _____
  Loans & Notes _____
  Other _____

  8. **Enter. & Recreation** _____
  Eating Out _____
  Baby Sitters _____
  Activities/Trips _____
  Vacation _____
  Other _____

  9. **Clothing** _____

  10. **Savings** _____

  11. **Medical Expenses** _____
  Doctor _____
  Dentist _____
  Drugs _____
  Other _____

  12. **Miscellaneous** _____
  Toiletry, cosmetics _____
  Beauty, barber _____
  Laundry, cleaning _____
  Allowances, lunches _____
  Subscriptions _____
  Gifts (incl. Christmas) _____
  Cash _____
  Other _____

  13. **School/Child Care** _____
  Tuition _____
  Materials _____
  Transportation _____
  Day Care _____

  14. **Investments** _____

  TOTAL EXPENSES _____

  INCOME VS. EXPENSES
  Net Spendable Income _____
  Less Expenses _____
  _____

  15. **Unallocated Surplus Income** [1] _____

[1] This category is used when surplus income is received. This would be kept in the checking account to be used within a few weeks; otherwise, it should be transferred to an allocated category.

Individual Account Page

	ACCOUNT CATEGORY		$ ALLOCATION		$ ALLOCATION	

DATE	TRANSACTION	DEPOSIT		WITHDRAWAL		BALANCE	

Budget Percentage Guidelines

Salary for guideline = _____/year [1]

Gross Income Per Month _____

1. Tithe   (__ % of Gross)   (_____)   = $ _____
2. Tax   (__ % of Gross)   (_____)   = $ _____

Net Spendable Income   _____

3. Housing   (__ % of Net)   (_____)   = $ _____
4. Food   (__ % of Net)   (_____)   = $ _____
5. Auto   (__ % of Net)   (_____)   = $ _____
6. Insurance   (__ % of Net)   (_____)   = $ _____
7. Debts   (__ % of Net)   (_____)   = $ _____
8. Entertain.   (__ % of Net)   (_____)   = $ _____
   & Rec.
9. Clothing   (__ % of Net)   (_____)   = $ _____
10. Savings   (__ % of Net)   (_____)   = $ _____
11. Medical   (__ % of Net)   (_____)   = $ _____
12. Miscellaneous (__ % of Net)   (_____)   = $ _____
13. School/   (__ % of Net)   (_____)   = $ _____
    Child Care
14. Investments   (__ % of Net)   (_____)   = $ _____

Total   (Cannot exceed Net Spendable Income) $ _____

15. Unallocated Surplus Income   (__N/A__)   = $ _____

Income Allocation

		INCOME SOURCE/PAY PERIOD			
INCOME					
BUDGET CATEGORY	**MONTHLY ALLOCATION**				
1. TITHE					
2. TAX					
3. HOUSING					
4. FOOD					
5. AUTO					
6. INSURANCE					
7. DEBTS					
8. ENTERTAINMENT & RECREATION					
9. CLOTHING					
10. SAVINGS					
11. MEDICAL/DENTAL					
12. MISCELLANEOUS					
13. SCHOOL/ CHILD CARE					
14. INVESTMENTS					
15. UNALLOCATED SURPLUS INCOME					

16
Estate Planning for Retirees

Not planning for after-death asset distribution is poor stewardship. . . . A small amount of time and money invested now can result in a huge savings in time, money, and grief (for your loved ones) later.

Are Wills Necessary?

MOST PEOPLE, RETIREES included, don't like to discuss death, so they delay talking about it until it's too late. And if they die without a will, no one, including their spouses, can make one for them.

If you die without a valid will (or trust), the state in which you lived will decide how the assets of your estate are distributed, which may be totally contrary to what you personally would have chosen. Therefore, if you want things done your way, make a will as soon as possible; none of us knows what the future holds.

Additional hardship may result for your loved ones who are handicapped (or become so) if you die without a will or trust. Having your lifelong spouse placed in an institution may be the last thing on your mind, but that could happen if the decision is left to the state.

Some couples argue that they don't need a will because all their possessions are in joint ownership with right of survivorship. True, joint ownership with right of survivorship will transfer property to the surviving spouse automatically at the death of the first spouse. But if both spouses die at the same time, such as in an auto accident, there will be no surviving joint owner to inherit the property. Without wills, the estate distribution will be decided by the state, none of which will go to God's work.

Who Needs a Will?

Mention the word estate and most people think of the wealthy who live in elaborate homes with servants and well-manicured lawns but, according to the law, virtually everyone has an estate. Some are large; others are small. Your estate consists of everything you own. Cars, furniture, antiques, jewelry, savings accounts, and even books are considered a part of your estate. Many people have larger estates than they realize when things like retirement benefits, life insurance policies, and homes are added up. And remember that the value of your estate is not what you paid for those things; it's their fair market value at the time of your death. With the current value of land, houses, and even furniture, it's entirely possible for retirees with average means to have an estate worth hundreds of thousands of dollars.

A common comment about wills is, "I don't need one; I'm not worth enough." That's poor stewardship of what God has entrusted to a Christian. Whatever you're worth, it should be managed well.

What Are the Requirements for Preparing a Will?

For a will to be valid, it must meet the legal requirements of your state of primary residence. The process of determining a will's validity is called *probate,* which means to prove or to testify. Legal requirements for valid wills can vary from state to state so you should have your will reviewed by a competent attorney to be certain it complies with the laws of the state in which you live.

It's a good idea to review your will on a regular basis—certainly any time your circumstances change substantially. Periodically, ask your attorney if there are new federal or state laws that would require your will to be updated.

In order to probate a will, the original copy must be delivered to the court. For that reason, the original copy should be kept in a safe location, such as your attorney's office or maintained in a secure file with other important papers. A note in your home files should indicate where the original copy is stored. It's also good to keep a copy of the will handy for future reference.

Changing circumstances may require an update of your will.

Many people place their original wills in a safe deposit box. Depending on the state in which you live, your bank officer may be allowed to enter the box after your death and search for your will. Other states may have more strict guidelines for entering safe deposit boxes. If you live in one of those states, you will need to authorize another person to enter the box. Otherwise, a court order may be needed to enter it, which could delay the probate process. Furthermore, if no one knows about your safe deposit box, it may be impossible to locate the will.

Do It Yourself?

A question often asked is, "Can I do my own will, or do I need an attorney?" The law allows a person to prepare his or her own will. One example is a *holographic* will, which must be entirely in the handwriting of the person drafting it.

However, if you draft your own will, you may be increasing the risk of it being contested or declared invalid. What's worse, if you do it wrong, it's too late to correct it after you die.

Will kits (which are fill-in-blanks wills), available in most bookstores, are another option for preparing your own will. A will "kit" generally is accepted in most states, particularly if the kit uses computer software to generate the will.

With a computerized will kit the will can be printed out, which reduces the possibility of errors. Be certain to verify the validity of will kits in your state by checking with your local probate court. It's also a good idea to have your will reviewed by a competent attorney. An hour of an attorney's time may well save your estate (and your heirs) thousands of dollars and a lot of inconvenience.

Will Updates

As I mentioned before, changing circumstances may require an update of your will. If this occurs, it is not necessary to make an entirely new will. Instead, these changes could be made through the use of a *codicil,* or supplement. The codicil is subject to the same laws of probate as the will, so it must be drafted properly, and only the original is valid in court. Attach all codicils to the original will and store them together. If you have previous wills in existence, you should specify that your latest will or codicil supersedes all previous drafts.

Witnesses

The laws for validating a will vary from state to state, usually requiring two or more witnesses. It is a good idea to use more witnesses than required by law, just in case one or more of the witnesses have died or cannot be located when your will is probated. It is also a good idea to use witnesses you know so they can be located if necessary. If your will is challenged and the legal number of witnesses cannot be located, your will may be declared invalid.

The Executor

One of the most unfortunate errors associated with planning a will is choosing the wrong *executor.* A common misconception is that the executor is simply a legal requirement that anyone can satisfy. As a result, some believe the primary responsibility of settling an estate falls on the attorney. However, the reverse is true.

Often your spouse is the best selection for the position of executor.

Some of the many duties of an executor include:

- Locating the will and studying it.
- Conferring with the attorney who drew the will.
- Locating witnesses and notifying creditors.
- Locating all the decedent's property.
- Obtaining all canceled checks for the past several years.
- Authorizing appraisals for real estate.
- Evaluating leases and mortgages.
- Filing an income tax return for the deceased person.
- Filing estate tax returns.
- Preparing information for the final accounting, including all assets, income, and disbursements.
- Disbursement of estate assets as specified in the will.

Note: If a will simply specifies the assets (unnamed) are to be divided equally among the heirs, an executor has broad discretionary powers.

The selection of an executor(s) is a very important function. Select an executor with the same degree of caution you would if he or she were your own guardian.

Multiple Executors

Often your spouse is the best selection for the position of executor. In your will(s), you and your spouse would simply name each other as executor.

It's also a good idea to name an alternate executor who can take over if the spouse can't serve. This alternate could be another family member, a CPA, or an attorney who is familiar with your circumstances and assets and knows where you keep important documents.

You could also select a third alternate, such as a major bank with a trust or estate department that you know could serve if all the alternates failed. Professional executors charge fees but, in return, they offer an established method of administering estates.

If you don't name an executor in your will, or if the person you choose fails to serve and you have no alternates, then the court will appoint someone to fill the position. Before you name someone as executor, be sure you talk with him or her first to ensure that the person is willing to accept all the responsibilities. It's also a good idea to stay in contact with your intended executors to verify that they're still willing and able to do the job.

Paid Executors

Compensation for the executor is another issue that needs to be considered. If you and the executor agree that he or she will serve without compensation, you can specify that in your will. You can also request that the executor serve without the usual required bond.

If you die without a will and the court appoints an executor for your estate, that individual could receive a percentage of your estate as compensation. In Georgia, for example, this percentage may be as high as 5 percent. However, the executor may choose to waive compensation if he or she desires.

No matter whom you appoint as executor, you can make his or her job easier by maintaining a detailed inventory of all your assets (see the Location of Important Documents at the end of this chapter). One of the executor's duties will be to locate your assets; a detailed inventory can reduce the time and trouble required to perform this service. As a result, you can save unnecessary expenses and delays in settling your estate.

Inheritance Taxes

As I discussed previously, your estate is potentially subject to federal and/or state taxes at your death; and, depending on how you make your will, the state where you reside, and other factors, your tax burden can be very low or very high.

Fortunately, there are ways to escape some, or even all, of the federal estate tax burden at the death of one's spouse. One of these ways is to prepare a simple will, in which the husband leaves everything to his wife and she leaves everything to him. As a result, their estates are qualified for the *unlimited marital deduction,* which means the surviving spouse won't owe a penny of estate tax when the other spouse dies.

Another provision that can be used to reduce the federal estate tax is the *unified credit.* This provision allows a person to make transfers during life or after death of up to $600,000 to people other than his or her spouse and pay no estate tax on that amount. If properly used, this is an excellent provision to use in leaving property to children, other relatives, or friends.

For people with large estates, these gifts are a means of reducing the estate's size, which reduces the assets that are potentially taxable. This can be very helpful to widows with large estates.

State Death Taxes

As I also discussed earlier, although the federal Estate Tax Code exempts all assets left to a spouse and up to $600,000 left to other beneficiaries, the same is not necessarily true of state death taxes. Many states have adopted the same code as the federal government, but others have not. If you happen to live in one of the states that tax an inheritance, the financial shock can be severe. See the table in Chapter 8.

Paying the Tax

The amount of federal estate taxes and state death taxes can have a significant impact on heirs because the taxes must be paid *in cash*. Illiquid assets may have to be sold in order to raise enough money to pay these taxes. And due to the urgency of the situation, heirs may have to settle for less than the real value of the assets.

For that reason, it's wise to arrange for estate liquidity during your lifetime. One option for achieving this goal is life insurance, but you must plan carefully so that insurance proceeds won't increase the inheritance taxes and probate costs.

Trusts can be set up so that the insurance proceeds are owned by an irrevocable trust, thus they are not part of the decedent's estate.

What Is a Trust?

Simply stated, a trust is an entity for owning and managing assets. You create a trust, transfer assets into it, and choose a trustee to manage the assets and disburse them to beneficiaries.

A trust can be *inter vivos* (during life) or *testamentary* (at death). Just as the name implies, an inter vivos trust is drafted and implemented during a person's lifetime. These trusts are also referred to as *living trusts*. In contrast, a testamentary trust is set up to begin when a person dies.

A trust may also be *revocable* or *irrevocable*. If it is revocable, the *trustor* (trust maker) reserves the right to modify or even cancel the trust and to remove or substitute property as long as he or she is alive.

An irrevocable trust means exactly that; it is irrevocable and cannot be changed once established. In addition, property assigned to the trust cannot be recovered by the trustor, who is bound by the terms of his or her trust.

Generally speaking, assets held in a revocable trust are still the property of the trustor and, as such, are subject to federal and state inheritance taxes (although they would bypass probate costs). Assets held in an irrevocable trust are not part of the decedent's estate. Therefore, they are not subject to federal or state inheritance taxes. However, assets assigned to irrevocable trusts may be subject to gift taxes if they exceed the annual exemption ($10,000) or the cumulative exemption ($600,000). Also life estates held in trust and trustor beneficial interests (such as an annuity income from the assets) may be subject to tax.

Note: If you feel you need a trust to help protect your estate assets, always consult a competent estate planning attorney.

A trust is normally meant to handle and disburse amounts for a long time.

Unlike wills, living trusts are "private" documents and, as such, do not require probate. As a result, the terms of the trust won't be available for the public to read. To some people the privacy afforded by a trust justifies the cost.

Out of State Property

Another situation in which trusts can be valuable is one in which you own property outside your state of residence. This involves *ancillary jurisdiction,* which can result in separate probate proceedings—one in your own state and other proceedings in the state or states where you may have owned a vacation home or other property.

Ancillary jurisdiction can be very expensive, requiring separate attorneys in each of the states where you own property. But if all your property is in a trust, you can avoid problems with ancillary jurisdiction and also reduce the cost of transferring assets to your heirs at death.

The Trustee

Unlike the duties of an executor, which are over once the administration of the estate is settled, the *trustee's* duties can last for a much longer term. A trust is normally meant to handle and disburse assets for a long time and requires periodic accounting and tax reports. Thus, naming a trustee is somewhat more complicated and should be done only after careful evaluation of the skills and experience necessary.

Trustees can be empowered to buy and sell trust assets and transact any business necessary in the name of the trust. The powers of the trustee should be spelled out in the trust document. *Cotrustees* can be named, and it is often desirable to appoint *successor trustees.* It may be a good idea to name a professional trustee as the final successor trustee in the event that none of your other trustees is able to serve.

2503(C) Trust

One of the most common needs for a trust is to set aside funds for your children's or grandchildren's education, and the *2503(C) Trust* (IRS Tax Code identification) is often used for this purpose. The trustor can make periodic gifts to the trust that are gift-tax free under the annual exclusion provision of the Tax Code. And when the trust beneficiaries reach college age, the trustee disburses money to cover education costs.

The advantages of the 2503(C) Trust are that the assigned assets are no longer a part of your estate, and the accumulated earnings will be taxed at a lower percentage.

I would emphasize that not planning for after-death asset distribution is poor stewardship. As best I can tell, death is not an option—it's a fact. A small amount of time and money invested now can result in a huge savings in time, money, and grief (for your loved ones) later.

You can only decide how and where your assets will be disbursed while you are living. Keep in mind Solomon's admonition: *"When there is a man who has labored with wisdom, knowledge and skill, then he gives his legacy to one who has not labored with them. This too is vanity and a great evil"* (Ecclesiastes 2:21).[4]

Living Wills

If you have a will or trust, you probably feel assured that your estate will be settled easily when you die. After all, you've established guidelines to eliminate possible confusion. But instead of dying, you might possibly spend years in a hospital bed, suspended at some point between life and death.

In the case of serious, irreversible brain damage, your body might require the help of machines to continue functioning. These animated functions would be the only signs of life while you were held in limbo, unaware of your surroundings and unable to manage your affairs.

If all your estate plans were set to begin at death, your assets also would be in limbo while doctors, relatives, and perhaps even the courts debated about removing your life-support systems. A new federal law called the *Patient Self-Determination Act* is aimed at dealing with these situations before they happen.

Effective December 1, 1991, the act requires all hospitals, nursing homes, and other facilities receiving Medicaid or Medicare funds to inform adult patients of their right to complete *an advance directive*—a legal document allowing the patient to specify his or her choices about medical care.

One type of advance directive is the *living will,* which is recognized in most states. It can be used to request that life-prolonging techniques be withheld or withdrawn in the event of a situation like that described above.

---

[4] Adapted from the *Financial Planning Organizer,* © 1992 Christian Financial Concepts, Inc., Gainesville, GA.

To some, this represents the right of self-determination but to others, it is man's attempt to make a decision reserved only for God. As would be expected, Christians and right-to-die advocates are on opposite sides of the fence. But there is division over the issue even in the pro-life and evangelical communities.

At the heart of the debate is the question of how far to go in preserving life, even if the patient has no hope of recovery. This question also has doctors taking sides. For example, one doctors' association said treatment should be continued only as long as there's a chance for improvement. Another said treatment should be continued regardless of the life-prolonging treatment. That's why it's wise to discuss the issue with your doctor before making a living will.

If you are interested in making a living will, you should contact your state health department or department on aging because requirements for living wills vary from one state to another. And if you move to another state or spend a lot of time there, it's a good idea to create a living will for that state.

When completed, your living will should name someone you trust who can speak for you and, if necessary, defend your choice of medical treatment in court. This individual is called a *proxy*, and in the same way you name alternate executors and trustees, you should name an *alternate proxy* as well.

Sign your living will before two witnesses—other than relatives or proxies—but give proxies and family members a copy of the will. Once your living will is completed, it's a good idea to initial and date it at least once a year.

As already noted, living wills can be used to request that you not be kept on life-support systems. But you can also use them to ask that life support be continued.

Depending on the state in which you live, you may be able to execute a *Durable Power of Attorney for Health Care.* This is a document that allows you to appoint an agent (typically a spouse) to make health care decisions for you in the event you are not able to make those decisions yourself.

Unlike a living will, which only covers a terminal condition, the Durable Power of Attorney for Health Care covers a broad range of health care problems. It is actually required in some states as a supplement to living wills.

Even if your state doesn't have a health care power of attorney, all states will allow you to execute a *General Power of Attorney,* in which you can appoint someone to handle your business if you become incapacitated.

Regardless of what plans you make, you need to be as specific as possible. For example, you might become comatose or vegetative and unable to eat by mouth. To keep you alive, a feeding tube could be surgically inserted into your stomach. If you would not be opposed to tube feeding, you need to affirm that in your living will.

Several states already have living will statutes that say you can't refuse tube feeding. But in the opinion of many state courts, you can still reject it even if a statute says you can't. Other life-prolonging treatments that you may want to cover in your living will include respirators, kidney dialysis machines, and ventilators. Make your instructions as clear as possible. Persons who don't want to remain on life support indefinitely may place a time limit on how long they would want to continue in a comatose or vegetative state. If family members are left with this decision, it can be emotionally devastating, and there may be disagreement. That's why you need to state your desires beforehand.

Consideration of a living will brings up some difficult questions. The following are examples.

1. At what point is man usurping God's authority to determine who lives and who dies? Some would say that point is reached when life-support systems are removed. But what about patients who have been kept alive for years in a vegetative state with no hope of recovery? If they would die without life support, are doctors also usurping God's authority by continuing their body functions?

2. Should families be concerned about the devastating financial impact of continuing life support for years and years? One argument for making a living will is that it saves family members from suffering through this financial nightmare. However, others argue that the value of human life does not depend on its quality or its cost.

3. If someone has suffered irreversible brain damage and has no awareness of his or her surroundings, does this person reap any benefits from being kept alive for years in that condition?

4. Is it less humane to remove food/water tubes than to shut off a respirator or other type of life-support system? As already stated, some states have laws prohibiting the removal of food/water tubes. If the patient requires no other form of life support, the only means of dying is starvation, which could take up to two weeks. The pain of hunger is a sight that has always touched Americans, as in the Ethiopian famine several years ago. But that pain would be greatly multiplied if a loved one were involved.

It is at this point that euthanasia, the most critical issue associated with living wills, arises. For example, consider the case of a patient who required no life support except food/water tubes. Because removal of the tubes would cause starvation, and death might require two weeks, some would support giving the patient a lethal injection instead.

In a 1990 survey, individuals were asked what choices they would make in the case of an unconscious terminally ill patient who had left instructions in a living will. Over 80 percent said the doctor should be allowed to remove life-support systems. However, 57 percent went as far as saying the doctor should be allowed to give the patient a lethal injection or lethal pills.

Some fear that if right-to-die measures become too lax, the result will be involuntary euthanasia, in which death is forced upon those people who are considered a "burden" to society.

As a Christian, you need to consider all the questions and issues associated with living wills. Some twenty-one million Americans die each year, and most of those deaths occur in hospitals or nursing homes, where life-prolonging techniques are often used.

Without instructions from you, doctors in these institutions and members of your family must debate this difficult issue. If for no other reason, you should state your wishes in advance.

For further information on living wills, ask your family physician or contact a hospital in your area.

I trust that you have found this book a useful and even valuable guide in helping you to make some difficult decisions about retirement. I am not naive enough to believe it is all-inclusive.

First, I don't even know all the questions about retirement, much less all the answers.

Second, space limitation forced me to make a compromise between detail and the number of topics covered. I sincerely pray that I reached the right balance for the majority of readers.

I have sacrificed several additional pages to a fairly comprehensive Appendix because there are many other materials available which focus on specific areas in much greater detail than I have.

I will leave you with this parting message from our Lord: *"Do not be anxious then, saying, 'What shall we eat?' or 'What shall we drink?' or 'With what shall we clothe ourselves?' For all these things the Gentiles eagerly seek; for your heavenly Father knows that you need all these things. But seek first His kingdom and His righteousness; and all these things shall be added to you. Therefore do not be anxious for tomorrow; for tomorrow will care for itself. Each day has enough trouble of its own"* (Matthew 6:31–34).

LOCATION OF IMPORTANT DOCUMENTS

WILLS

Will For	Dated	Attorney	Location of Will

POWER OF ATTORNEY

Power of Attorney For	Power Given To	Date	Location of Document

BIRTH CERTIFICATES

Certificate For	Date of Birth	Certificate Number	Location of Certificate

DEATH CERTIFICATES

Certificate For	Date of Death	Certificate Number	Location of Certificate

MARRIAGE LICENSES

License For	Date of Marriage	Certificate Number	Location of Document

DIVORCE DECREES

Divorce Decree For	Date of Divorce	Decree Number	Location of Document

SOCIAL SECURITY RECORDS

Social Security Records/Card For	Social Security No.	Date Received	Location of Document

REAL ESTATE RECORDS

Records For Property Located At	Type of Record	Dated	Location of Document

AUTOMOBILE RECORDS

Title & Registration For Vehicle	Title Number	Dated	Location of Document

LIFE INSURANCE POLICIES

Policy on Life Of	Policy Number	Company	Location of Document

BANK, SAVINGS & LOAN, OR CREDIT UNION RECORDS

Name of Institution	Type of Account	Account Number	Location of Document

SAFETY DEPOSIT BOXES

Box Registered In Name Of	Name of Institution	Box Number	Location of Keys

CHURCH RECORDS

Type of Record	Record For (Name)	Date of Event	Location of Document

MILITARY RECORDS

Type of Record	Record For (Name)	Date of Event	Location of Document

OTHER IMPORTANT PAPERS

Type of Record	For	Dated	Location of Document

Appendix A:
Glossary

Annuity

An annuity is a contract between a person and an insurance company. The insurance company promises to pay monthly payments either immediately or at a point in the future.

There are two types of annuities: *fixed* and *variable*.

A fixed annuity earns an interest rate that may fluctuate as interest rates change.

A variable annuity allows an investment in various stock, bond, or government security funds. Monthly payments may be received, based upon the returns of the investments chosen.

All annuities are tax deferred. Penalties may be imposed if there is an early distribution.

Certificate of Deposit

A deposit account issued by savings and loan associations, banks, and credit unions.

Charitable Gift Annuity

An annuity plan offered by many charities. Essentially, money or property is exchanged for annuity payments.

Charitable Lead Trust

This type of trust is similar to a charitable remainder trust except the income payments go to a designated qualified charity, and at a specified

time the principle reverts back to the donor or
designated non-charitable beneficiary.

Charitable Re-
mainder An-
nuity

Similar to a charitable remainder unitrust, except the income payments to the beneficiary are
designed to be a fixed amount annually.

Charitable Re-
mainder Uni-
trust

A trust whereby donors can gift highly appreciated assets, such as stocks, bonds, or real estate.
Beneficiaries can receive periodic payments
from the trusts for life. Upon the death of the
donors, all remaining proceeds will go to a qualified charitable organization.

Federal De-
posit Insur-
ance Corp
(FDIC)

This agency is backed by the full faith and credit
of the U.S. government. It guarantees depositors
of member banks coverage of up to $100,000
per account.

Federal Farm
Credit

These securities include obligations of the Federal Land Banks, Banks for Cooperatives, and
Federal Intermediate Credit Banks. They are not
guaranteed by the U.S. government and are subject to federal taxes, but not state and local
taxes.

Federal Home
Loan Banks
(FHLB)

Securities are offered in minimum denominations of $10,000, are not guaranteed by the U.S.
government as Treasuries are, and are subject to
federal taxes, but not state and local taxes.

Federal Home
Loan Mort-
gage Corp
(FHLMC)

Securities are available in two options: *mortgage*
participation certificates (PCs) are available in
denominations beginning at 100,000; *guaran-*
teed mortgage certificates (GMCs) are also avail-

able in denominations starting at $100,000. They are not guaranteed by the U.S. government and are subject to federal, state, and local taxes.

Federal National Mortgage Assoc (FNMA)	Securities, known as "Fannie Maes," offered in two forms: *short-term discount notes* with minimum purchase at initial offering of $50,000; *debentures* are issued in book-entry only with minimum purchases of $10,000. Not guaranteed by the U.S. government and subject to federal, state, and local taxes.
Government National Mortgage Assoc (GNMA)	The most popular of the government agency securities, "Ginnie Maes" are available in denominations of $25,000, are guaranteed by the U.S. government, and are subject to federal, state, and local taxes.
Money Market Deposit Account	An account available at banks, savings and loans, and credit unions, normally paying a slightly higher rate of interest than a passbook savings account and allows an individual to write up to three checks per month. Insured by the FDIC up to $100,000.
Money Market Mutual Fund	In competition with money market deposit accounts. Offered by investment companies, they are short term in nature and invest in jumbo CDs, commercial paper, or T-bills. There is no federal insurance on these accounts.
Mutual Funds	These investment vehicles are offered by investment companies who pool many people's money to invest in securities. There are over

3,000 different mutual funds to choose from, with new ones being offered continuously.

National Credit Union Administration

An agency of the U.S. government that insures each account at member credit unions up to $100,000.

Pension Benefit Guaranty Corp (PBGC)

A corporation administered by the U.S. Department of Labor to provide an insurance program for pensioners of companies that have gone out of business.

Real Estate Investment Trust (REIT)

Similar to an investment company (mutual fund company) in that investors pool their money to invest in real estate properties or mortgages.

Retirement Plans (Tax-Deferred)

401(k). Named after Section 401(k) of the Internal Revenue Code, a salary reduction plan whereby an employee may make tax-deferred contributions. The employer may also participate by contributing a percentage. Total contributions are limited to the lesser of 25 percent of salary or $30,000 per year. Distributions prior to age 59½ may be penalized.

403(b). Also referred to as a Tax Sheltered Annuity or a TSA. Named after Section 403(b) of the Internal Revenue Code, these plans are available to employees of public school systems and religious, charitable, educational, scientific, and literary organizations. Contributions are made by salary reduction on a tax-deferred basis. Total contributions are limited to the lesser of 16⅔

percent of salary or $9,500. Distributions prior
to age 59$\frac{1}{2}$ may be penalized.

IRA. Individual retirement accounts are available
to everyone with earned income. The maximum
contribution is $2,000 per year. There is also a
provision for a non-working spouse, which is
limited to $250 per year. IRAs for single individu-
als are limited to those with adjusted gross incomes of $25,000 or less; married individuals,
$40,000 or less; married individuals filing sepa-
rately, $10,000 or less. Distributions prior to age
59$\frac{1}{2}$ may be penalized.

Keogh. A retirement plan for self-employed, unincorporated business owners, partners who
own more than 10 percent of a partnership, and
employees of either. Contributions are limited to
25 percent of earned income or 15 percent if it
is a profit-sharing plan. Distributions prior to age
59$\frac{1}{2}$ may be penalized.

SEP-IRA. Simplified Employee Pension Plans can
be employer or employee funded. Eligible businesses may be incorporated or unincorporated.
Total contributions, including any employee
contributions, are limited to the lesser of 15 percent of net income or $30,000. Distributions
prior to age 59$\frac{1}{2}$ may be penalized.

Pension Plans. These are funded by and
through the employer. Employees may be able
to contribute under some circumstances. They
are formal written plans that have defined rights,
eligibility standards, and use predetermined for-
mulas to calculate benefits.

Profit-Sharing Plans. Profit-sharing plans allow the employer the flexibility to contribute funds into the plan only when there are profits. Contributions are made tax deferred. Distributions prior to age 59½ may be subject to a penalty.

Securities Investor Protection Corp (SIPC)

A corporation established to protect investors up to $500,000 per account against the loss of securities due to failure of a broker/dealer.

U.S. Government Securities

Series EE Savings Bonds—In face value denominations of $25 to $10,000, series EE bonds are issued at a discount and are redeemable at the face value at maturity; thus no actual interest is paid.

Series HH Savings Bonds—Sold at par and the interest is paid semi-annually. Denominations range from $500 to $10,000 and may be redeemed six months after the issue date.

Treasury Bills—T-bills are short term in nature. The maximum maturity is one year, the most common maturities are 91 and 182 days. Sold at a discount-to-face value, the minimum unit is $10,000. T-bills are direct obligations of the U.S. government.

Treasury Bonds—These have the longest maturities of the treasuries with maturities of seven to twenty-five years. Like Treasury notes, they provide direct interest and are sold in denominations of $1,000 and higher. Treasury bonds are direct obligations of the U.S. government.

Treasury Notes—Intermediate term securities ranging from one to seven years. They provide direct interest and are sold in denominations of $1,000 and higher. Treasury notes are direct obligations of the U.S. government.

Appendix B:
Resources

Alternate Health Care Services

(1) Brotherhood Newsletter
PO Box 29
Barberton, OH 44203
330/848-1411

(2) The Good Samaritan
PO Box 279
Beech Grove, IN 46107

Asset Management Services

(1) Ron Blue & Company
1100 Johnson Ferry Rd Ste 600
Atlanta, GA 30342 (fee charged)
(*Note:* This is the firm discussed in Chapter 11 which utilizes
the Frank Russell Company for maximum diversification.)

Banks, Saving, and Loans, Credit Union
Rating Services

(1) Veribanc Inc Report
PO Box 461

Wakefield, MA 01880
617/245-8370 (fee charged)

(2) Weiss Research Inc
PO Box 109665
Palm Beach Gardens, FL 33410
800/289-9222 (fee charged)

Better Business Bureaus

(1) Council of Better Business Bureaus Inc
4200 Wilson Blvd
Arlington, VA 22203
703/276-0100

Buying Clubs

(1) Amway Corporation
7575 Fulton St E
Ada, MI 49355-0001

Cafeteria (Sec. 125) Plan

(1) R J Colbert Company
PO Box 90121
Sioux Falls, SD 57105-9061
605/331-0508 (fee charged)

Credit Bureaus

(1) Equifax
PO Box 740241
Atlanta, GA 30374 (fee charged)
(Note: This group also does background investigations.)

(2) Trans Union Credit Information
555 W Adams
Chicago, IL 60661 (fee charged)

(3) TRW Inc
1900 Richmond Rd
Cleveland, OH 44124-3760 (fee charged)

Federal Trade Commission

(1) Correspondence Department
Federal Trade Commission
Washington, DC 20580
(written complaints only)

(2) Public Reference Branch
Federal Trade Commission
Washington, DC 20580
202/326-2222
(publications)

General Financial Newsletters

(All the following publications have subscription fees.)
(1) The Cornerstone Investment Newsletter
297 Herndon Pky Ste 302
Herndon, VA 22070

(2) Sound Mind Investing Newsletter
2337 Glen Eagle Drive
Louisville, KY 40222

Insurance Companies (Auto, Home, Life)

(1) American Association of Retired Persons (AARP)
601 E St NW
Washington, DC 20049
202/434-2277

(2) Government Employees' Insurance Company (GEICO)
5260 Western Ave
Chevy Chase, MD 20076-0001
800/841-3000

Insurance Company Rating Services

(1) A.M. Best Company
Ambest Rd
Oldwick, NJ 08858-9988

(2) Duff & Phelps Inc
55 E Monroe St Ste 3600
Chicago, IL 60603

(3) Moody's Investor Service Inc
99 Church St
New York, NY 10007-2787

(4) Standard & Poor's Corp
25 Broadway
New York, NY 10004-1064

(5) Weiss Research Inc
PO Box 109665
Palm Beach Gardens, FL 33410 (fee charged)

(Note: This service normally is not available in public libraries.)

Long-Term Care Insurance Underwriters

(See your local telephone directory.)

AAL
AMEX Life
Atlantic & Pacific
Blue Cross & Blue Shield
CNA
CONSERV
Finger Lakes Long Term Care
First Penn-Pacific
IDS
John Hancock
Life Investors
Lincoln National
Medical Life
Penn Treaty
Prudential—AARP
Security Connecticut
Time
Travelers
United Security Assurance

Medicare Supplements

(Note: Continental General, United American, and others are available through your local agent.)

(1) American Republic
Sixth and Keo Sts

Des Moines, IA 50334
800/247-2190

(2) Golden Rule
712 11th St
Lawrenceville, IL 62439
800/937-4740

Memorial Societies

(1) Funeral & Memorial Societies of America
PO Box 10
Hindsburg, VT 05461
800/458-5563
(*Note:* This organization will provide the telephone numbers
of chapters in your locale.)

Ministries Providing Assistance on Wills, Trusts, and Annuity Programs

(1) Back to the Bible Broadcast
PO Box 82808
Lincoln, NE 68501
402/474-4567

(2) The Bible League
16801 Van Dam Rd
South Holland, IL 60473
708/331-2094

(3) Billy Graham Evangelistic Assoc
1300 Harmon Pl
Minneapolis, MN 55403
612/338-0500

(4) Campus Crusade for Christ
100 Sunport Lane
Orlando, FL 32809-7875
407/826-2000

(5) Compassion International
3955 Cragwood Dr
PO Box 7000
Colorado Springs, CO 80933
719/594-9900

(6) Focus on the Family
8605 Explorer Drive
Colorado Springs, CO 80920
719/531-3400

(7) Friends of Israel Gospel Ministries
PO Box 908
Bellmawr, NJ 08099
609/853-5590

(8) Joni and Friends
PO Box 3333
Agoura, CA 91301
818/707-5664

(9) Moody Bible Institute
820 N LaSalle Blvd.
Chicago, IL 60610
312/329-4000

(10) The Navigators
PO Box 6000
Colorado Springs, CO 80934
719/598-1212

(11) Prison Fellowship Ministries
PO Box 17500
Washington, DC 20041-0500
202/265-4544

(12) Wycliffe Bible Translators
PO Box 2727
Huntington Beach, CA 92647
714/969-4600

(13) World Vision International
800 West Chestnut Ave.
Monrovia, CA 91016-3198
626/303-8811

Mutual Fund Companies

(1) American (Load)
333 S Hope St
Los Angeles, CA 90071-1447
800/421-0180

(2) Fidelity (No-load and Low-load)
82 Devonshire St
Boston, MA 02109-3605
800/544-8888

(3) Franklin (Load)
777 Mariners Island Blvd
San Mateo, CA 94404-1585
800/632-2180

(4) Janus (No-load)
PO Box 173375

Denver, CO 80217-3375
800/525-3713

(5) Kemper (Load)
222 South Riverside Plaza
Chicago, IL 60606
800/621-1148

(6) Massachusetts Financial Services (Load)
500 Boylston St
Boston, MA 02116
800/343-2829

(7) Phoenix (Load)
101 Munson St
Greenfield, MA 01301
800/243-1574

(8) Pioneer (Load)
60 State St
Boston, MA 02109-1975
800/225-6292

(9) Scudder (No-load)
Two International Place
Boston, MA 02110-4103
800/225-2470

(10) T. Rowe Price (No-load)
100 E Pratt St
Baltimore, MD 21202
800/638-5660

(11) Templeton (Load)
700 Central Ave

St Petersburg, FL 33701
800/237-0738

(12) American Century Investments (No-load)
PO Box 419200
Kansas City, MO 64141-6200
800/345-2021

(13) USAA (No-load)
USAA Bldg
9800 Fredricksburg Road
San Antonio, TX 78288
800/531-8181

(14) Vanguard (No-load)
Vanguard Financial Center
PO Box 2600
Valley Forge, PA 19482-2600
800/662-7447

Mutual Fund Services

(Fees charged for all material.)

(1) Guide to Mutual Funds (general—all types)
Investment Company Institute
1401 H St. NW
Ste. 1200
Washington, DC 20005

(2) Income and Safety (income-oriented funds)
Institute of Econometric Research
2200 SW 10th St.
Deerfield Beach, FL 33442

(3) Mutual Fund Forecaster (growth mutual funds)
Institute of Econometric Research
2200 SW 10th St.
Deerfield Beach, FL 33442

(4) Mutual Fund Values Newsletter (general—all types)
Morningstar Inc
225 West Wacker Drive
Suite 400
Chicago, IL 60606

(5) No-Load Fund-X (all types of No-load funds)
235 Montgomery St, Ste. 662
San Francisco, CA 94104

(6) Sound Mind Investing Newsletter (general—all types)
2337 Glen Eagle Drive
Louisville, KY 40222

Pension Benefits

(1) Pension Benefit Guaranty Corp
1200 K St NW
Washington, DC 20005
202/326-4000

Programs for Older People

(1) American Association of Homes for the Aging (AAHA)
(national organization of not-for-profit nursing homes, senior
housing, continuing care retirement communities, and community services for the elderly), 901 E St NW Ste 500, Washington, DC 20004-2011—202/783-2242

(2) American Association of Retired Persons (AARP)
(members entitled to group health insurance, group travel
program, investment program, discounts on pharmacy services—membership 50 and older), 601 E St NW, Washington, DC 20049—202/434-2277

(3) Mobility International USA
(promotes travel among the elderly and disabled by offering
information on how to make traveling easier and less expensive), PO Box 10767, Eugene, OR 97440—541-343-1284

(4) National Association for Home Care (NAHC)
(trade association representing home health agencies, home-
maker-home health aide organizations, and hospices—to promote and protect the well-being of the nation's sick, disabled, and elderly), 228 7th St. SE, Washington, DC 20003—
202/547-7424

(5) National Citizens' Coalition for Nursing Home Reform
(NCCNHR)
(made up of twelve citizen advocacy groups—to improve
care and life for nursing home residents and provide information and leadership in legislation and government policy),
1424 16th St NW, Ste. 202, Washington, DC 20036—202/
332-2275

(6) National Council of Senior Citizens (NCSC)
(an advocacy group dedicated to protecting the rights of
senior citizens), 8403 Colesville Road, Ste. 1200, Silver
Springs, MD 20910 301/578-8800

(7) National Council on Aging (NCOA)
(individuals and organizations interested in making society
more equitable for older persons—protecting their rights,
making sure their needs are met), 409 3rd St SW, Ste. 200,
Washington, DC 20024—202/479-1200

(8) National Hispanic Council on Aging (NHCOA)
(promotes well-being of Hispanic elderly, working to eliminate the social, civic, and economic inequalities experienced
by elders of Hispanic descent), 2713 Ontario Rd NW, Washington, DC 20009—202/265-1288

(9) National Hospice Organization (NHO)
(concerned with supportive services for terminally ill people
and their families to make final weeks or months of life as
pain-free, dignified, and meaningful as possible), 1901 N
Moore St Ste 901, Arlington, VA 22209—703/243-5900

(10) National Senior Citizens Law Center (NSCLC)
(provides legal services on behalf of elderly poor clients
and client groups—litigation assistance, research and consulting support, national policy representation, and on-site
training manuals on legal matters), 1815 H St NW, Ste. 700,
Washington, DC 20006—202/887-5280

(11) Older Women's League (OWL)
(national grassroots organization focusing exclusively on aging women), 666 11th St NW, Ste. 700, Washington, DC
20001—202/783-6686

(12) Pensions Rights Center
(seeks solutions to problems of current private and government pension systems—ultimate goal to bring about retirement income system that is economically feasible while
meeting individual needs), 918 16th St NW, Ste. 704, Washington, DC 20006—202/296-3776

(13) The Salvation Army
(has special program that addresses physical, emotional,
and spiritual needs of senior citizens), 120 W 14th St, New
York, NY 10011—202/337-7200

(14) Service Corps of Retired Executives (SCORE) (administered by Small Business Administration; counsels individuals starting small business), 409 3rd St SW, Washington, DC 20024—202/205-6762

Recommended Reading

(1) *The Complete Financial Guide for Single Parents*
Larry Burkett—Victor Books

(2) *Debt-Free Living*
Larry Burkett—Moody Press

(3) *Encyclopedia of Investments*
Jack P. Friedmon—Warren, Gorham & Lamont

(4) *One Up on Wall Street: How to Use What You Already Know to Make Money in the Market*
Peter Lynch—Simon & Schuster (hardback), Viking Penguin (paperback)

(5) *Personal Financial Planning*
G. Victor Hallman & Jerry S. Rosenbloom—McGraw-Hill Book Co

(6) *The Templeton Plan: 21 Steps to Personal Success and Real Happiness*
James Ellison—Harper & Row

(7) *The Thoughtful Christian's Guide to Investing*
Gary Moore—Zondervan Books

Resource Materials on Wills and Trusts

(1) *A Second Start: A Widow's Guide to Financial Survival*
Judith N. Brown and Christina Baldwin—Simon & Schuster

(2) *The Essential Guide to Wills, Estates, Trusts, and Death Taxes*
Alex J. Soled—Scott, Foresman: Lifelong Learning Division

(3) *Family Guide to Estate Planning*
Theodore E. Hughes—Scribner

(4) *Living for Today, Planning for Tomorrow*
Shelly Lynch—World Wide Publications

(5) *Plan Your Estate with a Living Trust* and *Nolo's Simple Will Book*
Denis Clifford—Nolo Press

(6) *Thy Will Be Done: A Guide to Wills, Estates, and Taxation for Older People*
Eugene Daly—Prometheus Books

Savings Bonds

(1) *The Savings Bond Informer*
PO Box 09249
Detroit, MI 48209
800/927-1901

Social Security Guides

(1) *What You Should Know About Your Social Security Now*
The Research Institute of America Inc, 90 5th Ave, New
York, NY 10011 (a free publication)

(2) *Social Insecurity*
Dorcas Hardy—Villard Books, 201 E 50th St, New York, NY
10022

Stock Services

(Both publications have subscription fees.)

(1) *The Dick Davis Digest*
PO Box 350630
Fort Lauderdale, FL 33335

(2) *The Value Line Investment Survey*
220 East 42nd St.
New York, NY 10017